Crossroads After Communism

Binio S. Binev's book offers an innovative interpretation of the relationship between economic liberalism and political illiberalism in contemporary Eastern Europe and Latin America. Focusing primarily on the former region, he emphasizes linkages between the legacies of early market reform and the adaptive strategies of subsequent populists. By integrating elements of path dependency and human agency, this book advances a distinctive explanation of illiberals' electoral viability and behavior in power. It uses both quantitative analysis of region-wide patterns and in-depth case studies informed by interviews from fieldwork in both regions to offer a comprehensive and nuanced perspective on the long-term effects of building capitalism, the political Left, and the persistent appeal of populist forces after the end of communism. It also identifies intriguing cross-regional parallels connecting early market reforms, societal reactions to neoliberalism, and illiberals' prospects of dominating politics and contesting democracy.

Binio S. Binev is Assistant Professor in the Department of Political Science at Virginia Tech, where his work covers institutions, political economy, and cross-regional perspectives. He was educated in Bulgaria and the United States, studied languages in Germany, Mexico, and Kyrgyzstan, and has conducted research in Eastern Europe, South America, and Central Asia.

Crossroads After Communism

Neoliberal Legacies in Eastern Europe and Parallel Paths in Latin America

BINIO S. BINEV

CAMBRIDGE
UNIVERSITY PRESS

CAMBRIDGE
UNIVERSITY PRESS

Shaftesbury Road, Cambridge CB2 8EA, United Kingdom

One Liberty Plaza, 20th Floor, New York, NY 10006, USA

477 Williamstown Road, Port Melbourne, VIC 3207, Australia

314–321, 3rd Floor, Plot 3, Splendor Forum, Jasola District Centre, New Delhi – 110025, India

Cambridge University Press is part of Cambridge University Press & Assessment, a department of the University of Cambridge.

We share the University's mission to contribute to society through the pursuit of education, learning and research at the highest international levels of excellence.

www.cambridge.org
Information on this title: www.cambridge.org/9781009706650
DOI: 10.1017/9781009706643

First published 2026

Cover image: People queuing to buy bread in Sretenka Street, Moscow, USSR. Photo: ITAR-TASS / Sergei Mamontov; Alexander Nemyonov (c) TASS / Mary Evans.

A catalogue record for this publication is available from the British Library

A Cataloging-in-Publication data record for this book is available from the Library of Congress

ISBN 978-1-009-70660-5 Hardback
ISBN 978-1-009-70665-0 Paperback

For my mother and my grandma Rossa

Contents

Figures

Tables

Acknowledgments

The conception, research, and writing of this book have taken its author on quite a journey. It all began long ago with a fascination provoked by a vague and mystifying sense of parallelism between two very different settings that had recently gone through similar pains of economic crisis and austerity – the place where I grew up, Bulgaria, and the place where I was learning Spanish at the time, Mexico. This fascination eventually led me to graduate school, to research that allowed me to venture into completely new experiences in Eastern Europe and South America, and ultimately – to the realization of this project, which studies the links between neoliberalism and illiberalism in these two regions. On the way, I accumulated many debts – to teachers, colleagues, and loved ones, to friends both old and new, people who gave help when I needed it, engaged with me on the substance, and offered support in previously unfamiliar lands.

My dissertation advisors at Georgetown University played important roles in terms of my professional trajectory, affording me opportunities to pursue my interests, bailing me out whenever I got in trouble, and always encouraging me to stay the course. Marc Howard consistently inspired and motivated me with his remarkable ability to create both impactful scholarship and positive change in others' lives. Diana Kapiszewski provided precious opportunities for intellectual and professional growth, including the kind of mentorship that junior scholars only dream of. Jeff Anderson was a steady rock who never stopped believing in me and always extended a helping hand. Charles King set a standard of what it means to be an outstanding author and teacher. I am lucky to have had these four mentors in my corner.

Four other scholars have been notably impactful with regard to the development of core ideas that constitute the backbone of this book. Ken Roberts' body of work on democracy, market reform, and populism in Latin America has influenced the evolution of my own thinking about Eastern Europe. Kevin

Deegan-Krause's scholarship on party competition and political divides, Mitch Orenstein's contributions on economic liberalization and its social consequences, and David Ost's arguments about the political effects of neoliberal dislocation have helped shape my own understanding of post-communism. These colleagues also offered valuable guidance as I completed this project, for which I sincerely thank them.

The book was written at Virginia Tech, where I was fortunate to work alongside friends and associates of goodwill. Besnik Pula was an inexhaustible spring of solidarity, intelligent input, and encouragement. Andy Scerri was generous with his time, advice, and intellectual engagement. The esteemed Tim Luke, who was my chair throughout the writing process, gave needed backing at all times; Karin Kitchens helped navigate questions of strategy and method; and Paul Avey kindly shared useful insights. Yannis Stivachtis, Mauro Caraccioli, and Nick Copeland offered friendship and good cheer. Colleagues from whose comments at a workshop this book benefited include Nick Goedert, Karen Hult, Wayne Moore, Deborah Milly, Fabian Wendt, and Dan Gibbs. Ilja Luciak, Edward Weisband, Scott Nelson, Laura Zanotti, Caitlin Jewitt, Bettina Koch, François Debrix, Farida Jalalzai, Michael Moehler, Desirée Poets, Audrey Reeves, Brandy Faulkner, Aaron Brantly, Priya Dixit, Lillian Frost, Clara Suong, Bikrum Gill, Kim Hedge, Elizabeth Long, Sarah Harvey, Phoebe Peterson, and Patrick Salmons also helped in various ways.

A few close and solid individuals provided encouragement and counsel at critical moments on the way to realizing this project – especially Shannon Kelleher, whose big heart and sharp mind steadily aided my cause; Leo Valentine, who has been like a brother to me; Raushan Abduldaeva, whose care, authenticity, and love put fresh wind in my sails; and Zacc Ritter, whose grasp of world affairs made him an ideal sounding board. Others whose kindness made a difference include Boyana Spasova, Zoya Delcheva and the late Nedyalko Delchev, Maria Repnikova, Marios Antoniou, John Mills, Onur İşçi, Gamze Ergur, Harry Merritt, Bo Anders Knutson, Alesia Sedziaka, Belinda Cofield, and Barbara and Alan McWhirter. The following people were particularly helpful during fieldwork – Ivan Borimechkov, Michał Kotnarowski, Maria Kapiszewska, Alicja Majczak, and Justina Duda in Poland; Michal Polák and Dalibor Roháč in Slovakia; Segundo Enrique Cabrera, Marlon Armando Espinoza, Alfonzo Aguilar, David Tejada, and Lorena Montellanos O'Diana in Peru; and Luigina Fosatti, Jacobo García, Franklin Ramírez, and Luis Verdesoto Custode in Ecuador. I also thank Gary Maris, Eugene Huskey, Bill Nylen, and the late T. Wayne Bailey for fostering my interest in comparative politics and languages many years ago. And I applaud Kevin Gunn for creating an excellent index for this book.

The project benefitted from institutional support, including from the Council for European Studies based at Columbia University, which sponsored my fieldwork in Eastern Europe, Georgetown University's Department of Government, which subsidized my research in Latin America, and Virginia

Tech's Department of Political Science and College of Liberal Arts and Human Sciences, which afforded me course releases to complete the manuscript. At Cambridge University Press, I am especially lucky to have been able to work with a team of professional and considerate people. I am particularly grateful to Executive Publisher John Haslam for his confidence and generosity – for giving this project a chance, for finding constructive reviewers whose incisive comments improved the book, and for letting me write as many words as I needed to. I am also thankful to Senior Editorial Assistant Carrie Parkinson for being so attentive and for shepherding this volume masterfully through the publication process, as well as to Content Manager Laura Blake and the editorial and design teams for their careful work. Much deserved appreciation goes to Jayavel Radhakrishnan and Srishti Prakash for their accommodating manner and eye for detail.

Parts of this book draw on ideas and data from earlier articles that I wrote, and I thank the publishers of the following works for granting me permission to reuse and adapt textual and illustrative material: "Post-Communist Junctures, the Left, and Illiberalism: Theory with Evidence from Central and Eastern Europe," *Comparative Political Studies* 56(4): 465–502 (2023); "Post-Neoliberal Populism in Latin America and Eastern Europe: Recognizing Family Resemblance," *Studies in Comparative International Development* 59(3): 517–81 (2024); and "The Social Bases of Populist Domination: Market Reforms and Popular Reactions in Latin America and Post-Communist Europe," *Government and Opposition* 59(1): 23–46 (2024).

Not least of all, I owe boundless gratitude to two strong-minded women whose resilience and sacrifices have sustained and amazed me for a long time. I dedicate this book to my mother and my grandma.

PART I

THE BIG PICTURE

I

Illiberal Outcomes and the Weight of Recent History

On September 29, 2011, former Solidarity trade union leader and Polish president Lech Wałęsa celebrated his sixty-ninth birthday at an award ceremony in Gdańsk, which was attended by another onetime labor organizer – Brazil's former (and future) president Luiz Inácio Lula da Silva. Taking the stage and looking Lula in the eye, Wałęsa made the following confession:

In the early days of Solidarity, when we were struggling for our freedom, you and I disagreed. I wanted to move towards capitalism and you – towards socialism. I was a capitalist and you disagreed. And I was certain you were wrong and I was right. Yet once we had capitalism and communism was gone, I noticed capitalism was not so tasty. What we needed was a third way. Like what you have achieved in Brazil. Yes, Brother Lula, it turns out you are right and I was wrong. And today we must think ahead … for tomorrow will not be today, and what we needed yesterday will not be what we need today.[1]

The Brazilian leader's response to this humble self-criticism was generous, affirming the righteousness of Wałęsa's struggle for solidarity in the 1980s and reminding his Eastern European "brother" that "under communism, the market system was an appropriate goal and true symbol."[2] Yet, if Lula's reassurance provided any comfort, it was not for long. Just ten days after Wałęsa's birthday that year, an illiberal political party that vilified his legacy won – yet again – nearly a third of the vote in the Polish parliamentary election. That party, Law and Justice (PiS), not only routinely smeared the anti-communist hero's name but also rebuked the very market system whose building blocks he had scrupulously defended as president in the early 1990s. Twenty years after Poland's most critical market reforms and a decade into the twenty-first

---

[1] Barber (2011).　　　　　　　　　　[2] Barber (2011).

century, Lech Wałęsa could personally feel the weight of recent history on his country's political present.

The basic intuition of one of Eastern Europe's most emblematic reformers – that political leaders take one side or another during periods of dramatic historical change – is both correct and thought provoking. It is indeed true that such political agents take sides – sometimes at will, other times by chance – as history unfolds. Yet to what extent, under what conditions, and how, if at all, the sides they take are historically consequential are separate issues. While Wałęsa's self-awareness as a key agent of transformation is admirable, his concrete effect on ensuing historical developments remains an open question. So does the impact of many other political agents who took sides – as either prominent reformers or opponents to reform – at the time when postcommunist countries made their most decisive steps toward building capitalism.

The difficult relationship between political agency and historical legacy has been at the core of debates on Eastern Europe ever since the 1989 revolutions, when much of the region transitioned from dictatorship and state-led development to democracy and the market. On one side of this argument were prominent thinkers of various ideological stripes, such as neoliberal reform advocate Anders Åslund and (former) analytical Marxist Adam Przeworski, who highlighted the capacity of agents to make history-shaping decisions during periods of significant change. On the other side were influential scholars, such as Ken Jowitt, Andrew Janos, and Herbert Kitschelt, who insisted that historical legacies – of either pre-communist or communist experiences – heavily constrained political possibilities after 1989. While this key intellectual disagreement evolved in the context of early postcommunist developments, its relevance certainly reverberated well into the present century. Indeed, as a range of highly personalistic political agents – like those in charge of Poland's illiberal PiS – rose to prominence, and even power, by pledging to redress the historical injustices of the "not so tasty" liberal capitalism, the relationship between voluntarism and the shadow of the past has remained largely unsettled.

The present book contributes to this foundational debate by making the case that political agency and historical legacies – not of the distant past but rather of major market reforms after communism – interactively shaped illiberal outcomes in Eastern Europe, and that developments in this region are both illuminated by and instructive regarding post-neoliberal experiences in Latin America. Most generally, I advance and test a new theory of institutional development, according to which contingent political configurations during *postcommunist junctures* of neoliberal deepening conditioned divergent path dependencies that reflected distinct societal reactions expressed predominantly at the ballot box. As the legacies of junctures shaped political opportunities and constraints to which highly adaptive, yet fallible, critics of liberalism adjusted as they actively sought popular support, the viability of contemporary illiberalism was scarcely the result of historical determinism. Its varying expressions were, rather, the probabilistic effects of contingencies during prior junctures of market reform.

Given the essence of this core proposition, the specifics of which I detail later, this book joins other scholarship that draws linkages between neoliberal economics and illiberal politics. Two such works are Kenneth Roberts' major analysis of Latin American party systems in the neoliberal era and Maria Snegovaya's recent study of the decline of the Left and the rise of the populist Right in postcommunist Europe.[3] While my argument is very much in line with the former's analysis – which also explores the linkages between market reform and societal reactions from a critical juncture perspective informed by the work of Karl Polanyi – it differs in several important ways. Unlike Roberts' contribution, I develop an explicitly probabilistic approach to critical juncture analysis, advance an entirely different core argument, one centered on leftist parties as spheres of institutional reproduction in Eastern Europe, and apply insights cross-regionally. As I show in this book, while parallels with Latin America can be theoretically appropriate and analytically illuminating, making sense of Eastern European dynamics requires an original theoretical framework. And although my account concurs with Snegovaya's that populism in contemporary Eastern Europe rises "when Left moves Right," it diverges from her argument, which focuses on shorter-term outcomes of policy choices and emphasizes parallels with the more developed democracies of Western Europe. By contrast, I prioritize the historical context of longer-term trajectories and identify more counterintuitive parallels between postcommunist Europe and Latin America – two less developed regions at the periphery of global capitalism, where, as Aldo Madariaga has convincingly demonstrated, the transition to market liberalism molded political futures in uniquely comparable ways.[4]

Identifying illiberal outcomes as legacies of postcommunist junctures is important, especially considering that illiberal parties took what used to be Eastern Europe's most advanced democracies and boldest market reformers – for example, Hungary and Poland – in troubling authoritarian directions. Indeed, as the conventional wisdom that decisive liberalization would produce stable democracies[5] now seems to have been unduly optimistic, a reassessment of the recent past can shed much light on the region's contemporary predicament with the illiberal challenge. By offering a nuanced account of developments after communism, this book, then, joins others that have questioned the strategies and choices of political forces in charge of early and decisive market reforms.[6] Yet with its focus on how the junctures of the 1990s consistently shaped political trajectories in the first two twenty-first century decades, it breaks new theoretical and empirical grounds. The remainder of this introduction presents the central puzzle of the study and the analytical framework used to address it. After discussing postcommunist illiberal outcomes and my innovative perspective on critical junctures, I highlight the methods and data deployed in the comparative analysis and offer a brief preview of the book's organization.

---

[3] Roberts (2014); Snegovaya (2024).
[4] Madariaga (2020).
[5] For example, Åslund (2001); Fish (1998).

[6] For example, Greskovits (1998); Orenstein (2001); Ost (2005).

I.I ILLIBERAL OUTCOMES IN POSTCOMMUNIST EUROPE

Although political competition in Eastern Europe tends to be structured along relatively stable party programs,[7] this has not made liberal democratic politics in this region particularly coherent or robust. Indeed, especially as mainstream parties have generally been perceived as poor representatives of the electorate's preferences, there has been little to celebrate about Eastern Europe's state of democratic accountability.[8] If the social and ideological divisions on which voters and parties align issue preferences have been rather stable, the same cannot be said about the relationship between Eastern European constituents and their political representatives. As a clear symptom of this problem, party system instability in the region has been both "self-reinforcing" and significantly higher than in Western Europe.[9]

Such poor institutionalization of linkages between popular and political classes has, of course, driven the rise and consistent salience of populism[10] – a concept that prominent commentators now associate with democratic illiberalism.[11] Often conflated with illiberal democratic regimes,[12] however, illiberalism, when not defined empirically, can be a highly subjective notion, as I have argued elsewhere.[13] It is for this reason that I follow the standard scholarly intuition, which posits that the populist rejection of liberal ideas occurs largely on the ideational level.[14] Because this rejection manifests itself in both culture and economics as two standard dimensions of political competition, this study understands illiberalism as the programmatic mix of social conservatism and economic statism[15] – both of which contest, in their own ways, the core classical liberal belief of maximizing individual freedom of choice.[16]

Illiberalism is of course nothing new in Eastern Europe, where multiple layers of past legacies have long conditioned skepticism of individualism in economic and social life. For example, communism conditioned popular preferences for generous welfare[17] – a standard product of the state's intervention in the economy. Meanwhile, the delegitimization of Marxism meant that after the Cold War, material concerns in this region were often transmuted into cultural and identity antagonisms,[18] which, in turn, regularly drew on the scarcely liberal heritage of pre-communist conservatism and nationalism.[19]

---

[7] Kitschelt et al. (1999); Rohrschneider and Whitefield (2009).

[8] Haughton and Deegan-Krause (2020); Kitschelt (2000); Wineroither and Seeber (2018).

[9] Haughton and Deegan-Krause (2015); Powell and Tucker (2014); Rovny and Polk (2017).

[10] For recent contributions, see Engler et al. (2019); Orenstein and Bugarič (2022); Vachudova (2020).

[11] Mudde (2016; 2021); Pappas (2016b).

[12] Zakaria (1997).

[13] Binev (2024a).

[14] Mudde (2004; 2021).

[15] Inglehart and Norris (2016); Kriesi and Pappas (2015).

[16] McLean and McMillan (2003: 309).

[17] Pop-Eleches and Tucker (2017).

[18] Ost (2005).

[19] Bunce (2005).

If Eastern Europe's complex past makes available the ideological resources underpinning contemporary illiberalism, it also "conditions the relationship between economic hardship and the degree and form of citizen response," as Béla Greskovits showed early in the postcommunist transformation.[20] During the 1990s, illiberalism may have shown its teeth, but it did so mostly as an undemocratic phenomenon, as seen in Slobodan Milošević's Yugoslavia, Vladimír Mečiar's Slovakia, and Ion Iliescu's Romania. While many Eastern Europeans frustrated with neoliberal reforms – the so-called transition "losers" – tended to support illiberal parties mixing socially particularist and economically statist and redistributionist messages,[21] the most successful of these were led by authoritarian ex-communists. Unlike Latin American publics, who vigorously protested structural adjustment and punished traditional parties at the ballot box, Eastern Europeans remained impressively patient – with both market reforms and their former overlords from the political Left. One decade after communism, then, Eastern Europe was a very different place from the Latin America of the late twentieth century.[22]

Everything changed as the new millennium marked a shift from the crisis-ridden and quasi-democratic years of early post-communism to the region's Europeanization. As much of Eastern Europe achieved the economic and democratic stability required of European Union (EU) aspirants, freshly salient issues of immigration, integration, and trade structured a new "transnational cleavage." This, in turn, strengthened new parties – often, but not always, on the radical Right – which "absorbed leftist distributional concerns" as they competed in democratic elections.[23] By articulating both socially and economically based critiques in their struggle against the liberal establishment,[24] these *democratic illiberals* helped define a central line of contestation in the Eastern Europe of the early twenty-first century.

Although many parties in the region do not fit standard patterns of contestation[25] – a reason why it remains unclear whether the conflict shaped by illiberals represents a true Rokkanian cleavage[26] – scholars of post-communism have offered convincing evidence that "economic issues constitute the common basis for party competition in the region."[27] Indeed, as material concerns "loom sufficiently large everywhere," most political contenders are inevitably forced "to show their cards and take position" on economic questions.[28] Of course, this does not mean that radical leftist challenges to liberalism have been feasible in a region where both the traumatic memories from communism and the fiscal

[20] Greskovits (1998: 69).
[21] Kitschelt (1992: 42).
[22] Greskovits (1998).
[23] Hooghe and Marks (2018: 124).
[24] Marks et al. (2006); Rohrschneider and Whitefield (2009); Whitefield and Rohrschneider (2015).

[25] Engler (2020); Hanley and Sikk (2016); Haughton and Deegan-Krause (2020); Pop-Eleches (2010).
[26] Casal Bértoa (2014); Haughton and Deegan-Krause (2020).
[27] Rohrschneider and Whitefield (2009: 298).
[28] Kitschelt (2015: 86–7).

discipline required of EU members and aspirants limit such alternatives. Unlike in Latin America and Southern Europe, where serious economic concerns can inspire openly leftist rebellion,[29] opposition to liberalism in Eastern Europe during the neoliberal era has thus far been predominantly articulated by illiberal parties that typically supplement their nationalism and conservatism with economically "leftist" positions or posturing.

Take, for example, the two paradigmatic cases of Eastern European illiberalism – the conservative nationalists of Poland's PiS and Hungary's Fidesz. While as incumbents these parties promoted targeted and even nativist welfare programs,[30] they also enacted interventionist economic policies after campaigning for financially nationalist, statist, welfarist, and anti-austerity solutions.[31] Whereas Fidesz resisted pressures for austerity, nationalized pension funds, transportation, and telecommunication companies, and imposed a high bank tax, after 2015 PiS adopted pro-welfare policies, reduced inequality, and made efforts to "re-polonize" parts of the economy.[32] As such policies provoked the conservative Heritage Foundation to downgrade the business freedom, property rights, and limited government rankings of Hungary and Poland, the economic heterodoxy of Fidesz and PiS clearly alarmed proponents of free markets. Along with the conservative and nationalist critique of social liberalism, then, the statist challenge to liberal economics defines the illiberal society–economy nexus in postcommunist Europe.

Hungary and Poland may be the most prominent cases of illiberalism in power,[33] but electoral support for illiberalism is a much more widespread phenomenon in postcommunist Europe. Figure 1.1a aggregates results for illiberal parties from eighty-seven parliamentary elections in fifteen postcommunist countries during the 2000–20 period by using expert survey data on parties' social and economic positions. Notably, in my empirically based conceptualization, illiberal parties combined socially conservative and economically "leftist" positions, were "antiestablishment" at some – usually early – point of their development, and gained at least 1 percent of the vote. To be clear, such parties are distinct from "mainstream reformist" antiestablishment parties,[34] which take liberal economic or social positions, as well as from more traditional parties with illiberal positions, which were, however, integral to the communist or early postcommunist "establishment." Overall, while my measure does not capture all antiestablishment and illiberal voting in the region, it does capture illiberalism with antiestablishment origins. (Appendix A details the coding procedure and lists all ninety parties categorized as illiberal in relevant parliamentary elections.) Based on this empirical and dynamic

---

[29] Hooghe and Marks (2018); Roberts (2014).
[30] Szikra (2018).
[31] Johnson and Barnes (2015); Orenstein and Bugarič (2022).

[32] Krekó and Enyedi (2018: 44–5); Toplišek (2020).
[33] Pirro and Stanley (2022).
[34] Hanley and Sikk (2016).

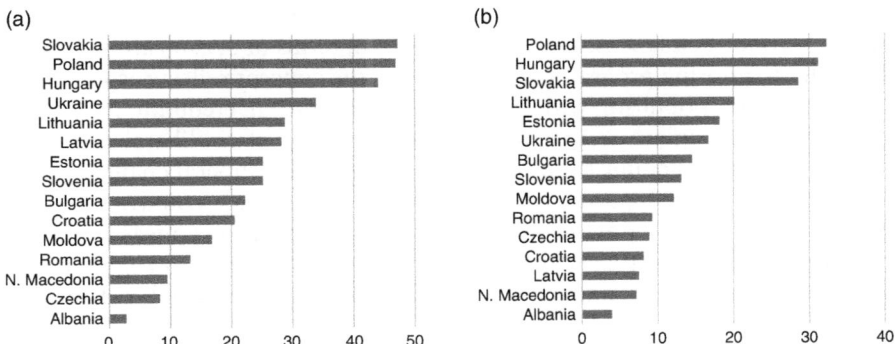

FIGURE 1.1 Illiberalism and post-neoliberal populism in Eastern European parliamentary elections, 2000–20. (a) illiberalism, average vote share and (b) post-neoliberal populism, average magnitude

measure,[35] Figure 1.1a confirms, unsurprisingly, that illiberalism routinely gained support at the ballot box in the first two decades of twenty-first century postcommunist Europe[36] – a quarter of the vote (24.4 percent), on average. More puzzlingly, however, the figure shows considerable variation across the region – while illiberal parties were most viable at the ballot box in Slovakia, Poland, and Hungary,[37] they were somewhat less electorally successful in Estonia, Slovenia, and Bulgaria, and significantly less so in Romania, Czechia, and Albania.

If Figure 1.1a illustrates that support for illiberalism varied across contemporary postcommunist Europe, Figure 1.1b shows that so did the salience of *post-neoliberal populism* – a related but distinct category, which I understand as a highly adaptive challenge to the neoliberal doctrine "that market exchange is an ethic in itself."[38] As I have defined it in prior work, post-neoliberal populism is a family resemblance concept that integrates various interactive dimensions of contemporary antiestablishment actors. As an empirically based construction, it is specifically grounded in economic statism while, however, also incorporating sociocultural conservatism as well as personalism and out-siderness relative to party systems as two strategic-organizational attributes of those disputing neoliberalism.[39] There are three reasons why the multidimensional concept of post-neoliberal populism is particularly useful for making sense of the illiberal challenge in contemporary Eastern Europe. First, given that not all populism is critical of the free market,[40] a subtype centered on

---

35 As expert survey scores vary over time, parties can be illiberal in some elections but not in others.

36 Engler et al. (2019); Inglehart and Norris (2016).

37 Fidesz, the only party coded differently over time in my dataset, is treated as illiberal

and post-neoliberal populist beginning in 2010 and as mainstream prior to 2010. For details, see note 4 in Chapter 3.

38 Harvey (2005).

39 Binev (2024a).

40 Rovira Kaltwasser et al. (2017); Weyland (1999).

economic statism foregrounds the high salience of material questions in the region. Second, as it is sensitive to adaptations in terms of organizational strategy without ignoring programmatic positions, the concept reflects aspects that endow modern populism with efficacy and contrarian credibility.[41] Third, from a methodological perspective, the category of post-neoliberal populism offers an additional empirical baseline for assessing the illiberal challenge.

More concretely, Figure 1.1b ranks Eastern European countries by the average *magnitude of post-neoliberal populism* as a distinct measure based on weighting by vote shares the intensity of relevant parties' programmatic and strategic-organizational attributes.[42] Like the measure of illiberalism, the measure of post-neoliberal populism not only excludes "traditional" parties from the 1990s but also captures evolution over time based on multiple expert survey waves and my own coding of dynamic organizational attributes. Most importantly, and reflecting that illiberalism and post-neoliberal populism are neither identical nor conflicting concepts, Figures 1.1a and b feature both differences and similarities.

Indeed, with only two countries (Slovenia and Albania) achieving the same ranking, it should be clear that illiberalism and post-neoliberal populism are distinct from one another. The difference between the former, which weights social conservatism and economic statism equally, and the latter, which prioritizes economic statism and incorporates organizational aspects, is perhaps best seen in the case of Latvia. Because of the strong electoral performance of parties like the National Alliance (NA), which were socially conservative without, however, basing their appeals on economic statism, personalism, or outsiderness, this country ranks markedly higher on illiberalism (sixth) than on post-neoliberal populism (thirteenth). The two constructs, therefore, are not identical.

And yet the tendencies of the average illiberal vote share and average magnitude of post-neoliberal populism point generally in the same direction. Indeed, while Poland, Hungary, Slovakia, and Lithuania are in the top third, Slovenia and Bulgaria appear in the middle, and Albania, Czechia, and North Macedonia are in the last third in both Figures 1.1a and b. The rankings of most other countries are relatively stable too, with Ukraine being sixth on post-neoliberal populism and fourth on illiberalism, Estonia – fifth and seventh, Croatia – twelfth and tenth, Moldova – ninth and eleventh, and Romania – tenth and twelfth, respectively. The two measures are in fact strongly correlated ($r = 0.88$), thereby suggesting a crucial takeaway: *The economic statism typically associated with the post-neoliberal populist critique of market liberalism[43] is a key element of democratic illiberalism in contemporary Eastern Europe.*

[41] Barr (2009); Levitsky and Loxton (2013); Roberts (2006a).

[42] See Binev (2024a) for details regarding conceptualization and measurement. Unlike the measure of illiberalism, which includes

parties that gained at least 1 percent, this measure requires 2 percent of the vote in parliamentary elections.

[43] Binev (2024a); Ruckert et al. (2017).

The last point is crucial and requires additional clarification. As this study conceptualizes illiberalism and post-neoliberal populism as multidimensional concepts, it facilitates comparisons of both the interactions among and relative salience of their various constituent features. Whereas my construction of the latter category incorporates more facets, as noted earlier, both illiberalism and post-neoliberal populism include not only economically statist and culturally conservative dimensions but also – when they find themselves in a position of power – a political aspect defined by maneuvers relative to liberal democracy. While these three illiberal and populist dimensions – the economic, the cultural, and the political – can certainly have affinities for one another under some circumstances, they are, in fact, distinct and do not always go hand in hand. This, in turn, suggests that even if populist parties are economically or culturally illiberal, or both, they are not necessarily autocratic when in power. Although illiberalism is often conflated with democratic backsliding, the two come together only under some historical conditions, as the case studies of evolving institutional dynamics will convey. More relevantly for the book's main argument, it is specifically economic illiberalism as a reaction to processes of marketization that is central to political trends across contemporary postcommunist Europe. *The economic dimension is often downplayed relative to the cultural and political aspects of postcommunist populism, but it is, in fact, key for understanding developments in the region.*

In sum, the popular rejection of liberalism in Eastern Europe can be understood in two related ways – (1) as the vote share of parties with socially and economically illiberal positions and (2) as the magnitude of post-neoliberal populist reactions grounded in economic statism. While conceptually distinct, these two constructs uncover largely comparable tendencies in terms of illiberal outcomes. The viability of the populist challenge, itself largely driven by economic considerations, varied widely across postcommunist Europe in the first two decades of the twenty-first century.

1.2 THE LATIN AMERICAN CONNECTION AND THE WEIGHT OF RECENT HISTORY

The uneven salience of illiberal outcomes has certainly provoked the interest of many scholars, who have explained it with reference to standard factors in comparative politics. Most generally, these include (1) "demand-side" arguments focused on economics (e.g., crisis or inequality), politics (e.g., perceived corruption), or culture (e.g., attitudes against minorities); (2) "supply-side" accounts prioritizing institutions of governance (e.g., the electoral system) and representation (e.g., unresponsive parties), or voluntarism (e.g., leadership charisma and manipulation); (3) explanations emphasizing the international environment (e.g., leverage and diffusion); and (4) those underscoring how the legacies of longue-durée history shaped contemporary cleavages and institutions. As I discuss in detail and demonstrate empirically in Chapters 2 and 3, this scholarship, although offering important insights, does not explain convincingly the overall patterns of variation discussed earlier. There are three reasons for this. First, suffering from a scarcity of appropriately measured concepts, much of the literature tends to equate illiberalism with radical right parties and thus ignores the considerably more nuanced nature of developments in Eastern Europe. Second, as authors tend to focus on a limited set of troubled countries, particularly Hungary and Poland, narrowness of comparative scope often results in a fragmented view of more general institutional patterns. Third, since standard explanations ignore the crucial linkages between political agency and past legacy, they usually fail to recognize both the dynamism and historical context of illiberal outcomes.

This book overcomes such limitations by developing a theory of postcommunist European institutional development, which draws insights from the Latin American experience. On the face of it, this may seem counterintuitive – after all, the two regions are fundamentally different in terms of history, structure, culture, institutions, and international environments, and if there are any similarities, those were already analyzed in classic studies of the transitions to democracy and the market.[44] Nevertheless, subsequent scholarship has problematized the similar long-lasting effects of the neoliberal revolutions that Latin America and postcommunist Europe experienced, usually under the guidance of the International Monetary Fund (IMF), late in the twentieth century.[45] Indeed, both regions transitioned from state-led development – socialism in the East, import substitution in the South – into neoliberal regimes similarly defined by "Washington Consensus" policies of privatization, free trade, deregulation, and spending cuts.[46] Without doubt, the neoliberal revolutions followed different scenarios in the two regions. Whereas in Latin America the historically high inequality dating back to Iberian colonialism and the perceptions of exploitative international financial institutions contributed to the politicization of reforms, in the relatively more egalitarian Eastern Europe economic liberalization was enacted in a context of communist stigmatization, pressures of renewed nation-building, and EU conditionality.[47] Despite these differences, which molded divergent ideological environments where the popular reactions to market reform would later play out, neoliberalism produced large-scale popular disenchantment and raised the salience of material concerns in these two world regions.

If the economic transformation unsettled societies in Latin America and Eastern Europe, political developments reinforced historical parallels. As both regions exited dictatorial rule, democratization, often an elite-driven process,

---

[44] For example, Greskovits (1998); Linz and Stepan (1996); Przeworski (1991).
[45] Madariaga (2020); Pop-Eleches (2009).

[46] Greskovits (1998: 106); Ruckert et al. (2017: 1585).
[47] See Pop-Eleches (2009).

typically failed to produce institutional stability.[48] Operating within shaky party systems with weak links to organized civil society, important mainstream parties continued relying on corrupt practices of patronage and clientelism rather than prioritize building programmatic linkages with voters.[49] In turn, as citizens disaffected with the transformation became ever more suspicious of political parties and liberal democratic institutions more generally,[50] they often turned to antiestablishment entrepreneurs who denounced the entire system. In their fight against liberalism, these populist challengers operated within the ideological environments that, as noted earlier, had been shaped by prior experiences. If their illiberalism was typically associated with Bolivarian left-wing nationalism in the South, it tended to attach itself to more traditional ethnic nationalism after communism. In sum, the recent economic and political challenges of Eastern Europe mimicked and even mirrored those of Latin America, where, however, both the peak of neoliberal reforms and the populist counter-reaction generally occurred a decade earlier.

What precisely does such analogousness imply, and how does the Latin American experience illuminate developments in Eastern Europe? To answer this question, I turn to the idea of critical junctures – the central concept of a research tradition traceable to Max Weber, informally launched by Seymour Martin Lipset and Stein Rokkan, and substantially developed by Ruth Berins Collier and David Collier in their landmark work on the labor movement and regime dynamics in Latin America.[51] More recently, the critical juncture framework was fruitfully deployed by Roberts in his analysis of the linkages between market reform and party system stability in that region. In his formulation, the transition from state-led development to market capitalism across Latin America constituted *neoliberal critical junctures* – "periods of heightened uncertainty and potential institutional discontinuity," during which crises "can unsettle existing institutions and force actors to make contested decisions about policy or institutional innovations that have durable (though often unintended) consequence."[52] With an emphasis on the role of political actors during such watershed moments of market reform, Roberts' insights are especially relevant for the Eastern European context, where the choices of political elites were absolutely central for the management of early economic crises and the shaping of capitalist orders.[53] Indeed, building capitalism here was not simply a product of socialism's end; rather, as noted by Åslund, strategic policy choices had to be made.[54] Early in the postcommunist transition, political elites exercised their agency as they followed advice, usually offered to them by international experts, to choose wisely in ways shielding neoliberal reforms

48 Przeworski (1991).
49 Grzymała-Busse (2002, 2008); Levitsky and Roberts (2011); Mainwaring and Torcal (2005); O'Dwyer (2006).
50 Doyle (2011); Mishler and Rose (2001).

51 Collier and Collier (1991); Collier and Munck (2022: 1).
52 Roberts (2014: 6–7).
53 Bohle and Greskovits (2012: 56).
54 Åslund (2001).

from popular backlash.[55] Their policy choices, in turn, conditioned important "path-contingent" institutional legacies, as Juliet Johnson showed in her study of early economic liberalization in Eastern Europe.[56]

If political agency molded neoliberal reform legacies, these legacies next shaped subsequent agents' choices. Illiberal actors in the early twenty-first century are such ensuing agents whose options are significantly conditioned by the long-term effects of prior market building efforts. For example, as populist parties tend to be highly personalistic, their leaders played definitive roles in terms of deciding policy positions, including on the highly salient economic issues of the neoliberal era.[57] Far from random, however, these positions were strategically chosen to fit particular environments conditioned by the legacies of neoliberal reform. Yet, if such legacies shaped strategies, they did not determine them. As recognized by Kitschelt, historical legacies may explain how "parties find themselves facing specific political predicaments and opportunities," but they do not "account for all the learning that takes place, once parties encounter new challenges of the postcommunist era."[58] Thus, as the highly autonomous leaders of populist parties made strategic choices – often, but not always, the most fitting ones given the legacy within which they operated – they exercised their agency in the probabilistic shadow of earlier events. As legacies were both inherited from the past and constructed in the present,[59] illiberalism and post-neoliberal populism must be understood as the strategic constructions of positions most likely to be viable given the specific opportunities molded by the recent past.

1.3 CORE ARGUMENTS AND CONTRIBUTIONS

This book thus contends that illiberal outcomes in Eastern Europe are the probabilistic results of path dependencies defined by the interplay of political agency and the legacies of early critical periods of neoliberal deepening, or what I call *postcommunist junctures*. By using the building blocks of critical juncture analysis,[60] Figure 1.2 sketches the study's basic explanatory framework, which I substantially elaborate theoretically in subsequent chapters (particularly Chapters 2 and 7). As postcommunist junctures resolved crises provoked by historical antecedents and triggered institutional innovation, the political agency that defined them shaped environmental opportunities and constraints within which subsequent antiestablishment agents adapted by making choices – a process that culminated in varying probabilities of illiberal outcomes. Crucially, while this framework is cross-regionally informed, it is deployed in an original manner germane to the specificity of Eastern Europe.

---

[55] Hanson (1998).
[56] Johnson (2001).
[57] Haughton and Deegan-Krause (2020: 128–35); Rohrschneider and Whitefield (2009).

[58] Kitschelt (2002: 14–5).
[59] Kubik (2015).
[60] Collier and Collier (1991).

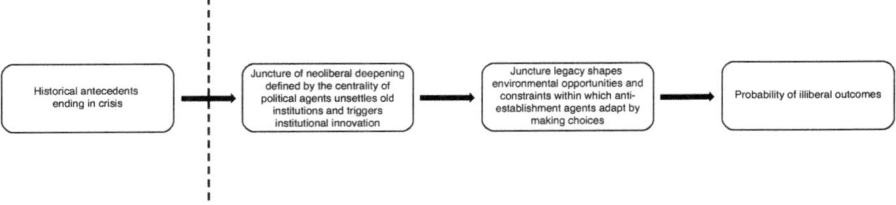

FIGURE 1.2 The basic critical juncture framework

Indeed, postcommunist junctures – conceptualized as the earliest watershed moments of neoliberal deepening after second competitive national elections (see Chapter 2) – were neither the same as Latin America's neoliberal junctures nor did they trigger identical reactive sequences of what Collier and Collier call "institutional production and reproduction."[61] Although historical processes in the two regions unfolded in corresponding ways, Eastern Europe experienced distinctive developments.

These developments are captured by the following core argument, which focuses on the links between leftist politics, societal coalitions, and populist strategies in postcommunist Europe. First, as the pressures of building capitalism during the early transition years forced political actors to adapt, the Left found itself at a crossroads – it could openly embrace neoliberal policies, repudiate them, or adopt a less clear position. Far from historically determined or the product of free choice, the positions leftist or labor-based parties adopted were contingent on the political roles in which they found themselves during the postcommunist juncture, when intense reforms were typically enacted in response to real or perceived economic crises. Where the Left led the parliamentary opposition at the time, the juncture was *aligning* – meaning that leftist parties acted consistently with ideological tenets, voiced strong opposition to neoliberalism, and generally upheld their commitment to redistribution and protectionism in the long term. By contrast, where pro-worker parties – such as communist successors or, in the case of Poland, the labor-based Solidarity – found themselves in charge of economic reform, the juncture was defined by *bait-and-switch* dynamics, which signaled not only broken campaign promises but also the Left's persistent embrace of neoliberal prescriptions in the future. Where leftist parties found themselves in charge neither of the reforms nor of the parliamentary opposition – an *ambiguous* juncture – their positioning on economic issues was more intermediate. Crucially, as leftist parties had incentives to reproduce their positions, their stances on economic issues would persist well after postcommunist junctures.

Second, the Left's persistent programmatic positions had serious and long-lasting political implications as the region dealt with considerable economic

---

[61] Collier and Collier (1991: 30–1).

dislocations. As both the crises of the 1990s and the neoliberal responses to them produced uniquely negative consequences for Eastern European societies, many experienced worsening life prospects, including downward mobility, unemployment, and impoverishment, among other struggles.[62] Whereas during the communist years ruling parties could not be punished at the ballot box for their failures, postcommunist publics could vote in elections with real consequences. Of particular significance in this new context defined by both economic dislocation and democratic sanction was the positioning of the Left – the expected defender of the social segments most hurt by the neoliberal crises and shocks. Where leftist parties were positioned as credible moderators of neoliberalism, the social coalitions they represented rewarded them at the ballot box. Where they were perceived as architects of economic orthodoxy, leftist parties lost support as key constituencies in need of protection abandoned them.

Third, the relationship between the political Left and those who comprised the social coalition seeking respite from seemingly endless neoliberal adjustment mattered a great deal for the electoral prospects of illiberal or post-neoliberal populist parties. As the commodification of labor, land, and capital in postcommunist Europe provoked the rise of a reactive Polanyian countermovement, not all leftist parties could channel into the political system the demands of those seeking defense from marketization. Where such parties remained strong, the long-term loyalty of their social coalitions constrained illiberals' electoral prospects. Where the Left crumbled, however, many victims of neoliberalism – including, among others, workers, post-peasants, lower middle-class citizens (and sometimes national capitalists)[63] – gave their votes to challengers of liberalism. As populist parties are distinguished by peculiar adaptive capacities and incentives for opportunism, they could take electoral advantage of the Left's weakness by strategically promising statist solutions to societal problems and even enacting policies that reshaped the social relations molded by the neoliberal revolutions.

In sum, where leftist parties led the parliamentary opposition to rightist reformers during postcommunist junctures, as in Czechia and Romania, their consistent positions as credible critics of neoliberalism translated into subsequent electoral strength, which consistently constrained opportunities for illiberal success at the ballot box. By contrast, where postcommunist junctures were defined by bait-and-switch dynamics, as in Slovakia and Poland, the Left's embrace of neoliberalism conditioned its subsequent weakening, thus enhancing chances for illiberals' electoral viability in the long run.

Yet, if junctures of market reform triggered reactive sequences specific to Eastern Europe, they also shaped developments, which, though not identical, were highly analogous to patterns seen in Latin American countries. Once again, it was the juncture contingencies of political agency that made the difference. First, those who engaged in bait-and-switching during junctures were

---

[62] Ghodsee and Orenstein (2021).

[63] See Scheiring (2020b) and Chapter 2 for a discussion.

either standard leftist parties or populist personalists. In the first scenario, seen in Slovakia and Ecuador, subsequent illiberals mobilized highly extensive electoral coalitions centered around former leftist voters, based on which they delivered popular public goods associated with good governance – and, as a result, dominated in the long run. By contrast, where the bait-and-switching agent had been a populist personalist who politicized regional divides, as in Poland and Peru, ensuing illiberals mobilized considerably more segmented electoral coalitions, based on which they governed less cohesively and effectively – a reason why they failed to be as dominant. Second, anti-neoliberal protest was only sometimes institutionalized during junctures. Where this happened, as in Poland and Ecuador, subsequent radicalism and party system upheaval amid the solidification of the neoliberal consensus incentivized illiberals to adopt contestatory strategies vis-à-vis liberal democracy. Where, by contrast, anti-neoliberal protest was not institutionalized during the juncture, as in Slovakia and Peru, the subsequent weakness of radical alternatives and relative party system stability encouraged illiberals to embrace moderation.

As it approaches both regional distinctiveness and cross-regional parallels from a perspective preoccupied with the general historical context defined by momentous neoliberal deepening and its legacies, this comparative study makes theoretical, methodological, and empirical contributions to critical juncture research. First, it adds to theoretical debates in three ways – (1) by extending to the post-communist European region a framework that conceptualizes concrete periods of market reform as critical junctures; (2) by developing, based on Eastern European cases, a more nuanced understanding than prior research of how political agents acted during these junctures and adapted thereafter, and then applying the refined theory back to Latin American cases; and (3) by integrating the oft-debated aspects of agency and legacy into a common causal mechanism.[64] Second, from a methodological perspective, I avoid the "inevitability framework" usually associated with the determinism prevalent in historical institutionalism[65] by accommodating voluntarism and demonstrating – with a combination of qualitative and quantitative techniques – probabilistic causality. As I show, even though junctures imposed certain restrictions on the subsequent choices of agents,[66] their legacy "entails causal patterns that are strong enough to yield a substantial interval of persistence, yet are not fully deterministic."[67] Third, the study advances empirical knowledge by developing and analyzing data that substantiate how the linkages between junctures and illiberal outcomes materialized in the reality of Eastern Europe in ways both unique and analogous to Latin American experiences. The following section discusses considerations of methodological nature.

---

[64] See Capoccia and Kelemen (2007) and Mahoney (2001b) for arguments underscoring voluntarism, Faletti and Lynch (2009) and Slater and Simmons (2010) for an emphasis on legacy, and Soifer (2012) for an attempt to reconcile the two.

[65] Dunning (2017: 41).

[66] Mahoney (2000: 513).

[67] Collier and Munck (2017: 8).

1.4 RESEARCH DESIGN

1.4.1 Mixed Method Empirical Approach

To investigate empirically the linkages between agency and legacy from a perspective that incorporates intra-regional and cross-regional comparisons, this book combines qualitative and quantitative methodological approaches. The various analytical techniques and wide array of data used offer considerable leverage in terms of making sense of the varying causes, effects, and processes associated with critical junctures. Generally, the logic of inquiry involves three major steps. First, having developed a new theory that accounts for the variation identified earlier, I deploy large-N analysis to perform an initial plausibility probe vis-à-vis alternative explanations of illiberal outcomes. Second, as the findings from these tests support my theory, I next scrutinize causal mechanisms by tracing historical processes in four Eastern European countries (Czechia, Poland, Romania, and Slovakia) that exhibit crucial variation in terms of key explanatory factors. Third, after elaborating the critical juncture framework based on insights from postcommunist Europe, I assess the cross-regional validity of the refined theory by tracing processes in two Latin American countries (Ecuador and Peru).

In terms of scope, the book covers developments up through 2020, a year after which Eastern Europe faced new and dire challenges – the peak of COVID-related casualties (2021) and the start of the war in Ukraine (2022) – whose ramifications on political trajectories are yet to be understood. Additionally, as I analyze postcommunist junctures' electoral effects during the first two twenty-first century decades, I focus on countries considered to have consistently held relatively meaningful democratic elections[68] and safe from serious statehood challenges[69] in the aftermath period between 2000 and 2020. As a result, the large-N study assesses developments in 130 parliamentary elections, eighty-seven of which took place in the twenty-first century, from 1990 to 2020, in the following fifteen postcommunist countries: Albania, Bulgaria, Croatia, Czechia, Estonia, Hungary, Latvia, Lithuania, Moldova, North Macedonia, Poland, Romania, Slovakia, Slovenia, and, until 2012, Ukraine.[70] As it renders a sufficiently large number of observations to be analyzed by means of standard statistical techniques for cross-sectional

---

[68] Operationalized here as elections taking place in years for which countries received a Polity score of six or above, or, if the Polity score was five (as in Albania in 2001), the overall Freedom House score was at most 3.5. Despite their "democratic" scores for some election years, Armenia, Belarus, Georgia, Kyrgyzstan, and Russia are excluded due to lack of democratic consistency.

[69] I exclude Bosnia and Herzegovina, Kosovo, Montenegro, and Serbia due to the high salience of statehood problems, which largely overshadowed economic concerns.

[70] Ukraine after 2012 is excluded from the analysis due to political instability and statehood problems, as epitomized by the 2014 Maidan Revolution and the Russian annexation of Crimea.

and time series data, this broad empirical scope facilitates the identification, in Chapter 3, of strong correlational patterns that invite further investigation in case studies.

1.4.2 Case Studies

To assess causal inferences and the validity of mechanisms in a more focused manner, this study engages in qualitatively driven and quantitatively informed comparisons that emphasize both similarities and differences on two levels – intra-regionally and cross-regionally. Beginning with the within-regional assessment, I trace processes in Slovakia, Poland, Czechia, and Romania – a choice driven by several methodological factors. To begin, and incorporating insights from both Evan Lieberman and Sidney Tarrow, these four cases, nested in the statistical tests, are grouped in two pairs – the first two versus the latter two just mentioned – that are strongly representative of contrasting tendencies in terms of both theoretical predictions and statistical findings.[71] Indeed, as Slovakia and Poland experienced a type of postcommunist juncture opposite to that seen in Czechia and Romania, illiberal outcomes in the former two countries were significantly more viable than in the second pair.

Furthermore, these four cases represent a wide variation in terms of the theoretically consequential agency – that is, of labor-based or leftist actors, as explained in Chapter 2 – during critical market reform periods. For example, whereas in Poland the agent bearing the main political responsibility during the juncture was a labor-based personalist, in Slovakia this role was played by the ex-communist party. And if in Czechia and Romania crucial economic liberalization was enacted, respectively, by more and less cohesive right-leaning coalitions, opposition to reforms was led by social democrats with noncommunist roots in the first case and by ex-communists in the second.[72] Moreover, as the four countries feature both developmental similarities (e.g., imperial domination, EU membership, and even, in the Czech and Slovak cases, common statehood during most of the twentieth century) and, as detailed in Chapter 4, considerable differences in terms of historical antecedents (e.g., pre-communist and communist experiences),[73] transitions out of communism, and crises preceding junctures, the four-way comparison helps to evaluate a range of competing hypotheses, including those prioritizing distant history, as discussed in Chapter 6.

In addition to providing opportunities to assess the book's core theory, the case studies of Eastern European historical trajectories also offer insights that facilitate refining it. Indeed, while Slovakia and Poland featured the basic building blocks and path-dependent linkages underpinning the theorized core

---

[71] Lieberman (2005); Tarrow (2010). [73] Kitschelt et al. (1999).
[72] Orenstein (2001); Pop-Eleches (2009).

causal mechanism, as I show in Chapter 5, reactive sequences in these two cases were far from identical. Even though both saw *quantitatively* high illiberal outcomes at the ballot box without undergoing significant democratic erosion (as in Hungary),[74] the two countries still had *qualitatively* different experiences with illiberalism. For example, whereas Slovakia's leading illiberals dominated politics in the long term while embracing a strategy of relative moderation, Poland's failed to be as dominant, yet they seriously contested liberal democracy. It is based on these two case studies that I refine the theory by linking nuanced differences between generally similar junctures to the peculiar institutional environments to which illiberals adapted via strategic choices in the aftermath period.

Having elaborated, in Chapter 7, how the contingencies of agency – both in charge of and against neoliberal reforms – during junctures shaped durable path dependencies in Eastern European countries, I test the validity of the refined framework by tracing processes in two Latin American cases – Ecuador and Peru. Although these two comparable Andean countries saw, after similar neoliberal junctures, an upsurge of electoral support for post-neoliberal populist projects that neither originated as bottom-up movements (as in Bolivia) nor consolidated authoritarian rule (as in Venezuela), their experiences with illiberalism diverged widely. If the leading illiberal project of Ecuador was both hegemonic and contestatory vis-à-vis liberal democracy, its Peruvian counterpart both moderated and disintegrated. As demonstrated in this paired comparison – which adds to previous scholarship by offering, in Chapter 8, an innovative reinterpretation of developments – the nuanced contingencies of neoliberal junctures shaped varying illiberal tendencies in ways strikingly parallel to those seen in Eastern Europe. Obvious regional specificities notwithstanding, the linkages between critical periods of economic liberalization and subsequent political developments were historically grounded in analogous ways.

1.4.3 Data

The study draws on a large body of data that generally fall into three categories. First, I use the specialized secondary literature on (1) historical institutionalism; (2) Eastern Europe, with a particular attention to Czechia, Poland, Romania, and Slovakia; and (3) Latin America, especially Ecuador and Peru. Second, the project extensively employs available quantitative data, which are too many to list here and which I discuss, usually in footnotes, in the course of the book. Briefly, I constructed key variables by relying on economic, national

---

[74] While Hungary's elections qualify as relatively democratic per the above threshold, democratic erosion after 2010 makes this country a weaker candidate in terms of case selection for the purposes of studying illiberalism under democratic conditions, as this book does. Although Poland experienced limited democratic deconsolidation toward the end of the aftermath period, this was much less pronounced and successful than in Hungary.

election, and expert survey data, which have many advantages for "measuring empirical information on policy positions across a wide range of countries,"[75] and I conducted empirical tests by utilizing a large variety of data on economic, political, societal, institutional, and international developments, available from reputable international and research organizations. Crucially, I also developed new datasets in order to assess illiberalism, post-neoliberal populist magnitude,[76] and party system volatility in postcommunist Europe. Likewise, to measure the territorial extensiveness of electoral coalitions – or party nationalization – in Slovakia, Poland, Ecuador, and Peru, I assembled a dataset based on subnational-level election data obtained from central electoral bodies and previous research.[77] Constructed by following Daniel Bochsler's mathematical method for calculating weighted Party Nationalization Scores (PNSw),[78] this dataset helps me assess the relative coalition extensiveness of all political actors competing in all national elections from the transitions to democracy to the year 2020 in the four countries at the core of the cross-regional comparisons.

Third, these four case studies are significantly informed by extensive fieldwork. Specifically, I travelled to Krakow and Warsaw in Poland, Bratislava in Slovakia, Lima in Peru, and Quito in Ecuador, where, in 2015 and 2016, I conducted a total of 101 interviews with individuals involved in or impacted by the processes I study.[79] In each country, I carried out between twenty and thirty interviews ranging from thirty minutes to over three hours, attended party meetings, and visited with numerous individuals willing to share with me memories and interpretations. While I cite them in the case studies, the most crucial function of these "refracted context" interviews is to inform my comprehension of historical processes through the reconstruction of "narrative structures" and the uncovering of "landscapes of meaning."[80] All interviews, listed in Appendix B, were semi-structured yet open-ended in order to give interlocutors opportunities to discuss their own opinions and understandings.

Although I conducted interviews based on nonrandom "convenience sampling" due to my research priority – "to gain information about context, process, and mechanism"[81] during a finite time in each country – I nevertheless

---

[75] Wiesehomeier and Benoit (2009: 1437).

[76] See Appendix A; Binev (2023); Binev (2024a).

[77] Data for Slovakia and Poland come, respectively, from the Statistical Office of the Slovak Republic (SOSR) and the National Election Commission (PKW). For Ecuador, I use data from the National Election Council (CNE), John Polga-Hecimovich (2014), and Thomas Mustillo's (2012) dataset in the Latin American Electronic Data Archive (LAEDA). For Peru, the data are from the National Office of Electoral Processes (ONPE) and Fernando Tuesda Soldevilla's "Data Política" collection. Where necessary, I supplemented with data from the Constituency-Level Election Archive (Kollman et al. 2024).

[78] Bochsler (2010).

[79] Whereas I carried out interviews in Central Europe with the assistance of interpreters or, where possible, in English, in the Andes I conducted them in Spanish.

[80] Tavory (2020).

[81] Mosley (2013: 19).

maximized diversity of perspectives by talking to a wide range of individuals, as recommended by qualitative methodologists.[82] My informants thus included those of various economic circumstances and educational levels, women, who constituted about one-third of interviewees, and a number of young and older adults. Furthermore, as I explored linkages between political adaptations and societal forces, I interviewed at both the elite- and non-elite levels. Consequently, interviewees can generally be divided into three categories – (1) national-level politicians, including parliamentarians, former presidential candidates, and ministers; (2) experts such as social scientists, journalists, high-level government officials, and leaders of nongovernmental organizations; and (3) regular citizens, most of whom were political activists and some of whom had experience in local-level politics. These categories, however, are not strict, as a number of individuals belong to more than one. Whereas national-level figures typically expressed comfort with their names appearing in this project, all others were guaranteed confidentiality.

Finally, in my quest for balanced insights into the divisive political phenomena I study, I interviewed both supporters and opponents of leading illiberal or post-neoliberal populist projects. While I was in the field at a point when such phenomena were similarly salient in postcommunist Central Europe and the Andes, however, my interview schedule reflected adjustments based on the particular political circumstances of each country at the time. For example, as my trips to Slovakia (2015) and Ecuador (2016) coincided with the last year during which illiberals ruled with legislative majorities, in these countries I interviewed equal shares of pro- and anti-government individuals. I did the same in Peru but, since my visit here (2015–16) was at a time when the leading post-neoliberal project was disintegrating irreversibly, opportunities to engage with activists committed to it were diminishing. And as my trip to Poland (early 2015) was during a period when PiS, then in opposition, was actively organizing to recapture national power, here I interviewed the largest number of individuals aligned with illiberalism. Indeed, this was especially helpful for understanding developments in the Polish context since PiS, being the only explicitly rightist, and indeed anti-communist, illiberal project under study, was the least likely case of a post-neoliberal critique of capitalism. Overall, then, rather than being randomized and identical, the groups of individuals I interviewed in each country facilitate making sense of political processes in specific contexts,[83] while still representing a reasonable diversity of views.

In sum, the study uses a wide variety of methods and data, both quantitative and qualitative, in order to develop, test, and elaborate its core theoretical claims. As this mixed method approach is used to both make sense

---

[82] Bleich and Pekkanen (2013); Kapiszewski   [83] See Tansey (2007).
et al. (2015: 230).

of path-dependent developments in Eastern Europe and draw cross-regional parallels with Latin America, the book offers a truly innovative perspective on comparative research in the critical juncture tradition.

1.5 ORGANIZATION OF THE BOOK

The study is structured in three main parts. The first revolves around "big picture" theoretical and empirical considerations. Having presented the main puzzle and overall framework above, in Chapter 2 I discuss relevant prior work on historical legacy, agency, and illiberalism; develop, by drawing on both Polanyian scholarship and the Latin American experience, an original theory that links agency and legacy; and identify postcommunist junctures in fifteen Eastern European countries as well as the causal mechanisms that the theory posits. Chapter 3 offers a quantitative analysis, which includes the development and assessment of key variables; a demonstration of how empirical linkages between variables support the core theoretical propositions; and a discussion of why my argument is superior to alternative explanations of illiberal voting.

Having found strong correlational patterns in support of the main theory, in the second part of the study I trace processes in the four Eastern European case studies by following the conventions of critical juncture analysis.[84] By comparing historical antecedents, crises, and postcommunist junctures in Czechia, Poland, Romania, and Slovakia, Chapter 4 demonstrates that junctures indeed unsettled prior institutions and constituted moments of significant change. While Chapter 5 uncovers overall similarities in terms of the general mechanisms linking bait-and-switch junctures to the electoral viability of illiberalism in Slovakia and Poland, it also shows that reactive sequences in these two countries were, in fact, not identical. Chapter 6 traces how opposite junctures to those seen in Slovakia and Poland tended to produce persistently lower likelihoods of illiberal voting in Czechia and Romania; reassesses, based on the four Eastern European case studies, the soundness of the core theory relative to standard explanations; and concludes by briefly discussing how developments in the rest of the region also validate the theory.

If the book's first two parts focus on Eastern Europe, the third offers a cross-regional perspective. In Chapter 7, I refine the theoretical framework by focusing on the long-term effects of the more nuanced differences between otherwise similar junctures in Slovakia and Poland; justify a comparison involving Ecuador and Peru; and discuss why standard explanations of dominant illiberalism and contestatory illiberalism do not sufficiently account for tendencies in these four countries. Chapter 8 then traces processes in the two Andean

---

[84] Collier and Collier (1991); Collier and Munck (2022).

countries and discusses how developments and patterns there were analogous to those seen in Eastern Europe in ways anticipated by the refined theory. Chapter 9 closes the book by briefly discussing its main findings, its implications regarding Polanyian scholarship and the dual transition to democracy and the market after 1989, and its relevance for discussions about neoliberalism, illiberalism, and the Left.

From Neoliberal Reform to Illiberalism in Eastern Europe

Historical Legacies, Polanyian Perspectives, and Latin American Lessons

Why were illiberal forces more electorally viable in some Eastern European countries than in others during the first two decades of the twenty-first century? And how can we make sense of divergent trends from a perspective sensitive to both historical path dependency and agency as an autonomous and adaptive force in politics? This chapter elaborates the book's theoretical framework in three steps. First, after explaining why longue-durée historical legacies cannot account for the variation identified in Chapter 1 and how political agency was central in the postcommunist transition to democracy and the market, I discuss the linkages between the active and politically enabled building of capitalism and subsequent illiberalism in Eastern Europe by integrating perspectives influenced by the work of Karl Polanyi. Based on insights from political economy, sociology, and anthropology, I both elaborate on why postcommunist illiberalism and post-neoliberal populism are best understood as representing a countermovement to the marketization intensified during postcommunist junctures and clarify how my approach differs from other scholarship with a similar message.

Second, having placed the overall message of this book in the Polanyian tradition, I advance a theoretical perspective that focuses on the interactive relationship between historical legacy and political voluntarism. Concretely, I identify the legacies of neoliberal reform as both shaped by political agency and having the potential to condition subsequent agents' choices. By arguing that this interplay between path-dependent developments and voluntarism is central for making sense of political trajectories in Eastern Europe, I contend that illiberal outcomes at the ballot box are best understood as probabilistic, rather than deterministic, phenomena. Importantly, this novel proposition is informed by lessons I draw from Latin America, where critical junctures of neoliberal reform shaped subsequently divergent political consequences.

Third, after drawing insights from the Latin American experience, I develop my own argument about the path-dependent sources of illiberalism's electoral viability in Eastern Europe. To begin, I define postcommunist junctures of neoliberal reform as the earliest decisive periods of building capitalism sometime after second competitive election, and I identify three types of such junctures in fifteen postcommunist countries based on key political configurations that characterized these periods. Next, having discussed important similarities with and differences from the Latin American experience, I argue that while cross-regional insights are highly instructive, Eastern Europe's peculiar context requires its own theoretical framework. Finally, I elaborate this framework by linking postcommunist junctures, path-dependent programmatic and electoral developments on the political Left, and the strategic choices of subsequent antiestablishment actors with unique incentives and capacities for adaptation. As it integrates political agency and postcommunist juncture legacies into a unified explanation of institutional outcomes, the theoretical framework developed in this chapter locates the electoral viability of Eastern European illiberalism during the 2000–20 period in its proper historical context.

2.1 HISTORICAL LEGACY, NEOLIBERAL AGENCY, AND THE ILLIBERAL REACTION

The liberal revolutions of 1989 may have represented the closure of a cycle of world-historic significance,[1] but history has continued weighing heavily on Eastern Europe – the reason why its legacies have long constituted "the primary explanation of divergent outcomes in the region."[2] While authors prioritizing the past as a causal force disagree regarding just what legacies truly matter for subsequent developments,[3] a brief discussion of historically informed scholarship must be the starting point of a study seeking to make sense of popular support for liberalism's contemporary challengers, for three reasons. First, as there is a natural affinity between legacy explanations and historical institutionalist arguments, including those focused on critical junctures,[4] a consideration of such work can be informative regarding potentially competing historical causes. Second, scholarship in this tradition problematizes the persistent effects of modernization and political socialization on voting behavior.[5] Third, a longer historical horizon is well-suited for the analysis of cleavages and party system developments, which, as noted in Chapter 1, have been central in discussions of postcommunist illiberalism and populism.[6]

[1] Tismaneanu (1999: 1).
[2] LaPorte and Lussier (2011: 637).
[3] See Beissinger and Kotkin (2014); Bernhard and Jasiewicz (2015).
[4] LaPorte and Lussier (2011); Lussier and LaPorte (2022).
[5] Pop-Eleches and Tucker (2017).
[6] See Kitschelt et al. (1999); Kriesi (2014); Pop-Eleches and Tucker (2017).

2.1.1 Historical Legacy: Perspectives from Political Science

Political science scholarship prioritizing historical factors as shaping postcommunist institutions can be divided into two major categories. The first of these emphasizes the deleterious heritage of communist regimes. Advanced in Ken Jowitt's influential *New World Disorder*, which was published just a year after the dissolution of the Soviet Union, the idea of a systematic, singular, and pernicious Leninist legacy suggested a bleak future. Because communist rule had largely ruined societal capacities for mutual trust, toleration, and self-reliant behavior, Jowitt predicted "an authoritarian, not a liberal democratic capitalist, way of life" as the most likely outcome across the postcommunist world.[7] Following his lead, scholars focused on the Leninist past introduced important conceptual refinements, such as Stephen Hanson's disaggregation of the communist heritage into component dimensions,[8] and conducted fruitful analyses of, for example, communism's material,[9] attitudinal,[10] or revolutionary[11] legacies. Although such scholarship has yielded important insights into the long-term structural impact of Leninism, its tendency to emphasize unity among countries with a communist past and their distinctiveness from those with no such experience[12] represents a considerable handicap when it comes to explaining intra-regional diversity and cross-regional similarities, as this study does.

A notable – and relevant for the theory advanced here – exception within this analytical tradition is Anna Grzymała-Busse's argument that certain communist practices shaped elite skills and subsequent transformation strategies, which, in turn, allowed some ex-communist parties to liberalize, "redeem the communist past," and become electorally successful after 1989. This pathbreaking work offers two correctives to the literature on communist legacies. First, it accounts for intra-regional variation by examining the conditions under which some aspects of the communist past can become "usable" under post-communism. Second, it shows that legacies are mediated through deliberate political action, including choices made during the early transition years.[13] Grzymała-Busse thus engages productively with the role that political agency can play in terms of shorter-term effects after 1989 – a perspective further developed in her subsequent work.[14] Nevertheless, while *Redeeming the Communist Past* accounts for important dynamics during communism and early post-communism, it faces both empirical and theoretical difficulties. From an empirical point of view, the book explains developments in the Visegrád countries more convincingly than outside of Central Europe.[15] From a theoretical perspective, the importance of what can be understood as multiple critical junctures in Grzymała-Busse's model[16] – for example, the crises corresponding to the communist takeover in a coup d'état,

---

[7] Jowitt (1992).
[8] Hanson (1995).
[9] Barany and Volgyes (1995).
[10] Howard 2003; Pop-Eleches and Tucker (2017).
[11] Kopstein and Bernhard (2015).
[12] Pop-Eleches (2015).

[13] Grzymała-Busse (2002).
[14] Grzymała-Busse (2007).
[15] Smyth (2005). For an additional discussion of Grzymała-Busse's work, see the section on leftist paths in this chapter.
[16] See Lussier and LaPorte (2022).

the Prague Spring, and the democratic transition in Czechoslovakia – suggests that crucial choices of key political agents might well depend less on historical legacies and more on contemporaneous contingencies.

The second category of historically based arguments offered by political scientists focuses on the legacies of the pre-communist past. Originating with the work of Andrew Janos,[17] this scholarship emphasizes the longue-durée resilience of pre-communist political, economic, and cultural differences, which survived communism and then shaped divergent postcommunist trajectories. While a number of scholars have furthered this research tradition, explaining, for instance, nationalism,[18] political partisanship,[19] and democratization[20] under post-communism, the contribution most relevant to the argument advanced here is *Postcommunist Party Systems*, which Herbert Kitschelt and a group of Central European scholars published a decade after 1989. Concretely, the authors of this theoretically sophisticated and empirically rich study traced varieties of postcommunist party system structuration back to early twentieth century developments. Originating in pre-communist times, clientelist (e.g., Bulgaria), national-accommodative (e.g., Poland), and bureaucratic-authoritarian (e.g., Czechia) communist varieties weighed heavily on party systems in the 1990s. Because national-accommodative communism had already partially reformed itself, ex-communists could intensify market reforms in the 1990s, thus limiting partisan competition on economic issues and strengthening it along cultural lines. Where ex-communists were less reformed – after bureaucratic-authoritarian and patrimonial varieties of communism – socioeconomic cleavages dominated subsequent party systems.[21]

While Kitschelt and coauthors correctly identify key structural forces driving cleavage formation and institutional coherence in the first postcommunist decade, the predictive power of their argument diminishes with the subsequent evolution of party systems. As in Latin America, where longue durée history does not explain shorter-term variations in party system stability,[22] the cleavages inherited from the past do not map onto more recent trends in Eastern Europe.[23] For instance, national-accommodative communism may have structured partisan competition along sociocultural cleavages in Hungary, Poland, Slovakia, and Lithuania in the 1990s, but long-distance history does not explain why subsequently successful populists in these countries challenged the liberal establishment by instrumentalizing leftist positions and posturing on economic issues. While evolving and varying cleavages have been discussed in the party systems literature as related to institutionalization, illiberal outcomes correspond neither to a specific type of dominant cleavage nor to degree of institutionalization, as seen in Hungary, Slovakia, and Poland, which vary considerably on both dimensions.[24] As the number, type, and formation of cleavages do not explain

[17] Janos (1994; 2000).
[18] Bunce (2005).
[19] Wittenberg (2006).
[20] Pop-Eleches (2007).

[21] Kitschelt et al. (1999).
[22] Roberts (2014).
[23] Bakker et al. (2015); Rovny (2015).
[24] Casal Bértoa (2014).

support for illiberalism and the magnitude of post-neoliberal populism – both of which entail elements of cultural conservatism (salient where religious and ethnic cleavages dominate) *and* economic statism (prevalent where materially based cleavages are primary) – it remains unclear what facets of party system institutionalization affect the varying outcomes discussed in Chapter 1.[25]

Overall, then, the longue durée is unlikely to have determined party system development and illiberal outcomes in the Eastern Europe of the early twenty-first century. If, from the perspective of history, the region's party systems were expected to become more institutionalized with social modernization, proximity to the West, and simply the passage of time, their consolidation remains only partial[26] and its relationship with illiberal outcomes – unsettled. Although pre-communist and communist legacies undeniably shaped politics and societies during the early postcommunist years, more recent trends must be the result of developments of somewhat closer historical proximity. As I discuss next, such developments were characterized by the centrality of political agents acting in ways shaped less by long-distance history and more by the contingencies of the economic crises that overwhelmed Eastern European societies in the 1990s.

2.1.2 Neoliberal Agency and the Illiberal Reaction: Insights from Political Economy, Anthropology, and Sociology

If political scientists have tended to focus on the institutional legacies of the distant past, other disciplinary perspectives have been more attentive to the role political agency played in the shaping of developmental paths as Eastern Europe embraced economic liberalism. Fundamental in this regard are two pioneering works in sociology, which examine the passage from socialism to capitalism from opposite path-dependent perspectives. In *Postsocialist Pathways*, David Stark and László Bruszt related the diversity of institutional "rearrangements, reconfigurations, and recombinations" to crucial political choices made at the time of extraction from socialism. By linking resulting patters of democratization and privatization to political configurations, electoral competition, and compromise involving partisan agents in power and opposition, these authors underscored democratic accountability and policy coherence as fundamental for success in the transformation.[27]

Adopting an approach opposite to Stark and Bruszt's institutionalism, which identified the breakup of communism as the dawn of a new political and economic order, Gil Eyal, Iván Szelényi, and Eleanor Townsley analyzed how individuals responded to institutional changes by adjusting trajectories rooted in dispositions from the past. By arguing that postcommunist capitalism was built by strategic elites endowed with cultural capital, their *Making Capitalism*

[25] For further engagement with Kitschelt's work, see the section on leftist paths in this chapter and Chapter 6.

[26] Enyedi and Casal Bértoa (2018).

[27] Stark and Bruszt (1998).

Without Capitalists emphasized the social action, political alliances, and negotiated compromises of three fractions – managers able to govern the economy, reformist ex-communist technocrats who embraced monetarism, and
anti-communists dissidents based in civil society. As the balance of power
within this new power bloc varied, so did the potency of the communist legacy
and the character of the new capitalist order.[28]

Although these interpretations identify different origins of postcommunist
European divergence, their common preoccupation with the transformative
nature of agency and political configurations when embryonic capitalism was
being built echoes palpably in the arguments advanced here. On the one hand,
Stark and Bruszt's insistence on the importance of *democratic accountability*
and *policy coherence* is central to the causal story I develop. On the other
hand, Eyal, Szelényi, and Townsley's sociology illuminates key dynamics not
only between political elites but also between political elites and the social coalitions that the capitalist transformation conditioned. Of particular relevance
is the relationship between the postcommunist Left, often headed by former
communist technocrats who, after being temporarily sidelined, joined the new
political elite in some countries by the mid 1990s, and the Right, typically
associated with former dissidents for whom the liberalization of civil society
meant the depoliticization and exclusion of popular social groups.[29] In Eastern
Europe, it was these very groups – many ex-communists, industrial and agricultural workers, the less educated, the self-employed, and those working in small
businesses – that experienced the most significant dislocation and downward
mobility as those in power enacted neoliberal reforms.[30] These perspectives on
the early transition years resonate with my arguments about the nature and
timing of political configurations and about the effects of top-down political
action on the constitution of newly disenfranchised societal segments during
key periods of building capitalism.

Elites may have been instrumental in the building of postcommunist capitalism, but the questions regarding the origins and consequences of their actions
have been far from settled. Yet these are crucial questions, especially for arguments centered on agency-based critical junctures. Regarding origins, because
transformations can result not only from contingent moments that open up possibilities but also from incremental processes during which prior legacies constrain
choice, a consideration of how decision-making is affected by the immediate
context becomes crucial for building valid critical juncture arguments.[31] Indeed,
from a perspective focused on the fact of economic reform in Eastern Europe, it
may seem that postcommunist liberalization was a mere continuation of prior
developments. As shown by sociologists, including Johanna Bockman, Besnik
Pula, Adam Fabry, and Agnes Gagyi, the region served as a laboratory of neoliberal globalization well before the end of communism. Having originated in

---

[28] Eyal et al. (1998).
[29] Gagyi (2021: 14–24).
[30] Eyal et al. (1997; 1998).
[31] Capoccia and Kelemen (2007).

transnational networks preceding the Cold War,[32] proto-neoliberal concepts gained traction and drove the economic policies of a number of communist regimes after the 1960s. In this context, late communist technocrats embraced economic orthodoxy not only as a response to the exhaustion of Stalinist industrialization and 1970s oil crisis[33] but also, in Jerzy Szacki's words, as "a whip" against the collective will and economically progressive ideas of the democratic opposition.[34] As these technocrats also led economic liberalization after 1989 in some of the same countries that had been at the forefront of reform under socialism, incrementalism seems like a plausible explanation of the origins of and agency behind the neoliberal revolutions of the 1990s.

Nevertheless, a postcommunist juncture perspective provides a more convincing explanation of developments. Even if capitalism had been in the making in communist Poland, Hungary, and Yugoslavia, this was capitalism "by default," "from below," and rather limited. In contrast, post-1989 capitalism was "by design," "from above," and quite unlimited.[35] This is a crucial distinction with theoretical and empirical relevance. From a theoretical perspective, it illuminates why prior liberalization policies are best understood as what Dan Slater and Erica Simmons call "conditioning antecedents" – developments which do not produce causal effects without the exogenous force of the critical juncture itself.[36] In line with these authors' argument, because designs from above in the permissive post-1989 context corresponded to the expansion of both agency and divergence options, postcommunist reforms are causally more significant than prior liberalization, which had occurred during more restrictive conditions under dictatorship. This expansion of possibilities after 1989 also corresponds to the empirical reality that whereas Hungarian and Polish ex-communists continued leading neoliberal efforts, their similarly reformist counterparts in former Yugoslavia found themselves in more ambiguous positions, whereas the ex-communist Left in Romania tended to moderate neoliberalism after long-standing integration with the West and austerity in the 1980s. As shown later in this chapter, because postcommunist junctures varied across countries in terms of both timing and the overall parliamentary balance of powers – including not just the Left but also the political Right – the prior dispositions and policies of former communists do not satisfactorily predict political configurations and top-down action during crucial moments of neoliberal reform.

Unlike the pre-1989 past, contingent events from the first postcommunist decade mattered a great deal for the future because they sowed the seeds of illiberalism as a Polanyian counterreaction to neoliberalism. To begin, postcommunist capitalism created, in the 1990s, a historically unique social structure of stratification.[37] Within this structure, neoliberal technocratic and reformist elites pushed for self-regulating markets from a relatively autonomous political

---

[32] Bockman (2011).

[33] Fabry (2019); Pula (2018).

[34] Szacki (1995: 142–5). See also Gagyi (2021).

[35] Eyal et al. (1998: 177).

[36] Slater and Simmons (2010).

[37] Eyal et al. (1998: 7).

sphere, whereas social forces subsequently sought to resist subordination to the market. As in previous waves of marketization in the West, the supply of market reforms and the demand for social cohesion together defined key questions concerning political legitimacy and appropriate forms of protectionism in Eastern Europe after 1989.[38] In the Polanyian framework, the outcomes that become institutionalized as a result of this double movement varied based on specific historical conditions shaping class struggle and who organized the interests of the social groups – anti-capitalists and capitalists alike – that paid, in their own ways, the price of building market societies.[39]

The dynamics between major political actors and social groups implicated in and responding to what Michael Burawoy identified as a third Polanyian wave of marketization[40] have been productively studied by political economists, sociologists, and anthropologists concerned with the repercussions of economic liberalism in postcommunist Europe. As marketization disembedded Polanyi's three fictitious commodities – labor, land, and money – from their necessary social supports,[41] those whose livelihoods were affected – workers, peasants, and domestic capitalists, among others – had to be politically organized in order to manage market reform and its consequences. Therefore, questions regarding what political agents represented various societal, domestic, and transnational business interests, how they acted when it counted most, and how social forces counteracted become critical. Although a Polanyi-inspired analysis moves beyond an understanding of class in purely economic self-interest terms,[42] the political evolution of social groups hurt in the process of marketization is central.

Pioneering in this respect has been scholarship that uncovers how the identity shifts triggered by early neoliberal reforms played a role in the illiberal counterreaction. Based on extensive fieldwork in manufacturing centers in Poland, David Ost's *The Defeat of Solidarity*[43] showed that in the early 1990s left-liberal elites embraced neoliberalism, thereby driving an angry working class toward right-wing nationalism. In subsequent work, Ost also explained how, as the language of class was intentionally jettisoned amid the politically engineered disempowerment of labor and public embrace of individualism,[44] industrial workers and the marginalized small-city precariat came to rationalize their opposition to egalitarianism and indifference to the formal institutional niceties of liberalism.[45] Working from an anthropological perspective to assess how social class experiences shaped identities, Don Kalb similarly recognized the early neoliberal years as a "critical junction of devaluation and dispossession,"[46] during which a "class struggle without class" truly began in

---

[38] Bohle and Greskovits (2012: 13–14); Burawoy (2013).

[39] Burawoy (2003: 238–9).

[40] Burawoy (2010; 2013).

[41] Burawoy (2019: 214); Hann (2019a; 2021b).

[42] Block and Somers (1984); Hann (2018).

[43] Ost (2005).

[44] Ost (2009; 2011; 2015a; 2015b).

[45] Ost (2018; 2022).

[46] Kalb (2009); Kalb and Halmai (2011).

Eastern Europe. As the region was increasingly integrated into global supply chains and some social democrats capitulated to transnational finance, Kalb argued, those who bore the brunt of neoliberal reforms – large swaths of the fractured working class, the provincial bourgeoisie, and the post-peasantry[47] – were ultimately mobilized by illiberals promising to strengthen the state and counter globalization.[48] Another anthropologist, Chris Hann, has "repatriated" Polanyi to the Central European countryside, where the neoliberal reforms of the 1990s produced the disintegration of collective farms and rural communities, to show how a sense of "moral dispossession" gave rise to nationalist identities and receptiveness to populist promises for a return of morality and fairness through workfare programs.[49] Based on half a century of fieldwork, Hann has not only shown how early neoliberalism disembedded provincial civil society after decades of socialist embeddedness, but also that crucial values, such as the peasant ethics of re-embedding the economy into the rural household, have persisted over time.[50]

This research tradition has been further developed by a number of scholars seeking to correct dominant narratives of the postcommunist transition as an unmitigated success story and to show how neoliberalism, the strategies of political elites, and illiberalism are linked in contemporary Eastern Europe. Some political economists have connected the formation of illiberal social coalitions to the failures of political agents to defend the interests of key constituencies – above all, labor, post-peasants, and national capitalists – as the region developed dependence on foreign capital. For Stuart Shields, for instance, after transnationally oriented social forces coopted Poland's Solidarity and postcommunist Left in order to deregulate the economy, a "recombinant" populist social force – including manufacturing, agricultural, and mining workers, among others – first emerged as a defensive reaction and then sought to "domesticate" neoliberalism.[51] Analyzing how a very different social force benefits from foreign investment in Fidesz's Hungary, Samuel Rogers has also emphasized the key role political agency plays in mobilizing and managing national capitalists previously unhappy with the country's postcommunist integration with the West.[52] Gábor Scheiring has argued persuasively that as left-wing technocrats sought to institutionalize the accumulation of transnational capital, a dual countermovement, including the working class "left behind in the Hungarian rustbelt" and the domestic bourgeoisie, rebelled against neoliberal elites and sought to re-embed the economy – a process that ultimately facilitated authoritarian statism.[53] Specifically analyzing variations in international economic integration and the dynamic relations among social coalitions, this author has

---

[47] Rural populations that seek to revive household-based economies after the end of collective farming. See Buzalka (2007); Hann (2021b); Szombati (2021).

[48] Kalb (2018; 2019).

[49] Hann (2011; 2018; 2019a).

[50] Hann (2019b; 2021a; 2021b).

[51] Shields (2007a; 2007b; 2012; 2015; 2021).

[52] Rogers (2019; 2020a; 2020b; 2024).

[53] Scheiring (2020a; 2020b; 2021a).

also explained different populist models in dependent economies, including mutations motivated by new compromises between transnational and national capitalists and strategically managed from the top down.[54]

Others have offered convincing ethnographic details regarding how ordinary people's subjectivities and everyday experiences matter for understanding the links between marketization and illiberalism under post-socialism as a distinctive material reality shaping human lives.[55] While some have attributed authoritarianism at the European periphery directly to skillful politicians' abuse of financialization as a system of social relations,[56] others have been more explicitly Polanyian in their interpretations. Emphasizing the collective working class memory of both socialism and neoliberalism in Hungary, Eszter Bartha has drawn attention to the Left's complicity in implementing austerity and promoting the interests of foreign capital at the expense of industrial labor, which turned to nationalism as a result.[57] As Kristóf Szombati has shown, the left-liberal elite's economic policies not only helped to destroy working class communities in Hungary's former industrial centers but also inspired a "revolt of the provinces," where the "de-peasantization" of agriculture undermined collective goods, provoked a sense of abandonment, and resulted in support for illiberal paternalism.[58] Extending research on the populist reaction to the transformation of agrarian and provincial communities, other anthropologists have emphasized the cognitive foundations and historical interpretations charging the Polanyian countermovement. Thus, whereas Anna Malewska-Szałygin has argued that social imaginaries inherited from the past have translated into a normative critique of neoliberalism and support for populism in rural Poland,[59] Juraj Buzalka has traced how the post-peasantry's nostalgia for a self-sufficient "people's economy" first developed when capitalist agrobusiness replaced collective farming and later contributed to the making of "village fascism" as a cultural economy of protest in Slovakia.[60]

What unites all these accounts, of course, is a Polanyian understanding of illiberalism as a countermovement that is collectively shaped by societal forces reacting to the particularly aggressive wave of marketization triggered by the end of communism. From this perspective, moreover, these reactive forces are shaped by purposeful and strategic political agents – main protagonists in terms of both driving marketization and managing the diverse social forces seeking protection from the reforms. Thus, rather than portray the rise of postcommunist illiberalism as a simplified story of supply or demand, scholars inspired by Polanyi prioritize a relational framework, according

---

[54] Scheiring (2021b; 2022).

[55] Borelli and Mattioli (2013); Gagyi (2016); Hann and Scheiring (2021); Scheiring and Szmobati (2020); Wyss (2021).

[56] Mattioli (2018; 2020).

[57] Bartha (2011; 2013); Bartha and Tóth (2021).

[58] Szombati (2018; 2021).

[59] Malewska-Szałygin (2017; 2021).

[60] Buzalka (2007; 2018; 2021a; 2021b).

to which an autonomous political sphere and reactive societal forces inter-acted in dynamic ways as postcommunist elites and regular people dealt with the neoliberal shocks of the 1990s and their consequences thereafter. As it emphasizes how some political agents shaped societies by enacting neoliberal policies while others adapted to the societal coalitions reacting to marketi-zation, this analytical tradition stresses the continued historical significance of early postcommunist political economy developments for making sense of subsequent illiberalism.

This book advances this dynamic and relational Polanyian perspective in terms of both its substantive arguments and methodological approach, which integrates subjective experiences and interpretations gleaned from scores of interviews into a historical-institutionalist analysis. Nevertheless, it does so in ways that make its contributions distinct from those of most sociologists, anthropologists, and political economists working within this tradition. First, by offering a political science interpretation, which relies on correspond-ing standard methods for comparative analysis, I adopt an institutionalist approach, which, as Fred Block and Margaret Somers have explained, is indeed central in Polanyian historical analysis.[61] While, unlike some sociologists, my inquiry does not explicitly focus on class interests and relations, I remain atten-tive, especially in the case studies, to how various social categories experienced the stratifying effects of marketization and were politically mobilized as they sought to defend themselves from neoliberal dislocations.

Second, although I deny neither the significance of transnational capital for unsettling and molding social relations, as argued by political economists, nor the importance of deeper historical forces for constructing populist narra-tives, as emphasized by anthropologists, I remain focused on domestic politi-cal dynamics during the first three postcommunist decades. On the one hand, while I consider historical legacies (above and in subsequent chapters) and international trade with the West, in which transnational capital plays a key role (in Chapter 3), I do not find evidence that such factors explain the concrete patterns of variation analyzed in this study. On the other hand, whereas much has been written about how foreign capital and longue durée history shaped populist politics in one or a few countries, the intricate dynamics concretely between domestic political agents and Polanyian countermovements have not been explored from a broader comparative perspective, as in this book. Third, by drawing on knowledge from scholarship on the movements countering marketization in Latin America and by assessing comparability with devel-opments in Eastern Europe, I advance an original Polanyian perspective that accounts for both the contextual uniqueness and historical generality of the neoliberal revolutions and post-neoliberal reactions across the world. It is to such cross-regional insights that I turn next.

---

[61] Block and Somers (1984).

2.1.3 Learning from Latin America's Recent History

As the above discussion made clear, distant history does not explain illiberal outcomes in Eastern Europe, whereas the top-down supply of strategic agency and bottom-up demands of social coalitions have been interactive in the historical reality of the region after 1989. Indeed, as unique postcommunist legacies supersede previous ones and as the salience of political issues can be driven by both legacy and agency,[62] it is recent history that can illuminate how illiberal outcomes are the product of interactive dynamics between historical path dependencies *and* political agents' strategies. To understand how such interactions materialized in the postcommunist context, I turn for insights to Latin America, where the interplay between political agency and the legacies of recent history also defined politics in the early twenty-first century. Indeed, the postcommunist context may in many ways be particular, but it can nevertheless be approached in generalizable and contextually holistic ways based on theoretically justified cross-regional comparisons.[63] As I next argue, the Latin American experience, which provided useful points of reference for Eastern Europe early in the economic and political transition,[64] still offers valuable comparative lessons for the postcommunist context.

As acknowledged in Chapter 1, these two regions are undeniably different from one another. Historically, the Eastern European legacies of empire, communism, and highly contentious state- and nation-building at various historical stages are very different from Latin America's experiences with Iberian colonialism, military dictatorship, and relatively more stable borders. Geopolitically, one region is located between East and West, while the other is in the global South. Eastern Europe, as a whole, is characterized by relatively less pressure for economic redistribution due to its lower inequality, greater skepticism of openly leftist alternatives to neoliberalism, more intense forms of ethnic nationalism, and weaker and less mobilized civil societies.[65] Whereas Latin America's republics are presidential systems, postcommunist countries are mostly parliamentary republics. Even if these generalities do not define all countries in each region, the basic historical, economic, sociocultural, and institutional contrasts between Eastern Europe and Latin America are innumerable.

More interesting than the obvious differences, however, is a theoretically relevant development from the not-so-distant past – the shared legacy of historically recent waves of political and economic liberalization. Yet although both regions underwent elite-driven transformations to democracy and the

---

[62] Whitefield and Rohrschneider (2015); Wittenberg (2015).

[63] Kubik (2015).

[64] Greskovits (1998); Jowitt (1992); Linz and Stepan (1996); Przeworski (1991).

[65] Greskovits (1998: 103); Howard (2003).

market,[66] the long-term effects of the political dynamics that defined critical moments of neoliberal reform have been more systematically studied for the Latin American context. For instance, depending on what political forces were in power and in opposition during neoliberal critical junctures, Roberts distinguishes between two general scenarios with long-term consequences. Under *contested liberalism,* conservatives spearheaded market reforms while facing congressional opposition from left-of-center parties – a predictable dynamic that programmatically aligned and stabilized party systems. By contrast, where champions of labor – whether worker-based and leftist parties or independent populist actors – found themselves in charge during junctures, *neoliberal convergence* undermined party programs, increased voter uncertainty, and destabilized party systems.[67] As economic shocks forced governing leftwing parties to renege on programmatic commitments and as voters abandoned such parties,[68] leftist ideology and branding became resources available for subsequent populist mobilization.[69] Overall, the highly contingent roles political actors played during neoliberal junctures triggered reactive sequences, thereby channeling societal reactions to neoliberalism, conditioning subsequent variation in party system stability, and creating different opportunities for resourceful antiestablishment actors to exploit nationalist and statist economic platforms.[70] As the *type* of critical juncture – itself defined by who led and opposed reforms during crucial moments of neoliberal deepening – was independent from historical antecedents, it was recent, rather than longue-durée, history that shaped subsequently varying effects in contemporary Latin American party systems.[71]

Although this scholarship does not specifically theorize the mechanisms shaping linkages between opportunity structures conditioned by junctures and the electoral viability of strategic antiestablishment actors, the path dependency framework is highly relevant for making sense of illiberal outcomes at the ballot box in postcommunist Europe. As in Latin America, political and technocratic elites played key roles during critical periods of market reforms in Eastern Europe.[72] In both regions, for example, high-level political choices and arrangements were centrally important for managing economic crisis under the guidance of international financial institutions during the early years of the economic transition.[73] Even if subsequent antiestablishment reactions in Eastern Europe were not under explicitly anti-neoliberal banners, as in Latin America, they nonetheless featured riots, mass demonstrations, citizens' exit from formal politics,[74] and "the strange death of the

[66] Pop-Eleches (2009); Przeworski (1991); Roberts (2014).
[67] Roberts (2014).
[68] Lupu (2016).
[69] Cyr (2017); Handlin (2017).
[70] Roberts (2013: 1440).
[71] Roberts (2014: 89–134).
[72] Bohle and Greskovits (2012: 56).
[73] Pop-Eleches (2009).
[74] Bohle and Greskovits (2012: 5–6).

liberal consensus."[75] As the legacies of early postcommunist political strategies, competition patters, and balance of partisan power conditioned subsequent institutional outcomes,[76] I next explain how political dynamics during
postcommunist junctures shaped trajectories and outcomes in ways both
similar to and different from the Latin American experience.

2.2 PATH-DEPENDENT SOURCES OF EASTERN EUROPEAN ILLIBERALISM

2.2.1 Postcommunist Junctures

Postcommunist junctures are crucial periods of building capitalism in Eastern
Europe. Similarly to Latin America's neoliberal junctures, they can be
understood as moments of intense neoliberal deepening, when, in response
to impending crises, governments "attempted an ambitious package of
market-based stabilization and adjustment designed to dismantle historical
forms of state intervention."[77] Of course, such attempts varied significantly
across the region as reformist governments adopted different approaches to
welfare, industrial deregulation, and privatization policymaking.[78] This, in
turn, resulted in greatly varying patterns of reform intensity and effectiveness. While Poland, Estonia, and Albania chose shock therapy early on,
Lithuania, Hungary, and Slovenia experimented with gradualism. If reforms
were deemed successful relatively fast in Poland, Estonia, Slovenia, Lithuania,
and Hungary, their effectiveness in Ukraine, Moldova, and across the Balkans
was more delayed and questionable. While such differences corresponded to
unique domestic conditions, including the intensity of the crises that austerity
was meant to counteract, what all postcommunist junctures had in common
was the consolidation of neoliberalism by means of significant budgetary roll-
backs and welfare retrenchment.

   Yet the implementation of market reforms does not by itself constitute a critical
juncture, which, as noted in Chapter 1, is associated with institutional unsettle-
ment and innovation. After all, economic liberalization featuring various forms of
austerity was an ongoing process that in most cases had begun under communism,
as discussed earlier. In this context, what made postcommunist junctures harbin-
gers of change was the link between elected politicians' choices relative to credible
campaign platforms and voters' ability to hold such agents accountable in competitive elections – a historical novelty for countries in the region. Yet, while first competitive elections may have been important for early political trajectories,[79] they
were less crucial for long-term illiberal outcomes, as they did not trigger postcommunist junctures. The reason for this is that initial competitive elections neither
were genuinely democratic nor offered much choice on the most relevant questions

---

[75] Krastev (2007).

[76] Frye (2010); Grzymała-Busse (2002); McFaul (2002).

[77] Roberts (2013: 1430).

[78] Bohle and Greskovits (2012).

[79] Bunce (2003); Fish (1998).

when building capitalism – those of economic salience. Indeed, initial competitive elections – for the Polish Sejm (1989), for the Supreme Soviets of the Baltics, Moldova, and Ukraine (1990), or for constitutional assemblies in Bulgaria (1990) and Albania (1991) – revolved around issues of the imminent political transition, statehood, and constitutionalism, not questions about the economy.

By contrast, subsequent elections – held after limited restructuring and its attendant social dislocations – featured debates and platforms of more obvious economic relevance. It was, thus, beginning with *second competitive elections* that voters in better consolidated democracies – with "electoral rules identical to the ones that brought the incumbent to office"[80] – could hold elected politicians accountable for economic policies relative to prior campaign promises. As the salience of questions about market-making and social welfare grew under improved democratic conditions, postcommunist junctures occurred sometime after second nationwide competitive elections. Triggered by a sense of crisis, junctures generally transpired at different points throughout the first postcommunist decade, beginning in Poland in 1990 and ending everywhere by 2002, when many countries successfully completed negotiations for European Union membership after sufficient liberalization.

In sum, postcommunist junctures are the earliest decisive periods of neoliberal deepening sometime after second competitive nationwide elections in Eastern European countries. Returning to the centrality of political agency and relying on data from the annual reports of the European Bank for Reconstruction and Development in order to gauge the relevant depth of neoliberal reforms over time, Table 2.1. groups countries based on the type of postcommunist juncture they experienced.[81] Loosely based on Roberts' categorizations of neoliberal junctures in Latin America, it identifies leading reformers (prime ministers and, for countries with relatively strong presidencies, presidents) and their parliamentary opponents during relevant reform periods. Importantly, because the phase of most intense economic reforms tended to correspond to the erratic timing of crisis, the political configurations defining postcommunist junctures were contingent rather than determined by prior developments.[82]

---

[80] Cheibub et al. (2010: 69).

[81] Postcommunist junctures typically represent the largest absolute change toward economic liberalization – as measured with EBRD's "Transition Indicators" – achieved under a single government sometime after the second competitive election. See Binev (2023) for a list of key reform events in overall liberalization, market-making, and the social sector during each country's juncture.

[82] While some of the variation in configurations could be potentially explained with reference to Eyal et al.'s (1998) perspective focused on legacies and elite strategy – according to which former dissidents, having initially tried to squeeze ex-communists out of power immediately after 1989 but soon realizing they could not govern alone, allowed former communist pragmatists back in the ruling elite by the mid 1990s – this is not sufficient, for two reasons. First, as Eyal et al.'s analysis covered few countries in East Central Europe, there is not enough evidence that such dynamics occurred in the broader postcommunist region. Second, as the timing of the crises that triggered the most intense market reforms could not be predicted and as junctures occurred sometime – but not necessarily immediately – after second competition elections, the political configurations at the time were highly idiosyncratic.

TABLE 2.1 *Postcommunist junctures*

Country	Second competitive election	Juncture period	Politically responsible leaders	Elected parties/actors in charge	Leading opponents
Aligning junctures					
Albania	1992 (parl.)	1992–1996	Meksi (PM)	Democratic Party (right)	Socialist Party of Albania (ex-communist)
Bulgaria	1991 (parl.)	1997–2001	Kostov (PM)	Union of Democratic Forces (right)	Bulgarian Socialist Party (ex-communist)
Czechia	1992 (parl.)	1992–1996	Klaus (PM)	Civic Democratic Party (right)	Czech Social Democratic Party (historical left), Communist Party of Bohemia and Moravia
Moldova	1994 (parl.)	1998–2001	Ciubuc, Sturza, Braghiș (PMs)	Alliance for Democracy and Reforms (right)	Communist Party
N. Macedonia	1994 (general)	1998–2002	Georgievski (PM)	VMRO-DPMNE (right)	Social Democratic Union (ex-communist)
Romania	1992 (general)	1996–2000	Constantinescu (Pres.), Ciorbea, Vasile, Isarescu (PMs)	Romanian Democratic Convention (right)	Social Democratic Party (ex-communist)
Ambiguous junctures					
Croatia	1992 (parl. & pres.)	1992–1995	Tuđman (Pres.), Šarinić, Valentić, Mateša (PMs)	Croatian Democratic Union (right)	Fragmented opposition, including Social Democratic Party (ex-communist)
Estonia	1992 (parl. & pres.)	1992–1995	Laar, Tarand (PMs)	Governing coalition led by Pro Patria (right) and including the relatively weak Moderates (center-left) for most of the period	Fragmented opposition eventually joined by the Moderates, who withdraw support for cabinet and facilitate Laar's ouster in 1994

Latvia	1993 (parl.)	1993–1995	Birkavs, Gallis (PMs)	Latvian Way (right)	Various, with relatively weak Harmony for Latvia (leftist)
Slovenia	1992 (parl. & pres.)	1992–1996	Drnovšek (PM)	Grand Coalition led by Liberal Democracy (right of center) and including Social Democrats for most of period	Various, including Social Democrats (ex-communist) after 1995
Ukraine	1994 (parl. & pres.)	1994–1998	Kuchma (Pres.), Marchuk (PM)	Rightist president elected with support from Communist Party	Various, including Communist Party and Socialist Party

Bait-and-switch junctures

Hungary	1994 (parl.)	1994–1998	Horn (PM)	Socialist Party (ex-communist)	Hungarian Democratic Forum (right)
Lithuania	1992 (parl.)	1992–1996	Brazauskas (Pres.), Šleževičius, Stankevičius (PMs)	Democratic Labor Party (ex-communist)	Sajudis (right)
Poland	1990 (pres.)	1990–1993	Wałęsa (Pres.), Bielecki, Suchocka (PMs)	Labor-based populist president retains shock-therapy Finance Minister for a year after entering office and appoints reformist prime-ministers for most of period	Various/fragmented opposition
Slovakia	1992 (parl.)	1998–2002	Dzurinda (PM)	Party of the Democratic Left (ex-communist) is largest single party in reformist coalition government and in charge of key ministries (Finance and Labor and Social Affairs)	People's Party – Movement for a Democratic Slovakia (national populist)

Depending on who led, on the one hand, efforts at economic liberalization and, on the other hand, the parliamentary opposition during these critical reform periods, postcommunist junctures set in motion dynamics of varying degrees of predictability and voter certainty about political commitments. In countries where rightist incumbents were in charge and leftist rivals led the parliamentary opposition, consistency with party brands and campaign promises triggered predictable patterns of political competition and highest certainty. Although neoliberal deepening occurred under very different conditions in these six countries – earlier in democratic Czechia and competitive-authoritarian Albania, and later in Romania, Bulgaria, Moldova, and North Macedonia[83] – they all experienced aligning junctures associated with clear programmatic differentiation, or what Roberts identified (for the Latin American context) as contested liberalism. By contrast, more ambiguous political dynamics during junctures provoked lower levels of predictability and voter certainty in the second set of countries. While rightist forces here also led important reforms – whether by shock-therapeutic (Estonia and Ukraine) or more moderate means (Croatia and Slovenia)[84] – the relative feebleness of leftist alternatives conditioned programmatic ambiguity. The Left did contest elections in Croatia, Estonia, and Latvia but it was not sufficiently strong to lead the parliamentary opposition to market reforms during junctures. Leftist parties waivered in Ukraine, where the Communists ended up opposing Kuchma's reforms after first helping him win the 1994 presidential election, and Slovenia, where the Social Democrats withdrew from the reformist coalition after participating in it for most of the juncture period. Even if leftist alternatives to rightist reformers existed in these five countries, ambiguous dynamics were less conducive to clear programmatic differentiation.

Bait-and-switch junctures, finally, were distinguished by counterintuitive dynamics of neoliberal convergence. In Hungary, Lithuania, and Slovakia, it was leftist parties that bore the main responsibility for deepening neoliberalism during the juncture. They may have pledged in their campaigns to slow down reforms and relax the socially punishing policies of previous conservative governments, but socialists led the charge on both "the most radical adjustment program ever implemented in Hungary" and the currency board and flat tax in Lithuania.[85] Having also promised socialist solutions yet ending up in charge of the Ministry of Finance as the de facto largest party in their country's first reformist government to complete a full term,[86] Slovakia's ex-communists enacted austerity by significantly tightening the

---

[83] Levitsky and Way (2010); Pop-Eleches (2009).
[84] Bohle and Greskovits (2012).
[85] Bohle and Greskovits (2012: 109–12); Cook and Orenstein (1999: 92).

[86] For details regarding why this period, rather than Dzurinda's second government (2002–6), corresponds to Slovakia's juncture, see Chapter 4.

budget.[87] Poland's first democratically elected president, Lech Wałęsa, may have been an anti-communist hero, but he also engaged in similar about-face after credible prolabor rhetoric as the leader of the largest labor union, which had recently demanded higher wages. Having stoked "anti-capitalist anger" as he ran for the presidency against Tadeusz Mazowiecki, the prime-minister who had initiated shock therapy, Wałęsa was then instrumental for sustaining neoliberal reforms as president.[88] Although Poland's configuration was somewhat idiosyncratic – because a weakened Left led neither reforms nor, during most of the juncture, the parliamentary opposition – it, too, entailed dynamics and consequences similar to those in other bait-and-switch cases, as detailed in Chapters 4 and 5. As critical liberalization was either spearheaded by or implemented with crucial support from leftist or labor-based political forces, postcommunist junctures in these four countries produced lowest levels of predictability and certainty about political commitments.

2.2.2 Key Similarities with and Differences from Latin America

As noted earlier, the perspective focused on political roles during key periods of postcommunist market reform suggests interesting parallels with the Latin American experience, where neoliberal junctures conditioned, earlier than in Eastern Europe, varying degrees of predictability and uncertainty.[89] As in Latin America, moreover, the type of juncture in postcommunist Europe was contingent not on historical legacies or ideology but rather on more coincidental political configurations at a critical time of economic crisis management. For example, if both Bulgaria and Ukraine had come out of patrimonial communism, shock therapy was administered by the anti-communist Right in the first case and a "red director" in the second. Estonia and Lithuania may have shared important historical similarities, but they experienced opposite types of junctures. And if the social democratic Left criticized neoliberal deepening in Czechia, it was in charge of it in Slovakia. As adversarial economic circumstances – hyperinflation (Poland, Ukraine, Bulgaria), impending debt crisis (Hungary), or economic stagnation (Lithuania, Slovakia, North Macedonia) – required those in power at the time to intensify reforms and allowed those in opposition to voice criticism, postcommunist junctures were periods of pronounced contingency.

This general similarity in terms of contingency, however, does not mean that neoliberal junctures in Eastern Europe triggered processes of production and reproduction[90] identical to those in Latin America. To the contrary – Eastern Europe's junctures are uniquely *postcommunist*. Because here the exit from state socialism and totalitarianism was even more drastic than Latin America's transition away from import substitution industrialization and authoritarianism, the rupture with

---

[87] Bohle and Greskovits (2012: 170); Fisher (2002); Vachudova (2005).

[88] Ost (2005: 60–93).

[89] Roberts (2014).

[90] Collier and Collier (1991: 30–1).

the past was even more pronounced. In Latin America, where the antecedent foundations of multiparty regimes conditioned varying dynamics during the transition years – with labor-mobilizing party systems experiencing greater disruptions than elitist ones – neoliberal junctures triggered institutional continuities or changes in the aftermath period.[91] By contrast, throughout Eastern Europe, where labor had been mobilized more rigidly under one-party systems, institutional discontinuities were the norm as postcommunist junctures coincided with the formation of new multiparty systems everywhere. Therefore, if Latin America's neoliberal junctures had implications for overall party system stability relative to the past, without necessarily affecting traditional leftist and conservative parties differently,[92] this general mechanism cannot apply to Eastern Europe, where liberals and conservatives had been banned from competing under communism.

Figure 2.1 clarifies relevant similarities and differences in terms of the development of party system stability in the two regions. Based on Roberts' data for Latin America and my own dataset for Eastern Europe, it compares

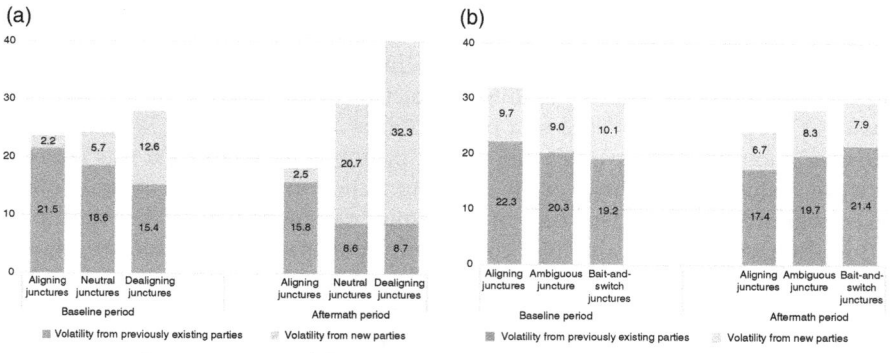

FIGURE 2.1 Party system stability in Latin America and postcommunist Europe.
(a) Latin America, (b) postcommunist Europe
(1) Whereas I adopt Roberts' nomenclature for "aligning" junctures, "ambiguous" and "bait-and-switch" junctures in postcommunist Europe correspond, respectively, to "neutral" and "de-aligning" junctures in Latin America. I prefer distinct terms for these types of junctures in postcommunist Europe because the political configurations that define them were not identical to the ones discussed by Roberts for the Latin American context. (2) The figures are for the purpose of a general comparison, as aggregation techniques are somewhat different for the two regions. Volatility in Latin America is calculated based on results from legislative and presidential elections, while volatility in Eastern European countries, one-third of which do not hold presidential elections, is calculated based on parliamentary elections. Whereas for Latin America the baseline period is 1980–2000 (before and during junctures) and the aftermath period is 2000–10 (see Roberts 2014), for Eastern Europe the two periods are defined separately for each country (see Table 2.1).

---

[91] Roberts (2014: 89–110).   [92] Roberts (2014: 103–10, 125–32).

the evolution of electoral volatility from previously existing and new parties during baseline periods preceding junctures and aftermath periods following them. Although the baseline period in Eastern Europe – from the end of communism to the beginning of junctures throughout the 1990s – is necessarily shorter than the baseline period in Latin America, where volatility in multiparty system contexts can be more meaningfully studied for a longer period, this comparison is nevertheless instructive as it reveals key patterns of theoretical significance.

Figure 2.1a illustrates the central point of Roberts' argument for Latin America. Whereas aligning junctures stabilized overall party systems (reducing overall volatility by 23 percent), the neoliberal convergence associated with programmatic ambiguity under neutral junctures, and, above all, bait-and-switch tactics under de-aligning junctures clearly destabilized them (increasing overall volatility by 21 percent and 46 percent, respectively), particularly as voting for new parties – such as those led by anti-neoliberal populist outsiders – exploded in the aftermath period. In Eastern Europe, too, the baseline similarity of relative instability in the three groups of countries was followed by a divergence in the aftermath period, as seen in Figure 2.1b. If aligning junctures tended to stabilize party systems relative to the baseline period (reducing overall volatility by 25 percent, a downward trend very similar to the one in Latin America), ambiguous and bait-and-switch junctures did not. If contested liberalism similarly stabilized party systems in both regions, neoliberal convergence did not.

And yet the comparison of evolving volatility shows that the Eastern European experience is also different, in three important ways. First, party system instability during the baseline period – when early liberalization was unfolding throughout the region – was generally higher than in Latin America, with nearly a third of the electorate in Eastern Europe switching votes between elections. This is unsurprising given that in the 1990s democratic choice was a novelty for postcommunist European publics, now finally free to switch their votes from one election to the next. Second and relatedly, as ambiguous and bait-and-switch junctures were notably less disruptive than similar junctures in Latin America (where baseline volatility had been comparatively lower), they seem to have conditioned persistent, rather than increasing, party system instability in Eastern Europe. Third, if neoliberal convergence was associated with the rise of new parties in Latin America, volatility from older parties tended to be more prevalent in Eastern Europe.

Of course, such differences can be partially explained by regionally specific factors such as, for example, electoral institutions incentivizing the development of new parties under Latin America's presidentialism.[93] More importantly, however, the cross-regional comparison illuminates both theoretically

---

[93] On the relationship between electoral institutions and volatility, see Birch (2001) for Eastern Europe and Carreras (2012) for Latin America.

informative parallels and key differences. If junctures of deepening neoliberalism corresponded to somewhat parallel dynamics in party systems, such
dynamics were far from identical in Eastern Europe and Latin America. Having
emerged out of its communist past, the former region not only differed from
the latter with its more conservative reactions to neoliberalism; it also experienced more contextually specific party system developments after junctures.
While overall tendencies of volatility do not unlock the mechanism linking
postcommunist junctures and persistently varying illiberal outcomes, they do
suggest that – unlike in Latin America – mainstream, or established, parties
continued being central for party system instability after junctures in Eastern
Europe. I next focus on the region's historically best-established parties – those
left-of-center – as key spheres of institutional reproduction.

2.2.3 Leftist Paths

The fate of the postcommunist Left has been subject to much analysis, with
authors often relating electoral performance to the capacity for ideological
adaptation to a new set of norms soon after the end of communism.[94] Leftist
parties could adapt ideologically on two dimensions – by distancing themselves
from communist economics and by embracing culturally liberal ideas.[95] In
turn, their capacity to adopt liberal democratic programs in the early transition
years has been linked to mutually related organizational and historical factors.
By emphasizing organization, Grzymała-Busse attributed communist successor
parties' "regeneration" to reform-minded elites, who not only had access to
organizational resources inherited from the communist past but also managed
to block resistance from party conservatives by centralizing power in the early
transition period.[96] On the other hand, Kitschelt saw national-accommodative
communism – itself possible where the strength of pre-communist political
society and the professionalization of civil service had been neither too strong
(as in East Germany and Czechia) nor too weak (as in the Balkans) – as conducive to the social democratization of ex-communists. Where long-distance factors shaped more orthodox paths for communist successor parties, it was new
statehood in search of Western protection (as in the Baltics, Slovenia, Slovakia,
Croatia, and, to a lesser extent Moldova, North Macedonia, and Ukraine) that
could possibly induce reformist currents.[97]

Although this foundational scholarship convincingly explains the programmatic and electoral tendencies of communist successor parties in the first
postcommunist decade, it is less persuasive when it comes to subsequent developments and nuances. To begin, the organizational approach takes a holistic

---

[94] E.g., Grzymała-Busse (2002); Tavits and
Letki (2009).
[95] Bozóki and Ishiyama (2002).

[96] Grzymała-Busse (2002).
[97] Kitschelt (2002).

view of ideology – if ex-communist party organizations are reformist, they adopt economically *and* culturally liberal programs. Yet outside of Central Europe, which was the main focus of the accounts noted above, the picture has been more mixed. Although they all share similar organizational heritage and centralizing tendencies, Albania's and North Macedonia's ex-communists subscribe to culturally liberal values and are thus more reformed than communist successors in Romania and Moldova. Likewise, the programmatic positions of important leftist parties without communist organizational origins also remain poorly understood, as Czechia's Social Democrats have been not only consistently more economically leftist than their Estonian, Latvian, and Lithuanian counterparts but also as leftist as Bulgaria's and Romania's ex-communists.[98] Such programmatic trends in the early twenty-first century can be explained with reference to neither organizational resources inherited from the past nor credible social democratic commitments, as per Grzymała-Busse's argument. Kitschelt's historical approach, on the other hand, makes highly correct predictions regarding the economic and cultural programs of communist successor parties throughout the region. At the same time, however, it is less predictive in terms of the varying popularity of ex-communist parties after national-accommodative communism in the twenty-first century. Indeed, the longue-durée historical approach may have anticipated high electoral support in all such cases, but only some of these reformed ex-communists experienced electoral strength (Croatia) or stability (Slovenia) in the 2000–20 period relative to the 1990s, with others undergoing ballot box losses (Slovakia, Lithuania, Poland). In sum, the approaches prioritizing organizational factors and longue-durée history do not explain the programmatic *and* electoral tendencies of leftist parties – whether ex-communist or not – in the first two decades of the twenty-first century.

And yet these tendencies mattered in Eastern Europe, where economic issues became increasingly salient across the region after the first postcommunist decade[99] – that is, when the long-term effects of the neoliberal revolution started to be truly understood and felt by publics.[100] It is here that the postcommunist juncture approach illuminates developments as it pays close attention to how particular political configurations during key moments of market reform shaped links between leftist parties' credibility on economic matters and their electoral performance in the long run. Indeed, whether they are communist successors or more traditional social democrats, leftist parties in Eastern Europe have historically based their legitimacy on socialist rhetoric and policies. With an average age of eighty-seven years as of 2020 and most tracing their origins to the pre-communist era, Eastern Europe's leftist parties were long associated with socialist redistribution aimed at promoting equality through "modern welfare systems, functioning pension schemes, and adequate

---

[98] Bakker et al. (2015); Lindberg et al. (2022); Polk et al. (2017).

[99] Rohrschneider and Whitefield (2009).
[100] Ghodsee and Orenstein (2021).

healthcare and educational institutions."[101] Although leftist parties displayed ideological diversity after communism, even the most reformed among them – those that embraced "new social democracy" – were expected to pursue active government policy as a solution to problems arising from the weakening of social safety nets.[102] Especially as the system of state-socialist redistributive policy collapsed, the Left's credible interventionist appeal attracted significant popular support in the early phases of the transformation – the "deep recession" years of inflation, unemployment, impoverishment, and homelessness.[103]

As postcommunist junctures generally occurred after initial but incomplete reforms, when the deeply felt social effects of the economic transformation raised the salience of economic issues in Eastern Europe, the policy stances the Left took at the time had significant consequences. Because their political positions – in opposition or in government – represented either conformity with or a major departure from historically established programmatic tendencies, the role in which leftist parties found themselves during the juncture had major implications for their future relationship with constituencies. Crucially, the juncture shaped the Left's programmatic positions – and thus its linkages with voters – in the long term. As noted by Paul Pierson, "actors have strong incentives … to continue down a specific path once initial steps are taken in that direction."[104] Specifically, as structural crises raised the salience of economic concerns after second competitive elections, as discussed earlier, parties came "to 'own' issues in the public mind" by acquiring reputations for the stances they took. In turn, "once established, various mechanisms work to keep these initial party alignments in place."[105] While mechanisms of ideological reproduction may vary, junctures were especially critical for subsequent developments – because the reforms undertaken during these periods usually led countries out of preceding crises or at least out of the economic swamps of the early transition years. Since competent reformers were rewarded with concrete material benefits – for example, superior trade and investment flows sanctioned by international financial institutions or improved prospects for EU membership[106] – those in charge of reforms developed reputations for competence. As Western linkage and leverage created virtuous cycles and domestic stakeholders,[107] postcommunist junctures thus shaped reputational incentives with implications for long-term programmatic consistency.

The incentive to cultivate reputations charted distinct paths of ideological reproduction for leftist parties in different political roles during junctures. Those that found themselves in a position of incumbency "had strong incentives to implement fiscal austerity because they needed to prove their dissociation from socialism and their ability to operate in a democracy and market

---

[101] Ladányi and Szelényi (2002: 45–6).
[102] Ladányi and Szelényi (2002).
[103] Ghodsee and Orenstein (2021: 32–3); Ladányi and Szelényi (2002: 45–6); Tucker (2006).

[104] Pierson (2000: 254).
[105] Whitefield and Rohrschneider (2015: 4).
[106] Pop-Eleches (2009); Vachudova (2005).
[107] Levitsky and Way (2005: 24).

economy."[108] Once competent reformers of the Left proved liberal credentials, they continued on, rather than resisting, the neoliberal path. By contrast, leftist parties leading the opposition during junctures distinguished themselves as long-term critics of neoliberalism. Of course, this is not to say that such parties were against all market reforms; in fact, some had already engaged in limited liberalization earlier in the 1990s, as in Bulgaria, North Macedonia, and Romania. Yet, because it was their rightist competitors who first established reputations for neoliberal reform competence during junctures, the best option for the Left, as a leader of the parliamentary opposition, was to emphasize policy differentiation. As branding divergence from political competitors also "maximizes ranks" and strengthens partisan attachments,[109] such leftist parties had long-term incentives to highlight the deleterious effects of market deepening on welfare.

In sum, depending on the political role in which it found itself during junctures, the Left had reputational incentives to either continue acting as a credible reformer or keep differentiating itself from those in charge of deepening neoliberalism. In between were leftist parties whose relative weakness during junctures assigned them more secondary roles in government and opposition, thus shaping more ambiguous positions on economic issues over time. Since contingent roles during junctures in turn shaped varying degrees of voter uncertainty about policy consistency, leftist parties' durable positions on economic issues affected their long-term prospects at the ballot box. As junctures disrupted or sustained the Left's traditional programmatic linkages with constituencies, they conditioned either persistent voter loyalty – to leftist parties with reliably socialist positions, or exit[110] – from leftist parties with pro-market tendencies at odds with historical commitments. The Left's persistent positioning on economic issues and electoral performance were thus two mutually related legacies of postcommunist junctures.

2.2.4 Legacies, Strategic Choices, and Probabilistic Outcomes

If leftist path dependencies constitute the first component of my two-step argument highlighting the interaction between legacy and agency, subsequent strategic choices represent the second. Indeed, postcommunist junctures had powerful conditioning effects, either as resources or constraints, on political environments to which subsequent actors – specifically, anti-establishment parties – adapted by making choices.[111] More specifically, whereas the Left's programmatic consistency and relative electoral strength limited the viability of illiberalism and post-neoliberal populism, its programmatic inconsistency and relative electoral weakness can be understood

---

[108] Tavits and Letki (2009: 555).
[109] Lupu (2013: 61).

[110] Hirschman (1970).
[111] See Mahoney and Snyder (1999: 24).

as resources that enhanced it. Two characteristics of antiestablishment parties account for this link between environmental legacies bequeathed by postcommunist junctures and subsequent illiberal outcomes at the ballot box – (1) organizational capacity for adaptation and (2) unique incentives to maximize contrarian legitimacy.

First, antiestablishment parties are often personalistic formations,[112] which tend to concentrate decision-making in their leadership. Highly autonomous from the civil society pressures traditionally associated with organized labor, itself in poor shape across postcommunist Europe, modern antiestablishment parties are typically unconstrained by programmatic linkages[113] and thus ideologically flexible. As such parties have considerable leeway to pick and choose ideas and programmatic positions that they interpret as strategically advantageous, their leadership autonomy endows them with key organizational capacities for adaptation to the environmental context.[114] Second, antiestablishment parties' actual choice of economic positions is guided by particular incentives to maximize contrarian legitimacy by differentiating themselves from the liberal establishment. While many such parties adopt culturally illiberal positions, only some exploit economic interventionism as a successful electoral strategy. As environmental opportunities after postcommunist junctures vary, antiestablishment parties are likely to pursue different economic positions as adaptive strategies for differentiation.

Of course, antiestablishment parties do not always choose the positions best fitting their particular political contexts. While such parties are generally characterized by the capacities and incentives just noted, their leadership autonomy is not always limitless, and neither are the fallible individuals at their helm always capable of optimizing learning opportunities.[115] Thus, as the strategic choices of actual programmatic positioning are conditioned, rather than fully determined, by the environmental legacies of postcommunist junctures, they shape probabilistic illiberal outcomes.

Figure 2.2 captures how antiestablishment parties' strategic choice of economic positions is both enabled by unique incentives and organizational capacities for adaptation and conditioned by the environmental legacies of postcommunist junctures. As junctures conditioned path dependencies linking the Left's economic positioning and electoral performance, as explained earlier, their environmental legacies provided varying opportunities for ideologically adaptive and eager to differentiate themselves antiestablishment parties to succeed by exploiting economic positions or posturing critical of neoliberalism. Whereas a programmatically consistent and electorally resilient Left constrained opportunities for the strategic exploitation of such positions, a programmatically inconsistent and electorally weaker Left enhanced the electoral

---

[112] Mudde (2007: 260–4).
[113] Kitschelt (2000).

[114] See Burgess and Levitsky (2003).
[115] See Kitschelt (2002).

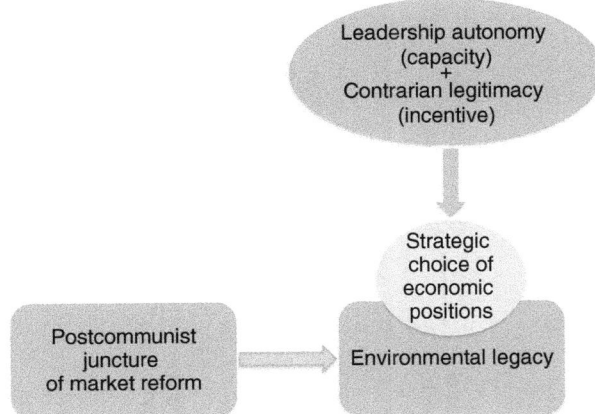

FIGURE 2.2 Strategic choices of economic positions by antiestablishment parties

viability of parties betting on illiberalism, both cultural and economic. If such parties had uneven viability at the ballot box across Eastern Europe in the first two twenty-first century decades, their electoral success depended on the strategic – but not always perfect – choice of economic positions most suitable for the environmental conditions in which they operated. As these contexts had been shaped by prior junctures, illiberal outcomes were the probabilistic products of postcommunist agency and history alike.

2.2.5 Overall Argument

The overall argument linking postcommunist junctures to subsequent leftist path dependencies and illiberal electoral outcomes is sketched in Figure 2.3, which borrows concepts from James Mahoney's work on critical junctures of liberal reform in Central America. With its attention to "how actor choices create institutional structures, which in turn shape subsequent actor behaviors ... and new institutional and structural patterns,"[116] this analytical framework is highly relevant for the analysis of Eastern Europe's challenge to liberalism as a probabilistic outcome shaped by the institutional legacies of political configurations during prior postcommunist junctures.

Throughout much of Eastern Europe, as in Latin America, key periods of neoliberal deepening after the fall of Cold War dictatorships proved critical for understanding subsequent institutional outcomes. As the earliest periods of decisive market reform amid crisis sometime after second competitive elections, postcommunist junctures featured varying degrees of predictability

---

[116] Mahoney (2001a: 11).

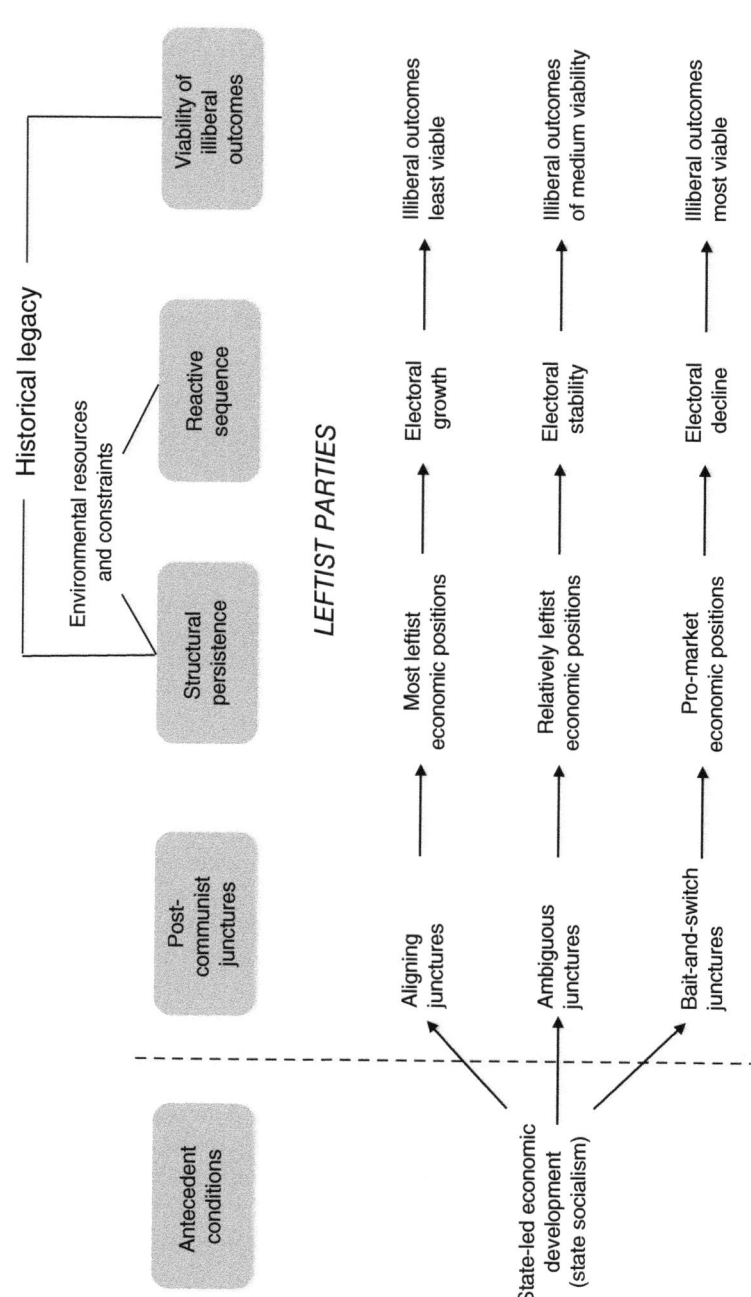

FIGURE 2.3 Divergent legacies of postcommunist junctures

and uncertainty, depending on who happened to be in power and opposition at the time. Where rightist incumbents enacted significant reforms, junctures were either aligning – if a strong Left established a predictable pattern of political competition by leading the parliamentary opposition, or ambiguous – if relative weakness prevented leftist parties from articulating clear economic policy alternatives. Where leftist or labor-based actors deepened neoliberalism contrary to credible historical commitments and prior campaign promises, bait-and-switch junctures occurred, triggering highest uncertainty regarding the Left's fidelity to its own policy priorities. As these political configurations were contingent less on prior history and more on coincidental power balances at the time, and as they shaped subsequent legacies, postcommunist junctures were events undetermined by the past and critical for future developments.

Unlike in Latin America, where analogous junctures generally shaped divergent patterns of overall party system stability, however, political configurations during critical periods of building capitalism triggered somewhat more particular institutional processes in Eastern Europe. Here, political roles during postcommunist junctures conditioned powerful incentives for the region's historically best-established parties – those left-of-center – not only to take positions on the most pressing issues at a time of economic crisis and reform, but also to stick to these positions thereafter. As postcommunist junctures left environmental legacies by shaping interlinked programmatic and electoral path dependencies specifically on the Left, they conditioned linkages between divergent institutional persistence and reactive sequences, as shown in the figure. Put simply, where leftist parties more consistently positioned themselves as critics of neoliberalism, they tended to be electorally successful in the long term; where they persisted on a pro-market path, they were likely to decline. The Left's stance on economic questions and its electoral performance constitute, together, the central legacies of postcommunist junctures.

Finally, these varying legacies conditioned different institutional environments for subsequent political actors whose unique incentives to maximize contrarian legitimacy and organizational capacities for ideological flexibility drove likely choices of programmatic positions. Where path dependencies created restrictive opportunities due to the Left's brand consistency and electoral strength, economically leftist positions were less viable as a successful electoral strategy for parties critical of liberalism. Where environmental legacies created permissive opportunities due to the Left's ideological inconsistency and electoral decline, illiberalism featuring economically leftist positions or posturing was electorally viable. As they left distinct legacies that opponents of liberalism could then exploit strategically – yet not always perfectly – by choosing economic positions most suitable for different environments, postcommunist junctures shaped the probability of illiberal outcomes at the ballot box in the first two decades of the twenty-first century.

2.3 CONCLUSION

The unevenness of illiberalism's electoral viability across Eastern Europe in the first two twenty-first century decades raises important questions about the direction in which postcommunist politics has gone and about the sources of divergence. In this chapter, I have developed the book's core argument by integrating Polanyian perspectives from political economy, sociology, and anthropology, by drawing lessons from the Latin American experience, and by highlighting how crucial early periods of neoliberal deepening, leftist politics, and the electoral viability of illiberalism were linked during the three decades between 1989 and 2020. Having identified postcommunist junctures as key moments of intense market reform and focused the analysis on the interactions between the historical legacies of junctures and political agency, I developed a theoretical framework that integrates elements of both path dependency and voluntarism.

As critical moments of deepening neoliberalism, postcommunist junctures featured varying political configurations, which were less contingent on the past than on more coincidental power balances at a time of economic crisis and decisive reform. While these configurations were in important ways similar to ones seen in Latin America, Eastern Europe's contextual peculiarity implies more unique paths of subsequent institutional development. Indeed, as postcommunist junctures molded the long-term programmatic and electoral fortunes specifically of leftist parties, they conditioned varying political opportunities for liberalism's subsequent challengers – parties equipped with particular incentives and capacities for adaptation. As environmental conditions made it relatively more or less likely for antiestablishment parties to appropriate for electoral success programmatic positions traditionally "owned" by the Left, varying illiberal outcomes materialized in the probabilistic shadow of postcommunist junctures.

Overall, the two-step argument developed in this chapter highlights the causal importance of both political agency and the legacy of key market reform periods. If political configurations during postcommunist junctures shaped leftist politics over the long run, those claiming to represent an alternative to the liberal establishment still had important choices to make if they were to be electorally viable. As the choice of whether and to what extent to embrace economically statist positions in addition to culturally conservative ones was shaped – yet not fully determined – by the legacy of early periods of building capitalism, postcommunist junctures conditioned varying likelihoods of illiberal electoral success across Eastern Europe.

3

The Long Shadow of Postcommunist Junctures

An Empirical Baseline

Having theorized that political configurations during critical periods of market reform engendered path-dependent trajectories culminating in varying illiberal outcomes in Eastern Europe, in this chapter I offer a quantitative analysis of the legacies of postcommunist junctures and contend with alternative arguments. The goal here is to operationalize variables, probe theorized relationships, and assess the postcommunist juncture theory against rival explanations, thereby establishing the empirical baseline for the subsequent case studies. After defining and identifying mainstream parties on the Left and Right, I first analyze both their long-term economic and cultural stances, on the one hand, and their electoral performance after postcommunist junctures, on the other. The findings support the theoretical expectation that leftist parties' economic positions and electoral performance in the aftermath period are two mutually related legacies of the most crucial periods of neoliberal deepening, a relationship that does not hold for rightist parties. Next, after developing a set of variables in order to compare long- versus short-term electoral dynamics, I demonstrate – while also alleviating potential concerns about reverse causality – that the persistent effect on the Left is the more important predictor of illiberal outcomes after postcommunist junctures.

Having unveiled strong correlational patterns in support of my theory, in the second part of the chapter I consider standard explanations of antiestablishment and illiberal voting, which fall in several broad categories – economic, political, and cultural demand, as well as institutional supply and international factors, including conditionality, leverage, and diffusion. While I recognize that such accounts have enriched our understanding of developments in postcommunist Europe, I explain why they are individually unreliable for making sense of the variation identified in Chapter 1. Finally, I deploy traditional statistical methods for time series cross-sectional data to test the postcommunist juncture theory against rival hypotheses. Concretely, I use an original dataset that covers 130 parliamentary elections in fifteen postcommunist countries in the 1990–2020 period and that includes a number of unique variables that I developed based on expert survey data, ballot box results, and my own coding. The analytical strategy, data sources, operationalizations, and statistical tests are available in Appendix D. The results from the quantitative analysis unequivocally point to the conclusion that the postcommunist juncture theory has considerably higher explanatory power than rival explanations. Although short-term electoral dynamics are not irrelevant, it is the long-term, path-dependent effects on the Left, themselves rooted in postcommunist junctures, that explain varying illiberal outcomes in the most substantive, significant, and consistent manner.

3.1 LEFT AND RIGHT IN POSTCOMMUNIST EUROPE

As argued previously, contingencies during postcommunist junctures conditioned varying path dependencies, whereby leftist parties' economic positions and electoral performance ought to be understood as mutually related legacies. In this section, I offer empirical evidence in support of this proposition by analyzing expert survey data and election results for relevant parties. As my argument centers on the mainstream Left as an intervening variable linking postcommunist junctures and illiberal outcomes in the long run, I also demonstrate that mainstream rightist forces were neither as impacted by prior junctures nor as impactful in terms of subsequent outcomes.

The standard, or mainstream, Left in postcommunist Europe is comprised of social democratic and communist parties, all of which originated before postcommunist junctures. The majority – eleven of them – are "reformed" parties that were either previously communist or founded by ruling communists and that claimed socialist or social democratic identities and titles after communism. These include the Socialist Party of Albania (PSS), the Bulgarian Socialist Party (BSP), the Social Democratic Party of Croatia (SPH), the Hungarian Socialist Party (MSZP), the Democratic Labor Party of Lithuania (LDDP), North Macedonia's Social Democratic Union (SDSM), the Democratic Left Alliance (SLD) organized around the Social Democracy of the Republic of Poland (SdRP), Romania's Social Democratic Party (PSD), Slovakia's Party of the Democratic Left (SDĽ), Slovenia's Social Democrats (SD), and the Socialist Party of Ukraine (SPU).

Not all standard leftist parties are reformed ex-communists, however. Three are unreformed communist parties – the Czech Communist Party of Bohemia and Moravia (KSČM), which was important after communism, as well as the Party of Communists of the Republic of Moldova (PCRM) and the Ukrainian Communist Party (KPU), which were the dominant parties on the Left in Moldova and Ukraine. Additionally, five leftist parties are neither communist nor ex-communist. Three parties are "historic" social democratic parties that had been electorally significant before communism – the Czech Social

Democratic Party (ČSSD), which was incorporated into the Czechoslovak communist regime, as well as the Latvian Social Democratic Workers' Party (LSDSP) and the Social Democratic Party of Lithuania (LSDP), both of which operated in exile during communism. Finally, two leftist parties have roots in Baltic pro-independence fronts – the Estonian Social Democratic Party (SDE) and the Latvian Social Democratic Party "Harmony" (SDPS). While none of these five parties has communist roots, they all gained considerable electoral support and, except for the Latvian Social Democratic Workers' Party (LSDSP),[1] became the leading leftist parties of their countries after communism. Overall, while the nineteen standard leftist parties noted here have different origins and histories, each of them originated and gained at least 5 percent electoral support before postcommunist junctures. They all also gained at minimum 10 percent of electoral support in at least one national postcommunist election.

Although the mainstream Right is harder to define in contemporary Eastern Europe due to the banishment of rightist forces under communism, standard rightist parties "seek broad electoral support for programs fusing elements of liberalism and varieties of conservatism."[2] By relying on previous scholarship[3] and my own dataset, I identify the standard Right as liberal and conservative parties with origins before postcommunist junctures. Whereas six countries (Albania, Bulgaria, Croatia, Latvia, Lithuania, and Ukraine) have a relatively uniform Right consisting of one or two parties, six others (Czechia, Estonia, Hungary,[4] North Macedonia, Romania, and Slovenia) have a more divided Right consisting of three parties. Exhibiting even greater fragmentation, the Right was least uniform in Moldova, Poland, and Slovakia. While some rightist parties have been relatively stable over time (e.g., the Democratic Party of Albania, the Croatian Democratic Union, and Liberal Democracy of Slovenia), others are de facto coalitions (e.g., the Slovak Democratic Coalition of 1998) or mergers of previously autonomous rightist parties (e.g., Lithuania's Homeland Union – Lithuanian Christian Democrats), and still others are best understood as party lineages (e.g., Poland's Democratic Party as the heir to Freedom Union, which, in turn, succeeded the Democratic Union). In general, and mirroring the strategy used for the Left, I define standard rightist parties as having originated before postcommunist junctures and having, with few

---

[1] This party led an alliance which gained 12.9 percent in the 1998 parliamentary election and briefly participated in the governing coalition in 1999.

[2] Hanley (2004: 22–3).

[3] Hanley (2004), Hanley and Szczerbiak (2006), Vachudova (2008a).

[4] Following convention, I treat Fidesz as a mainstream party before 2010 (e.g., Pop-Eleches 2010) and as an illiberal party beginning in 2010. As this coding decision, which is unique for Fidesz, contributes to a stronger correlation between center-right electoral decline and illiberal upsurge, it creates a harder test for my theory. Coding Fidesz as either only conservative or only illiberal would have *strengthened* my results.

exceptions,[5] gained at minimum 5 percent electoral support before junctures as well as 10 percent in at least one national postcommunist election. A full list of leftist and rightist parties included in the study is available in Appendix C.

3.2 FROM POSTCOMMUNIST JUNCTURES TO LEFTIST PATH DEPENDENCIES

Having identified the standard Left and Right in the fifteen postcommunist countries under analysis, I next measure policy positions on economic and cultural questions. To do so, and as I did when measuring illiberalism and post-neoliberal populism in Chapter 1, I rely on expert survey data. Namely, and for the purpose of consistency, I utilize the same two surveys that I used previously – the Chapel Hill Expert Survey (CHES)[6] and the Democratic Accountability and Linkages Project (DALP).[7] While CHES is ideal for capturing the temporal evolution of policy positions because it collected relevant data in five standard waves (2002, 2006, 2010, 2014, and 2019) and two EU candidate country waves (2007 and 2014), DALP – which was administered in 2008–9, or roughly the midpoint between junctures and 2020 – is useful where CHES data are unavailable (as for parties in Moldova and Ukraine) as well as for cross-validation purposes.

Conveniently, both of these expert surveys score parties' economic and cultural positions on a left-right scale. In CHES, the two most relevant variables are *lrecon*, which measures economic statism versus liberalism, and *galtan*, which measures cultural liberalism versus conservatism. Because DALP does not provide such aggregated scores, I develop two measures, both of which I transform from DALP's original scale from one to five into a scale from zero to ten for comparability with CHES data. While I measure economic stances by averaging policy position scores for social spending (DALP variable $d1$), state role in the economy ($d2$), and public spending ($d3$), I identify cultural positions by averaging scores for national identity ($d4$) and traditional authority, institutions, and customs ($d5$). Finally, I average the relevant scores of standard leftist and rightist parties for the elections in which these parties participated in the 2000–20 period. Representing parties' average positions on economic and cultural issues, these scores are particularly informative with regard to the hypothesized effects of postcommunist junctures on programmatic stances.

---

[5] There are five exceptions, which I include as important rightist parties because, having originated before junctures, they all participated in subsequent governing coalitions – Albania's Republican Party (PRSH), which gained neither at least 5 percent before the juncture nor at minimum 10 percent support in any election, Czechia's Civic Democratic Alliance (ODA), Latvia's Christian Democratic Union (KDS), and Moldova's Party of Democratic Forces (PFD), all of which gained more than 5 percent before junctures but never at least 10 percent, as well as Moldova's Liberal Party (PL), which gained more than 10 percent in several elections but less than 5 percent before the juncture, when it was known as the Reform Party (PR).

[6] Bakker et al. (2015); Polk et al. (2017).

[7] Kitschelt (2013).

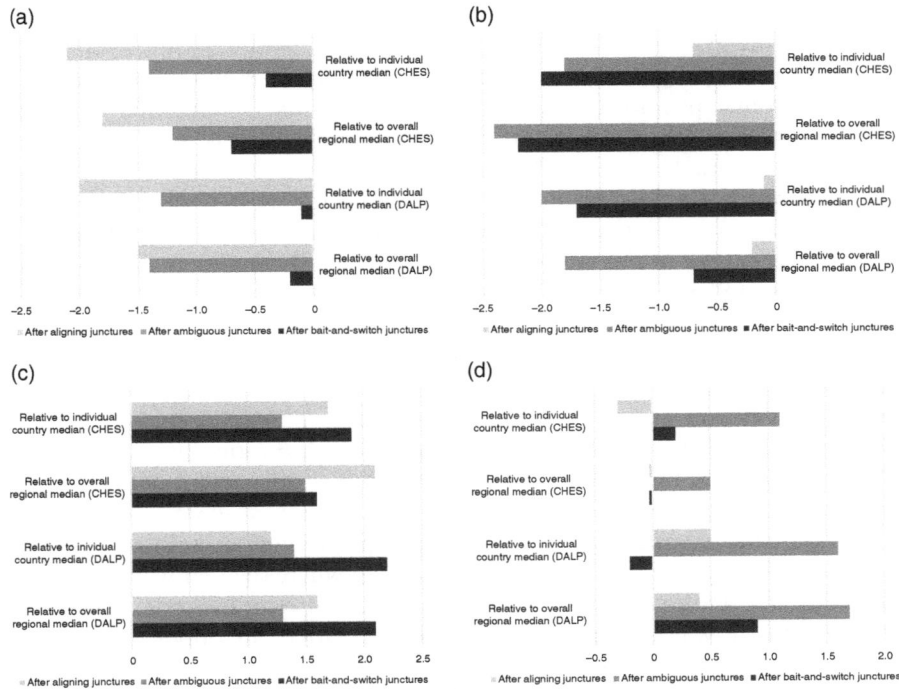

FIGURE 3.1 Average position on economic and social issues of the Left and Right after postcommunist junctures (relative to country and regional medians), 2000–20. (a) The Left, economic issues, (b) the Left, social issues, (c) the Right, economic issues, (d) the Right, social issues
The aggregations are based on 75 (58 CHES and 17 DALP) survey scores for leftist parties and 106 (82 CHES and 24 DALP) survey scores for rightist parties, each score being the average of all ratings assigned by experts participating in survey waves after postcommunist junctures.

Figure 3.1 locates party positions on economic and social issues relative to country-specific and regional medians[8] (represented by 0) after the three types of postcommunist junctures. As expected, the Left tended to reproduce programmatic positions that had originated during junctures, as seen in Figure 3.1a. While its economic positions were the most statist and redistribution-ist where the Left had led the parliamentary opposition to market reform under aligning junctures, they tended to be somewhat less progressive where the Left had been ambiguous during the key period of neoliberal deepening. Finally, the Left's economic positions were consistently most pro-market[9] after

---

[8] See Acemoglu et al. (2013: 772) for an approach that compares positions relative to the median.

[9] I prefer the term "pro-market" rather than "neoliberal" when referring to the positions of

leftist parties that embraced economic reform-ism. As Scheiring and Szombati (2020: 726) explain, because such parties also maintained some redistributive policies, it would be an oversimplification to label them "neoliberal."

bait-and-switch junctures – a finding valid regardless of data source and measurement strategy.[10]

This durable programmatic divergence certainly does not mean that the Left's economic positions were static over time. As documented in prior scholarship, even leftist parties after aligning junctures – as in Bulgaria and Romania – eventually embraced elements of market reformism.[11] Yet despite such dynamism, the long-term positioning of such parties tended to be economically statist in relative terms – compared to both domestic rivals and to other leftist parties in the region. By contrast, social democrats in Hungary, Lithuania, and Slovakia embraced more unambiguously pro-market economic positions after bait-and-switch junctures. In the more peculiar case of Poland, when ex-communists returned to power after labor-based Lech Wałęsa's about-face during the juncture, they also embraced economic reformism,[12] as detailed in Chapter 5.

While this evidence supports the idea that the Left's positioning on economic issues tended to be reproduced over the long run as a legacy of political configurations during junctures, Figure 3.1b suggests that an identical statement cannot be made regarding the Left's long-term positioning on cultural matters. First, while it is true that in some of the countries where the Left was most economically statist – for example, after aligning junctures in Bulgaria, Moldova, or Romania – it was also quite culturally conservative, the opposite tendency is not observable following the converse, that is, bait-and-switch, junctures. As the most pro-market leftist parties – in Hungary, Poland, or Lithuania – were not the most culturally liberal ones, their positioning on cultural questions did not result from prior junctures. Postcommunist junctures thus conditioned the Left's positioning on economic questions, but not on cultural ones.

Moving to the mainstream Right, Figure 3.1 also presents data on its average positioning on economic and cultural issues during the aftermath period after the three types of junctures. As seen, varying junctures did not affect the Right's subsequent programmatic stances over the long run. Regarding economic questions, Figure 3.1c shows that rightist parties were decisively pro-market across the board, with no coherent pattern emerging based on prior junctures. A somewhat similar picture emerges regarding positioning on cultural questions, seen in Figure 3.1d, with the Right appearing most culturally conservative after ambiguous junctures and relatively less so after aligning and bait-and-switch junctures. Overall, while the Eastern European Left tended to reproduce divergent economic positions rooted in the political contingencies of critical periods of neoliberal deepening, the Right did not experience similar programmatic reproduction originating in prior junctures.

---

[10] As seen, the results based on CHES and DALP data are similar. Regarding measurement strategy, I assessed average positions not only relative to medians but also relative to country-specific and regional means.

[11] Tavits and Letki (2009).

[12] Markowski (2002).

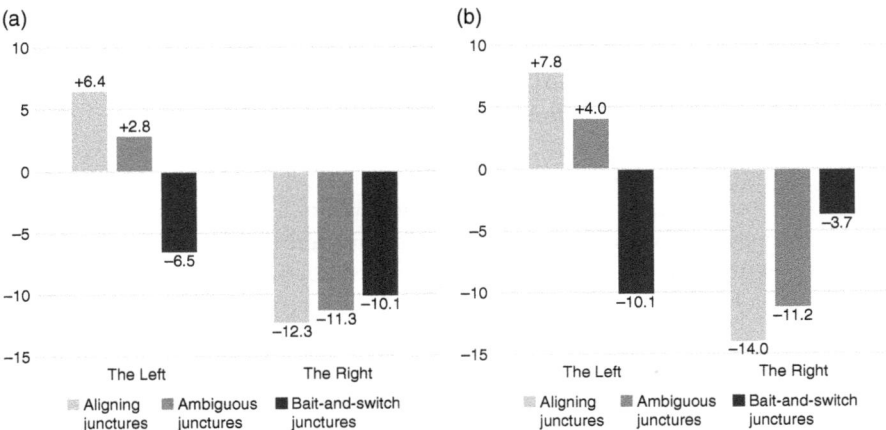

FIGURE 3.2 Average change in net electoral performance of the Left and Right.
(a) Change from 1990s to 2000–20 period, (b) change from pre-juncture to aftermath
period
Calculations based on results from 130 legislative elections. Whereas 43 of these
elections took place in the 1990s and 87 in the 2000s, 28 were before junctures and
102 after junctures.

The Left's programmatic divergence on economic matters, in turn, resulted
in varying electoral outcomes in the long run, as documented in Figure 3.2,
which registers change in electoral support for the Left and Right based on
postcommunist juncture type. Concretely, the figure traces electoral change in
two ways – (1) more generally, that is, between the 1990s, when postcommunist junctures typically occurred, and the 2000–20 period (Figure 3.2a) and (2)
more specifically, that is, between the period before junctures and the aftermath
period in each country (Figure 3.2b). While the Left made net electoral gains of
6.4 percent in the 2000–20 period after leading the parliamentary opposition
during aligning junctures, such gains tended to be more modest, on average
(2.8 percent), after ambiguous junctures. And while some leftist reformers initially benefited after adopting pro-market positions[13] following bait-and-switch
junctures, their electoral support in the 2000–20 period declined by 6.5 percent
relative to the 1990s. Although this downward trajectory varied in particular
contexts – from the total collapse of Slovakia's ex-communists, through more
(in Lithuania) or less (in Poland) immediate erosion, to eventual decline following initial stability under Hungary's idiosyncratic electoral systems – the Left
faced long-term electoral losses following bait-and-switch junctures.

Crucially, the mainstream Right did not experience comparable divergence in terms of its long-terms electoral performance, as it tended to decline

---

[13] See Tavits and Letki (2009).

regardless of the type of juncture. Notably, while those that had played the roles of reformist incumbents during junctures were generally punished by voters in the long term regardless of their ideological colors, it was leftist parties that had led the parliamentary opposition to neoliberal reform during junctures that tended to benefit at the ballot box over time. Finally, a comparison of changes in net electoral support based on, on the one hand, the more general periodization of the 2000–20 period relative to the 1990s, and, on the other hand, a more specific periodization accounting for the exact timing of junctures in each country provides further support to the argument. As Figure 3.2 demonstrates, these changes are magnified – and in the expected directions – when comparisons are made based on country-specific pre- and post-juncture periods (Figure 3.2b) rather than based on the more general periodization (Figure 3.2a). Indeed, the more specific periodization focused on the exact timing of junctures in each country shows even greater gains for the Left and losses for the Right after aligning junctures, as well as greater losses for the Left and less dramatic decline for the Right after bait-and-switch junctures.

Moreover, these trends are unlikely to have resulted from prior organizational endowments or potentially undemocratic tactics, as an analysis of actual electoral performance, as opposed to electoral shifts, suggests. As shown in Figure 3.3a, the Left's electoral fortunes diverged sharply after having been roughly equal, on average, before aligning (25.6 percent) and bait-and-switch (26.6 percent) junctures. While organizational endowments and authoritarian tactics in the 1990s may have potentially contributed to subsequent leftist gains after aligning junctures in Albania or Moldova, the Czech social democrats transformed themselves from an electorally meager organization in the early 1990s to a party that won four elections after the aligning juncture (see Chapter 6 for details). Mainstream leftist parties also made relative gains after ambiguous junctures in democratic Croatia and Latvia, where they had been rather weak in the early 1990s. Meanwhile, although the Left had been strong in Lithuania, where it had commanded a towering 44 percent support in the first democratic election, and organizationally endowed in Poland and Hungary,[14] it faced eventual decline after bait-and-switch junctures.

Turning to the Right, Figure 3.3b communicates two ideas. First, while the Right experienced greatest losses, on average, after junctures in countries where it had been previously strongest, it declined the least where it had been weakest. This is not surprising. The Right had the most to lose where, as a result of its prior electoral strength, it had led key neoliberal reforms from a position of incumbency (aligning junctures), and the least to lose where it had not assumed the main responsibility for such reforms (bait-and-switch junctures). Second, while rightist parties tended to decline across the board, their average electoral

---

[14] Grzymała-Busse (2002).

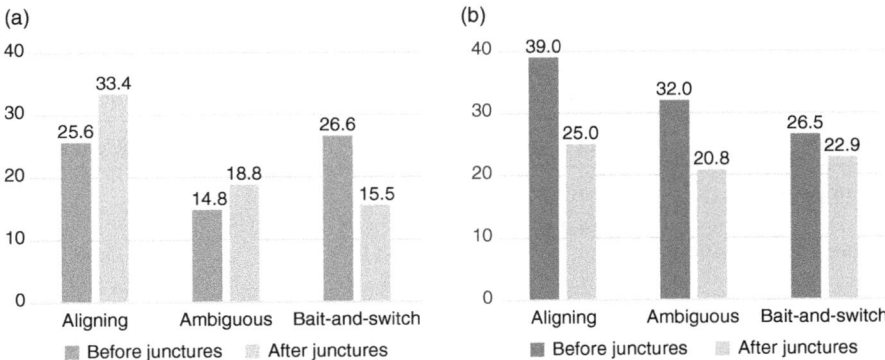

FIGURE 3.3 Average electoral performance of the Left and Right before and after junctures. (a) The Left, (b) the Right

performance after the three types of postcommunist junctures was much less varied (between 20.8 percent and 25.0 percent) than was the case for the Left.

The above discussion suggests that political roles during junctures were much more consequential for the Left than for the Right, not only in terms of relative gains or losses over time but also in terms of actual electoral performance after junctures. If electoral strength before junctures was somewhat predictive of subsequent electoral results for the Right, it was not important for the Left.[15] By contrast, how the Left did electorally after junctures was driven not by electoral strength before junctures but rather by postcommunist juncture type. This is clearly shown in Table 3.1, which presents the results of regressing electoral support for leftist and rightist parties in the aftermath period on the conceptually opposite aligning and bait-and-switch types of junctures.

As seen, whereas juncture type is not an important predictor of the rightist vote, it is, as expected, a statistically significant predictor of the leftist vote in the aftermath period. Concretely, aligning and bait-and-switch junctures are associated with similarly substantive coefficients with opposite signs (+16.2 and −13.4, respectively). While electorates rewarded the Left for its continued programmatic faithfulness to statist and redistributionist economic positions after aligning junctures, they tended to punish it for its pro-market stances after bait-and-switch junctures. As different political configurations during key periods of neoliberal deepening implied persistent divergence in terms of the Left's mutually related programmatic and electoral trajectories, postcommunist junctures certainly shaped subsequent developments.

---

[15] While regressing electoral performance after 2000 on average electoral performance before junctures produces a positive and somewhat statistically significant coefficient for the Right ($\beta = 0.300$, SE $= 0.143$, $p < 0.1$, $R^2 = 0.08$, $N = 87$), it produces a weaker coefficient ($\beta = 0.088$) that is not statistically significant for the Left.

TABLE 3.1 *OLS regression analysis of the vote share of leftist and rightist parties (2000–20) based on opposite types of prior junctures*

Variables	(1) Left vote	(2) Left vote	(3) Right vote	(4) Right vote
Aligning juncture	16.17*** (4.14)		3.38 (6.02)	
Bait-and-switch juncture		−13.41** (5.72)		−0.61 (4.67)
Constant	17.49*** (3.35)	27.73*** (2.93)	20.28*** (3.15)	21.84*** (3.71)
Observations	87	87	87	87
R-squared	0.32	0.18	0.01	0.00

Robust standard errors in parentheses
*** $p < 0.01$, ** $p < 0.05$, * $p < 0.1$

3.3 FROM LEFTIST PATH DEPENDENCIES TO ILLIBERAL OUTCOMES AFTER POSTCOMMUNIST JUNCTURES

These subsequent developments certainly include the varying illiberal outcomes – that is, the illiberal vote share and post-neoliberal populist magnitude – discussed in Chapter 1. As the mutually related persistent economic positioning and overall electoral fortunes of leftist parties were the key legacy of postcommunist junctures, they also constituted the environmental contexts in which subsequent illiberal outcomes unfolded. Figure 3.4 presents the relationships between, on the one hand, electoral support for mainstream parties on the Left and Right, and, on the other hand, the illiberal vote share (Figure 3.4a) and the magnitude of post-neoliberal populism (Figure 3.4b) in the 2000–20 period. As seen, the electoral performance of the Left is negatively and strongly correlated with illiberalism and post-neoliberal populism. Notably, while the Right's electoral performance is also negatively correlated with illiberal outcomes, when the measures for illiberalism and post-neoliberal populism are regressed on the Right's vote share, both the coefficients and R-squared values are considerably smaller than when the Left's vote share is used as the regressor. The electoral performance of the Right is thus a substantively weaker predictor of illiberal outcomes than the electoral performance of the Left.

This is, of course, consistent with prior research showing that leftist reformers alienated traditional constituencies, who then shifted support to populist alternatives in Eastern Europe.[16] Crucially, however, although my

---

[16] Bagashka et al. (2022); Snegovaya (2022; 2024).

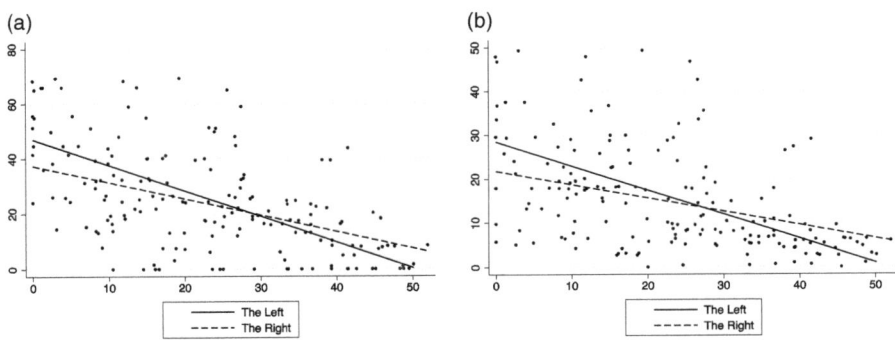

FIGURE 3.4 The electoral performance of the Left and Right versus the illiberal vote share and post-neoliberal populist magnitude after postcommunist junctures, 2000–20. (a) Illiberal vote share, (b) post-neoliberal populist magnitude

The regressions represented by the fitted lines for the illiberal vote share (Figure 3.4a) yield coefficients of –0.931 (SE = 0.103), R^2 = 0.49 for the Left and –0.599 (SE = 0.132), R^2 = 0.19 for the Right. The regressions represented by the fitted lines for post-neoliberal populist magnitude (Figure 3.4b) yield coefficients of –0.549 (SE = 0.069), R^2 = 0.43 for the Left and –0.306 (SE = 0.087), R^2 = 0.13 for the Right. N = 87 for all regressions.

findings confirm the insight that the Left's varying electoral fortunes corresponded to divergent illiberal viability, they go an important step further – because they also identify the historical rootedness of illiberal outcomes in prior junctures. While electorates either rewarded or punished the Left for its persistent positioning on economic issues, it was postcommunist junctures – where these positions had originated – that ultimately shaped the durable legacies that culminated in illiberal outcomes. This is illustrated in Figure 3.5, which offers two types of comparisons in support of my argument. First, the figure compares the net illiberal vote share as well as the magnitude of post-neoliberal populism after the three types of junctures. Second, it also disaggregates electoral support for illiberalism into low- and high-intensity components.

Most generally, the figure shows that both illiberal voting and post-neoliberal populist magnitude were, on average, lowest after aligning and highest after bait-and-switch junctures. As leftist parties rose or fell because of economic positions reflecting political configurations during prior junctures, parties critical of the liberal establishment encountered varying odds of electoral success. Moreover, observed patterns of voting for parties taking low- and high-intensity illiberal positions further substantiate the proposed causal mechanism linking the Left's programmatic positioning and electoral success after junctures, on the one hand, and illiberal outcomes, on the other. As shown, illiberalism tended to be not only most electorally viable but also of highest intensity specifically after bait-and-switch junctures. It was where the Left lost most support after clearly embracing pro-market positions following bait-and-switch

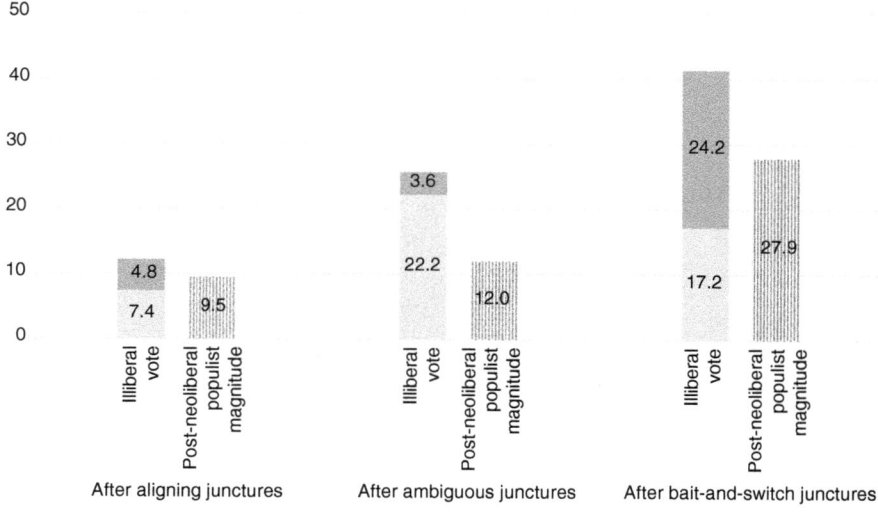

FIGURE 3.5 Illiberal legacies of postcommunist junctures
Based on results from 87 legislative elections after postcommunist junctures and
author's dataset. As I coded illiberal parties by adding scores derived from expert
survey results regarding their economic and social issues, each on a scale of zero to
three (see Appendix A), low-intensity illiberalism corresponds to total scores of three
and four, while high-intensity illiberalism corresponds to total scores of five and six.

junctures that high-intensity illiberalism was particularly viable at the ballot
box in the aftermath period. In sum, as postcommunist junctures conditioned
divergent path dependencies on the Left, they shaped clearly varying illiberal
outcomes in the 2000–20 period.

3.4 LONG- VERSUS SHORT-TERM ELECTORAL DYNAMICS

Having provided some evidence in support of the theory linking postcommunist junctures, the Left, and illiberal outcomes, I next discuss the main explanatory variables that I use in subsequent empirical tests. Specifically, I offer a
comparison between, on the one hand, post-juncture long-term electoral trends
relative to pre-juncture periods and, on the other hand, short-term electoral
fluctuations. This comparison is important for the assessment of the hypothet-
ically durable effects of postcommunist junctures. As I demonstrate, long-term
dynamics are indeed a superior predictor of divergent illiberal outcomes across
Eastern Europe.

While I showed above that the leftist vote share is negatively and strongly
correlated with the viability of illiberal outcomes, analyzing it as an intervening variable between junctures and outcomes requires some additional

consideration, for two reasons. First, as electorates vote for a variety of reasons, it is possible that varying trends in support for leftist parties may possibly not represent a historical effect of prior junctures. Second, reverse causality is a potential problem due to the possibility that the viability of illiberal outcomes at the ballot box may plausibly be empirically prior to the decline of the mainstream Left.

To alleviate the first concern and focus more squarely on the effect of junctures, I develop a *proportional measure* of standard parties' electoral performance after junctures relative to their average electoral performance before junctures. I do so by dividing mainstream leftist and rightist parties' vote shares after junctures by their average vote shares between 1989 and junctures. The advantage of this approach, which gauges how well mainstream parties did electorally during the aftermath period relative to the postcommunist period before junctures, is that it zooms in on how junctures may have affected durable patterns of electoral continuity or change. Unlike vote shares, which correspond to the relative electoral strength of parties and can fluctuate widely, the proportional measure, with a much narrower range,[17] indicates whether a party overperformed (scores higher than 1.0) or underperformed (scores lower than 1.0) relative to the period between 1989 and postcommunist junctures. Thus, the proportional measure captures more readily than simple vote shares long-term electoral dynamics and tendencies, specifically relative to pre-juncture periods.

These proportional measures strengthen the case for the Left's electoral performance as an intervening variable between postcommunist junctures and illiberal outcomes. First, there is a much stronger relationship between the proportional measure developed for the Left and the actual vote share of leftist parties after junctures ($r = 0.85$) than between corresponding variables for the Right ($r = 0.47$). It thus appears that vote shares reflect not only the Left's relative power at the ballot box after junctures but also, and more importantly, persistent and divergent electoral tendencies relative to pre-juncture periods. Overall, the comparison of proportional measures and vote shares lends further support to the notion that varying electoral trends on the Left, but not the Right, had been shaped by the conditioning effects of prior junctures.

Second, while concerns about reverse causality are more thoroughly addressed in the case studies in following chapters, I also develop an additional estimate that is sensitive to such concerns by lagging my proportional measure by one election. This lagged proportional measure is correlated with the original (concurrent) proportion measure similarly for both the Left ($r = 0.73$) and the Right ($r = 0.68$).[18] Crucially, as it captures

---

[17] The standard deviations are 14.1 and 13.8 for the leftist and rightist vote shares, respectively, and 0.66 and 0.67 for the proportional measures for the Left and Right, respectively.

[18] Likewise, the lagged and concurrent vote shares are similarly correlated for both the Left ($r = 0.73$) and the Right ($r = 0.76$).

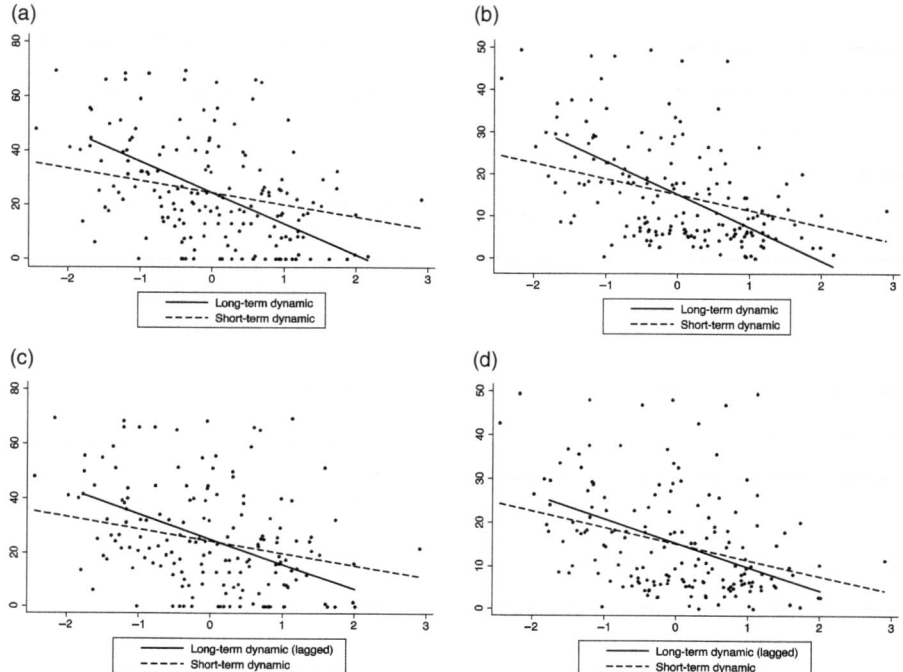

FIGURE 3.6 Illiberal outcomes and long- versus short-term electoral dynamics on the Left. (a) Illiberal vote share, (b) post-neoliberal populist magnitude, (c) illiberal vote share (lagged measure for long-term dynamics), (d) post-neoliberal populist magnitude (lagged measure for long-term dynamics)

subsequent ballot box performance relative to the pre-juncture period via the polls immediately preceding elections under analysis, the *lagged proportional measure* not only helps address concerns about reverse causality but also can be especially useful for assessing the effects of longer-term electoral dynamics vis-à-vis shorter-term ones. Indeed, an important difference between the concurrent measure of electoral performance and the lagged proportional measure is that the latter allows for better comparisons specifically between, on the one hand, the effect of longer-term trends relative to pre-juncture periods, which it captures, and, on the other hand, the more transient effect of vote shifts from anterior elections, which it does not capture.

Figure 3.6 presents a comparison of the relationships between illiberal outcomes and persistent versus transient electoral dynamics on the Left. Because the measures capturing long-term (*proportional measure*) and short-term (*vote change from one election to the next*) dynamics are scaled differently, I use standardized Z-scores to explicitly compare persistent effects with the more transient fluctuations between successive elections. While Figure 3.6a and Figure 3.6b operationalize long-term electoral trends by using the original proportional measure for the Left, Figure 3.6c and Figure 3.6d do so by relying on the lagged proportional measure.

As seen clearly, long-term trends relative to pre-juncture periods are always more strongly correlated with illiberal outcomes than short-term fluctuations at the ballot box. Although using the lagged measure results in somewhat weaker relationships, long-term tendencies remain more strongly, and negatively, associated with illiberal outcomes than transient electoral shifts. These relationships are additionally compared in Table 3.2, which provides concrete statistics regarding the relationships between the variables discussed earlier and illiberal outcomes, and which also serves as the empirical baseline for additional tests vis-à-vis rival explanations. Notably, the first two regressions show that the leftist vote share is a stronger predictor of illiberal outcomes than both the rightist vote share and short-term electoral shifts on the Left and Right. The third and fourth regressions demonstrate that the original proportional measure of long-term electoral dynamics on the Left is the only significant predictor of the illiberal vote share and post-neoliberal populist magnitude.

Crucially, the fifth and sixth regressions, which use standardized Z-scores for direct comparability of coefficients, indicate that while short-term shifts gain significance when the measures of long-term effects are lagged, persistent post-juncture electoral dynamics on the Left are still the most substantively consequential predictor.[19] Finally, the last four regressions confirm the strong and contrasting effect of opposite juncture types – while, as expected, aligning junctures are negatively associated, bait-and-switch junctures are positively associated with illiberal outcomes.[20]

Overall, then, while short-term electoral dynamics on the Left clearly make some difference for illiberal outcomes, the long-term effect of prior junctures remains the most substantive and significant predictor. As postcommunist junctures conditioned leftist parties' economic positions and subsequent electoral fortunes in the long run, their durable legacies are crucial for understanding varying patterns of illiberal outcomes in Eastern Europe during the 2000–20 period.

---

[19] The relative power of these effects is confirmed by fixed and random-effects estimations, which explicitly address the time series nature of the data and produce even larger coefficients for the variables measuring long-term trends compared to those measuring short-term shifts. For a discussion of these two types of estimations, see the "Analytical Strategy" section in Appendix D.

[20] As a robustness check, I also ran random-effects regressions, which are more appropriate than fixed-effects regressions because junctures do not vary within countries. The estimations confirm the relationships seen in Table 3.2.

TABLE 3.2 *OLS regression analysis of illiberal outcomes based on electoral dynamics and opposite types of prior junctures*

Variables	(1) Illiberal vote share	(2) Post-neoliberal populism	(3) Illiberal vote share	(4) Post-neoliberal populism	(5) Illiberal vote share	(6) Post-neoliberal populism	(7) Illiberal vote share	(8) Post-neoliberal populism	(9) Illiberal vote share	(10) Post-neoliberal populism
Leftist vote	-0.87*** (0.13)	-0.49*** (0.09)								
Rightist vote	-0.32** (0.12)	-0.13 (0.14)								
Left/juncture			-17.14*** (3.96)	-11.16*** (1.51)						
Right/juncture			-3.31 (3.02)	-0.96 (1.88)						
Left/juncture, lag (std)					-12.05*** (2.64)	-7.83*** (1.07)				
Right/juncture, lag (std)					-0.65 (2.26)	-0.42 (1.41)				
Left short-term shift	0.09 (0.14)	-0.08 (0.10)		-0.13 (0.10)						
Right short-term shift	-0.13 (0.18)	-0.12 (0.13)		-0.15 (0.13)						
L short-term shift (std)					-9.15*** (1.62)	-7.15*** (0.99)				

R short-term shift (std)					-5.29^{**} (2.10)	-3.10^{**} (1.41)				
Aligning juncture							-20.43^{***} (4.34)	-9.73^{**} (3.54)		
Bait-and-switch juncture									23.21^{***} (4.83)	17.30^{***} (2.81)
Constant	52.11^{***} (3.09)	29.21^{***} (3.26)	45.51^{***} (5.10)	27.87^{***} (2.77)	25.12^{***} (2.70)	15.25^{***} (1.63)	32.89^{***} (3.54)	19.18^{***} (3.26)	18.30^{***} (2.54)	10.58^{***} (1.20)
Observations	87	87	87	87	82	82	87	87	87	87
R-squared	0.56	0.47	0.41	0.47	0.47	0.52	0.29	0.16	0.30	0.42

Robust standard errors in parentheses

*** $p < 0.01$, ** $p < 0.05$, * $p < 0.1$

3.5 COMPETING EXPLANATIONS

Having elaborated how the main explanatory variables relate to the two illiberal outcomes, in the remainder of this chapter I identify five categories of alternative explanations based on the scholarship on antiestablishment and illiberal voting in postcommunist Europe. Reflecting debates in the broader field of populism studies, the major arguments that I focus on include (1) economic demand, (2) political demand, (3) cultural demand, (4) institutional supply, and (5) international factors. Below, I sketch these accounts and briefly discuss why they are individually insufficient for explaining the variation discussed in Chapter 1. In Appendix D, I detail my analytical strategy for empirically assessing rival arguments vis-à-vis my theory, review data sources and operationalizations of variables, and present results from statistical tests, which clearly confirm the superiority of the postcommunist juncture theory.

3.5.1 Economic Demand

Explanations focused on structural demand have a long lineage in the study of populism, as they can be traced back to early theories of political development. For example, by focusing on the inability of late industrializing nations to meet the rising material expectations of newly activated – yet insufficiently incorporated politically – publics, modernization theorists understood populism as a function of developmental gaps.[21] While dependency theorists focused on a different gap – one defined by trade relations between core and peripheral countries – they, too, understood populism as a product of rapid socioeconomic change, crisis, and underdevelopment.[22]

Although structuralist theories have been less influential since the end of the Cold War, economic factors, such as "globalization shocks," remain pertinent in the literature on populism.[23] Their significance makes sense in the context of Eastern Europe, which experienced a drastic change in the form of political and economic liberalization after state-led development,[24] as well as persistent underdevelopment in comparison to Western Europe.[25] Indeed, and taking a cue from the thesis that "globalization losers" – that is, the unskilled, unemployed, and underemployed victims of post-industrialism – are more likely to vote for radical right parties,[26] a variety of authors with very different perspectives have issued warnings about a populist backlash to neoliberal reforms, economic insecurity, and

---

[21] Di Tella (1965); Germani (1978); Lipset (1960).

[22] Cardoso and Faletto (1979); O'Donnell (1979).

[23] See Hawkins et al. (2017) for an elaboration and criticism. Also, Rodrik (2018).

[24] Greskovits (1998); Przeworski (1991).

[25] Bohle and Greskovits (2004).

[26] Betz (1994); Jackman and Volpert (1996); Kitschelt and McGann (1995); Kriesi et al. (2012).

inequality throughout the postcommunist period.[27] Similarly to scholars who emphasized the Great Depression as conducive to "classical populism" as well as to those who linked hyperinflation to the rise of "neoliberal populism" in the late twentieth century,[28] authors emphasizing the economy view the Great Recession of 2008–9 as a trigger of a twenty-first century "populist explosion."[29]

Arguments focused on the economy are commendable due to their sensitivity to material circumstances, but the picture they paint is too broad brushed. For example, as globalization and neoliberalism "triumphed and endured" throughout the postcommunist world,[30] economic insecurity heightened across the entire region. Additionally, some of the countries that experienced greater economic declines (e.g., Bulgaria, North Macedonia, and Latvia) rank lower on illiberal outcomes than countries with superior economies (e.g., Poland, Hungary, and Slovakia).[31] Finally, the Great Recession of 2008–9 explains neither support for antiestablishment alternatives throughout most of the twenty-first century's first decade nor differences between strongly impacted countries such as Albania, Czechia, Bulgaria, North Macedonia, and Romania, where support for antiestablishment illiberalism remained relatively low, and weakly impacted and prosperous Poland, where it remained much higher.[32] Economic demand, therefore, remains unconvincing as an explanation of persistently divergent illiberal outcomes.

3.5.2 Political Demand

If economic demand reflects changes in material circumstances, political demand channels popular dissatisfaction with poor governance and democratic institutions.[33] Sometimes triggered by large-scale scandals, such as the admission by the Hungarian prime minister that his government systematically lied before the 2006 election, demands to "throw out the bums" have resulted in protest voting in postcommunist Europe.[34] While perceptions of poor governance and corruption typically are associated with increased distrust in governments and liberal democratic institutions more generally, distrust in parliaments and parties can also be a chronic symptom of failing institutional representation and, thus, not be triggered by singular economic or political crises. No matter its origins, institutional distrust often results in voting for antiestablishment actors presenting themselves as champions of the pure people

---

[27] For example, Appel and Orenstein (2018), Balcerowicz (1995); Epstein (2020); Kriesi and Pappas (2015); Ost (2005); Przeworski (1991); Sachs (1990).
[28] Conniff (1999); Weyland (1999).
[29] Judis (2016).

[30] Appel and Orenstein (2016).
[31] See Ghodsee and Orenstein (2021).
[32] See, for example, Kriesi and Pappas (2015).
[33] Kriesi (2014); Kriesi and Pappas (2015).
[34] Pop-Eleches (2010).

against a corrupt or incompetent political elite.[35] As a number of analysts of Eastern Europe have underscored dissatisfaction with governments perceived as ineffective and corrupt,[36] as well as distrust in parties, parliaments[37] and the EU bureaucracy,[38] the role of political demand has the potential to drive populist voting in the region.

Although political demand is relevant in Eastern Europe, where perceptions of poor governance and high corruption go hand in hand with distrust of liberal democratic institutions, arguments that prioritize it have shortcomings. First, protest voting based on the perceived governance failures of mainstream parties has a temporal dimension, as convincingly shown in Pop-Eleches' "third generation elections" argument.[39] Yet, if dissatisfaction with governance and institutional distrust remained high, the actual reasons for this shifted with the changing circumstances over time. For example, if publics were discontent with mainstream parties rotating in government in the early 2000s, the Great Recession and immigration were more likely to be sources of political distrust thereafter.[40] Corruption, on the other hand, seems to have been a consistent reason for antiestablishment voting in the region.[41] However, as corruption concerns during the 2000–20 period were consistently more prevalent in Albania, North Macedonia, Bulgaria, and Romania, countries that ranked lower on antiestablishment illiberal outcomes, than in high-ranking Hungary, Poland, Slovakia, and Lithuania,[42] corruption cannot be an explanation for long-term differences in illiberal outcomes across the region. Neither is trust in the EU, which despite generally dropping levels, was, on average, equal over time in countries ranking on the opposite ends of the antiestablishment illiberalism spectrum.[43] Finally, as political demand factors are predominantly focused on institutions of governance rather than questions of political economy, they cannot explain the statist economic positions or posturing of electorally successful illiberal parties.

3.5.3 Cultural Demand

Cultural demand explanations focus on societal characteristics and developments. Once again originating in modernization theory, particularly the idea that "the social situation of the lower strata, especially in poorer countries with lower levels of education, predisposes them to view politics as black and

---

[35] Hanley and Sikk (2016); Haughton and Deegan-Krause (2015); Hawkins (2010); Klašnja et al. (2016); Mudde and Rovira Kaltwasser (2012: 8).

[36] For example, Engler (2020); Hanley and Sikk (2016); Pop-Eleches (2010); Tavits (2005).

[37] Rupnik (2018: 34).

[38] Whitefield and Rohrschneider (2015).

[39] Pop-Eleches (2010).

[40] See Armingeon and Ceka (2014); Jeannet (2020).

[41] Hanley and Sikk (2016).

[42] See Holmes (2013).

[43] See Armingeon and Ceka (2014).

white, good and evil,"[44] one such explanation can be traced even further back to Gustave Le Bon's and Sigmund Freud's theories of group hysteria in mass society. Concretely, when media exposure is widespread, opportunistic populists can more successfully exploit the poorly educated via unmediated channels of communication.[45] A second societal explanation focuses on the health of civic life and the potential for Durkheimian *anomie*.[46] Specifically, where "civil society is strong and densely organized," citizens are unlikely to sacrifice their political autonomy "to an autocratic figure with top-down visions of political organization, however charismatic or messianic such a figure might be."[47] As postcommunist Europe has been known for weak associational life,[48] civil society weakness is a potential cause of populist voting.

A third set of cultural explanations centers on the concept of post-materialism, which can work in two opposite ways relative to illiberal outcomes. On the one hand, as societies transition from materialist to post-materialist values, popular demand for participatory democracy grows.[49] Although such value shifts occur slowly, many Eastern European countries were exposed to post-materialist values rather abruptly with their incorporation into the European Union, which espouses liberal norms. Relatedly, as debates about the EU's "democratic deficit"[50] became exacerbated, particularly in the context of the 2008 economic crisis,[51] publics that demand better democracy may be especially attracted to populist calls for direct democracy.[52] On the other hand, Eastern European illiberalism can also be interpreted as a reaction against post-materialism. For example, the cultural backlash thesis argues that populism represents a rejection of the openness to cultural diversity, refugees, and gender equality spurred by the progressive "silent revolution.[53] Indeed, while some authors have argued that Eastern European illiberalism was especially stimulated by the 2015–16 refugee influx,[54] others have associated it with a cultural opposition to the empowerment of women.[55]

Cultural demand explanations are powerful, as they emphasize the evolution of values to which Eastern Europe has sought, and at times struggled, to adapt itself. Yet they are unpersuasive. First, theories of mass societies do not account for illiberal outcomes, as educational systems, which are similarly affected by the legacies of communism and insufficiently supported across the region, still produce comparably educated publics.[56] Similarly unconvincing

---

[44] Lipset (1960: 100).
[45] Hawkins (2010: 137–8).
[46] See Hawkins et al. (2017: 269).
[47] Roberts (2000).
[48] Howard (2003).
[49] Inglehart (1990); Offe (1985).
[50] Hix and Follesdal (2006); Majone (1998); Moravcsik (2002).
[51] Varoufakis (2012).

[52] Hawkins (2009).
[53] Inglehart and Norris (2016: 13–6).
[54] Vachudova (2020).
[55] See Grzebalska and Pető (2018).
[56] Gawlicz and Strarnawski (2018); Sondergaard and Murthi (2012). While differences in educational attainment exist, these do not correspond to varying illiberal outcomes (Halász 2015).

are explanations focused on civil society, which is weak across Eastern Europe in terms of associational life and labor unionization,[57] as well as those prioritizing post-materialist demands for participatory democracy provoked by the EU's technocratic governance. First, Eastern European countries directly affected by the EU's democratic deficit – that is, those that are EU members – score both high and low on illiberal outcomes. Second, appeals for direct democracy do not account for the attraction of most successful antiestablishment or illiberal parties, which typically did not make such calls.

Finally, the cultural backlash thesis does not explain the variation in Chapter 1. A key reason for this is that Eastern European illiberal or post-neoliberal populist parties are not necessarily "radical right" – the central preoccupation of Ronald Inglehart and Pippa Norris for the European context as a whole.[58] Indeed, while resentment against ethno-liberal parties may explain the rise of the radical right in Eastern Europe,[59] illiberal and post-neoliberal populist parties tended to be more successful in homogenous countries with weaker ethnic parties (e.g., Hungary, Poland, and Lithuania) than in more diverse countries with more relevant ethnic parties (e.g., North Macedonia, Estonia, and Latvia). Additionally, while resentment against refugees can possibly explain developments after the 2015 migrant influx, it cannot account for illiberal outcomes in Eastern Europe during the first fifteen years of the 2000–20 period. Finally, as publics across the region are rather uniformly unsupportive of gender equality[60] and as the adoption of affirmative and antidiscrimination policies does not correspond to trends in illiberal outcomes,[61] women's empowerment is an improbable explanation of varying illiberal trends.

3.5.4 Institutional Supply

Opposite to demand-side explanation, arguments focused on political supply underscore top-down factors. The first set of explanations here focuses on the institutional rules of the game. For example, plurality electoral systems and high electoral thresholds have been hypothesized to reduce "vote wasting" on new or relatively minor parties,[62] thus diminishing the electoral potential of many antiestablishment populist and illiberal players. For the Eastern European context, some authors have argued that direct presidential elections[63] or high district magnitude in proportional representation systems[64] are associated with increased electoral volatility, which, especially when extra-systemic,[65] can theoretically correspond to the electoral success of new or previously minor antiestablishment parties.

---

[57] Crowley (2004); Howard (2003).
[58] See Inglehart and Norris (2016).
[59] Buštíková (2014).
[60] Pop-Eleches and Tucker (2017: 221–2).
[61] See Beloshitzkaya (2021).

[62] Jackman and Volpert (1996); Riker (1982).
[63] Filippov et al. (1999).
[64] Tavits (2005).
[65] See Powell and Tucker (2014).

The second set of supply side explanations can be traced back to the work of Samuel Huntington, who considered political institutionalization as predictive of stability and governance quality.[66] Some scholars in this tradition argue that under-institutionalized party systems – namely, those with weak programmatic discipline and linkages, less policy content, and less clear partisan divides[67] – can motivate voters to seek populist alternatives promising better representation.[68] This is the message of recent work arguing that leftist constituencies turn to populism when social democratic parties supply neoliberal policies.[69] A different line of argumentation emphasizes party organization as a more concrete institutional supply factor. Yet, as many populist parties distinguish themselves electorally precisely due to their lack of coherent organization,[70] some supply side accounts emphasize these parties' personalistic tendencies[71] and, more specifically, the role of charismatic appeals and manipulation for shaping voters' preferences.[72]

Supply side accounts are crucial, as they direct attention to the strategies of political elites. But they are either unconvincing or incomplete. Neither institutional rules nor personalism or charisma can tell us why challengers of liberalism adopt particular ideological positions. Moreover, as there is evidence that party system over-institutionalization, rather than under-institutionalization, can pave the way to populist success, as seen in Hungary and Greece,[73] the concrete effects of party systems, which are complex and multi-faceted agglomerations, remain unclear. And while the argument linking social democratic parties' pro-market turn and populist voting is compelling, especially as it posits a trend similar in the Eastern and Western parts of Europe,[74] it does not tell a convincing story regarding the reasons for such parties' adoption of such policies in the first place. Indeed, as Eastern Europe is characterized by distinct historical legacies, political economies, and party systems,[75] the reasons for leftist parties' positions and policies on economic issues are likely motivated by somewhat different dynamics than in Western Europe. In short, supply side explanations neither specify what aspects of party systems lead to varying illiberal outcomes nor sufficiently consider postcommunist Europe's concrete historical context.

3.5.5 International Factors

Arguments focused on international factors emphasize external forces as an explanation of electoral reactions against liberalism. For example, constructivists have made the case that "reinforcement by reward," featuring

---

[66] Huntington (1968); Kaufman and Stallings (1991).
[67] Kitschelt (2003).
[68] Mainwaring and Scully (1995); Mair (2002).
[69] Bagashka et al. (2022); Snegovaya (2024).
[70] Burgess and Levitsky (2003); Levitsky (1999); Mudde (2007).
[71] Weyland (1999).
[72] Engler (2020); Haughton and Deegan Krause (2020).
[73] Enyedi (2016); Pappas (2014).
[74] Berman and Snegovaya (2019); Snegovaya (2024).
[75] Bohle and Greskovits (2012); Pop-Eleches and Tucker (2017); Powell and Tucker (2014).

persuasion, learning, and socialization, can strengthen liberalism domestically. Emphasizing EU conditionality as a key element of Western leverage, scholars in this tradition argue that prospects for EU membership constrain illiberal discourses at odds with popular pro-European attitudes and aspirations across the postcommunist region.[76] Relatedly, Eastern Europe has also experienced increasingly dense linkages with the West. While, according to Levitsky and Way, such linkages are expected to enhance the position of antiauthoritarian adherents to international norms,[77] thus logically limiting the salience of illiberalism, others see more pernicious effects. As discussed by Rodrik, for example, exposure to trade – a key element of both Western linkage and economic globalization – can intensify calls for protectionism and populist voting, mostly due to its uneven redistributive and labor market effects.[78] A final argument focused on international factors emphasizes spatial diffusion as fundamental for the spread of norms, resources, and institutions under post-communism.[79] Specifically, as voters learn by observing foreign policies on top of domestic ones,[80] they have the power to "change their regimes" in ways matching those of their "contiguous neighbors."[81] As such a domino effect has been observed by scholars of Latin American and Western European populism,[82] and as the populist challenge has been prevalent in neighboring countries in postcommunist Europe, diffusion can be a contributor to illiberal outcomes in the region.

Although such explanations are attractive because they emphasize the international environment to which Eastern Europe has sought to adapt itself after communism, they do not account for the uneven patterns identified in Chapter 1. First, Western leverage fails to explain varying outcomes not only because EU members are found on both sides of the illiberalism gamut but also because EU accession solidified, rather than disrupted, already existing divergences between, for example, Poland, Lithuania, and Slovakia, on the one hand, and Czechia, Romania, and Croatia, on the other. Likewise, the role of Western trade remains ambiguous both in theory, as noted earlier, and in practice, as seen in countries at opposite ends of the antiestablishment illiberalism spectrum, yet engaged in comparably high (e.g., Czechia and Slovakia) or lower (e.g., North Macedonia and Lithuania) levels of trade with the West.[83] Also unconvincing is the spatial diffusion argument – because for every country where illiberal reactions could have been learned from contiguous neighbors (e.g., Poland, Hungary, Slovakia, Lithuania), there is a counter example

---

[76] Innes (2002); Pridham (2002); Schimmelfennig and Sedelmeier (2004: 670); Vachudova (2008b).

[77] Levitsky and Way (2005: 23; 2010).

[78] Rodrik (2021: 141–8, 162–5).

[79] Kopstein and Reilly (2000).

[80] Kishishita and Yamagishi (2021).

[81] Brinks and Coppedge (2006).

[82] Corrales (2007); Rydgren (2005).

[83] Author's calculations based on IMF data on trade as a share of GDP.

where such contagion did not materialize in comparable ways (e.g., Czechia, Romania, Croatia, Slovenia).

In sum, standard explanations focused on demand side, supply side, and international factors are individually unsatisfying in terms of making sense of postcommunist illiberalism. As I demonstrate with systematic empirical tests in Appendix D, such factors do not account for patterns of illiberal outcomes at the ballot box across Eastern Europe in the 2000–20 period. Indeed, these tests point to one basic conclusion – electoral support for the challengers of liberalism in the fifteen countries under analysis is best predicted by the long-term electoral trends of the Left. They also show that while short-term electoral shifts contributed somewhat to illiberal outcomes, the difference they made is less substantial than the effect of the path dependencies posited by the theory developed in Chapter 2. Because the durable trajectories of leftist parties originated in postcommunist junctures, as the first part of this chapter demonstrated, they are best understood as the crucial link between critical prior moments of neoliberal deepening and the persistently varying illiberal outcomes that these moments ultimately conditioned.

3.6 CONCLUSION

In this chapter, I have moved from an exploration of theoretical considerations to an initial assessment of the empirical evidence. First, having identified the mainstream Left and Right in contemporary Eastern Europe and considered the programmatic evolution and electoral performance of such parties, I showed that postcommunist junctures bequeathed distinct long-term legacies that ultimately shaped illiberal outcomes. As programmatic and electoral dynamics on the Left were largely rooted in prior critical moments of market reform, these dynamics should be understood as the connecting link between the postcommunist junctures from which they emerged and the illiberal outcomes that they conditioned. Second, having identified competing accounts, I discussed why economic, political, and cultural demand, as well as institutional supply and international factors, cannot explain sufficiently well the puzzle of illiberalism in Eastern Europe. Indeed, this is empirically documented in Appendix D, which demonstrates unambiguously that the postcommunist juncture theory has higher explanatory power than rival arguments precisely because it focuses on the long-term dynamics that consistently made the most substantive and significant difference in terms of illiberal outcomes in the region.

While the evidence presented in this chapter lends support to the theoretical propositions developed previously, it is, of course, best understood as an initial feasibility probe of the postcommunist juncture argument. This empirical baseline, in turn, suggests the need for a deeper exploration of the causal mechanisms linking the legacies of political configurations during crucial moments of neoliberal deepening in the 1990s and institutional outcomes thereafter. The second part of this book (Chapters 4–6) explores historical antecedents, postcommunist junctures, and path-dependent developments in four case studies, demonstrating how key mechanisms of production and reproduction were both the products of contingencies independent from longue-durée history and the makers of political futures across contemporary Eastern Europe.

PART II

CASE STUDIES FROM EASTERN EUROPE

4

Antecedent Conditions and Postcommunist Junctures in Poland, Czechia, Slovakia, and Romania

If region-wide statistical patterns confirm strong relationships between types of postcommunist junctures, leftist party politics, and illiberal outcomes, how did the mechanisms linking these factors play out in the actual experiences of various Eastern European countries? This and Chapters 5 and 6 answer this question by comparing historical developments in four countries where political configurations during junctures produced varying long-term effects. Because I have posited that postcommunist junctures were products of historical contingency rather than determinism, and because to qualify as "critical" these junctures have to meet certain criteria, in this chapter I assess questions of contingency and "criticalness" by tracing processes leading up to and during the most crucial moments of neoliberal reform in four case studies.

A comparison of Poland, Czechia, Slovakia, and Romania is analytically advantageous due to the confluence of both differences and similarities in terms of historical, political, economic, and societal developments. Indeed, these four cases represent the diversity of Eastern European pre-communist, communist, and early postcommunist experiences, as well as the variety of transitions between these periods. As I show, while long-term historical developments conditioned the central political divides in different countries soon after 1989 as well as the crises that would ultimately be resolved during postcommunist junctures, they did not determine types of junctures. In turn, postcommunist junctures – occurring sometime after second competitive elections, when main political actors offered to the electorate alternative political visions on economic policy – were products of highly uncertain events that could not have been predicted in advance. Entailing key choices and considerable institutional innovations during neoliberal deepening, the postcommunist junctures discussed in this chapter correspond to varying political configurations and dynamics. While in Czechia and Romania those in charge and in opposition during junctures acted in alignment with prior electoral commitments, key reformers in Slovakia and Poland used bait-and-switch tactics. By tracing historical developments and identifying and analyzing the crucial political configurations that would shape future politics in the four countries, the chapter lays the basis for the subsequent comparative analysis.

4.1 HISTORICAL ANTECEDENTS AND CRISES

While all Eastern European countries underwent consequential junctures of neoliberal deepening, these critical periods occurred against the backdrop of a wide range of historical experiences. Because Poland, Czechia, Slovakia, and Romania are representative of the great diversity of such experiences across the region, in this section I focus on their trajectories before postcommunist junctures. As these four countries were characterized by both important similarities and crucial differences in terms of political, societal, and economic developments before, during, and soon after communism, this discussion is an ideal starting point for the case-based comparative analysis. This section makes two important contributions. First, it helps drive the point that long-term historical experiences, which varied widely, did *not* determine types of postcommunist junctures, which varied less and were, as argued in Chapter 2, highly contingent in nature. Second, it demonstrates that historical antecedents ultimately culminated not only in political divides, as correctly identified by previous historical institutionalist work,[1] but also in considerable crises, the resolution of which would correspond to postcommunist junctures shaping new trajectories. In addition to following historical developments with an eye toward key similarities and differences across countries, the section also discusses why early attempts at market liberalization after communism did *not* constitute postcommunist junctures.

4.1.1 Poland

Ever since its foundation in the Middle Ages, Poland has been distinguished by a tradition of bottom-up societal mobilization. Having originated with the gentry's nationalist program of *polonization* and then organized against Russian, Prussian, and Austrian imperial dominance following the eighteenth-century partitions,[2] civil society here became known for its unusual for the region strength. By the early 1900s, it had matured into a powerful force organized by the social democratic and nationalist parties and movements that crystallized as industrialization unsettled the traditional agrarian economy.[3] This force was indeed so irrepressible that it survived not only authoritarian rule

---

[1] Kitschelt et al. (1999).
[2] Castle and Taras (2002: 2–18).

[3] Kitschelt et al. (1999: 97); Pankowski (2010: 15–31); Rae (2008: 35).

during the Second Polish Republic (1918–39)[4] but also renewed partition and genocide during World War II. With the country's resistance being among the strongest in Europe,[5] the mobilizing capacity of its civil society transcended unprecedented privation.[6]

Beginning in the mid 1940s, the externally imposed communist regime attempted to fundamentally reconfigure Polish politics and society. Yet although it sought domination through a number of Stalinist maneuvers,[7] the communist Polish United Workers' Party was unpopular from the beginning.[8] This, in turn, provoked multiple waves of protest mobilization[9] – in 1956, 1968, 1970, 1976, and 1980–81 – which forced significant concessions to the anti-communist opposition, including "a rollback of land reforms, considerable autonomy for the Catholic Church, and a circumscribed area of civil liberties."[10] Although the communist state increasingly used heavy-handed repression against dissidents,[11] collective protests ultimately forced it to adopt a national-accommodative, rather than totalitarian, approach to its relationship with society.[12] When Poland began experiencing economic crisis in the 1970s, the state-society cleavage became increasingly apparent. As failed efforts at economic liberalization resulted in mounting food prices, deficit, and debt, as well as steep national income decline and triple digit inflation,[13] Poland experienced violent working class uprisings. Instantly becoming a symbol of labor resistance, these protests both inspired the development of new societal organizations, such as the Workers' Defense Committee (KOR),[14] and highlighted the central importance of economic issues during the final two communist decades.

If labor-based mobilization laid the basis for anti-communist protest in the 1970s, the cleavage between the state and a civil society mobilized around the defense of workers' interests[15] only deepened in the 1980s. The key social actor by then was Solidarity, a trade union whose origins in KOR and ten million members constituted a united front of intellectuals and workers demanding both political and economic rights.[16] Looking for an accommodation after first imposing martial law and banning Solidarity,[17] the regime, now led by General Wojciech Jaruzelski, experimented with new attempts at reform, which,

---

4 Castle and Taras (2002: 18–23); Kitschelt (2002: 18); Pankowski (2010: 16); Rae (2008: 37).
5 Castle and Taras (2002: 25–5); Linz and Stepan (1996: 259).
6 See Kitschelt et al. (1999: 36–7).
7 Castle and Taras (2002: 31); Ekiert (1998: 17–8); Grzymała-Busse (2002: 42–4); Kitschelt (2002: 18).
8 Grzymała-Busse (2002: 41).
9 Ekiert (1998: 15).
10 Kitschelt et al. (1999: 18–9, 97–9); Linz and Stepan (1996: 253–61).
11 Kitschelt et al. (1999: 40).
12 Ekiert (1998: 28–32); Kitschelt et al. (1999); Linz and Stepan (1996: 255–9).
13 Connor and Ploszajski (1992: 18); Ekiert (1998: 30–1); Grzymała-Busse (2002: 49); Rae (2008: 46).
14 Ekiert (1998: 28–31).
15 Castle and Taras (2002: 52–62).
16 As Solidarity activists from the 1980s underscored, the union's central mission was to protect workers' rights (Interviews POL-09; POL-17).
17 Ekiert (1998: 35–7).

however, resulted in more indebtedness, inflation, and real wage declines.[18] When yet another round of price hikes triggered a new wave of strikes in 1988,[19] the government finally budged to Solidarity's demands. The round-table talks of early 1989 concluded with the communists not only agreeing to hold semi-free elections but also conceding to calls for wage increases and employment security.[20]

Yet these measures, adopted as a response to labor mobilization at a time of already high inflation, immediately provoked hyperinflation.[21] As the negotiated transition brought a Solidarity-led government headed by Tadeusz Mazowiecki, Poland found itself in a deep economic crisis. It was in this context that the cabinet's most influential member, Finance Minister Leszek Balcerowicz, planned a radical economic transformation.[22] Known as the Balcerowicz Plan, the shock therapy reforms introduced a variety of liberalization measures beginning on January 1, 1990. Although these measures did include deflationary policies, stubborn macroeconomic instability featuring declines of industrial output, real wages, and consumption persisted throughout 1990.[23]

The major reforms of 1990, however, did not constitute a postcommunist juncture – because alternative economic visions had not been contested in the country's first competitive election,[24] which had preceded the Balcerowicz Plan. Indeed, as parties "had little time to prepare full-fledged electoral campaigns" for the "competitive but not confrontational elections" held just two months after the 1989 roundtable, Solidarity won the competitive 35 percent of lower-house seats simply by claiming that it was the "more competent, democratic, and viable alternative."[25] This electoral result, however, forced the communists to focus on their party's reformation.[26] It also transformed Solidarity into a standard political actor vested with policymaking powers – a new reality that would soon lead to the trade union's undoing.

In sum, if civil society mobilization defined Polish history before and during communism,[27] the divide between society and the state deepened amid economic crisis in the 1970s and 1980s. As attempts to accommodate societal demands, which reflected important labor concerns, ultimately resulted in significant concessions, Poland emerged from communism having yet to solve its deep economic problems. If the socially painful shock therapy initiated by the first Solidarity government represented a major step in this direction, it would also deepen nascent economic and cultural divides[28] amid crisis during the first

[18] Rae (2008: 48).
[19] Connor and Ploszajski (1992: 20); Rae (2008: 38).
[20] Baka (2005: 51–5); Myant and Drahoukopil (2011: 38); Orenstein (2001: 27–8).
[21] Kołodko (1991).
[22] Castle and Taras (2002: 84–5); Greskovits (1998: 58); Orenstein (2001: 29–30); Rae (2008: 53–4).
[23] Myant and Drahokoupil (2011: 56–8); Rae (2008: 60).
[24] Kitschelt et al. (1999: 99).
[25] Castle and Taras (2002: 81); Taras (1995: 138–42; 1998: 51).
[26] Grzymała-Busse (2002).
[27] Ekiert (1997).
[28] Kitschelt et al. (1999: 79).

postcommunist year. As Poland approached its second competitive election – this time for president – in late 1990, these divisions set the tone for the major changes ahead.

4.1.2 Czechia and Slovakia

Having spent most of the twentieth century as one state, Czechia and Slovakia experienced both divergent and convergent tendencies. To begin, pre-communist Czechoslovakia may have been the most economically prosperous and only consistently democratic country in interwar Eastern Europe,[29] but these accomplishments were mostly due to progress in the Czech lands of Bohemia, where early industrialization under the Hapsburgs conditioned developments unlike those in agrarian and impoverished Slovakia, which had long been held back under Hungarian control. It was in Czechia where an active labor movement invigorated the social democratic and communist parties that helped structure a coherent party system.[30] In contrast to the more secular Czechia, predominantly rural and Catholic Slovakia had both one of the region's weakest civil societies[31] and an under-institutionalized party system revolving around questions of religion and national autonomy.[32] As Slovak disaffection with relative underdevelopment was additionally aggravated by the Czechs' domination of the state administration and all interwar governments, Slovaks became increasingly susceptible to nationalism. The beneficiary was a quasi-fascist party, which, under the leadership of Josef Tiso, first declared Slovak autonomy and then independence following the 1938 Munich Agreement.[33] After Tiso's regime collaborated with Nazism, Slovakia was reincorporated into Czechoslovakia in 1945.[34] The following year, the communists won a free and fair election. Although they lost in Slovakia, their dominance in Czechia[35] was sufficient for capturing control of the unitary state.

It was based on such historical differences that the communist dictatorship, which consolidated control with a coup in 1948 and lost power in 1989, featured somewhat different state-society relations in the two parts of Czechoslovakia. Having forcefully incorporated Czechia's historic Social Democratic Party, the communists instituted a regime whose despotism became especially pronounced in Czechia after the failed 1968 liberalization attempt known as the Prague Spring. If Czechs faced what Kitschelt and coauthors identified as bureaucratic-authoritarian communism, Slovaks endured a harder-to-classify

---

[29] Linz and Stepan (1996: 316).
[30] Hanley (2002); Kitschelt et al. (1999: 102).
[31] Interview SVK-19.
[32] Henderson (2002: 9); Linz and Stepan (1996: 328); Kitschelt et al. (1999: 36, 41, 101); Kitschelt (2002: 20).

[33] Henderson (2002: 7–12); Ward (2013: 166).
[34] Fisher (2006: 26); Henderson (2002: 13–8); Linz and Stepan (1996: 328); Ward (2013: 235, 253).
[35] Kitschelt et al. (1999: 101); Linz and Stepan (1996: 317).

communist experience, which combined national-accommodative and patrimonial elements.[36] However, as the regime here was harsher than in Poland,[37] where communists adjusted to societal pressures by taming repression, and as national accommodation – namely, administrative autonomy after federalization in 1968 – was instituted to satisfy regional elites rather than societal demands,[38] Slovakia's case was unlike more standard examples of national-accommodative communism. Instead, the state's cooptation of a passive civil society made Slovak communism rather similar to patrimonial experiences in the otherwise less developed Balkans.[39]

The differences between Czechia and Slovakia notwithstanding, the communist project did reverse some previously divergent trends in economics, politics, and society. Economically, after the regime modernized Slovakia through rapid industrialization,[40] the weaknesses of central planning eventually undermined both parts of the federation in similar ways.[41] Politically, Slovakia achieved considerable gains as it was rewarded for its passivity in 1968 with preferential treatment in terms of administrative appointments.[42] Societally, the communists were so harsh that they suppressed even limited pluralism everywhere across the country. Although dissident groups like *Charter 77* became active a decade after the Prague Spring – itself initiated not by bottom-up activism but rather by top-down technocrats hoping for economic modernization[43] – these groups were neither large nor well-organized.[44] If Czech civil society had been impressively active in the interwar period, by the 1980s communist repression had rendered it nearly as powerless as in Slovakia.

This combination of communist rigidity and civil society weakness, or what Juan Linz and Alfred Stepan called "frozen" post-totalitarianism, resulted in a democratic transition and economic conditions opposite to Poland's.[45] First, Czechoslovak communism ended not by negotiation but rather by implosion stemming from its incapacity to reform itself. While public protests – more large-scale and politicized in Prague than Bratislava[46] – did foreshadow the transition, popular mobilization in Czechoslovakia began later than in Poland and did not cause the regime's collapse.[47] Second, lacking societal feedback and pressure, the communists had failed to implement "anything beyond cosmetic" market reforms. As a result of this unwillingness to experiment with liberalization, by the 1980s Czechoslovakia's economy was both increasingly

---

[36] Kitschelt et al. (1999: 39).

[37] Deegan-Krause (2006: 195).

[38] Grzymała-Busse (2002: 36, 41); Kitschelt et al. (1999: 40–1).

[39] Kitschelt (2002); Kitschelt et al. (1999).

[40] Fisher (2006: 27); Henderson (2002: 18–21); Myant (2003: 11).

[41] Myant (2003: 11).

[42] Bunce (1999: 221); Grzymała-Busse (2002: 41); Henderson (2002: 21–6).

[43] Kitschelt et al. (1999: 102).

[44] Linz and Stepan (1996: 320–1).

[45] Linz and Stepan (1996).

[46] Whereas protests in Prague demonstrated significant working class support for regime change (Bunce 2003: 176; Orenstein 2001: 65), those in Bratislava were fewer, smaller, and "about other religious and ecological issues" (Henderson 2002: 29).

[47] Linz and Stepan (1996: 324–7).

stagnant and, ironically, more stable than Poland's, "avoiding budget deficits, generalized shortages, inflation, or a collapse in production."[48]

Thus, although their historical experiences were far from identical, Czechia and Slovakia underwent four decades of relative leveling in terms of political, economic, and societal trajectories. When the communist chapter ended in 1989, the suddenly democratic federation found itself grappling with new urgent questions about political and economic organization. As Czechoslovakia's Velvet Revolution produced a "government of national understanding," dissidents, such as the new president, Vaclav Havel, and reform communists, such as the new prime minister, Marian Čalfa, agreed that an electoral mandate was necessary if structural adjustment were to be accepted by the public.[49] With the anti-communist Civic Forum (OF) winning a majority in Czechia, its Slovak counterpart, the Public Against Violence (VPN), gaining a plurality in Slovakia, and both jointly taking most of the seats in the Federal Assembly, the 1990 election provided the mandate reformers had sought.

And yet the period between the Velvet Revolution, which ended Czechoslovak communism, and the Velvet Divorce, which ended Czechoslovakia itself, did not correspond to a postcommunist juncture. Since the dissidents and reform communists in government between December 1989 and the June 1990 election had agreed on an economic program, the election was "more a referendum on communism than a vote on programmatic issues of economic reform."[50] Moreover, although the government initiated, in January 1991, structural adjustment led by Finance Minister Vaclav Klaus, this program was based not on strictly neoliberal principles but rather on a social–liberal compromise that included protections for pensioners and the unemployed in addition to a nationalist approach to privatization and banking.[51] Because purer market reforms were postponed until more favorable political circumstances, these early policies are best understood as a neoliberal prelude rather than a juncture.

This prelude, however, unsettled the economic stability inherited from communism as it triggered a "transformation recession" featuring the loss of a third of industrial output, a fourth of agriculture, and a fifth of overall productivity.[52] Inflation, reaching over 70 percent in 1992, persisted at higher levels than anticipated. As domestic demand and GDP continued declining, so did industrial employment.[53] Whereas unemployment was lower in Czechia, it was in the double digits in Slovakia,[54] where "the social consequences of the Czech-led economic transformation" were especially severe.[55] With the 1992 elections producing newly dominant political actors with divergent ideas regarding

---

[48] Myant and Drahokoupil (2011: 37).
[49] Orenstein (2001: 64–73).
[50] Orenstein (2001: 73).
[51] Greskovits (1998: 139); Orenstein (2001: 73–9).
[52] Klaus (2014: 62–4).

[53] Myant (2003: 26–8).
[54] Mikloš (2014: 115). See also Bohle and Greskovits (2012: 76); Klaus (2014: 55).
[55] Bohle and Greskovits (2012: 76); Fisher (2006: 24).

the future – Czechia's Vaclav Klaus seeking speedier neoliberal deepening and Slovakia's Vladimír Mečiar calling for a slowdown of reforms[56] – the dissolution of the federation was spearheaded by leaders in pursuit of opposite visions. In the end, it was opportunistic political elites, and not the citizens they represented, that agreed to split Czechoslovakia.[57] As these leaders next enacted their visions, the two new countries would undergo very different trajectories. In Czechia, where the type of economic divides that had defined the interwar period reemerged as politically salient after communism,[58] the postcommunist juncture occurred immediately after the split. In Slovakia, where different issues gained salience, patterns from the past continued reproducing themselves – a reason why developments there between the Velvet Divorce and the postcommunist juncture deserve additional attention.

4.1.3 Slovakia's Persistent Past

Although by 1993 Slovakia had exited both communism and Czechoslovakia, a clear break with the past did not materialize here for nearly a full decade after 1989.[59] As prior patters of civil society weakness and quiescence continued well after the transition, with less protest activity than elsewhere in Central Europe,[60] Mečiar easily imposed a competitive-authoritarian regime[61] that "colonized" political and economic life through the patrimonial apparatus inherited from communism.[62] Because he persecuted opponents[63] and engaged in broad surveillance of political and civil society,[64] his regime was decidedly undemocratic. In the economic spere, Mečiar not only created a regime-friendly oligarchic business class through patrimonialism[65] but also enacted subsidies and protective regulations for industries, expansionary fiscal policies, and welfare paternalism.[66] These measures were buttressed by economically nationalist and leftist rhetoric, itself a legacy from Slovakia's communist past.[67] Such tactics facilitated the empowerment of his party, the ironically named Movement for a Democratic Slovakia (HZDS), and attracted widespread support for it,[68] mostly from constituents who would have otherwise voted for communists.[69] By hijacking the political and economic transformation, Mečiarism perpetuated communist-era practices of exchanging social security for acquiescence to

---

[56] Fisher et al. (2007); Henderson (1995); Innes (2001); Raimondi (1991: 7).
[57] Henderson (2002: 34); Orenstein (2001: 85).
[58] Kitschelt et al. (1999).
[59] Interviews SVK-16; SVK-20.
[60] Interview SVK-19; Ekiert and Kubik (1998).
[61] Levitsky and Way (2010: 93–4).
[62] O'Dwyer (2006: 6, 31, 99).
[63] Deegan-Krause (2006: 34–8).
[64] Levitsky and Way (2010: 91–2).
[65] Mikloš (2014: 116).
[66] Bohle and Greskovits (2012: 146); Haughton (2001: 748–54); Pop-Eleches (2009: 114).
[67] Interview SVK-20.
[68] Deegan-Krause (2006: 81–3); Fisher (2006: 151); Haughton (2001: 754–9); O'Dwyer (2006: 50–1).
[69] Interview SVK-08.

authoritarianism and corruption.[70] Rather than break with the past, "Mečiar was running the country Lukashenko style."[71]

As it polarized political and civil society, Mečiarism defined the central lines of contestation in the 1990s. Complex and multidimensional, the main political divide at the time can be described as a center-periphery cleavage revolving around questions of nationalism, state-building, Catholicism, and democracy.[72] Although economic considerations were not primary,[73] they were nevertheless far from irrelevant[74] as Mečiar's supporters – state administrators, corrupt business beneficiaries, and voters "nostalgic for communist times" – were all attracted to his "program of managed economic reform."[75] The regime's opponents, meanwhile, were those aspiring for democracy but divided over just which kind – liberal or social – was best.[76]

Although Slovak cleavages in the 1990s featured several dimensions,[77] the main political divide that emerged was between national-authoritarians and market-oriented reformists. Mečiarism, with a third of the vote, dominated the national-authoritarian field, with its two coalition partners between 1994 and 1998, the Slovak National Party (SNS) and Union of the Workers of Slovakia (ZRS), playing along. Against these forces of continuity with the patrimonial and national-collectivist past[78] were market-oriented reformists – represented by the Christian Democratic Movement (KDH),[79] the neoliberal Democratic Party (DS) and Democratic Union (DÚ), and the Party of the Hungarian Coalition (SMK–MKP)[80] – as well as social democrats led by the ex-communist Party of the Democratic Left (SDĽ).[81]

Even as the center-periphery cleavage dominated political competition at the time, it must be acknowledged that less than a third of Slovak voters in the 1990s preferred parties espousing neoliberalism. With more than half of the public supporting rather statist options, the left-leaning electorate was mostly split between Mečiar's populist HZDS, with an increasingly redistributionist agenda,[82] and the leftist SDĽ – the second most successful party in the first postcommunist decade. Importantly, if these popular preferences helped structure politics during the Mečiar era, they would certainly be key for understanding developments resulting from Slovakia's postcommunist juncture, as discussed later in this chapter.

---

[70] Interview SVK-20; Bohle and Greskovits (2012: 145).
[71] Interview SVK-07.
[72] Casal Bértoa (2014); Deegan-Krause (2000: 38); Evans and Whitefield (1998); Henderson (2004: 143–4); Markowski (1997).
[73] Deegan-Krause (2006).
[74] Markowski (1997: 231).
[75] Haughton (2004: 182–3); Pop-Eleches (2009).
[76] Interview SVK-04.

[77] See Casal Bértoa (2014: 26).
[78] Interview SVK-20.
[79] On KDH's "traditional free market agenda," see Deegan-Krause (2000: 43n8). Also, Grzymała-Busse (2002: 152).
[80] Fisher (2006: 154–5); Henderson (2002: 46–7); Mikloš (2014: 117n9); Wightman (2001: 132).
[81] Grzymała-Busse (2002: 159); Rybář and Deegan-Krause (2008: 501).
[82] Rybář and Deegan-Krause (2008: 512).

Finally, as the divides and problems spurred by Mečiarism deepened over time, so did the sense of national crisis. With corrupt patrimonialism fostering tax evasion, high indebtedness, and a "freezing of the economic system," what had been a healthy economy in the mid 1990s gradually turned into a "black hole" repelling foreign investors.[83] When the country was excluded from the Organization for Economic Cooperation and Development, the first round of eastward enlargement of the North Atlantic Treaty Organization,[84] and European Union accession negotiations, its international "pariah status" became "a central theme of domestic politics," prompting numerous government resignations and strengthening the opposition.[85] As the competitive-authoritarian regime faced a legitimacy crisis, by the 1998 parliamentary election Mečiar's opponents finally had a chance to break with Slovakia's patrimonial and nationalist past.

4.1.4 Romania

Having achieved independence and unification amid Great Power rivalries, by the early twentieth century Romania was an agrarian country with a pronounced urban–rural divide and an enormous gap between Francophile elites, typically represented by the Liberal Party, and impoverished peasants constituting four-fifths of the population and mobilized by the National Peasant Party.[86] As authoritarian regimes used, with the support of the royalty, the poorly bureaucratized state apparatus to rule over a weak civil society,[87] significant social democratic and communist movements and parties failed to develop during the interwar period.[88] When, following the government's collaboration in the Holocaust, communism was imposed from abroad in the mid 1940s, neither the generally Russophobe elites nor the rural population fearful of land seizures[89] were in a position to resist the dramatic transformations ahead.

The communists not only pursued aggressive industrialization and collectivization but also developed, under the leadership of, first, Gheorghe Dej and, later, Nicolae Ceauşescu, an idiosyncratically independent yet harsh version of totalitarianism[90] – a patrimonial communist regime[91] which combined elements of extreme sultanism and nationalist Stalinism and which remained unreformed until its demise.[92] Although he refused to support the 1968 Soviet-led aggression against Czechoslovakia, Ceauşescu was uninterested in relinquishing control over what was possibly Eastern Europe's most repressed and

[83] Fisher (2006: 151); Fisher et al. (2007); Mikloš (2014: 117); Pop–Eleches (2009: 115–6, 179).

[84] Mikloš (2014: 116).

[85] Levitsky and Way (2010: 94–6).

[86] Glenny (2012).

[87] Kitschelt (2002).

[88] Mungiu-Pippidi (2002).

[89] Glenny (2012); Mungiu-Pippidi (2002).

[90] Glenny (2012).

[91] Kitschelt et al. (1999).

[92] Linz and Stepan (1996).

alienated civil society.[93] With no space for even limited opposition, the personalist dictator implemented "draconian austerity measures" in an ambitious attempt to repay the country's debt, thereby significantly reducing consumption and social services in the 1980s.[94] Yet, as deepening poverty sharpened discontent in what had become a "society of survival," Ceaușescu suddenly lost control.[95] When the 1989 events across Eastern Europe precipitated the spectacular unraveling of his regime, Romania found itself in a revolutionary transition out of communism.[96]

Although the Romanian Revolution vanquished Ceaușescu's regime, it failed to elicit a true transition to democracy and the market.[97] As former communists reorganized in the National Salvation Front (FSN),[98] they quickly "captured" the revolution by instrumentalizing the tried-and-true methods of nationalism, to which they repeatedly turned in the following years,[99] and personalism, which continued "flattening" the political and social landscape.[100] Having crushed the democratic opposition in the first postcommunist – and unfair – elections in 1990, the ex-communists, now led by Ion Iliescu, imposed a competitive-authoritarian regime where "elements of the old authoritarian state persisted."[101] This regime was consolidated with the victory of Iliescu-led forces in the second election, in 1992, following FSN's splintering into rival factions.[102] As the ex-communist Party of Social Democracy in Romania (PDSR) enlisted the support of a "red–brown" coalition[103] reflective of persistent affinities between collectivism and nationalism,[104] the government resisted de-communization, re-centralized power, and repressed opponents.[105] With the best organizationally endowed party[106] in power and refusing to abandon the nationalist-communist past,[107] the prospects of democratization were dim. If the 1990s were defined by an authoritarian-democratic divide,[108] it was the authoritarians who dominated for most of the decade.[109]

As in Slovakia, Romania's competitive-authoritarian regime not only consolidated power by continuing the corrupt and clientelist practices inherited

---

[93] Glenny (2012); Linz and Stepan (1996); Mungiu-Pippidi (2001; 2002).

[94] Glenny (2012); Pop-Eleches (2009).

[95] Mungiu-Pippidi (2002).

[96] Glenny (2012); Linz and Stepan (1996); Mungiu-Pippidi (2002); Tismaneanu and Kligman (2001).

[97] Linz and Stepan (1996); Mungiu-Pippidi (2002).

[98] Pop-Eleches (2008).

[99] Mungiu-Pippidi (2002).

[100] Linz and Stepan (1996).

[101] Levitsky and Way (2010: 99); Tismaneanu and Kligman (2001).

[102] Gabor (2021); Pop-Eleches (2008).

[103] Bozóki and Ishiyama (2002); Linz and Stepan (1996); Mungiu-Pippidi (2002); Pop-Eleches (2008).

[104] Mungiu-Pippidi (2002).

[105] Linz and Stepan (1996); Mungiu-Pippidi (2002); Pop-Eleches (2001).

[106] Gherghina and Miscoiu (2014); Grzymała-Busse (2002); Ziblatt and Biziouras (2002).

[107] Gabor (2021); Stevenson Murer (2002).

[108] Matiuta (2018).

[109] The authoritarian parties comprising the "red–brown" coalition included the PDSR, Greater Romania Party (PRM), Socialist Party of Labor (PSM), and Romanian National Unity Party (PUNR).

from patrimonial communism[110] but also refused to enact significant economic liberalization.[111] Although reform-minded prime ministers attempted limited liberalization in the early 1990s, their policies only provoked social protests, further strengthening Iliescu's position.[112] While the 1992 election featured a clear divide between neoliberal reformers and advocates of economic statism,[113] it did not initiate a postcommunist juncture due to the victory of the latter.[114] Indeed, the ex-communists pursued a "populist neo-developmentalist" program focused on arresting de-industrialization, furnishing progressive taxation and universal benefits, and supporting basic needs.[115] Since such policies reflected popular aversion to economic pain following Ceaușescu's austerity,[116] they solidified the Social Democrats' reputation as a leftist party. As they created obstacles to privatization, subsidized industries, signed tripartite agreements meeting labor demands, and emphasized job security and social benefits,[117] these ex-communists stood out as proponents of neo-Keynesian statism[118] in a country where most citizens were skeptical of working in the private sector.[119]

These popular policies, however, culminated in a crisis conditioned by considerable structural problems. Affected by serious industrial inefficiencies inherited from communism, Romania had for some time been a "quasi permanent IMF pupil," albeit sometimes an insubordinate one. Although the country had previously been in a somewhat advantageous position due to Ceaușescu's aggressive debt repayment, its escalating current account deficit expressly required external financing, possible only with IMF approval. Yet, as the Social Democrats pursued a new round of expansionary policies to appease antireform allies in parliament and the electorate, they not only induced inflation above 50 percent but also provoked a retaliatory IMF to suspend Romania's standby agreement right before the 1996 election.[120] Since by then Romanians widely viewed the potentiality of isolation from Western institutions as unacceptable,[121] the suspension – taking place amid a stagnating economy[122] – undermined the Social Democrats. It also strengthened the electoral prospects of their economically liberal opponents, who finally found themselves in a position to set Romania on a new path after 1996.[123]

---

[110] Grzymała-Busse (2002); Kitschelt (2002); Mungiu-Pippidi (2001; 2002).

[111] Appel and Orenstein (2016); Bohle and Greskovits (2012).

[112] Pop-Eleches (2009).

[113] Kitschelt (2002); Pop-Eleches (2009).

[114] Tavits and Letki (2009).

[115] Ban (2016b).

[116] Pop-Eleches (2009).

[117] Bohle and Greskovits (2012); Kitschelt (2002); Mingiu-Pippidi (2002); Pop-Eleches (2009); Stevenson-Murer (2002).

[118] Ban (2016b).

[119] Mungiu-Pippidi (2002); Pop-Eleches (2008).

[120] Pop-Eleches (2009).

[121] Levitsky and Way (2010: 102).

[122] Stevenson Murer (2002).

[123] Bohle and Greskovits (2012).

4.1.5 From Historical Antecedents to Postcommunist Junctures

Although the historical portraits above are necessarily abbreviated, they capture the essence of developments prior to postcommunist junctures in Poland, Czechia, Slovakia, and Romania. These developments are summarized in Table 4.1, which compares the countries based on three periods, the transitions between them, and the type of crisis that would require resolution during subsequent postcommunist junctures. Beginning with the pre-communist period, whereas industrialized Czechia was the unquestionable leader in terms of economic and democratic development, and Poland featured strong social mobilization despite autocratic flirtations, Slovakia's and Romania's weaker civil societies lagged under the weight of rural underdevelopment and nationalist authoritarianism. When communism was imposed after foreign occupation (Poland and Czechia) or Nazi collaboration (Slovakia and Romania), it was by external diktat in Poland, whose citizens generally opposed it, as well as in Romania, where societal weakness blunted anti-communist opposition, and by a coup in Czechoslovakia, where two years earlier the communists had won elections in the Czech lands but lost in Slovakia.

The communist period likewise featured both divergences and convergences. First, dictatorial rule varied widely – from Czech bureaucratic authoritarianism, through Polish national accommodation, to patrimonialism either with national-accommodative allowances for elites, as in Slovakia, or with personalist and nationalist proclivities, as in Romania. With their radically different approaches to state-society relations and the economy, the Polish and Romanian regimes embodied opposite strategies – attempts at compromise and reform in the first case versus uncompromising totalitarianism and austerity in the second. Meanwhile, highly repressive Czechia and paternalist Slovakia experienced relative leveling in terms of developmental trajectories while also avoiding economic liberalization. When communism ultimately ended, transitions also differed – from a round table amid popular mobilization in Poland, through implosion accompanied by more and less public protest in, respectively, Czechia and Slovakia, to a revolution hijacked by the ex-communists in Romania. In turn, the transition brought relatively speedy political and economic liberalization in Poland, where market reformers chose shock therapy, and Czechia, where the first democratic government pursued more socially sensitive liberal reforms. In Slovakia and Romania, meanwhile, nondemocratic rule persisted after communism, perpetuating patrimonial and nationalist continuities with the past.

The historical record thus suggests that macro-historical similarities and differences across countries are best understood as shifting, rather than stable, over time – a great diversity and dynamism of experience. It is also true, however, that key patterns within countries reproduced themselves, thus conditioning the central political divides after communism as well as the crises

TABLE 4.1 *Historical antecedents and crises before postcommunist junctures in Poland, Czechia, Slovakia, and Romania*

Period	Poland	Czechia	Slovakia	Romania
Before communism	Strong civil society amid recurrent repression; industrialization stimulates nationalist and socialist participation in fragmented party system, in which Communists are marginal; Nazi and Soviet occupation	Strong civil and political society in democracy; highest levels of industrialization and economic development; well-institutionalized party system with popular Social Democrats and Communists; Nazi occupation	Weak civil society; impoverished agricultural economy; underdeveloped party system with Catholics and nationalists leading way to authoritarianism, independence, and collaboration with Nazism	Weak civil society; impoverished agricultural economy; somewhat institutionalized party system without social democratic or communist mobilization; authoritarian rule leads to collaboration with Nazism
Transition to communism	Imposed externally and largely opposed internally	By coup d'état following Communists' election victory	By coup d'état following Communists' election loss	Imposed externally and largely unopposed internally
During communism	National-accommodative regime with some bureaucratic-authoritarian elements; attempts at repressing mobilized civil society amid deepening economic crisis	Bureaucratic-authoritarian regime following Social Democrats' incorporation into Communist Party becomes especially repressive after 1968 Prague Spring; stable but unreformed economy	Patrimonial regime with national-accommodative elements at elite level; economic and political leveling with Czechia; stable but unreformed economy	Patrimonial regime with heavy personalist and nationalist tendencies; intense repression of civil society; draconian austerity measures liquidate foreign debt in 1980s

Transition out of communism	Round table negotiations amid widespread popular mobilization	Implosion followed by some popular mobilization during Velvet Revolution	Implosion without much popular mobilization during Velvet Revolution	Revolution "captured" by ex-communists
After communism	Quick democratization and shock-therapy style economic reforms amid public protests; delegitimated ex-communist Left begins reforming itself after losing first election to labor-based Solidarity	Quick democratization and social–liberal style economic reforms; historic Social Democrats decouple themselves from unreformed Communists, and both lose first election to Civic Forum	Patrimonial and nationalist persistence, and shallow economic reforms, under competitive authoritarianism after renewed independence; reforming ex-communist Left in opposition	Patrimonial and nationalist persistence, and shallow economic reforms, under competitive authoritarianism; unreformed ex-communist Left in power
Dominant divide(s) and type of crisis	Cross-cutting cultural and economic divides; economic crisis with hyperinflation	Economic divide re-emerges; relatively mild economic crisis amid Velvet Divorce	Center-periphery divide reinforced by Mečiarism; legitimacy crisis amid worsening economy and international isolation	Reinforcing political regime and economic divides; legitimacy crisis amid inflation and threat of IMF isolation

to be subsequently resolved. In Poland – where national-accommodative communism produced less polarization due to the complex crosscutting nature of political and economic divides – hyperinflation was largely the product of the communist regime's reformist strategy, adopted to pacify a chronically restive civil society. In Czechia – where the conservative communists' unwillingness to experiment with liberalization conditioned higher polarization based on economic divides – the crisis was also economic but much milder.[124] And in Slovakia and Romania – where historically weak civil societies were no match for new authoritarians who exploited economic insecurity – key political regime divides only worsened when the possibility of isolation from the West, itself due to insufficient democratization and economic mismanagement, provoked serious legitimacy crises.

Finally, although history conditioned salient divides and crises after 1989, it did not determine the roles that political actors – such as Solidarity, the reformist Right, or the various versions of the Left – would play during the resolution of these crises. With the exception of Romania's not-yet-reformed communists, leftist parties – the resurrected social democrats and unreformed communists of Czechia as well as the reforming ex-communists of Poland and Slovakia – were not in power soon after communism. Yet, as postcommunist junctures were highly contingent in nature, the tables would soon turn – but only in some countries. In turn, while political configurations – that is, who was in power and who led the parliamentary opposition – during junctures were historically undetermined and thus highly uncertain, they were absolutely crucial for subsequent developments, the reason why I turn to them next.

4.2 ALIGNING JUNCTURES IN CZECHIA AND ROMANIA

Czechia and Romania had been characterized by unlike long-distance historical trajectories, economic conditions, political dynamics and divides, and crises after the end of communism, but they both experienced aligning postcommunist junctures. While these junctures may have occurred at different times – later in Romania than Czechia – and produced distinct results – worse in Romania than Czechia – the crucial similarity was that in both cases it was the Right that was in charge of significant neoliberal deepening, while the Left led the opposition after national elections featuring contestation between contrasting economic visions. Notably, whereas the political configuration in Czechia had not changed fundamentally after the second competitive election and Czechoslovakia's dissolution in 1992 – because the rightist forces around Klaus remained in power, it had in Romania, where the 1996 election forced the Left, led by Iliescu, into parliamentary opposition. Despite the fact that leftist parties in these countries were very different at the time – historic social democrats and unreformed communists in

---

[124] Kitschelt et al. (1999).

Czechia, and at best partially reformed ex-communists in Romania – during the juncture they all distinguished themselves in parliament as clear opponents of neoliberal reformers on the Right.

4.2.1 Czechia

Although Czechia's liberalization policies between the Velvet Revolution and Czechoslovakia's split had been significant, the inclusion of social democratic measures had constrained neoliberalism in the first three years after communism. By contrast, the reforms enacted in Czechia immediately after 1992 corresponded to "a more pure form of neoliberalism."[125] Moreover, because these reforms were also implemented after the second competitive election, which, unlike the first, did feature a debate on economic issues, they corresponded to the country's postcommunist juncture, which lasted from the Velvet Divorce to 1996.

Indeed, the June 1992 election for federal and state assemblies was dominated not only by the issue of federalism but also by debates regarding the way out of the economic swamp provoked by the initial reforms.[126] On the economic Right were parties advocating liberalization, specifically speedier privatization. These included Vaclav Klaus' Civic Democratic Party (ODS), which had emerged as the largest conservative grouping, as well as the reformist Civic Democratic Alliance (ODA) and Christian Democratic Union – People's Party (KDU-ČSL). On the economic Left were the Czech Social Democratic Party (ČSSD) and unreformed Communist Party of Bohemia and Moravia (KSČM), both arguing during the campaign for more generous social insurance payments.[127] With the rightist parties forming a solid majority government in Prague in the summer of 1992 and with the more left-leaning Slovaks going their separate way in the winter, Klaus, now prime minister, was finally in a position to dismantle the earlier social–liberal compromise and pursue explicitly neoliberal policies in the new Czechia.[128]

These policies included an assault on the social welfare system, devaluation of the minimum wage, attacks on corporatist-style tripartite bargaining, strict budgetary discipline, rapid voucher privatization, and an open trade regime. Having pursued such measures incrementally but consistently, by 1996 "Klaus made significant progress in implementing a neoliberal agenda" that included privatizing the economy, integrating with Western markets, and achieving nearly total liberalization – feats that cemented his reputation "as one of the most prominent market reformers in Central and Eastern Europe."[129] As Klaus' policies resulted in a greater EBRD composite score improvement[130]

---

[125] Orenstein (2001: 79–81).
[126] Myant (2003: 25–31).
[127] Olson (1993: 304).
[128] Orenstein (2001: 85–6).

[129] Orenstein (2001: 86–8).
[130] See Chapter 2 for a discussion of how postcommunist junctures are identified.

between 1992 and 1996 than under any subsequent government, they corresponded to the heyday of Czech neoliberalism.

The political configuration during the juncture featured a clearly aligning logic. If the governing coalition was entirely comprised of parties on the Right, those spearheading the parliamentary opposition were clearly on the Left. For its part, the unreformed KSČM maintained an explicitly anti-capitalist and anti-Western stance, which reflected the ascendance of orthodox neo-communists and appealed to an older and narrow constituency.[131] Yet, as policy issues remained secondary to internal party questions, KSČM developed a reputation as an incompetent protest party out of touch with the broader electorate.[132] The opposite was true of ČSSD, which, although outpolled by KSČM in 1990 and 1992, became "the dominant force of the Czech Left" after the Velvet Divorce. Having reclaimed its social democratic identity (from the communists who had previously absorbed the party) and attracted many ex-communist elites and leaders from other leftist parties, ČSSD became "the functional equivalent of a broad-based social democratic ex-ruling party."[133] Specifically, the Social Democrats overcome their "difficult renewal" after 1989[134] by empowering a faction of party radicals around Miloš Zeman – a group that explicitly opposed cooperation with the Right,[135] denounced the government's "scorched earth" policies, and argued for an alternative economic model.[136] Of particular significance were ČSSD's criticisms of Klaus' signature voucher privatization and attacks on the welfare state, as well as its siding with striking public sector workers and the national trade union organization during labor disputes after 1994.[137]

Although Klaus' reforms did not lead to macroeconomic deterioration in the short term and were generally accepted by the public,[138] the period of neoliberal acceleration ended by 1996, as popular support for the Right began to wane due to a number of bank failures and scandals over ODS party finances.[139] By that time, the structure of political competition had further consolidated around a single economic cleavage,[140] with incumbent market liberals driving marketization and social protectionists voicing discontent from the parliamentary opposition.[141] Having assumed political roles that only reinforced the basic political divide after 1989, the main parties on the Left and Right would continue defining Czech politics in predictable and stabilizing ways well into the future.

---

[131] Hanley (2002).

[132] Grzymała-Busse (2002).

[133] Hanley (2002); Kopeček and Pšeja (2008).

[134] Kopeček and Pšeja (2008).

[135] Hanley (2002: 160–2).

[136] Kopeček and Pšeja (2008).

[137] Dangerfield (1997); Kopeček and Pšeja (2008: 324); Orenstein (2001: 87).

[138] Dangerfield (1997); Myant and Drahokoupil (2011).

[139] Orenstein (2001: 88).

[140] Kitschelt et al. (1999).

[141] See Casal Bértoa (2014: 24–5).

4.2.2 Romania

Without a doubt, the 1996 general election – the third after communism – constituted a rupture in Romanian political and economic life.[142] Indeed, it heralded not only the country's first democratic government, headed by President Emil Constantinescu,[143] but also the kind of neoliberal deepening that would correspond to the postcommunist juncture. Having won the election after campaigning for liberalization as a solution to the crisis resultant from the policies of Iliescu's Social Democratic government,[144] the Romanian Democratic Convention (CDR) launched dramatic economic reforms. Indeed, the new government's program, enacted in collaboration with the IMF, "was more radical than any of the previous shock therapy initiatives tried elsewhere in the region and included ... monetary and fiscal austerity, trade, exchange rate, and price liberalization, combined with ambitious privatization and restructuring measures."[145] With EU membership serving as a key incentive for their adoption,[146] the measures resulted in the reduction of social spending, the elimination of nonprofitable state enterprises (particularly in the steel and mining industries),[147] and a shift from domestically oriented to foreign-focused and export-oriented industrial policies favoring transnational capital.[148] As the country's economic liberalization scores, as assigned by the EBRD, Heritage Foundation, and Fraser Institute, improved more between 1996 and 2000 than during any other period, the reformist government reached two key milestones – (1) the institutionalization of EU conditionality as a solid anchor that would all but guarantee continuity in subsequent economic policy[149] and (2) the inauguration of a neoliberal regime that would, over time, fundamentally transform market-society relations.[150]

As in Czechia, Romania's postcommunist juncture was characterized by a predictable pattern of alignment. After all, CDR was an alliance led by the heirs of the two major parties, both center-right, from the interwar period – the anti-communist Christian Democratic National Peasants' Party (PNȚCD) and National Liberal Party (PNL). Although the ruling coalition also included the Romanian Social Democratic Party (PSDR) and still left-leaning Democratic Party (PD),[151] it was the forces of the Right that always controlled most portfolios, including the Ministry of Finance. Meanwhile, Iliescu's Social Democrats – having already distinguished themselves as Romania's unwavering Left during

[142] Tismaneanu and Kligman (2001).
[143] Levitsky and Way (2010); Mungiu-Pippidi (2002).
[144] Bohle and Greskovits (2012); Popescu (1997); Roper (2003).
[145] Pop-Eleches (2009: 228). Also, Appel and Orenstein (2016).
[146] Aligica (2001); Appel and Orenstein (2016); Bohle and Greskovits (2012); Vachudova (2005).
[147] Stevenson Murer (2002).
[148] Bohle and Greskovits (2012).
[149] Aligica (2001).
[150] Ban (2016b); Bohle and Greskovits (2012).
[151] Gabor (2021); Mungiu-Pippidi (2001).

the previous government – led, in a highly disciplined manner,[152] the parliamentary opposition, from where they criticized the cabinet's neoliberal policies[153] and demanded a slowdown of the privatization process.[154]

Indeed, there was much to criticize. As the CDR-led government lacked capacity, cohesion, and stability, its performance was disappointing, leading to a considerable economic recession[155] and the attendant problems of rising unemployment, poverty, and inequality.[156] With a new wave of miners' protests materializing by 1999,[157] the political landscape became increasingly polarized. In this context, the Social Democrats positioned themselves, along with the radical right,[158] on the side of Romania's working classes – particularly miners and heavy industry workers – and the rural population, which was perhaps hardest hit by the economic downturn.[159] In the end, if the policies during the 1996–2000 period restructured Romanian political life, they did so by further raising the salience of economic issues[160] at the expense of the previously dominant concerns about parties' democratic credibility.[161] As the postcommunist juncture came to an end in 2000, it would be the ex-communist Left's ability to keep "owning" the economic issues – and thus to continue differentiating itself from the neoliberal Right – that would shape the political landscape during the subsequent two decades.

4.3 BAIT-AND-SWITCH JUNCTURES IN POLAND AND SLOVAKIA

If historical contingencies – such as Klaus' ability to retain power after 1992 and Iliescu's loss of power in 1996 – generated aligning junctures in the otherwise different Czechia and Romania, they produced the opposite type of junctures in Poland and Slovakia. Although these two countries also diverged in terms of types of pre-communist and communist developments, transitions, economic conditions, and postcommunist regimes, divides, and crises, they both experienced bait-and-switch junctures. As in the previous two cases, the timing varied, with Poland being first in the region to sustain and deepen economic liberalization after communism and Slovakia being among the last. Yet in both cases the implementation of crucial market reforms depended on abandoning commitments central to prior electoral campaigns. Whereas in Poland, the earlier policies of radical marketization were sustained by a populist president who, having risen as an anti-communist yet labor-based

[152] Pop-Eleches (2001).
[153] Mungiu-Pippidi (2002).
[154] Mungiu-Pippidi (2001).
[155] Ban (2016b); Pop-Eleches (2009); Roper (2003).
[156] Pop-Eleches (2001).
[157] Mungiu-Pippidi (2001); Stevenson Murer (2002).
[158] Pop-Eleches (2001).
[159] Stevenson Murer (2002).
[160] See Mungiu-Pippidi (2002).
[161] Mungiu-Pippidi (2001).

candidate, engaged in a volte-face, Slovakia's neoliberal regime was initiated under the effective stewardship of the ex-communist Left. While those politically responsible for the reforms clearly differed from one another, it was the centrality of bait-and-switch dynamics that defined postcommunist junctures in these two countries.

4.3.1 Poland

The radical reforms implemented in Poland beginning in January 1990 and defining the period of "extraordinary politics" were initially tolerated by the electorate.[162] Yet, as the year progressed and unemployment, real wage declines, and the collapse of budgetary expenditure and social benefits led to a "drastic deterioration of living conditions,"[163] the public's patience began to run out. With nine of ten Poles assessing the economic situation as "poor" by the fall of 1990, a new series of protests signaled societal opposition to Balcerowicz's reforms.[164] As he sensed the potential political benefits of this protest wave, Lech Wałęsa, Solidarity's leader, launched a "war at the top" against Mazowiecki and the liberals behind him. By the summer of 1990, Wałęsa's supporters had begun integrating around the Center Accord, a new Christian-nationalist party led by Jarosław and Lech Kaczyński and critical of the high social costs of Balcerowicz's reforms.[165]

Notably, it was both political opportunism amid economic pain and the new lack of a clear political antagonist against whom anti-communists could unify that precipitated Solidarity's unravelling. Because communists had been incorporated into Mazowiecki's "grand coalition" government following the round table,[166] the Polish logic of negotiated transition meant that there had been no political opposition to shock therapy during the painful initial stages of the neoliberal transformation. With the ex-communists undergoing social democratization[167] after receiving a sobering 27 percent electoral support in the 1989 election[168] and with no other leftist party articulating an alternative economic vision, many of those discontent with shock therapy converged toward Solidarity's nationalist factions around Wałęsa.

By the time of the campaign leading up to Poland's second competitive election, societal agitation further fueled the already brewing conflict among Solidarity's leaders. The presidential election of November 1990 pitted Mazowiecki, the prime minister politically responsible for shock therapy, against Wałęsa, the long-term labor union leader representing "the frustration of the old Solidarity camp."[169] In marked contrast to Mazowiecki, who defended the economic

---

[162] Bell (2001: 6); Przeworski (1996).
[163] Bell (2001: 15); Orenstein (2001: 36–7); Przeworski (1991: 165).
[164] Bell (2001: 24, 54).
[165] Interview POL-10; Millard (1999: 82).
[166] Millard (1999: 15–7, 82).
[167] Grzymała-Busse (2002).
[168] Pienkos (2001: 432).
[169] Orenstein (2001: 37–9).

polices thus far, Wałęsa readily embraced populism not only by relying on nationalist, religious, and even antisemitic rhetoric but also by emphasizing class issues of worker suffering, inequality, and poverty.[170] As his appeals resonated especially among the social groups most hurt by the reforms, as discussed in Chapter 5, he handily defeated Mazowiecki in the first round and then Stanisław Tymiński in the second round of the presidential election.

Having won the presidency by capitalizing on the popular rejection of the Balcerowicz plan, Wałęsa then "turned one hundred and eighty degrees in the opposite direction from his campaign message"[171] and "settled for a government of economic policy continuity."[172] It is this deepening of neoliberalism that defined the bait-and-switch juncture after Poland's second competitive election, which, unlike the first, had been contentious on the key economic issues of the crisis-heavy early transition. First, Wałęsa made the retention of the unpopular Leszek Balcerowicz as minister of finance a condition for supporting a new government.[173] As this maneuver ensured the liberals' backing for a cabinet led by Jan Krzysztof Bielecki, one of Solidarity's most market-oriented liberal economists, the first government under President Wałęsa set and overachieved new economic program targets.[174] Second, neither the growing wave of labor protest nor the splintering of Solidarity's national-conservative wing – signaled by the Kaczyński brothers' dismissal from the president's office[175] – could reverse the logic of Poland's bait-and-switch reform dynamic. Indeed, having "campaigned strongly against the Balcerowicz Plan" in the lead-up to the 1991 parliamentary election, national-conservative Jan Olszewski, the next prime-minister, "had to accept Balcerowicz's provisional budget that contained drastic cuts and tax increases" under pressure from the IMF.[176] Finally, when Olszewski's government collapsed in the summer of 1992, the new coalition government led by Hanna Suchocka "continued the economic strategy launched in 1990"[177] – until a new round of labor unrest provoked a no-confidence vote, new elections, and the return of the ex-communists to power in 1993.[178]

Poland's postcommunist juncture thus occurred under the leadership of Solidarity, which – having represented the culmination of labor-based mobilization in civil society by previously fighting for workers' rights – embraced pro-market policies in the early 1990s. This "unexpected shift to neoliberalism" contradicted the trade union's long-held views about evolutionary transformation prioritizing labor self-management and the protection of workers from macroeconomic turbulence.[179] Beginning with Wałęsa's election

---

[170] Greskovits (1998: 110); Ost (2005: 60–93).

[171] Interview POL-10.

[172] Millard (1999: 17). Also, Ost (2005: 60–93); Weyland (1999).

[173] Millard (1999: 17); Orenstein (2001: 39–40).

[174] Greskovits (1998: 41); Stone (2002: 97–9).

[175] Santora (2019).

[176] Orenstein (2001: 45).

[177] Orenstein (2001: 46).

[178] Millard (1999: 22–3); Ost (2005).

[179] Orenstein (2001: 26–30).

to the presidency and ending by 1993, Poland's juncture featured distinct bait-and-switch tactics in defiance of campaign promises and popular demands. As the then-reforming ex-communists did not lead the parliamentary opposition for most of the period,[180] deepening neoliberalism faced no meaningful opposition from the institutional Left. With no leftist alternatives, it was the national conservatives who first began exploiting the popular anger that the "huge societal costs" of the reforms[181] provoked. As social protests around economic demands peaked in 1992,[182] Jarosław and Lech Kaczyński, twin leaders of the Center Accord, suddenly began criticizing those leading the transition. Having broken with the president, these national conservatives swiftly radicalized their rhetoric – by attacking both Solidarity's reformers, whom they viewed as too influenced by Mazowiecki's shock therapy ideas,[183] and the ex-communists,[184] whom they accused of benefitting from "out of control privatization"[185] and selling out to foreign investors.[186] With Solidarity splitting and facing electoral defeat – "because Wałęsa lied and did exactly what Mazowiecki had promised," as disappointed Solidarity activists saw it[187] – the effects of Poland's postcommunist juncture were only beginning to be felt.

4.3.2 Slovakia

With the threat of international isolation gaining salience by 1998, a sudden activation of nongovernmental organizations helped unite anti-Mečiar parties into the Slovak Democratic Coalition (SDK) for the watershed 1998 parliamentary election. Although it competed as a single "party" in an effort to overcome Mečiar's active attempts to undermine coalition formation, SDK was a de facto coalition of two marginal center-left parties (the Social Democratic Party of Slovakia and the Green Party) and three more prominent pro-market parties (the Christian Democratic Movement, Democratic Party, and Democratic Union).[188] While this coalition did not win the 1998 election, it gained nearly as many seats in the National Council (28 percent) as Mečiar's HZDS, which – with 28.7 percent of seats – was once again the victor and thus granted mandate to form a government first.

In these circumstances, the leftist SDĽ – having come in third, with 15.3 percent of the seats – was presented with a historic choice. As SDK "immediately rejected talks with the HZDS," it was SDĽ to which Mečiar turned as a

---

[180] Having at first shared power with Solidarity and then received fewer seats in the 1991 parliamentary election than the Democratic Union, which temporarily led the opposition, the ex-communists led the opposition only after the formation of a government led by the Democratic Union in July 1992. See Kitschelt et al. (1999: 111).

[181] Interviews POL-09 and POL-10; Ost (2005).
[182] Ekiert and Kubik (1998: 554, 561).
[183] Interview POL-08.
[184] Millard (1999: 60).
[185] Interview POL-13.
[186] Interviews POL-15; POL-16.
[187] Interview POL-11.
[188] Vachudova (2005: 170–5).

potential coalition partner.[189] An agreement with the Left would have guaranteed parliamentary majority support for a government also including either the populist right SNS, with which Mečiar had thus far been in coalition, or the new center-left Party of Civic Understanding, which had raised eyebrows by calling for a "reconciliation."[190] Moreover, such an agreement was clearly viable[191] as SDĽ had once saved the HZDS-led government from collapse in 1996.[192] Indeed, the two parties had "occasionally discussed the possibility of cooperation" throughout the 1990s[193] based on their "strikingly similar" appeals stressing solidarity, social justice, and the promotion of the health and economic well-being of working people.[194] As Mečiar even offered SDĽ the opportunity to form a one-party "minority government with tacit support from HZDS and SNS"[195] – a "toleration model" similar to the one agreed to in Czechia just three months earlier[196] – Slovakia's break with the past in 1998 was by no means guaranteed.

Yet, realizing that cooperation with Mečiar could have allowed the autocrat to continue dominating, which would have triggered popular unrest, the Left resisted what it saw at the time as a "big temptation,"[197] opting instead to participate in a coalition government with the right-leaning SDK. This decision was not easy for a party that, being less experienced and skilled than other reformed communists in Central Europe,[198] had made strategic blunders before.[199] Being "initially reluctant to cooperate with the center-right,"[200] SDĽ ultimately agreed to negotiate with SDK. While the EU's active leverage and the shared motivation to free the country from its pariah status[201] influenced this choice, the Left's willingness to engage with the Right was certainly not inevitable.[202]

Crucially, given the balance of powers after the 1998 election and the polarization between Mečiarism and its opponents, neither side could have formed a stable government enjoying parliamentary majority support without backing from the Left. Being a true kingmaker, SDĽ demanded – and received – "more cabinet positions than its election results warranted."[203] As the "the one standard party"[204] and, indeed, the single largest in a coalition government led by SDK – itself an alliance of five smaller parties, which would soon splinter into its constitutive elements – the Left gained control over nine ministerial portfolios out of twenty-one,[205] including those of finance, labor and social affairs, education, agriculture, and defense.[206]

---

[189] Fisher (2002: 134).
[190] Fisher (2006: 155); Vachudova (2005: 170).
[191] Levitsky and Way (2010: 96n89).
[192] Kopeček (2002: 246).
[193] Deegan-Krause (2006: 104).
[194] Haughton (2004: 183).
[195] Fisher (2006: 167).
[196] Fisher (2002: 130n17).
[197] Interview SVK-06.
[198] Grzymała-Busse (2002: 266).

[199] Haughton (2004: 184).
[200] Fisher (2006: 155).
[201] Vachudova (2005: 170–5).
[202] See Rybář and Deegan-Krause (2008: 513n7).
[203] Fisher (2002: 135). Also, Grzymała-Busse (2002: 248).
[204] Wightman (2001: 133).
[205] Grzymała-Busse (2002: 248).
[206] Fisher (2002: 135).

This was not the first time SDĽ had participated in a reformist government. Having quickly broken with the communist past,[207] the Left had already been "burned" during an IMF-sponsored "neoliberal intermezzo,"[208] when it participated in a coalition that had briefly dislodged Mečiar from power in early 1994.[209] Yet the election later in 1994 had not only reinstalled Mečiarism, thus once again reversing liberalization; it had also brought SDĽ its weakest electoral result yet. The lesson of 1994 had been clear. Under new party leader Jozef Migaš – who called "for taking Marx off the shelf and dusting him off" – the Left would stick to socialist principles by intensifying criticism of the market, emphasizing its newly acquired membership in the Socialist International, and shifting power to local organizations.[210] SDĽ would also make prosocial commitments – to increase wages and pensions, halt privatization, guarantee state participation in strategic firms and financial institutions, secure quality education and free healthcare for all, and provide housing for young and socially weak families.[211] It was based on such promises, which offered an alternative to the vision of rightist parties, that Slovakia's second most successful party of the 1990s had, by 1998, recovered support to its previously highest levels.

And yet it was the Left that, pressed by the circumstances of Mečiarism's crisis, led the deepening of neoliberalism after 1998 – an act that bore striking resemblance to the actions of Hungarian and Polish ex-communists.[212] Faced with a "deteriorating economic situation" involving GDP decline and two-digit inflation, SDĽ Finance Minister Brigita Schmögnerová took unpopular steps such as adopting a "tough fiscal package to reduce the budget deficit," increasing the price of rents and fuels,[213] and raising the minimum level of the value-added tax.[214] Under the Left's stewardship, the government not only "restored macroeconomic balances" but also reversed Mečiar's ban on the privatization of strategic state-owned enterprises – a cornerstone in the postcommunist transition to capitalism.[215] Banks were revitalized with taxpayer money and then sold to foreign investors,[216] who were more sophisticated and played a more important role in the building of Slovak capitalism than Mečiar's homemade capitalists.[217] Additionally, as the Ministry of Finance pursued austerity through the single greatest annual reduction in government spending in 2001 and oversaw a six-fold increase of foreign direct investment after selling large financial institutions and industrial firms to international buyers, the new

---

[207] Grzymała-Busse (2002: 92–9, 150–60, 197–204, 244–9).
[208] Pop-Eleches (2009: 178).
[209] Henderson (2002: 44).
[210] Grzymała-Busse (2002: 154–8); Rybář and Deegan-Krause (2008: 504).
[211] Fisher (2002: 129, 133).

[212] Interview SVK-17.
[213] Haughton (2004: 185). Also, Bohle and Greskovits (2012: 148).
[214] Fisher (2002: 136).
[215] Myant and Drahoukopil (2011).
[216] Interviews SVK-10; SVK-20.
[217] Interview SVK-12.

and "functional market economy" suddenly helped Slovakia move to the forefront of the EU accession competition by 2002.[218]

More than any other time in the country's history as an independent state, the 1998–2002 period – marking the transition from a nonfunctional to a functioning market economy[219] – corresponded to major institutional innovations.[220] While attempts at liberalization had been initiated before the breakup of Czechoslovakia and in 1994, Mečiarism had reversed both. And although major liberalization continued during Mikuláš Dzurinda's second – and explicitly center-right – government after 2002,[221] it was between 1998 and 2002 that Slovakia saw greatest strides in privatization, investment, financial freedom, and reduced government spending.[222] As one SDĽ minister in Dzurinda's first government argued, "the second period was clear neoliberal policy, but we really stabilized the economy and laid the groundwork to become successful."[223] Slovak liberals, too, agree that "the country's future successes were planted under the first Dzurinda government."[224] As the Left's bait-and-switch during the postcommunist juncture proved critical for breaking with the patrimonial and nationalist past, it allowed Slovakia to finally exit international isolation and truly enter the neoliberal era.

4.4 CONCLUSION

The long-term historical trajectories of Poland, Czechia, Slovakia, and Romania culminated in different types of political divides and crises after 1989, but they did not determine the types of postcommunist junctures these four countries experienced sometime after second competitive elections. While these junctures corresponded to efforts at economic liberalization meant to resolve different crises – hyperinflation in Poland, a milder economic crisis amid the Velvet Divorce in Czechia, and political legitimacy crises with varying degrees of economic downturn in Slovakia and Romania – they all combined elements of contingency and political choices that could not have been foreseen based on prior experiences. No one could have predicted, for example, that Poland's Solidarity, headed by Wałęsa, would embrace neoliberalism so wholeheartedly after 1989; that Czechoslovakia would split at the hands of opportunistic elites, which in turn allowed Klaus to implement his economic vision in Czechia after 1992; that the Romanian Right would defeat the Iliescu-led ex-communists

---

[218] Bohle and Greskovits (2012: 180); Henderson (2002: 123–4); Mikloš (2014: 118); Vachudova (2005).
[219] Interview SVK-08.
[220] Gould (2009: 6).
[221] Bohle and Greskovits (2012: 170, 180); Mikloš (2014).

[222] Author's calculations based on data from the Heritage Foundation and the European Bank for Reconstruction and Development.
[223] Interview SVK-06.
[224] Interviews SVK-07; SVK-15.

in 1996; or that the Slovak Left would end up making the choices it did after the 1998 election. Because of the highly contingent nature of these events, the "key choice points"[225] identifiable in all of them, and the significant institutional innovation[226] they engendered, such developments are best understood as critical junctures.[227]

These critical postcommunist junctures of significant neoliberal deepening all occurred sometime after second competitive election, when alternative visions regarding the role of the state vis-à-vis the market were contested at the political marketplace of ideas. Depending on the political configurations – that is, who was in power and who led the opposition – during postcommunist junctures, this chapter analyzed developments in two pairs of countries. In the otherwise historically, societally, and economically dissimilar Czechia and Romania, the Right spearheaded market reforms while the Left led the parliamentary opposition. As key parties' positions aligned with prior electoral commitments and brands, I identified these junctures as aligning. In the likewise very different Poland and Slovakia, meanwhile, those in charge of the reforms, different though they were – a labor-based populist in the first case and a leftist party in the second – made similarly significant U-turns, a reason why I identified these as bait-and-switch junctures.

Notably, the postcommunist transition to democracy and the market was in important ways unlike Latin America's. In Eastern Europe, some countries had to deal with questions of statehood, which in turn conditioned particular cleavages and crises, as seen in Slovakia. Indeed, the crises that required resolution via subsequent junctures were not always or purely economic, as the Slovak and Romanian cases showed. Nevertheless, and like in Latin America, junctures of neoliberal deepening were always defined by questions of political agency – what the political configuration at the time would be and what choices key political agents would make in crucial moments of uncertainty. Chapters 5 and 6 demonstrate that as these questions were answered differently for Slovakia and Poland than for Czechia and Romania, bait-and-switch and aligning postcommunist junctures left dissimilar institutional legacies.

---

[225] See Mahoney (2001b: 113–4).
[226] See Collier and Collier (1991).

[227] See Capoccia and Kelemen (2007: 360–3).

5

From Bait-and-Switch Junctures to Illiberal Reactions

Slovakia and Poland

If different postcommunist junctures ultimately culminated in persistently varying illiberal outcomes, they did so by shaping institutional path dependencies that defined their legacies. In this chapter, I trace path-dependent processes in Slovakia and Poland, two countries where the political configurations during the most important periods of market reform produced powerful illiberal reactions throughout the first two decades of the twenty-first century. Concretely, I unpack political and societal dynamics triggered by bait-and-switch tactics during junctures, link these dynamics to anti-neoliberal populist backlash in both countries, and emphasize how the vanishment of the mainstream Left created opportunities that illiberals skillfully exploited for electoral gain. Crucially, while reactive sequences in these two countries were not identical – with the Slovak Left collapsing quickly after reneging on prior commitments and the Polish Left declining gradually after a somewhat more unique political configuration during the juncture – mainstream leftist parties, having embraced economic liberalism, sooner or later lost their appeal among constituencies that had previously supported them. As the Left lost popularity amid the growing salience of economic issues, highly adaptive personalist parties with antiestablishment origins were able to capitalize by adopting not just culturally conservative but also economically statist positions. Although the link between leftist politics and illiberal outcomes in Poland was less straightforward, a reason why I examine developments there in somewhat greater detail, bait-and-switch junctures ultimately resulted in the sustained electoral viability of illiberalism during the 2000–20 period in both countries.

The chapter also shows that despite the overall similar institutional legacies, the trajectories of Slovakia and Poland nevertheless featured important distinctions. While bait-and-switch junctures were highly consequential in both countries, the political configurations defining them featured somewhat more nuanced differences – with an ex-communist party being in charge of moving

Slovakia in an economically reformist direction and a labor-based personalist facilitating Poland's neoliberal deepening. These distinctions, in turn, conditioned contextually specific subsequent dynamics. In Slovakia, the Left's about-face ultimately resulted in long-term illiberal domination enabled by a highly extensive electoral coalition with core support from former leftist voters. In Poland, by contrast, the bait-and-switch juncture produced a more complex legacy, whereby the solidification of societal divides had both enabling and constraining effects in terms of the electoral coalition-building potential of subsequent illiberals. Overall, by tracing processes after bait-and-switch junctures, the chapter is attentive both to crucial similarities and notable distinctions between Slovakia and Poland. While the patterns of likeness substantiate the main theoretical propositions advanced in Chapter 2, the differences not only illuminate contextual specificities but also lay the groundwork for the theoretical elaborations and cross-regional comparisons explored in Chapters 7 and 8.

5.1 SLOVAKIA

5.1.1 The End of the Left

The liberalization that the Party of the Democratic Left (SDĽ) spearheaded during the juncture immediately caused problems for Slovakia's ex-communists in terms of both organizational cohesion and popular appeals. First, SDĽ experienced a profound identity crisis as "radical socialists" around party chairman Josef Migaš confronted "modernists" supportive of pro-market policies.[1] This tension had existed since earlier in the 1990s, when liberal party elites had been blamed for the party's disappointing performance in the 1994 election following participation in Josef Moravčik's brief reformist government. Consequently, power within the party had shifted toward cadres at lower organizational levels. As reflected in Migaš's successful bid for the party chairmanship with the support of these local organizations, this relative decentralization had signaled greater skepticism of neoliberalism within SDĽ in the mid 1990s.[2] As one political strategist recalled, for example, "none of the SDĽ membership supported privatization."[3]

By the late 1990s, however, the power balance within SDĽ had shifted once again. As decentralization proved more symbolic than real and "party elites simply approved the existing programmatic line,"[4] it was once again the reformists from the upper echelons who – being fully aware of the negative consequences this would bring the party[5] – negotiated the terms of the post-Mečiar democratization with the Right and then enacted neoliberal policies.[6] Because

---

[1] Kopeček (2002: 246–7).
[2] Rybář and Deegan-Krause (2008: 504).
[3] Interview SVK-12.

[4] Grzymała-Busse (2002: 155–7).
[5] Interview SVK-16.
[6] Rybář and Deegan-Krause (2008: 504).

differences between the two wings of SDĽ appeared irreconcilable – with the "radical socialists" supported by the base attacking cadres at upper party levels for abandoning leftist principles and ultimately forcing the dismissal of "modernist" Finance Minister Schmögnerová" in 2002[7] – SDĽ splintered before the next election.

Since SDĽ had already been suffering a "dramatic decrease of popularity," as reflected in its plummeting approval ratings after just two years in government,[8] the rift foreshadowed its electoral collapse. Yet, whereas the Left's humiliating 1.4 percent in the 2002 election signaled popular disappointment with its role in the government, this certainly was not an indictment of the ruling coalition's overall performance. Indeed, the coalition had reasons to celebrate – while the SDĽ-controlled Ministry of Finance had initially struggled with two-digit inflation and productivity declines, the austerity it implemented appeared to have solved both problems by 2001, stabilizing the economy and opening Slovakia's road to EU membership. Meanwhile, however, the country also saw the largest spikes in income inequality experienced thus far in its independent postcommunist history,[9] as well as its highest unemployment rate, which stubbornly persisted at close to 20 percent. This state of affairs was particularly ironic for the leftist SDĽ, which had also assumed charge of the Ministry of Labor and Social Affairs.

It was in this context that voters reached conclusions regarding who should take credit for the government's achievements and the blame for its shortcomings. The difference lied in the perceived loyalty of parties to ideological commitments. As popular perceptions of the coalition's effectiveness improved and distrust in the government declined substantially when the economy recovered after 2000, it was only right-of-center coalition members that benefited at the ballot box in 2002. Indeed, having achieved a superior aggregate result than in the previous election, the three rightist parties – Dzurinda's Slovak Democratic and Christian Union (SDK's successor), the Christian Democratic Movement, and the Party of the Hungarian Coalition – continued in government for a second term after 2002. As one SDĽ minister at the time recalled,

> It was us, the Left, that suffered, because to save the banks, we could not pay the teachers and give the social allowances, as we had promised in the election. The Right was clear – doing the neoliberal policy, cutting social benefits was necessary to stabilize the economy. But we were not able to explain this to our voters – why we are participating in a policy like this.[10]

The importance of loyalty to ideological commitment is additionally underscored by the fact that SDĽ was not the only party that lost support. In fact, no left-of-center party that had been associated in any way with the reformist

---

[7] Kopeček (2002: 247–8).
[8] Kopeček (2002: 255).

[9] Interview SVK-20.
[10] Interview SVK-06.

government managed to even make it into the next parliament. This included the new Social Democratic Alternative (which had splintered from SDĽ), the Social Democratic Party (which had supported the government as part of the Slovak Democratic Coalition), and the more ambiguously center-left Party of Civic Understanding (which had been in charge of the Ministry of Privatization). While this outcome was at the time celebrated as a vindication of liberalism, the celebrations proved to be shortsighted, as one conservative political consultant acknowledged.[11] As Slovakia's Left collapsed under the pressure of neoliberal reform during the juncture, its former supporters would soon constitute the electoral core of one of Eastern Europe's most dominant populist parties in the early twenty-first century.

5.1.2 From Bait-and-Switch to Populist Backlash

Of all Slovak parties that embraced illiberalism in the first two decades of the twenty-first century, SMER – or Direction – was by far been the most successful. While several other parties at times fit the illiberal or post-neoliberal populist categories,[12] it was SMER that dominated the illiberal field in Slovak elections during the period, and particularly beginning in 2006. As shown in Figure 5.1, support for the party accounted for most of the overall illiberal vote share (Figure 5.1a) and most of the post-neoliberal populist magnitude (Figure 5.1b) – 64 and 68 percent, respectively – from 2000 to 2020.

The party, which did not truly embrace illiberalism until after 2002, had typical populist origins,[13] as readily recognized by one of its first-generation representatives in the National Council, who understood SMER as "positively populist" (in contrast with Mečiar's "negative populism").[14] Founded by the ambitious Robert Fico, who felt insufficiently appreciated in SDĽ,[15] SMER began as a brand new antiestablishment party[16] promoting "the rise of new faces to power,"[17] emphasizing "order, justice, and stability,"[18] and abandoning "traditional notions of mass party organization and ideology."[19] As Fico built a top-down organization, where "the central position of the leadership

---

[11] Interview SVK-05.

[12] Namely, the Movement for Democracy (HZD), Communist Party of Slovakia (KSS), Slovak National Party (SNS), True Slovak National Party (PSNS), Kotleba's People's Party Our Slovakia (ĽSNS), and We Are Family (SR). While two others – Mečiar's People's Party – Movement for a Democratic Slovakia (ĽS-HZDS) and the Hungarian coalition (SMK-MKP) – at times also took illiberal positions, these parties were somewhat less antiestablishment due

to their important roles in political life throughout the 1990s.

[13] Mesežnikov et al. (2008).

[14] Interview SVK-03.

[15] Rybář and Deegan-Krause (2008: 502).

[16] Učeň (2001: 407).

[17] Marušiak (2005); Učeň (2001: 407).

[18] Fisher (2002: 138); Haughton (2004: 187); Marušiak (2005: 165).

[19] March (2011: 144); Marušiak (2005: 165); Rybář and Deegan-Krause (2008: 498); Pop-Eleches (2010).

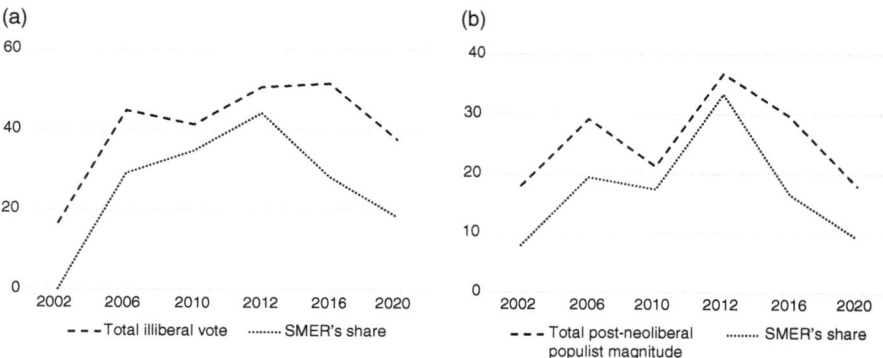

FIGURE 5.1 SMER's share of the total illiberal vote and post-neoliberal populist magnitude in Slovak parliamentary elections, 2000–20. (a) Illiberal vote share, (b) post-neoliberal populist magnitude

and the party leader in particular is accepted and undisputed," "it was the personality of the charismatic leader … that played the crucial role in formulating the party policy targets and in building the party image."[20] Meanwhile, SMER's ideology evolved over time, including calls not only for redistribution but also against the Roma, Hungarians, Muslims (during the 2015 European migrant crisis), and sexual minorities.[21] The party also subscribed to "standard Central European conservativism" regarding women's role in society.[22] It is for such reasons, as well as for the common belief that SMER's organizational beginnings were oligarchic[23] (as opposed to labor-based), that neither its critics nor its supporters typically take the "Social Democracy" label in the party's name seriously[24] and that Slovak experts distinguish it from "standard" parties.[25] Given both its organizational character and programmatic positions mixing economic leftism with ethnonationalism and Christian traditionalism,[26] SMER is best described as a post-neoliberal populist[27] party that embraced illiberalism.

Just like SMER's birth was the product of the organizational conflicts that overwhelmed SDĽ,[28] its electoral breakthrough – 13.5 percent in the 2002 parliamentary election – was a direct result of the Left's loss of popularity due to bait-and-switching during the juncture. While the fact that SMER's growing popularity coincided with the collapse of SDĽ raises the possibility of reverse

[20] Rybář and Deegan-Krause (2008: 513–4). Also, Marušiak (2005: 172).
[21] Malová (2017); Marušiak (2021: 42).
[22] Specifically, the three K's – "Kinder, Küche, Kirche," or "children, kitchen, church" (Interview SVK-19) – and as seen in what progressives describe as SMER's "cringeworthy" celebrations of International Women's Day (Interview SVK-20).
[23] Interviews SVK-05; SVK-07; SVK-15.
[24] Interviews SVK-01; SVK-04; SVK-15; SVK-20.
[25] Interview SVK-08.
[26] Interview SVK-09; Malová (2017: 11).
[27] See Binev (2024a).
[28] Kopeček (2002: 247).

causality – that is, that it may have been the establishment of SMER that contributed to the Left's decline[29] – the SDĽ-led economic reforms between 1998 and 2002 remain the key causal factor in the temporal sequence of events.[30] To begin, having once boasted the largest membership of all Slovak parties, by 1999 – that is, after a year of neoliberal deepening – SDĽ lost nearly a quarter (23.5 percent) of its members.[31] Indeed, as the reformist policies of dominant party elites clearly contradicted the will of the base – whose support of radical socialist ideas had been expressed in the 1996 elections of a party chairman known for "resolute advocacy of leftist positions"[32] – SDĽ was already hemorrhaging members before Fico's separation from the party. Given the availability of this leftist constituency for electoral mobilization, SMER, having started as a nonideological party that initially even stood for fiscal discipline and reduction of the social state,[33] "was quick to exploit the political opportunity structure"[34] by calling for a Slovak "Third Way" of "new social cohesiveness" and solidarity in the run-up to the 2002 election.[35] SMER's economic positioning – now more "leftist" than that of all other parties except for the unreformed communists – specifically targeted the Left's alienated members, who were unhappy with their party's role in the market-oriented governing coalition.[36] Indeed, SMER focused its criticism of the government on an issue to which this constituency was particularly sensitive – privatization.[37]

This "policy of pragmaticism and rationality"[38] paid off. As seen in data from the European Social Survey administered in Slovakia soon after the 2002 election, early SMER supporters were defined by both their high distrust of parties – registering their disappointment with the Left's volte-face – and their preference for redistribution and government regulation.[39] Because they were considerably more progressive economically than supporters of other major parties,[40] while at the same time being close to the national average on issues of immigration, religion, public safety, and dissatisfaction with democracy and the government, their overall views "showed considerable continuity with those who had previously voted for SDĽ." In the end, those who shifted from SDĽ to SMER "represented the largest single group" switching support from one party to another between 1998 and 2002, with the plurality of former SDĽ voters supporting SMER in 2002 and the plurality of SMER voters coming from SDĽ.[41]

---

[29] See Haughton (2003: 79–80), who recognizes the importance of market reforms enacted by the SDĽ-controlled Ministry of Finance.

[30] See Rybář and Deegan-Krause (2008: 514).

[31] See Kopeček (2002: 253).

[32] Kopeček (2002: 247); Učeň (2001: 409).

[33] Malová (2017: 10); Marušiak (2005: 167).

[34] Haughton (2004: 187).

[35] Marušiak (2005: 166–7).

[36] Grzymała-Busse (2002: 155–7); Rybář and Deegan-Krause (2008: 512).

[37] Interview SVK-12.

[38] Marušiak (2005: 165).

[39] After SNS voters, SMER voters were the second most distrusting of parties.

[40] Half of SMER's supporters self-identified as "left" or "center-left" and a third favored government reduction in income inequality.

[41] Rybář and Deegan-Krause (2008: 510, 514). See also Haughton (2003: 69; 2004: 186).

A look beyond this link between the decline of SDĽ and the breakthrough of SMER further supports the notion that it was the demise of center-left reformers that explains much of the antiestablishment vote in 2002. Indeed, neither was SDĽ the only left-of-center loser to come out of the reformist coalition, nor was SMER the only beneficiary of leftist protest voting. On the one hand, the Party of Civic Understanding – another left-leaning, though more ambiguously so, party – also lost a quarter of its supporters to SMER after being in charge of privatization during the juncture. On the other hand, the unreformed Communist Party registered its best ever electoral result in postcommunist Slovakia – and entered parliament for the first and only time – by attracting the second largest group of former SDĽ supporters.[42] Overall, as disaffected voters shifted support away from what they now saw as unreliably leftist parties, the antiestablishment critics of neoliberalism – above all, SMER – benefitted at the ballot box immediately after the juncture, thus embodying most of the post-neoliberal populist magnitude in 2002.

5.1.3 Illiberal Adaptation

SMER may have broken through in 2002, but its initial electoral result assigned the party only a secondary role in opposition. While party leaders interpreted it as a disappointment,[43] this early outcome gave SMER a valuable chance for the programmatic and organizational adaptations necessary for success in the new political context. As SMER strategically exploited the environmental opportunity shaped by the legacies of the postcommunist juncture, it began its evolution into the dominant illiberal force it would soon become.

The political environment bequeathed by the juncture was characterized by two relevant and mutually related aspects – (1) a shift in issue salience and (2) the decline of Mečiar's HZDS. The first of these was a major change resulting from the neoliberal transition under the Left's stewardship. Indeed, as the reformist government broke with the patrimonial and nationalist past, which had most recently been associated with HZDS's national populism, attention shifted away from issues of nationalism and democracy and toward concerns about the economy.[44] Second, coinciding with this shift was the growing availability for electoral mobilization of many voters who had previously supported Mečiar's now unraveling party. While HZDS was not an ex-communist party, it had shared the leftist constituency with SDĽ due to its redistributionist agenda in the 1990s, as discussed previously. Yet seeking to improve its image by adjusting to Slovakia's new context, in 2000 HZDS "rebranded itself as a center-right entity" in the image of German and British conservatives, even adding "People's Party" to its name[45] as an aspirational gesture to the EU's

---

[42] Haughton (2003: 69).
[43] Mesežnikov et al. (2008: 111).

[44] Rybář and Deegan-Krause (2008).
[45] Haughton (2001; 2003).

conservative party family. As HZDS shifted to the right, however, it experienced internal strife resulting in a splinter – the similarly named, and illiberal, Movement for Democracy (HZD). Following a familiar logic, HZD's leader rationalized the need to create a new party with a "leftist orientation" by citing HZDS's problematic evolution "into a party that appeared more centrist or rightist than leftist."[46]

While its shift to the right was understandable as HZDS searched for acceptance in the new context, the move proved detrimental for the party. Yet, despite the fact that nearly half of its 1998 voters abandoned HZDS by 2002 in favor of parties with more explicitly leftist positions – especially Fico's SMER, the new HZD, and the unreformed communists[47] – Mečiar's party kept shifting further to the right after 2002.[48] Given HZDS's new orientation, its supporters – who in 2004 were more dissatisfied than supporters of all other parties with both the government and the economy under Slovakia's now center-right administration (2002–6) – were unlikely to stay loyal. As neoliberal reform continuity further raised the salience of economic issues[49] and as HZDS appeared ever less capable of retaining its economically leftist yet also highly nationalist and religious voters,[50] SMER next strategically turned to illiberalism.

This pivot was two-pronged, involving a shift toward both economically redistributionist and ethnically nationalist positions.[51] Having begun as a party with rather centrist positions on both material and cultural issues[52] and having embraced a highly idiosyncratic law and order version of the "Third Way" in its early years, after 2002 SMER shifted further to the left. It did so specifically by intensifying criticism of the center-right government's "neoliberal value hegemony."[53] Arguing that if Mečiar had sold industries to his friends, Dzurinda was committing an even greater sin by "selling all of the country's golden eggs to foreigners,"[54] SMER blamed poverty and inequality on privatization, commercial banks, and international corporations.[55] As remedies to "a brutal economic regime" that, in the view of one SMER deputy, approximated Pinochet's Chile,[56] the party proposed "social democratic solutions" such as revoking the flat tax, lowering taxes on food and medicine, increasing the minimum wage, and canceling tuition fees at universities.[57] Yet in line with its "electoral-professional,"[58] rather than programmatic, character, SMER's

---

[46] Nicholson (2002).

[47] Haughton (2003).

[48] See the Chapel Hill Expert Survey's 2002 and 2006 waves (*lrecon* variable) for parties' relative positioning on economic issues (Bakker et al. 2015; Polk et al. 2017).

[49] Rybář and Deegan-Krause (2008: 513–4).

[50] Rybář and Deegan-Krause (2008: 514–6).

[51] Rybář and Deegan-Krause (2008: 505–8, 511).

[52] Interview SVK-09.

[53] Interview SVK-13.

[54] Interview SVK-11.

[55] Interview SVK-10.

[56] Interview SVK-14.

[57] Bohle and Greskovits (2012); Malová (2017: 10); Mesežnikov et al. (2008: 111).

[58] Rybář and Deegan-Krause (2008: 505).

supposed social democratization was more performative and particularistic than substantive and universal – the reason why the party would have a complicated, and often adversarial, relationship with the international socialist bodies that invited it to join their clubs for purely pragmatic reasons.[59] Indeed, SMER not only intensified attacks on the government's "anti-social" policies, including continued privatization and the flat tax favoring international corporations. It also stressed that it would be "neither more left-wing nor atheistic" and performed accommodationist gestures toward the radical Right by using nationalist and racist rhetoric against ethnic minorities, particularly Hungarians and the Roma.[60]

This illiberal shift was driven by efforts to showcase antiestablishment credibility in a context where minority scapegoating had become an outlet for social frustrations with growing inequality amid the establishment parties' continued market reforms.[61] As an electoral strategy, this move proved highly efficient[62] – especially "in a media environment that," as one SMER strategist remembered, "stigmatized as 'communist' any purely leftist criticism of the market."[63] Indeed, as a liberal politician described it, "If you do right-wing, pro-market reforms, someone will be hurt. Fico managed to convince these people – maybe more than 40 percent of voters – that he was the guy who would save them."[64] The result was that SMER not only kept "nearly all of its 2002 voters" in 2006 but also drew many new ones, especially from the "Slovak national" stream previously associated with HZDS – voters particularly attracted to SMER's "national element," understood as a commitment to supporting Slovak companies, products, and farmers.[65] Having positioned itself as an overall illiberal opponent of the government's neoliberal agenda – which continued raising the salience of economic issues – SMER, now seen as "the champion of the poor against the rich,"[66] handily won the 2006 poll, driving the most significant illiberal gains in a Slovak parliamentary election after 2000.

5.1.4 The Social Bases of Illiberal Domination

SMER's success in 2006 was the first in an impressive series of four consecutive parliamentary election victories, all of which the party won with large margins (20.5 points, on average) and by competing as an illiberal party. In this, SMER was a true pioneer. Unlike other parties that achieved similar feats in the postcommunist Europe of the early twenty-first century (e.g., Hungary's

---

[59] Interview SVK-02.
[60] Malová (2017); Marušiak (2005); Mesežnikov et al. (2008: 111).
[61] Bohle and Greskovits (2004).
[62] Interviews SVK-08; SVK-09.
[63] Interview SVK-10.
[64] Interview SVK-07.
[65] Interview SVK-11.
[66] Rybář and Deegan-Krause (2008: 515–6).

Fidesz after 2010), SMER defined a political "era" between 2006 and 2020[67] by "delivering certainty and without changing the rules."[68]

This illiberal hegemony over national politics was primarily due to the party's domination of the leftist field, which, in turn, had electoral and organizational consequences that benefited it in the long term. First, by attracting former SDĽ and HZDS supporters disillusioned with neoliberal reforms, SMER became the first party in the country's modern history to sustain electoral success while also overcoming long-standing regional divides.[69] Indeed, as Slovakia's electorate had been geographically segmented,[70] no party before the juncture had enjoyed both significant electoral strength and a highly nationalized – that is, geographically extensive, or well-balanced – coalition of voters.[71] Whereas the party with the most geographically extensive electorate in the 1990s, SDĽ, had not achieved particularly impressive results at the ballot box, support for Mečiar's dominant HZDS had been less nationalized due to disproportionate concentration in western and central Slovakia. SMER changed this, accomplishing both feats by 2006. Having attracted many former SDĽ voters, in 2002 it instantly became the most highly nationalized party in the country's postcommunist history. Although this nationalization waned minimally after attracting supporters from HZDS, SMER still sustained the most geographically balanced electorate of all major Slovak parties for over a decade.

Its agenda resonating with its extensive social coalition from the very start, SMER next developed the type of organizational structure that would both keep the party close to its voters across the country and enable the cohesion necessary to pass legislation that would keep these voters satisfied. Here, too, the effect of the postcommunist juncture proved beneficial. Indeed, neoliberal deepening had caused not only the collapse of the three standard social democratic parties (SDĽ, SDSS, and SDA), which had been associated with the reformist government, but also the gradual decimation of Slovakia's Confederation of Trade Unions, which had also supported the anti-Mečiar coalition in 1998.[72] Consequently, as the social democratic parties failed to build a left-wing non-populist alternative on the basis of trade unionism, they were either dissolved or, depending on the perspective, "incorporated into" or "annexed by" SMER,[73] with most of their members jumping ship. SMER took advantage of this opportunity strategically. If in 2002 the party had very

---

[67] Marušiak (2021: 38).

[68] Interview SVK-06. As one critic contended, SMER did not need to change the rules because it was sufficiently dominant (Interview SVK-15).

[69] Plešivčák (2013).

[70] Interview SVK-16; Krivý (1995).

[71] Only Public Against Violence (VPN), with 29.4 percent of the vote, achieved

both in 1990, but this movement quickly disintegrated.

[72] Pula (2020).

[73] Whereas those leaning left subscribe to the first interpretation (e.g., Interview SVK-13), those opposed to SMER prefer the latter (e.g., Interview SVK-08).

low membership and no municipal-level units, the situation quickly changed thereafter. On the one hand, by acquiring property from what had been an organizationally strong Left, SMER empowered its municipal structure. On the other hand, the way it accepted members – only with the approval of the party presidium – was specifically intended to stymie any potentiality of disunity based on alternative ideas that former members of the highly decentralized SDĽ might have entertained.[74] In sum, SMER significantly increased the density of its party organization across the country while remaining true to its autonomous leadership's aversion to internal discord.[75]

Organizational unity, in turn, proved highly advantageous after SMER assumed power in 2006. Indeed, the party proved to be "incredibly disciplined"[76] and cohesive, acting "in an extremely coherent manner, without open controversy," and enjoying unprecedented unity in parliament, with none of its deputies crossing the floor over the next decade.[77] Legislative cohesion, in turn, allowed SMER to enact demand-side and pro-social policies, even in the restrictive context of preparation for membership in the Eurozone, which Slovakia entered in 2009.[78] Having positioned itself as the "main caretaker of a strong social state," the first SMER-led government (2006–10) did not just distribute Christmas bonuses to pensioners and benefits to families having a first child. It also stopped all privatization and prioritized investment in state-owned companies, thereby keeping energy prices low and limiting "private ownership of public utilities, pension, and healthcare insurers."[79] And even when SMER's second government consolidated the budget after 2012, as required by the EU's Stability and Growth Pact, SMER not only significantly improved tax collection, particularly from corporations and banks,[80] but also implemented progressive taxation, three social packages, a labor code satisfactory to trade unions, cheaper natural gas for households, and free train tickets for students and the retired.[81] As such popular policies aimed at remedying some of the "ills of the market economy,"[82] they proved to be a powerful electoral instrument. As a party functionary explained, "We don't campaign for elections; we campaign continuously by providing for the people."[83]

Crucially, then, SMER's electoral success over the years is mostly attributable to its agenda seeking to soften the effects of neoliberal reform on Slovak

---

[74] See Marušiak (2005: 567).

[75] Rybář and Deegan-Krause (2008: 498, 504–6; 2009).

[76] Interview SVK-15.

[77] Malová (2017).

[78] Interview SVK-06. Notably, a SMER politician justified membership in the Eurozone as better for the national interest than a sovereign currency based on the argument that the latter could be an easier target for speculators (Interview SVK-18).

[79] Malová (2017).

[80] Interview SVK-20.

[81] Interview SVK-12; Malová (2017). As a party functionary argued, these tickets were not a populist measure but rather an incentive for Slovaks to support the national economy by spending at home rather than in Austria (Interview SVK-11).

[82] Rybář and Deegan-Krause (2008: 513).

[83] Interview SVK-11.

society. As the party fared equally well – 28.8 and 27.1 percent, respectively – when contesting parliamentary elections as a challenger (in 2002, 2006, and 2012) and as an incumbent (in 2010, 2016, and 2020), its long-term success was equally attributable to its criticism of rightist governments' neoliberal policies when in opposition and its delivery of material benefits when in power. Yet it was its initial criticism of market reforms, which SMER began voicing during the juncture and then intensified between 2002 and 2006, that helped the party mobilize the social bases necessary for its subsequent hegemony. Having acquired an impressively broad electorate (in terms of both sociological categories[84] and geographic distribution[85]), which included both rural voters and university educated urbanites,[86] SMER then sustained long-term popularity by supplying policies resonant with its supporters. Overall, as it strategically exploited the legacies of the postcommunist juncture, Slovakia's main illiberal party successfully built a highly extensive electoral coalition and, as SMER politicians emphasized, a unified organization even before rising to power for the first time in 2006.[87] These attributes, in turn, facilitated the legislative cohesion necessary for the delivery of public policies that strengthened party unity further[88] – a virtuous cycle that underpinned SMER's ability to dominate in the long term. I elaborate and discuss from a comparative perspective the mechanism underlying these dynamics in Chapter 7.

Finally, if SMER's rise and continued popularity reflected the centrality of economic issues for an extensive coalition of voters across the country, so did its eventual decline between 2016, when Fico's party still won the parliamentary election, albeit less convincingly, and 2020, when it finally lost. Although SMER's fall from power had much to do with the anti-corruption and anti-government protests of 2017 and 2018, the party started losing popularity as soon as it began turning away from economic issues in the run-up to the 2016 election. Indeed, as SMER once again turned to ethnonationalism, escalating anti-Muslim rhetoric during the 2015 refugee influx into Europe, it abandoned its traditional bread-and-butter issues. With the latest increases for pensioners being rather "measly" and with teachers and nurses striking for better pay,[89] Fico's party quickly lost popular support amid a strongly performing economy. While SMER still drove most of the total illiberal vote share in the 2016 election, as seen in Figure 5.1a, its xenophobic escalation only facilitated the strengthening of right-wing populists such as Kotleba's People's Party – Our Slovakia and We Are Family. Indeed, this latest flirtation with far right ideology was a strategic mistake, which resulted in the party losing what had been the most nationalized electorate in modern Slovak

---

[84] Interview SVK-09.
[85] Interview SVK-07.
[86] Who, in the words of one high-level SMER official, tended to vote for SMER more than for any one liberal party (Interview SVK-17).

[87] Interviews SVK-13; SVK-18.
[88] Interview SVK-09.
[89] Malová (2017: 8).

history. Having hemorrhaged supporters, SMER then also lost cohesion and splintered in 2020.

Overall, the popularity of Slovakia's most successful illiberal party rose and fell with its ability to, as one campaign strategist put it, "remain laser focused on the issues that matter most to regular Slovaks in terms of economic insecurity"[90] – issues that had become preeminent after the postcommunist juncture. Indeed, the prioritization of economic, rather than social, concerns was precisely the reason why even those not enthusiastic about the party usually saw no better alternative, as SMER politicians and supporters reasoned.[91] Thus, although SMER was involved in numerous corruption scandals,[92] voters, clearly more sensitive to economic questions,[93] continued rewarding it at the ballot box for most of the 2000–20 period. When SMER delivered where the ex-communist Left had failed, its extensive electoral coalition rewarded it. When it stopped delivering, the fracturing of its social bases foreshadowed its decline. While its cultural dimension complemented the economic one, Slovak illiberalism in the early twenty-first century was predominantly a socioeconomic phenomenon conditioned by the neoliberal legacies of the postcommunist juncture.

5.2 POLAND

5.2.1 The Polarizing Effect of the Juncture

The 1990 election, which elevated Lech Wałęsa to the presidency, was critical not only because it initiated Poland's bait-and-switch juncture but also because it activated political and economic cleavages of key significance for the future. By organizing popular anger through rhetoric emphasizing Polish nationhood and Christian values, as noted in Chapter 4, Wałęsa's was the first postcommunist electoral campaign to mobilize a "nationalist" versus "liberal" Poland.[94] As a result, he underperformed substantially where Tadeusz Mazowiecki received most support[95] – among city dwellers and the highly educated, as well as in the better industrialized western and northern territories that had once been part of Prussia after Poland's eighteenth century partition. Wałęsa attracted disproportionately high support among those with lower incomes, low-skilled workers, and rural communities,[96] as well as in the more religious southern and eastern territories that had once been dominated by the Austro-Hungarian and Russian empires.

In line with the theory developed in Chapter 2, the 1990 presidential election – Poland's second competitive poll – was more crucial for subsequent

---

90 Interview SVK-10.
91 Interviews SVK-14; SVK-18; SVK-20.
92 Interview SVK-15.
93 Interview SVK-09.

94 Ost (2005: 65–8).
95 Tworzecki (1996: 92).
96 Bell (2001: 91); Jasiewicz (1992: 191–2).

outcomes than the transitional 1989 parliamentary election, for several reasons. First, as explained previously, whereas the 1989 election was less confrontational, featuring virtually no debate on economic issues, the 1990 election was both confrontational and clearly focused on the economy. Second, although regional voting patterns in the transitional 1989 election had suggested the resurfacing of imperial partition patterns,[97] such patterns did not solidify until the 1990 presidential election. For example, while in 1989 Solidarity had overperformed in the south (Austrian partition) and the communists had gained strongest support in north-western areas (German partition), where Solidarity had been weakest, central and eastern Poland (Russian partition) had occupied an "intermediate position," with Solidarity performing rather poorly in some regions there.[98] In the 1990 presidential election, by contrast, Wałęsa overperformed in both the former Austrian and Russian partitions. By campaigning on a populist platform that resonated in both the South and the East, he was the first postcommunist politician to actively and successfully politicize for electoral gain the country's historical cleavages. Because these divides would resurface with a vengeance in the future, as I discuss later, their politicization by Wałęsa was highly consequential for subsequent developments in Poland.

Third, having primed voters with his populist message, Wałęsa then helped deepen neoliberalism, as explained in Chapter 4. Yet, as the reforms of the early 1990s brought real wage declines, unemployment, poverty, and inequality,[99] they had major destabilizing effects specifically for Wałęsa's core electorate. On the one hand, if Wałęsa's campaign had attracted many workers in 1990, the subsequent economic policies of his cabinets clearly provoked their protest,[100] with Poland experiencing the highest magnitude of contentious activity – particularly worker demonstrations and strikes organized by trade unions and focused on economic demands – in postcommunist Europe.[101] On the other hand, early market reforms resulted in particularly severe declines of agricultural production[102] and thus created highly differentiated effects in terms of regional development. As GDP per capita and incomes fell especially throughout eastern Poland[103] – where rural communities reliant primarily on farming are predominantly concentrated[104] – Polish farmers were the biggest "losers" of the early transformation.[105] Indeed, having disproportionately supported Wałęsa in 1990,[106] farmers and farm workers were the social group that experienced the greatest income losses. If their incomes had been above average when the juncture began in 1990, they were lowest by the time it ended

---

[97] Tworzecki (1996).
[98] For example, in Łódź, Kielce, Chełm, Białystok, and Siedlce. See Kowalski (2000: 13–4, 131–2).
[99] Bell (2001); Rae (2008); Shields (2007b: 167).
[100] Ost (2005).

[101] See Ekiert and Kubik (1998).
[102] Morgan (1992).
[103] Rae (2008: 73).
[104] See Bański (2003).
[105] Bell (2001: 2).
[106] Jasiewicz (1992: 191–220).

in 1993.[107] As a result, Polish farmers protested both more intensely than they had done in the 1980s[108] and more than their counterparts elsewhere in post-communist Europe.[109] As they accused Wałęsa of betrayal and demanded state intervention in the economy, by 1992 aggrieved farmers were increasingly mobilized by groups that often called for protest action. Yet, unlike workers' protests, which in most cases were "effective in gaining concessions, such as wage increases, from the government or employers,"[110] farmers' protests did not result in improved incomes. It was based on farmers' economic frustration that Andrzej Lepper, the leader of one of those groups, organized in 1992 a new political party, Self-Defense,[111] which would become especially relevant for understanding the subsequent salience of *contestatory illiberalism* in Poland, as I explain in Chapter 7.

Overall, as Wałęsa politicized divides between nationalists and liberals for electoral ends, and then facilitated neoliberal deepening that added an economic dimension to these divides, Poland's postcommunist juncture unleashed a powerful dynamic of polarization. Having persisted over time, this polarization has generally been understood as a multidimensional, yet single, regionally based cleavage between "Poland A" of the liberal North and West, urban centers, and transition "winners," and "Poland B" of the nationalist-conservative South and East, rural areas, and transition "losers."[112] While scholars have convincingly linked this "East/West Poland A/Poland B distinction"[113] to the structural and cultural legacies of imperial partition,[114] it was not until the early 1990s that these legacies were *politically triggered*. Indeed, as the communist regime had eliminated the gentry and enacted land reform, it had generally improved the economic position of workers and farmers by substantially reducing prior inequalities, including regionally based ones.[115] Although the inflation crises of the 1970s and 1980s had certainly been problematic, egalitarianism was still prevalent in the late 1980s,[116] as seen in Poland's low inequality levels and high farmers' incomes at the time. It was not until the early 1990s that both inequality and farmers' incomes quickly deteriorated amid deepening reforms, adding an economic aspect to the historical divisions that Wałęsa had activated for electoral gain.

It was thus the dynamics of electoral competition and market reform, which defined the postcommunist juncture in the early 1990s, that triggered the (re)activation of historically based divisions and spatial inequalities in

---

[107] Bell (2001: 122); Foryś and Gorlach (2002); Gorlach (2000: 73); Rae (2008: 71–3).
[108] Valdez (2011).
[109] Ekiert and Kubik (1998: 559).
[110] Osa (1998).
[111] Foryś and Gorlach (2002); Gorlach (2000: 70–6); Stanley (2015b).
[112] Stanley (2015b).
[113] See Kitschelt et al. (1999: 145).
[114] Grosfeld and Zhuravskaya (2013); Jańczak (2015); Zarycki (2015).
[115] Wesełowski and Wnuk-Lipiński (1992: 87).
[116] Wesełowski and Wnuk-Lipiński (1992: 88–90). Also, Bukowski and Novokmet (2021: 189).

contemporary Poland. Indeed, if "one of the unintended consequences of reform [was] high levels of unemployment[117] – which spiked to over 16 percent by the juncture's end in 1993 – the East and South of Poland were worst hit.[118] Already by the mid 1990s, there was a "growing awareness of a Polish East/ West divide," with the East suffering from "little opportunity for medium- to long-term investment, an agricultural-based economy, poor banking infra- structure, insufficient training opportunities, and few experienced business support agencies."[119] While the divide between the more "business-minded" Poland A and the "state-reliant" "Poland B[120] would assert itself in future elections,[121] it was the polarizing effects of the postcommunist juncture that truly breathed new life into it.

5.2.2 From Neoliberal Consensus to Populist Backlash

If the postcommunist juncture produced polarizing electoral and macroeco- nomic effects, these effects, in turn, contributed to the structuring of parti- san competition and cleavage formation. First, the electoral rivalry between Mazowiecki and Wałęsa resulted in the crystallization of two post-Solidarity partisan constellations – the secular and pro-market liberal democrats and the religious and virulently anti-communist national conservatives. Second, the social consequences of neoliberal reform contributed to the strengthening of parties with a social-protectionist orientation on economic issues. As these core partisan sectors consolidated, electoral competition in the 1990s revolved around two dimensions – a primary political-cultural divide revolving around attitudes about communism's legacy and religion, and a secondary economic divide centered on issues of market reform and development.[122]

The economic divide may have been secondary, but it was by no means peripheral throughout the 1990s, as most obviously seen in the overall elec- toral performance of parties "with non-negative perceptions of the communist regime"[123] – the Alliance of the Democratic Left (SLD), organized around the by-now social democratic ex-communist party, the Polish Peasant Party (PSL), which channeled farmers' discontent, and Labor Union (UP), a splinter from Solidarity.[124] While these parties entered the 1990s in a weak position, the deepening dissatisfaction with the ongoing neoliberal reforms resulted in a dra- matic improvement of their electoral fortunes by the 1993 parliamentary elec- tion, in which they finished first, second, and fourth, and as a result of which SLD and PSL governed in a coalition between 1993 and 1997.

As an ex-communist party that had neither spearheaded neoliberal deepen- ing nor led the parliamentary opposition during most of the juncture, SLD was

---

[117] Foley et al. (1996: 30).
[118] Shields (2007b: 167).
[119] Foley et al. (1996: 30).
[120] Interviews POL-04; POL-07.
[121] Tworzecki (1996); Zarycki (2015).
[122] Kitschelt et al. (1999).
[123] Casal Bértoa (2014: 27).
[124] Kitschelt et al. (1999: 114).

in a unique position relative to other leftist parties in Eastern Europe. First, although it emerged as the central actor in the social democratic field by 1993, SLD engaged in neoliberal reform continuity thereafter.[125] Second, rather than be punished for deviating from socialism, SLD experienced a decade-long upsurge by steadily improving its performance in both parliamentary and presidential elections. Influential scholarship on postcommunist party development has attributed this impressive resurrection to SLD's ability to "regenerate" itself by empowering reformist party elites who "broke with the communist past."[126] Indeed, as SLD controlled the budget, combatted inflation, and cut down expenditures between 1993 and 1997, it demonstrated competence in terms of following neoliberal policy and attracted many supporters, particularly secular and white-collar voters inhabiting Poland's more prosperous West.[127] Yet, while the "successful liberalization" argument certainly accounts for SLD's popularity among such transition "winners," it explains neither the party's inability to convince voters of its competence in the run-up to the 1997 election[128] nor its nontrivial attractiveness to more economically vulnerable social groups.

Indeed, the connection between the Left's economic profile and popular appeal in the first postcommunist decade is somewhat more complex.[129] Notably, as "the average Pole was quite supportive of a strong role for the state in the economy,"[130] SLD's two greatest parliamentary election gains relative to prior elections – the 70 percent and 51 percent improvements in 1993 and 2001 – were achieved not when the party embraced neoliberalism uncritically but rather when it opposed its deepening by reformist incumbents on the Right. In these election campaigns, the Left promised "a more sophisticated way to combat [the market's] negative side effects," particularly by means of "more state intervention, internal market protectionism, and higher taxes for the wealthy."[131] It was due to its support for "a progressive income tax and benefits for people adversely affected by the transition"[132] that SLD drew support not only from its traditional constituencies – pensioners and workers in the state sector – but also from blue-collar workers, who found the party increasingly attractive by the late 1990s,[133] and even from a considerable share of farmers, whom SLD poached from both Wałęsa and PSL.[134] As all these groups were opposed to fiscal austerity and structural adjustment,[135]

[125] Frye (2010: 220); Markowski (2002: 66–8).
[126] Grzymała-Busse (2002: 14–6, 45–9, 105–7); Tavits (2013: 184–5); Tavits and Letki (2009: 559–60).
[127] Markowski (2002).
[128] Szczerbiak (1998: 72).
[129] Bell (1997).
[130] Stanley (2015a: 271).
[131] Markowski (2002: 62–3). Relatedly, SLD's 2001 victory would have been

even larger had leading leftist politicians abstained from comments about impending austerity measures just weeks before the parliamentary election. See also Szczerbiak (2007).
[132] Pienkos (2001: 436).
[133] Markowski (2002: 59–63).
[134] Bell (1997: 1273–4); Szczerbiak (2002).
[135] Bell (1997: 1275).

the Left's social bases of support between 1993 and 2001 widened considerably, with the party overcoming historical, religious, and territorial divides in the early 2000s.[136] SLD thus not only dominated Poland's West and North but also consistently improved its electoral results in the poorer East, where a plurality of voters tended to choose leftist parties – above all, SLD – throughout the 1990s.

The other party that did well in eastern Poland throughout the 1990s was the agrarian PSL. Notably, PSL found disproportionately high support in rural areas with high concentrations of farmers, overperforming in the East mostly because of its advocacy of farmer subsidies as a corrective to the negative social effects of neoliberalism. Indeed, it was the agrarians that pulled the SLD–PSL coalition government (1993–97)[137] in the direction of national, as opposed to laissez-faire, capitalism through regulatory measures, protection of the agricultural sector from foreign competition, and "hybrid" forms of property.[138] Nevertheless, as their incomes remained stagnant during this period,[139] farmers ultimately punished PSL for failing to meet their demands and redistribute growing fiscal revenues to their liking.[140] Indeed, in 1997 the party lost more than half of its 1993 supporters, with a fifth of farmers voting for the Left and a third supporting the post-Solidarity coalition.[141]

If the two parties (SLD and PSL) that came out of the former regime saw divergent electoral fortunes by the second half of the 1990s, so did Solidarity's successors. First, although the liberal-democratic partisan sector, led by shock therapists Leszek Balcerowicz and Tadeusz Mazowiecki, was rather cohesive, it experienced diminishing electoral returns over time. Having coalesced into the Freedom Union (UW) by the mid 1990s, the liberal-democratic camp, which consistently underperformed in Poland's South and East, lost support throughout the 1990s[142] after leading several reformist governments in the early 1990s. By contrast, although national-conservative forces, especially those led by Jarosław Kaczyński and Jan Olszewski, were more prone to sectarian conflict and splintering, their electoral results did not generally suffer. Having exhibited overall stability during Wałęsa's presidency and then greater unity as the subsequently assembled Solidarity Electoral Action (AWS),[143] the conservative camp won the 1997 parliamentary election with more than a third of all votes.[144] As the split of Solidarity divided politics along multiple lines, the "populist leaning" national conservatives gained ground by positioning themselves against both liberals and the Left and by promising more "social solidarity" and subsidies for the countryside.[145]

---

[136] Szczerbiak (2002).
[137] Bell (2001: 36).
[138] Bohle and Greskovits (2012: 144); Kitschelt et al. (1999: 131); Markowski (2002: 65).
[139] Rae (2008: 73).
[140] Bell (2001: 37); Markowski (2002: 65).
[141] Szczerbiak (1998: 74–5).
[142] From 23 percent in 1991 to 15 percent in 1993 and 13 percent in 1997.
[143] Millard (2010: 83–4).
[144] Kitschelt et al. (1999: 112–5).
[145] Millard (2010: 52, 86).

Having attracted a plurality of voters across Poland's South and East, in 1997 AWS formed a governing coalition with the economically liberal Freedom Union. This coalition put Leszek Balcerowicz, the architect of shock therapy from the early 1990s, once again in charge of the Ministry of Finance, from where he led a new round of "difficult economic reforms in pensions, health care, and education."[146] As this maneuver was similar to what SLD had done just four years prior – rise to power by promising relief from neoliberalism and then deepen market reforms – a clear pattern had emerged in Poland. Indeed, with both the postcommunist Left and post-Solidarity Right staying the pro-market course that had been initiated in the early transition years, polarization throughout the 1990s was low.[147] Yet, as the neoliberal consensus among political elites appeared set in stone, an undercurrent of societal radicalization was gaining strength, particularly across the economically vulnerable sectors of Poland B.

Ever since the early 1990s, the growth of popular discontent with market reforms had resulted in large social groups losing trust in the system and the steady intensification of social anger through nationalist and populist discourses. As Solidarity, unable to deal with capitalist inequality, turned toward nationalist populism in the early 1990s[148] and as the Left did not particularly seek to mobilize the socially excluded thereafter, many workers, farmers, young people, and the religious became increasingly radicalized. Although radicalism was politically marginal throughout the 1990s, it was both politically and culturally significant. It began infecting the political system through parties – for instance, the Christian National Union (ZChN) and the Confederation of Independent Poland (KPN) – that joined the populist-leaning AWS for the 1997 election. Radicalism was also spreading throughout civil society, where a number of groups organized around ethnonationalist, antisemitic, and violent rhetoric and action. With access to a key resource of cultural mobilization – the well-financed Catholic-nationalist Radio Maryja – ethno-nationalist parties advocated economic autarky and the replacement of foreign owners with ethnic Poles as solutions to the problems of capitalism. These views were articulated especially prominently by two ethno-nationalist parties that, by 2001, would bring the populist reaction from the sidelines into the mainstream. One was the far-right League of Polish Families (LPR), whose anti-EU, anti-gay, and antisemitic posturing was specifically endorsed by Radio Maryja. The second, and even more prominent, was the radical populist Self-Defense (SO). Also given platform on Radio Maryja, this party had originated as an instrument for anti-neoliberal farmer protest in the early 1990s and then become a major organizer of anti-neoliberal contention by the late 1990s.[149]

The mainstreaming of popular radicalism is perhaps best embodied by the increased intensity of protest activity, particularly across Poland B, where,

---

[146] Frye (2010: 220).
[147] Frye (2010).

[148] Ost (2005).
[149] Pankowski (2010); Stanley (2015b).

as previously discussed, a key group most hurt by the economic transition – farmers – is concentrated. Indeed, while contentious action had generally waned after the postcommunist juncture ended in 1993,[150] it once again intensified by the late 1990s,[151] and this time it was farmers' grievances that constituted the focal point.[152] As continued neoliberal reforms had resulted in the elimination of subsidies, price controls, and trade barriers, Polish farmers, now facing competition from highly subsidized agribusinesses of Western Europe, continued suffering diminishing incomes in the late 1990s.[153] Notably, while agricultural cooperative reforms had been intended to facilitate rural adaptation to the new market economy, they, in fact, achieved the opposite effect, helping farmers overcome collective action problems and intensify their protest.[154] Led by Self-Defense, which Lepper had transformed into an "agrarian fundamentalist and populist" party, the farmers' protests of the late 1990s specifically targeted the Ministry of Finance led by "shock therapist" Leszek Balcerowicz. With Self-Defense's repertoire of contention now featuring highly disruptive new methods – road and cargo terminal blockades, clashes with riot police, and the destruction of imported grain – protest action in Poland had travelled a long way from the rather nonviolent days of mobilization against the Solidarity-led governments in the early 1990s.[155] As Lepper's Self-Defense increasingly dominated farmers' discourse and mobilization,[156] anti-neoliberal contention had found its own political vehicle.

It was in this context of growing societal radicalism that the 2001 parliamentary election fundamentally realigned the political landscape,[157] marking the collapse of Solidarity's direct heirs and bringing the populist reaction into parliament. Indeed, signs of change had already appeared in the presidential election of the preceding year, which had not only produced the easy reelection of the ex-communist Aleksander Kwaśniewski but also signaled public disenchantment with "the harsh brand of economic liberalism" of the post-Solidarity Right.[158] While the postcommunist Left achieved its best performance in 2001 by forming alliances with smaller parties, the post-Solidarity Right collapsed, with the bulk of its cadres and supporters veering toward either the new pro-market Civic Platform (PO) around Donald Tusk or the new anti-corruption Law and Justice (PiS) around the Kaczyński twins.[159] Whereas the liberal PO represented a sense of continuity, PiS was especially critical of AWS.[160]

While the competition between PO and PiS would define politics after 2005, it was the electoral breakthrough of the forces of populism – the radical

---

[150] Ekiert and Kubik (1998).
[151] Ekiert et al. (2017: 342).
[152] Gorlach (2000: 75–8).
[153] Rae (2008: 73).
[154] Valdez (2011).
[155] Gorlach (2000: 77–81).

[156] Foryś and Gorlach (2002: 61).
[157] Markowski (2008: 1058).
[158] Millard (2002: 362); Pienkos (2001).
[159] Szczerbiak (2002).
[160] Interview POL-02.

populist SO, which with 10.2 percent support came third in the 2001 election, and the far right LPR, which gained 7.9 percent of the votes[161] – that signaled the mood that had taken over large segments of the socially excluded after a decade of market reforms. Indeed, the 2001 electorates of SO and LPR shared a similar sociological profile, as they were concentrated in rural areas, villages, and small towns, as well as among those with relatively low levels of education and harboring antidemocratic attitudes.[162] While LPR's "radical right" voters tended to be religious and somewhat less motivated by purely economic concerns, their loathing of both the European Union and the "communist-liberalism" of the SLD, PO, and UW[163] betrayed deep frustrations with the convergence between leftist and rightist parties. Self-Defense, in turn, attracted many workers, unemployed citizens, some former leftist voters disillusioned with SLD's neoliberal policies, and especially farmers "who felt themselves to be among the greatest losers from the economic transformation and had become increasingly radicalized in recent years."[164] If LPR was disproportionately popular in the East and South, SO found most support in structurally impoverished areas in the Northwest and farmer communities in the East. As both appealed to transition "losers" – LPR to the religious elderly, SO to the economically disaffected and particularly farmers[165] – they channeled the undercurrent of radicalism that had grown in response to the liberal consensus of the 1990s[166] into a populist reaction that would define Polish politics during the following decades.

5.2.3 Illiberal Adaptation

The political breakthrough of Polish populism may have been associated with the two parties that embodied societal radicalization in the 2001 election, but it was Law and Justice (PiS) that dominated the illiberal field in the first two decades of the twenty-first century. Indeed, of the various parties that populated this space,[167] PiS was by far the most important over time. As seen in Figure 5.2, support for it represented both most of the illiberal vote share (Figure 5.2a) and most of the post-neoliberal populist magnitude

---

[161] Millard (2003); Szczerbiak (2002).

[162] Pankowski (2010).

[163] Millard (2003: 371).

[164] Szczerbiak (2002: 57). Also, Stanley (2015b).

[165] See Pankowski (2010: 97, 124–9, 146–8); Szczerbiak (2002).

[166] See Shields (2007b: 168).

[167] Other parties included in both categories at one time or another are the League of Polish Families (LPR), Self-Defense (SO), Labor Union (UP), and Left Together (LR). Whereas the parties and alliances around Janusz Korwin-Mikke – Janusz Korwin-Mikke's Platform (PJKM), Congress of the New Right (KNP), Coalition for the Renewal of the Republic of Liberty and Hope (KORWiN), and Confederation – fit only the illiberal category, Social Democracy of Poland (SDPL) fits only the post-neoliberal populist category. Although the Polish People's Party (PSL) also defended illiberal positions, it was somewhat less antiestablishment due to its governing role in the 1990s.

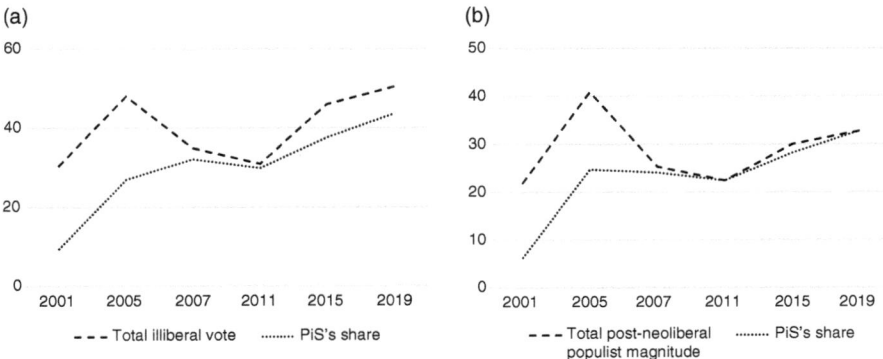

FIGURE 5.2 PiS's share of the total illiberal vote and post-neoliberal populist magnitude in Polish parliamentary elections, 2000–20. (a) Illiberal vote share, (b) post-neoliberal populist magnitude

(Figure 5.2b) – 74 percent and 80 percent, respectively – in parliamentary elections from 2000 to 2020. It was this popular support that enabled PiS to attack liberal institutions – including not only the independence of the Central Bank and Constitutional Tribunal but also the 1997 Constitution, which the party saw as epitomizing the consensus of the 1990s[168] – when it governed during this period. If a single party came to embody the essence of societal opposition to liberalism in Poland, this undoubtedly was PiS.

While the founders of PiS – the Kaczyński twins – had been key players in the national-conservative camp in the early 1990s, it was not until the 2000s that they achieved true success as an independent political force. Having participated in the increasingly unpopular AWS coalition, they established their new political project around a small circle of former Center Accord politicians, which was not particularly welcoming to outsiders.[169] Founded in 2001, PiS began as an antiestablishment "centrist" party, which, although focused on law, order, and the fight against corruption, was at first very similar to PO, as a former senator, who "could have been in either party," recalled.[170] Initially organized based on the personal popularity of Lech Kaczyński, who had built a tough-on-crime reputation as Minister of Justice between 2000 and 2001, and ultimately dominated by Jarosław Kaczyński, who led the party in a highly centralized manner, PiS was always a decidedly personalistic organization,[171] as admitted – and embraced – by its rank and file.[172] The high degree of top-down control, which encompassed all

---

[168] Interview POL-22; Bill and Stanley (2020: 283–4).
[169] Interview POL-06.
[170] Interview POL-18.

[171] Pankowski (2010: 151–60); Pytlas (2021); Tavits (2013: 236–7); Tworzecki (2012: 619).
[172] Interviews POL-02; POL-04; POL-11; POL-25.

party structures,[173] in turn facilitated PiS's adaptive capacity for effortless programmatic conversion after 2001. As it evolved toward what one activist described as "social democratic conservatism" – a mixture of, on the one hand, ethno-nationalist, antiabortion, and homophobic stances, and, on the other hand, economic interventionism[174] – the party became a paradigmatic example of both illiberalism and post-neoliberal populism in Eastern Europe.

The decision of the PiS leadership to abandon programmatic centrism in favor of illiberalism was driven by both strategic considerations and environmental factors. First, following a "disappointing start" in the parliamentary election of 2001, when it gained just 9.5 percent after eschewing ideological issues and anti-systemic appeals, PiS's leaders strategically changed the party's "rhetoric, policies, ideology, political allies, and sources of symbolic support."[175] This was not the first time the Kaczyński brothers had switched positions opportunistically. They had also done so in the early 1990s, when, having previously "supported the decision to leave communists in public life," they suddenly began arguing "for a punitive approach" to the ex-communists after falling out with Wałęsa.[176] (While the reasons for this break are complex, many PiS supporters believed that a key reason for the Kaczyński brothers' break with Wałęsa was their opposition to shock therapy and their anticipation of the selling of Polish industries to foreigners during the Solidarity governments in the early 1990s.[177]) Changing course again, the brothers now transformed PiS "from a fairly typical conservative ... into a radical nationalist and visibly populist-socialist" party. Unlike the gamble in the early 1990s, which had led to their marginalization, however, the "spectacular change" after 2001 proved successful, leading to victories in both the presidential and parliamentary elections of 2005.[178]

Two environmental factors – both missing in the 1990s but present by the early 2000s – conditioned this transformation and facilitated illiberal surge in 2005. The first was the electoral success of SO and LPR as catalysts of radicalism. Having gained a combined 18 percent of the 2001 vote by criticizing both social and economic liberalism and then having organized disruptive protests against Poland's impending EU membership,[179] the two anti-systemic parties next achieved even more impressive results in the 2004 European Parliament election – a whopping 26.7 percent of the vote. Seeing this populist tide as a potential opportunity, the Kaczyński brothers suddenly shifted to ethnonationalism and Euroscepticism in a bid to distance PiS from a political establishment uniformly uncritical of the EU and thus to compete for the radical parties' voters.[180] Having previously been a critic of Radio Maryja, PiS now

---

[173] Including the youth organization, where higher-ups select officers (Interview POL-21).

[174] Interview POL-22.

[175] Pankowski (2010: 157); Szczerbiak (2002: 58–9).

[176] Santora (2019).

[177] Interviews POL-01; POL-04; POL-06; POL-08.

[178] Markowski (2006: 820).

[179] Stanley (2015a).

[180] Interviews POL-27; POL-28.

endorsed it, increasingly adopting rhetoric against the West and specifically against Germany as the driver of the EU's economic integration.[181] By supplementing its newly found enthusiasm for a strong nation state with Christian fundamentalist and homophobic positions, by 2005 PiS absorbed many LPR defectors and former supporters. If in 2001 PiS received only 8 percent of votes cast by listeners of Radio Maryja, by 2005 it attracted 40 percent of this constituency – and 38 percent of former LPR voters.[182]

Second, PiS adopted an economically interventionist posture specifically in order to take advantage of SLD's decline amid the rising salience of economic concerns in Poland.[183] Notably, the Left's unpopularity after the 2001 election was due not only to the serious corruption scandals in which the ex-communists became enmeshed but also to the SLD-led government's multiple attempts at fiscal consolidation in an effort to overcome high stagnation, unemployment, and public debt as Poland prepared for fast-track adoption of the euro.[184] In line with the neoliberal consensus of the previous decade, SLD once again introduced austerity – this time to cut public spending, increase women's retirement age, and shrink the civil service.[185] However, if the maneuver had worked in the 1990s – when economic issues had been secondary to cultural ones – it spectacularly failed in the very different environment after 2001, by which time the economy had become "extraordinarily relevant" for most Poles.[186] As now "the public saw only expenditure cuts and loss of benefits,"[187] the austerity packages accelerated SLD's decline, as reflected both in public opinion polls and the European Parliament election results of 2004.[188] Consequently, PiS's "ideological and programmatic plans ... had to be changed" in a bid to attract economically vulnerable voters who had previously supported the Left and could potentially turn to the radical Self-Defense, now squarely focused on protesting the government's neoliberal agenda.[189] Since PiS responded not only by initiating a harsh attack on neoliberalism for "the general injustice done to the majority of the losers of the transformation"[190] but also by advocating a more "left-leaning approach to the economy, seeking state intervention for a more equitable distribution,"[191] it began "winning over leftist voters, mainly the retired and marginalized," in areas previously dominated by the Left.[192] As it now drew supporters both from communities with high unemployment,[193] where SLD had been strong in the 1990s,[194] and from the working class more

---

[181] Interviews POL-01; POL-08; POL-09.

[182] Pankowski (2010: 166).

[183] Markowski (2002); Rohrschneider and Whitefield (2009).

[184] Bohle and Greskovits (2012: 176).

[185] Shields (2015).

[186] Casal Bértoa (2014: 24); Markowski (2006: 817).

[187] Millard (2006: 1014).

[188] Markowski (2006).

[189] Stanley (2015b).

[190] Markowski (2006: 820–1). Also, Szczerbiak (2007).

[191] Pankowski (2010: 163); Szczerbiak (2002: 211).

[192] Markowski (2006: 820–1, 826).

[193] Shields (2007b: 166).

[194] Bell (1997).

generally, PiS's ideological pivot proved successful in attracting a wide range of voters disaffected with what they saw as the "wild capitalism" and "wild privatization"[195] that had begun with Solidarity's deviation from its original focus on workers.[196] In the words of some of the party's own politicians and activists, PiS was a consequence of the economic liberalization,[197] representing those hurt by reforms "forced" on society ever since the early 1990s[198] – a period of "total ruin"[199] and "huge injustice,"[200] when "Wałęsa made a lot of promises and disappointed a lot of people."[201] As one PiS activist summarized, "The Wałęsa presidency was a disaster for us, common people."[202]

Although PiS's illiberal adaptation after 2001 allowed it to win the 2005 elections, the party paid a price in terms of organizational cohesion. As its core support base was both initially unstable (shifting from relatively prosperous and well-educated urbanites to poorer and less educated rural voters[203]) and highly uneven geographically (mostly concentrated in southern and eastern Poland), during its formative period PiS was one of the parties with most under-developed organization[204] – and specifically with weakest local branches – across Poland.[205] As I elaborate in Chapter 7, PiS's then weak organization undermined legislative cohesion when the party first governed – initially with parliamentary support from, then in a coalition with, SO and LPR – between 2005 and 2007. While this government ended prematurely, primarily because of the unruly behavior of the junior parties, "the coalition partners were not the only source of strain."[206] For instance, when PiS governed alone (in 2005–6), its first prime minister, Kazimierz Marcinkiewicz, clashed with the party leadership over a number of ministerial appointees, including the minister of finance.[207] Additionally, while PiS's initial Speaker of the Sejm pursued a path independent from the party line, for which he was replaced, its second Speaker refused to cooperate with the PiS finance minister, for which he was suspended from the party.[208] In the end, "little was achieved legislatively."[209]

Having been supported by a segmented electorate with a core in Poland B and unable to govern in a cohesive manner, between 2005 and 2007 PiS neither delivered nationally relevant public goods nor governed effectively. Despite "its rhetorical commitments to social solidarity," it "did not undertake

---

[195] Interviews POL-11; POL-22.
[196] Interviews POL-15; POL-16.
[197] Interview POL-12.
[198] Interviews POL-05; POL-09.
[199] Interview POL-13.
[200] Interview POL-10.
[201] Interview POL-04. While some were disappointed by Wałęsa's failure to distribute the money obtained through privatization to the common people, as promised (Interview POL-20), others blamed him for high unemployment (Interview POL-23).

[202] Interview POL-14.
[203] Markowski (2006: 45–6); Szczerbiak (2002: 52).
[204] Interviews POL-03; POL-04.
[205] PiS's leaders even saw strong organization as a liability (Tavits 2013: 237).
[206] Millard (2008: 71).
[207] Millard (2008: 71).
[208] Nalepa (2016).
[209] Stanley (2016: 269).

ambitious economic reforms."[210] As the PiS-led government not only failed to reverse liberalization in the areas of healthcare and corporatist interest mediation but also reduced taxes and public spending,[211] "it provoked protests of doctors, nurses, teachers, police officers, miners, and other public sector workers."[212] Indeed, if PiS deviated from neoliberal norms – by attacking the National Bank and violating the deficit reduction requirement set for entry in the Eurozone[213] – such transgressions were rather performative, changing little in regular Poles' lives. Unable or unwilling to take action on key economic questions between 2005 and 2007,[214] PiS instead prioritized measures on the parochial issues – nationalism, de-communization, and moral traditionalism (especially opposition to abortion) – popular in Poland B.[215] Yet, as this contributed to even more government disfunction amid serious confrontations with both civil society and the Constitutional Tribunal,[216] PiS was ultimately forced out of office prematurely, having developed, as its own politicians complained, a reputation for controversy and incompetence.[217]

The immediate electoral result was dualistic. On the one hand, PiS lost the 2007 poll to PO by a large margin. On the other hand, however, it achieved its best parliamentary election result yet by hijacking the policy programs of its coalition partners. Having blended a nationalist and antidemocratic agenda with "a pro-labor and pro-social stance,"[218] PiS now became the "permanent home" of many of those who had previously supported the two radical parties.[219] As former SO and LPR voters rationalized, only PiS reflected these parties' preoccupation with both social values and solidarity with the poor.[220] Meanwhile, as it now openly contested liberal democracy, PiS became increasingly shunned by liberal voters[221] and mainstream parties.[222] Crucially, it was PiS's illiberal adaptation that politicized both cultural and economic questions and polarized the electorate,[223] thereby defining what was now becoming a persistent fault line in Polish politics – between "liberal" Poland A and "social-solidaristic" Poland B.[224] As it appeared to have reached what observers at the time erroneously saw as a limited electoral potential,[225] the party next spent the following two parliamentary terms leading the opposition

---

[210] Stanley (2016: 270).

[211] Several PiS politicians and activists argued that these tax reductions were at the time consistent with social justice objectives (Interviews POL-04; POL-08; POL-11; POL-22).

[212] Bohle and Greskovits (2012: 151); Stanley (2016: 267).

[213] Zubek (2008: 303–4).

[214] Interview POL-12.

[215] Interview POL-19.

[216] Stanley (2016: 269–70).

[217] Interviews POL-04; POL-13.

[218] Bohle and Greskovits (2012: 244).

[219] 44 and 26 percent, respectively, of those who in 2005 had supported LPR and SO, itself a recipient of many former SLD supporters (Pankowski 2010: 137).

[220] Interviews POL-03; POL-13.

[221] Pankowski (2010); Tworzecki (2019).

[222] Interview POL-07.

[223] Bill and Stanley (2020); Tworzecki (2019).

[224] Markowski (2006); Szczerbiak (2007).

[225] Interviews POL-24; POL-26; Markowski (2008).

to governments dominated by liberals. Yet, as this period also confirmed the seemingly irreversible decline of the Left amid the now undeniable importance of economic issues for regular Poles, PiS's uncontested hold over those desiring a more solidaristic Poland would facilitate yet another illiberal resurgence by the mid 2010s.

5.2.4 Illiberal Resurgence amid the Crisis of the Left

From a perspective focused on societal developments, Poland's 2007 election represented a turning point – not because it allowed liberal forces to success-fully unite[226] and thus temporarily deny PiS the opportunity to govern, but rather because it featured two developments that heralded PiS's future resurgence. First, with the electorates of all relevant parties exhibiting a preference for economically interventionist policies,[227] this was the first election in which economic, rather than cultural, questions clearly dominated the agenda.[228] Moreover, as the geographical dimension of the Poland A versus Poland B divide grew in salience,[229] the 2007 election was the first in a series of polls in which PiS overperformed relative to its overall national result not only in the country's South but also in the East. Indeed, PiS began to dominate electorally across Poland's East, where the social need for state interventionism was argu-ably greatest due to the inability of neoliberal measures – such as incentivizing foreign direct investment (FDI) inflows – to solve problems of poverty and persistent underdevelopment.[230]

In the years between 2007 and 2015, PiS consolidated and further expanded its hold on Poland B, understood as a broad concept borne out not only by historical divides but also by socioeconomic ones accelerated by the economic transition. (As one politician observed, "Poland A profited from the changing economy and Poland B lost out."[231]) An underlining reason behind this trend was the fact that although "more Poles felt themselves individually better off," the governing PO–PSL coalition's managerialist approach[232] ultimately proved insufficient in terms of solving persistent economic disparities. For example, while poverty and underdevelopment in rural areas – especially in eastern Poland's "belt of poor regions"[233] – remained significantly worse than in cities and the West,[234] the position of workers was becoming increasingly precari-ous as the country became a leader in part-time insecure contracts.[235] When the liberal-agrarian governing coalition announced new austerity measures, including raising the retirement age, abolishing early retirement privileges

[226] Stanley (2016).
[227] Markowski (2008: 1065).
[228] Gwiazda (2008: 762).
[229] Stanley (2015a: 284).
[230] Interviews POL-01; POL-09; POL-11; Bogumił (2009).

[231] Interview POL-25.
[232] Stanley (2023: 210).
[233] Ratazjac (2012).
[234] Rosner and Stanny (2017: 34); Żmija (2015); Żmija and Żmija (2014).
[235] Ost (2018: 114).

for some professions, and ending health insurance concessions to farmers, it immediately lost support among the majority of Poles.[236]

Second, while this situation might have been electorally beneficial for standard leftist parties in countries such as Czechia and Romania, as discussed in Chapter 6, Poland's SLD – having embraced neoliberal reformism and in freefall ever after its last tenure in government – was no longer attractive to the social groups that had previously elevated it to power. As the Left kept declining, even failing to enter parliament in 2015, PiS made overtures to leftist voters[237] and increasingly gained popularity among many of the economically vulnerable groups that had turned away from SLD after economic issues began gaining salience in the early 2000s. For example, if people with primary and vocational education, those over fifty years of age, pensioners, workers, and rural residents had predominantly voted for the Left in 2001,[238] by 2015 they disproportionately supported PiS.[239] Notably, these groups did not shift from SLD to PiS directly, as they also voted for other parties while Poland's new party system – now defined by the PO–PiS divide – was taking shape.[240] Yet, as PiS was the only party after SLD (in 2001) that managed to fuse all these groups in a single electoral coalition, the 2015 election represented the culmination of a political cycle that had begun with SLD's greatest electoral success and ended with its utter failure. With SDL – now perceived as socially leftist but economically rightist[241] – had proved increasingly unable to appeal to economically left-leaning social groups,[242] it was PiS, which even promised to implement SLD's welfare program,[243] that attracted them. Indeed, as some of its supporters explained in 2015, PiS was a "people's democratic," or de facto "leftist"[244] and "socialist," party "concerned with normal, ordinary people," and favoring domestic production, state ownership of utilities, and taxation in order to "give back to the people."[245]

Portraying itself as the party fighting on behalf of workers and against international corporations,[246] and now attracting Poles who believed that "the Washington Consensus was a big mistake,"[247] PiS won not only the presidency and a parliamentary majority in 2015 but also the following elections for parliament (in 2019) and president (in 2020). The key reason for these victories was the party's willingness to be more in tune than its competitors with the majority of Poles, specifically on economic questions. As perceived

---

[236] Rae (2016: 423); Stanley (2023: 209).

[237] Interview POL-27.

[238] Szczerbiak (2002: 52).

[239] Markowski (2016: 1317).

[240] Szczerbiak (2013).

[241] Interviews POL-01; POL-07.

[242] Szczerbiak (2013: 490; 2017: 421).

[243] Rosset (2011: 243).

[244] As one supporter explained, "people's democratic" was preferable to labels such as "leftist" and "socialist" due to the communist history (Interview POL-14). Indeed, PiS activists who reject such labels still describe the party as prioritizing the economically vulnerable (Interview POL-21) and criticize PO for having increased the retirement age (Interview POL-21).

[245] Interviews POL-17; POL-22; POL-23.

[246] Interview POL-19.

[247] Interview POL-25.

inequality remained extraordinarily high,[248] the public's preference for leftist economic policies had not changed since 2007, despite the generally favorable economy. By focusing on "bread and butter" issues – and concretely promising to reverse PO's unpopular policies on retirement and to introduce child benefits – in 2015 PiS attracted both older people sensitive to the retirement age question and many new younger voters prone to immigration due to subpar living conditions in the countryside.[249] Having once again returned to power, the party reversed the approach it had previously taken as an incumbent, now substantially increasing public spending. As its government implemented "leftist redistributive policies" – for example, a child benefits program especially favorable to poorer families, retirement age reduction, additional pensions and drug benefits for the elderly, construction of affordable housing, limitations of insecure short-term contracts, and an increase of the minimum hourly wage[250] – PiS effectively empowered "social groups that felt excluded from the post-1989 reforms."[251] Having fulfilled key 2015 election promises, the party then further improved its support among economically weaker social groups in the 2019 parliamentary election, attracting nearly two-thirds of those with primary education, rural inhabitants, and the oldest voters.[252]

In sum, PiS succeeded where the Left had not. As one of its former senators declared, "PiS is essentially socialist, and its program is a reaction to a situation where communists are capitalists."[253] Indeed, having failed to deliver socially sensitive policies to a broad electorate whose economic concerns had become prominent after a decade of the neoliberal consensus, Poland's ex-communist Left proved unable to draw the economically vulnerable after 2001. By making itself increasingly attractive to such social groups following its programmatic shift in the early 2000s, PiS ultimately consolidated its electoral hold on Poland B, understood both socioeconomically and geographically. Yet, even as the illiberal party expanded its electorate and attracted more support in western regions, this still did not translate into a substantial increase of the geographic extensiveness of its electoral coalition, as elaborated in Chapter 7. As PiS continued performing disproportionately better in the country's religious South and poor East – where, as one PiS activist put it, "most victims of the economic reforms live"[254] – Poland's divides persisted. These cleavages continued deepening as PiS confronted political, cultural, and economic liberalism after 2015.[255] While this latest illiberal challenge was more successful than the first due to the party's improved ability to control the parliamentary majority, it certainly originated in PiS's capacity to adapt – and thus exploit to its advantage the divides that had been activated during the postcommunist juncture.

[248] Tworzecki (2019: 114).
[249] Interviews POL-07; POL-09; POL-22.
[250] See Markowski (2020: 1516–7); Ost (2018); Toplišek (2020).
[251] Bill and Stanley (2020).

[252] Markowski (2020: 1520).
[253] Interview POL-18.
[254] Interview POL-17.
[255] Ost (2018).

5.3 CONCLUSION

Although the trajectories of Slovakia and Poland varied in significant ways, bait-and-switch junctures conditioned leftist parties' neoliberal embrace and vanishment, which in turn enabled the persistent electoral viability of illiberal forces in both countries. In Slovakia, the ex-communist Left collapsed soon after leading, as the de facto largest party in a reformist coalition, crucial market reforms that made economic issues most salient in political life. This volte-face triggered a reactive chain resulting in the long-term domination of a personalist party with antiestablishment origins that not only replaced the ex-communists but also, through a strategic illiberal adaptation, incorporated nationalist voters disgruntled with neoliberalism. In Poland, the trajectory of the Left was more complex, including electoral successes in the 1990s, when political-cultural divides were still central,[256] and a steady decline thereafter, when economic questions became dominant following a decade of the neoliberal consensus. Its decline might have taken some time and yet, having failed to lead the opposition to economic reforms during the bait-and-switch juncture under Wałęsa, Poland's Left remained associated with neoliberal policies over time – a serious liability when material concerns gained salience after 2001. While the link between the Left's electoral decline and illiberalism's viability here was more complex than in Slovakia – because Polish voters did not usually flow directly from SLD to PiS – the Left's decline still played a critical role. As seen, Poland's main populist project underwent, having begun as a centrist antiestablishment party, an illiberal adaptation precisely when the Left began to falter. It was this ideological pivot that ultimately helped PiS to disproportionately attract many of the vulnerable social groups that should have supported – and had, in fact, previously supported – the Left. In sum, although mainstream leftist parties in Slovakia and Poland declined at different speeds, their neoliberal drift and subsequent electoral failures were similarly exploited for electoral success by adaptive illiberals amid the rising salience of economic questions. Indeed, the most prominent illiberal parties of both countries strategically supplemented their original antiestablishment appeals with positions including not only cultural but also – and crucially – economic illiberalism.

Yet, while the legacies of bait-and-switch junctures culminated in high illiberal viability, path-dependent developments and outcomes in these two countries were not identical. If Slovakia's most successful illiberal project was embodied by a relatively moderate party, SMER, that dominated executive power for longer than a decade, its Polish counterpart, PiS, was less hegemonic yet more radical. Based on takeaways from the discussion in this chapter, these differences, too, can be traced back to developments during postcommunist

---

[256] Kitschelt et al. (1999: 223).

junctures. Whereas in Slovakia, market reforms during the juncture were enacted by a programmatic social democratic party with a nationalized electorate, in Poland it was the dynamics of polarization and radicalization, which originated during personalist Lech Wałęsa's bait-and-switch, that drove subsequent developments. In Slovakia, SMER mobilized an extensive electoral coalition with core support from the Left's former voters even before rising to power, built organizational capacity on the basis of this coalition, and provided popular public goods that reinforced its popularity over time. In more polarized Poland, by contrast, PiS mobilized a more segmented coalition around social groups that had previously supported Wałęsa, enjoying less cohesion while riding the wave of anti-systemic radicalism. Although these dynamics reversed after 2015 – with SMER losing ground and PiS overcoming some of its initial limitations – they nevertheless characterized the two countries for most of the 2000–20 period.

I return to these questions of varying illiberal tendencies in Chapters 7 and 8, where I analyze them more systematically and from a comparative perspective that also incorporates Latin American cases. Before doing so, however, I round off this part of the book by turning to a comparative assessment of path dependencies in the other two countries whose historical developments and key moments of neoliberal reform were discussed in Chapter 4. As I next show, postcommunist junctures left very different institutional legacies in Czechia and Romania than they did in Slovakia and Poland.

6

Divergent Legacies of Postcommunist Junctures

Czechia, Romania, and Beyond

Having traced political processes originating in bait-and-switch junctures, in this chapter I discuss developments shaped by opposite – that is, aligning – postcommunist junctures and engage in comparisons aimed at reassessing my theory vis-à-vis rival explanations of illiberal electoral viability. In Sections 6.1 and 6.2, I follow path dependencies in Czechia and Romania. Despite the many differences between these countries, political configurations during aligning junctures enabled standard leftist parties to differentiate themselves programmatically from rightist reformers in the long term. As a result of their persistent ability to distinguish themselves as moderators of neoliberalism, social democrats became the electorally strongest parties after junctures, consistently drawing economically vulnerable groups and thus limiting the viability of liberalism's challengers over time. Indeed, with an average vote share for illiberalism and post-neoliberal populist magnitude, respectively, four and three times lower than in Slovakia and Poland during the 2000–20 period, Czechia and Romania experienced very different postcommunist juncture legacies.

In Section 6.3, I analyze these differences from a comparative perspective that once again considers various demand and supply side factors, the legacies of long-distance history, and the possible relevance of the Right's positions on economic issues as well as of the Left's stances on social issues. As the comparative analysis shows, it was leftist parties' long-term positioning on economic questions, which sooner or later gained salience under neoliberalism, that mattered most in terms of illiberal viability. As path-dependent developments on the Left both affected antiestablishment parties' adaptive strategies and were more the product of relatively recent contingencies than of longue durée history, postcommunist junctures shaped probabilistic illiberal outcomes during the first two twenty-first century decades in Eastern Europe.

6.1 CZECHIA

Although two leftist parties competed in postcommunist Czechia – the Communist Party of Bohemia and Moravia (KSČM) and the Czech Social Democratic Party (ČSSD) – the following discussion focuses on ČSSD. The reasons for this have to do with the nature of these parties and the trajectories of electoral support for them. Support for KSČM – which is sometimes classified as unorthodox, protest, or populist – remained both limited and stable over time. Because average support for the Communists was virtually identical during the aftermath period (13–14 percent) to what it had been in 1990 and 1992, the postcommunist juncture (1992–96) did not affect KSČM's electoral trajectory – a reason why this party is less relevant for the following analysis, regardless of whether it is understood as leftist or illiberal.[1] The opposite is true regarding ČSSD, Czechia's conventionally leftist party. Indeed, having risen from obscurity to become the dominant player on the Left during the juncture, as discussed in Chapter 4, the Social Democrats ended up representing the bulk – or two-thirds – of the overall leftist vote share in the aftermath period. As this more electorally significant and mainstream leftist party experienced important electoral changes over time, it is far more relevant for the analysis of the relationship between postcommunist junctures and illiberal electoral outcomes.

Having distinguished itself as a "protest opposition party" during the juncture, ČSSD quadrupled its electoral support between 1992 and 1996, when it attracted more than a quarter of all voters after campaigning on "traditional social democratic issues such as solidarity, fairness, and the social dimension."[2] However, the Social Democrats' sudden popularity did not correspond to a shift in the general left-right orientation of the electorate. Rather, it reflected the crystallization of a "truly class-based political struggle," which largely aligned collective and material interests based on social class with political partisanship. Indeed, for the first time in postcommunist Czechia, workers and nonroutine manual personnel became significantly more likely to vote for leftist parties, especially ČSSD, whereas professionals and the self-employed tended to support rightist parties, particularly the Civic Democratic Party (ODS).[3] As the Left and Right developed opposite reputations regarding egalitarianism

---

[1] Even if it can be argued that illiberalism was mostly channeled via KSČM, the magnitude of illiberal outcomes in Czechia would still be twice lower than in Slovakia and Poland. Thus, if KSČM were coded as illiberal and post-neoliberal populist rather than as a leftist party of secondary significance, Czechia would rank tenth on illiberalism (with a 21.3 percent average illiberal vote share, or more than twice lower than in Slovakia and

Poland, and below the regional mean) and seventh on post-neoliberal populist magnitude (with an average score representing the regional mean) out of the fifteen countries discussed in the first three chapters. See Figure 1.1 in Chapter 1 for the relevant rankings.

[2] Fitzmaurice (1996: 576). Also, Kopeček and Pšeja (2008).

[3] Matějů and Řeháková (1997).

through state intervention and welfare during the years of Vaclav Klaus' government, the postcommunist juncture had an aligning effect on the relationship between social class and party choice.

Despite ČSSD's strong electoral performance in 1996, the rightist coalition led by ODS remained in power for two more years, this time forming a minority government, once again under Prime Minister Klaus. Although the cabinet was approved with the help of "two renegade deputies elected on the Social Democratic ticket," ČSSD still distanced itself from the Right. For example, when Klaus' new government, now dealing with a balance of payments and exchange rate crisis, introduced budgetary spending cuts in 1997,[4] ČSSD voiced opposition and even expelled the two renegades.[5] And after Klaus' government collapsed amid corruption scandals in late 1997, the Social Democrats still demanded a halt to the privatization pursued by Josef Tošovský's right-leaning caretaker cabinet.[6] Having also campaigned by continuing their radical criticism of the ODS program,[7] they won the early 1998 election, despite their own financial scandals. Indeed, the Social Democrats not only "repeated the pattern from the previous election" by mobilizing the pool of "stable working-class voters," but also drew transformation "losers" from the economically devastated North, who had previously supported Miroslav Sládek's extreme right Republicans.[8] By increasing its support by six points relative to the previous election – to nearly a third of the electorate in 1998 – ČSSD effectively destroyed the electoral base of Czechia's most successful illiberal party of the first two postcommunist decades, ending the parliamentary representation the Republicans had achieved in the two prior elections.[9]

Having won in 1998 but unable to construct a majority government, ČSSD formed a minority single-party cabinet led by Miloš Zeman and "tolerated" by ODS in exchange for electoral reforms.[10] Despite this opposition agreement, reached in a context of a deteriorating economy,[11] the Social Democrats, now in power for the first time, did not follow the standard neoliberal script. In fact, they challenged the independence of the Central Bank, whose restrictive policies they considered responsible for the weak recovery after the 1997 crisis,[12] and, pressured by the party's leftist faction, avoided the fiscal adjustment programs required for fast-track entry into the Eurozone.[13] They also initiated an economic policy shift including "better regulation of financial markets," improved social policy programs, and a new industrial policy that renationalized large enterprises.[14] In the

---

[4] Orenstein (2001: 88–91).
[5] Kopeček and Pšeja (2008: 328).
[6] Kopecký and Mudde (1999: 416).
[7] Plecitá-Vlachová and Stegmaier (2003: 776).
[8] Kopecký and Mudde (1999: 419).
[9] The Republicans gained 6 percent of the vote in 1992, 8 percent in 1996, 3.9 percent in 1998, and less than 1 percent in elections thereafter.
[10] Kopeček and Pšeja (2008).
[11] Kopecký and Mudde (1999: 416).
[12] Myant (2003: 111–2); Orenstein (2001: 90).
[13] Bohle and Greskovits (2012: 174–5).
[14] Orenstein (2001: 93–4).

lead-up to the 2002 election, ČSSD not only "promised to build an extensive welfare state and increase wages" but also clearly distanced itself from the opposition agreement.[15] As a result, and despite the weakness of its minority government, the party maintained stable electoral support between 1998 (32.3 percent) and 2002 (30.2 percent).

Although the 2002 election results suggested the possibility of forming an entirely leftist government based on the fact that the programmatically over-lapping Social Democrats and Communists had together drawn nearly half of the electorate and gained most parliamentary seats, ČSSD's new leader, Vladimír Špidla, chose to form a government with the Christian Democrats (KDU-ČSL) and the liberal Freedom Union – Democratic Union (US-DEU). Yet, pressured by ČSSD's leftist faction, which openly sought cooperation with the Communists, and amid the popular rejection of Špidla's coalition with the center-right – as reflected in ČSSD's disappointing result in the 2004 European Parliament election[16] – Špidla was quickly forced to step down.[17] After the next party chairman and premier, Stanislav Gross, also resigned in short order amid corruption scandals, in 2005 ČSSD appointed Jiří Paroubek as the head of both the party and the government. Although Paroubek, a formerly staunch anti-communist, renewed the governing coalition originally formed in 2002, he in fact actively cooperated with the Communists in parliament, passing laws that stalled the privatization of large hospitals and "significantly strengthened the position of employees and trade unions."[18]

Paroubek's leftist realignment paid off. Not only was he elected ČSSD chairman with 90 percent of party delegates supporting him at the 2006 party congress, but the Social Democrats once again received nearly a third of all votes (32.2 percent) in the 2006 parliamentary election. Although ODS was the winner, this result was an impressive feat for the Left, especially given both ČSSD's recent fall from grace under Špidla's and Gross' stewardship and the party's implication in yet another major scandal just days before the election. Notably, it was the ability to once again draw contrast with the Right that helped recover ČSSD's popularity. For example, if during the campaign ODS proposed the flattening or abolition of taxes, the reduction of state bureaucracy and welfare, and the further privatization of enterprises, the Social Democrats defended social welfare and promised childbirth benefits.[19] As a result, they even attracted voters who had supported the Communists in 2002.[20]

During the next four years, the Social Democrats once again stood in firm opposition to the Right, which eventually formed a coalition government led

---

[15] Kopeček and Pšeja (2008: 330).
[16] ČSSD received only 8.8 percent, while the Communists gained 20.3 percent.
[17] Kopeček and Pšeja (2008).

[18] Havlík and Voda (2018: 176); Kopeček and Pšeja (2008: 332–3).
[19] Plecitá-Vlachová and Stegmaier (2008).
[20] Kopeček and Pšeja (2008: 334).

by Mirek Topolánek.[21] First, ČSSD successfully undermined the prospects of any ODS-led government for more than half a year after the 2006 election and then expelled a deputy Topolánek had recruited for the confidence vote enabling the cabinet's inauguration in early 2007.[22] Second, in just two years ČSSD initiated five votes of no confidence against the right-leaning government, with the final of these ending its tenure and replacing it with a caretaker cabinet led by Jan Fisher (2009–10).[23] Third, ČSSD also distinguished itself from the Right in the lead-up to the 2010 election, which was held as the country was dealing with the effects of the Great Recession – namely, still rising unemployment after negative GDP growth in the previous year. For instance, if ODS proposed "reducing expenses through cuts in unemployment and pension benefits," "ČSSD advocated for increasing revenues in order to protect social programs."[24]

The 2010 election destabilized the party system as over a quarter of voters, wary of the economic and political crises that had by then engulfed Czechia,[25] turned to two new parties – TOP 09 and Public Affairs (VV) – that would provide backing for a center-right government under new ODS leader Petr Nečas. Although it still came out on top with 22 percent electoral support, ČSSD once again went into opposition, from where it critiqued the cuts in welfare and employment benefits, pension privatization, and value added tax hikes that the center-right government enacted as anti-recession measures. Because austerity led to the immediate erosion of public support for the government, when a new corruption scandal broke, the already unpopular Nečas had little choice but to resign.[26] With a snap election set in 2013, the Social Democrats campaigned by highlighting not only anti-corruption messaging but also the need for more effective regulation and social benefits provision,[27] as well as higher taxes for businesses and high-income earners, minimum wage increases, and inflation-indexed pensions, among other prosocial measures. While the political scene continued shifting dramatically – with two new parties, ANO and Dawn, again drawing over a quarter of the electorate and with the main party of the Right (ODS) collapsing to under 8 percent electoral support – ČSSD still came out on top in the 2013 election, with 20.5 percent support. As a plurality of voters perceived it as the party best able to solve economic problems,[28] the Social Democrats, like the anti-neoliberal Communists, experienced electoral stability amid the generalized party system flux between 2010 and 2013.

Led by a new Prime Minister, Bohuslav Sobotka, the Social Democrats then collaborated with the Right – and finally collapsed as a result. First, having formed a coalition government with billionaire Andrej Babiš's ANO and

---

[21] The government was led by ODS and included the Christian Democrats and the Greens.
[22] Plecitá-Vlachová and Stegmaier (2008: 183).
[23] Stegmaier and Vlachová (2011).

[24] Stegmaier and Vlachová (2011).
[25] Kriesi and Pappas (2015).
[26] Stegmaier and Linek (2014).
[27] Stegmaier and Linek (2014).
[28] Havlík and Voda (2018: 175).

having quickly approved accession to the EU fiscal pact requiring strict budgetary constraints,[29] Sobotka presided over the lowest unemployment and some of the strongest growth rates seen in postcommunist Czechia. Yet, as growing polarization within the government – mostly due to Finance Minister Babiš's instrumentalization of unlimited resources and his media empire in a context of weak campaign finance and parliamentary oversight – undermined democratic accountability after 2013,[30] the Social Democrats were unable to capitalize on the government's successes. When ČSSD finally collapsed to 7.3 percent of the vote in the 2017 parliamentary election, the by-now illiberal ANO and Freedom and Direct Democracy (SPD) drew a combined 40.2 percent. While the more successful of these parties, ANO, "practically cannibalized the left side of the political spectrum,"[31] they both attracted voters from the same peripheral and socioeconomically disadvantaged regions that had previously formed the main support base of Czechia's Left.[32]

Crucially, although antiestablishment parties had risen in prior parliamentary elections, illiberalism only surged in 2017, when the Social Democrats finally collapsed. Indeed, while TOP 09, VV, ANO, and Dawn had captured considerable electoral shares in 2010 and 2013, when the Social Democrats had still been the strongest party, they had done so without taking up leftist positions on the economy. Whereas TOP 09 was an explicitly center-right party, VV and ANO adopted centrist and ambivalent positions regarding the state's role in the economy before 2017.[33] Meanwhile, as the radical right Dawn and SPD, both led by Tomio Okamura and neither capturing a significant vote share,[34] were the only antiestablishment parties to mobilize around immigration, economic issues remained central even after the 2015 refugee crisis.[35] It was for this reason that, as the Left finally declined, both Babiš and Okamura repositioned their personalist parties from the economic right in 2013 to the left by 2017 – and thus improved their electoral results specifically by promising universalist and protectionist policies.[36] If in 2017 ANO attracted predominantly former ČSSD voters, SPD took over many former supporters of the Communists, who also declined.[37] Moreover, while ANO and SPD signaled the upsurge of Czech illiberalism and post-neoliberal populism in 2017,[38] the rise

---

[29] Guasti and Mansfeldová (2018: 77).
[30] Guasti (2020).
[31] Guasti (2020: 478).
[32] Lysek et al. (2021).
[33] Havlík and Voda (2018).
[34] 6.9 percent in 2013 and 10.6 percent in 2017.
[35] Bláha et al. (2022).
[36] Sirovátka et al. (2023).
[37] Lysek et al. (2021).
[38] While in 2013 ANO was post-neoliberal populist, the otherwise far-right Dawn (later

called SPD) was neither illiberal (because the addition of its economic and social scores, as calculated based on positioning relative to country-specific and regional medians, produced a total score of less than three) nor post-neoliberal populist (because its economic score was zero). Both ANO and SPD were illiberal and post-neoliberal populist in 2017. See Appendix A for details on scoring.

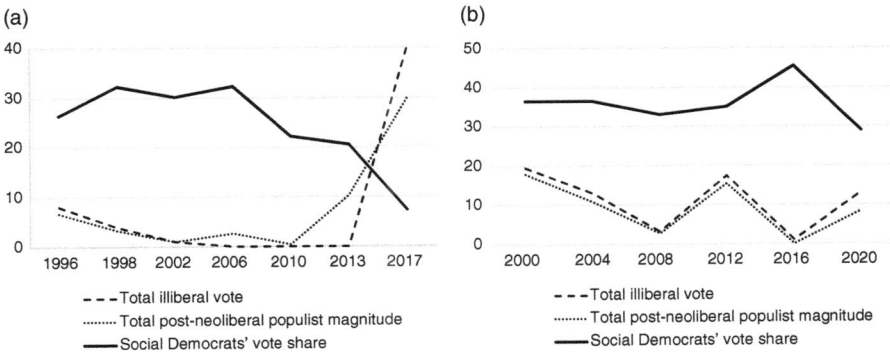

FIGURE 6.1 Illiberal outcomes and the social democrats' vote share in parliamentary elections after aligning junctures. (a) Czechia, (b) Romania

of the left-leaning Pirates – who also drew significant support from the Social Democrats' former voters[39] – contributed to the growth of post-neoliberal populism.[40] Finally, the electoral success of liberalism's challengers in the late 2010s was not limited to parliamentary elections. As incumbent president Miloš Zeman improved on his 2013 performance in the 2018 presidential election – by embracing economic and social illiberalism and with the support of both ANO and SPD – he, too, capitalized on the collapse of the Social Democrats, with whom he had previously competed for voters.[41]

The overall trends of illiberal outcomes at the ballot box and the Social Democrats' electoral performance after Czechia's aligning juncture are illustrated in Figure 6.1a. First, as ČSSD gained and maintained electoral strength in the first ten years after the juncture, it undermined support for critics of liberalism, particularly Sládek's Republicans, as explained earlier. While the Social Democrats' moderate decline after 2006 was followed by a modest rise of post-neoliberal populist magnitude in 2013 – when the not-yet fully illiberal ANO drew a limited share of ČSSD voters[42] – the Left's collapse in 2017 was accompanied by the dramatic upsurge of illiberal and post-neoliberal populist challengers. Crucially, although such parties rose only toward the end of the aftermath period, their viability had remained constrained in the long term.

In sum, having come out first four times and a close second twice in six parliamentary elections, the Social Democrats persisted as Czechia's most formidable party for two decades after the aligning juncture – despite corruption

---

[39] While half of the Pirates' 2017 supporters had previously abstained from voting, the plurality of their supporters who had previously voted came from ČSSD. See Pink and Folvarčný (2020: 188).

[40] Whereas I categorize ANO and SPD as both illiberal and post-neoliberal populist in 2017, the Pirates belong only to the latter category.

[41] Pehe (2018); Rybář (2014).

[42] Maškarinec (2017).

problems, frequent changes in leadership, and relatively low membership.[43] Notably, the party's electoral trajectory after the peak of market reforms was the product of ideological pragmatism characterized by programmatic proximity to the otherwise isolated Communists.[44] Unlike their counterparts in Slovakia and Poland, for whom pragmatism had the opposite meaning – namely, an embrace of market reformism[45] – Czechia's Social Democrats managed to credibly maintain their leftist positioning on economic issues, which differentiated them from the Right both during and after the aligning juncture. As a result, they were able to sustain relative popularity over multiple election cycles – and keep antiestablishment illiberals at bay for most of the aftermath period.

6.2 ROMANIA

If Romania's Left had entered the postcommunist juncture (1996–2000) as the leader of the parliamentary opposition after gaining just over a fifth of the overall vote in the 1996 parliamentary election, it exited it as a party of considerable – and consistent – electoral prowess. Indeed, the Social Democrats (or the electoral coalitions they led) won a plurality of the popular vote in every single parliamentary election after the juncture and led governments for half of the period between 2000 and 2020. Positioning themselves as clear opponents of market radicalism during election campaigns and governing by moderating neoliberalism, Romania's ex-communist Left steadily distinguished itself from the Right and routinely gained the support of over a third (34.4 percent on average) of the electorate. As the country's most successful party, the Social Democrats significantly limited opportunities for antiestablishment challengers of liberalism in the first two decades of the twenty-first century.

The story of the Left's long-term electoral success in Romania begins with the positioning of Ion Iliescu's party as a clear opponent of rightist reformers during the aligning juncture. This programmatic differentiation, in turn, lent credibility to the ex-communists' 2000 election campaign, during which they condemned the reforms implemented during the juncture[46] as "aggressive, or wild, liberalism," portrayed transnational capitalists as enemies of Romanian workers, promised to reverse austerity and slow down privatization, and called for a dialogue between the government and trade unions as a solution to the difficult economic situation.[47] Indeed, as the Left's "socially sensitive" approach to economic reform attracted a wide spectrum of pro-democratic constituents, its collectivist appeal proved significantly more popular than the individualist vision of market liberals in the 2000 election[48] – to the point where Iliescu's

---

[43] Bakke and Sitter (2021).
[44] See Kopeček and Pšeja (2008).
[45] See Grzymała-Busse (2002); Tavits and Letki (2009).

[46] Mungiu-Pippidi (2001).
[47] Popescu (2003); Stevenson Murer (2002).
[48] Kitschelt (2002); Mungiu-Pippidi (2001); Stevenson Murer (2002).

party did not even have to resort to the nationalism it had opportunistically exploited in the 1990s.[49]

Once again in power from 2000 to 2004, the ex-communists continued to distinguish themselves as credible leftists able to draw supporters attracted to both social democracy and communism. They did so both by absorbing smaller leftist parties and by enacting policies curtailing neoliberalism. First, if their 2001 fusion with the pre-communist Romanian Social Democratic Party (PSDR) licensed them to claim for themselves the historical heritage of Romanian social democracy,[50] their 2003 incorporation of the openly anti-market Socialist Party of Labor (PSM), which claimed links to the communist regime, enabled the ex-communists – now called the Social Democratic Party (PSD) – to attract voters nostalgic for communism.[51] Second, as the leader of the governing coalition between 2000 and 2004, PSD, now under the leadership of Adrian Năstase, slowed down market reforms and limited cooperation with the IMF, thus delivering on its 2000 campaign promises. Indeed, the PSD-led government curtailed privatization, raised the minimum and real wage,[52] and adopted a new and more progressive labor code that guaranteed social protections for workers.[53] In turn, these measures not only secured the loyalty of labor unions[54] but also brought PSD a considerable increase of support among voters preferring social democratic solutions.[55]

Having led the opposition between 2004 and 2008 – a period during which the rightist National Liberal Party (PNL)[56] presided over a "radicalized neoliberal regime" that adopted a 16 percent flat tax,[57] renewed efforts of privatization and deregulation (including of the labor market), and increased private indebtedness driven by import-driven consumption[58] – PSD once again distinguished itself as a leftist alternative in the lead-up to the 2008 parliamentary election. Now presided by Mircea Geoană, the party called for the redistribution of wealth, the doubling of the minimum wage, higher taxes for the wealthy, and more social protections for the marginalized.[59] Although following the election PSD did enter a grand coalition with Emil Boc's Democratic Liberal Party (PDL), a communist successor turned center-right after 2004,[60] it exited the Boc government after just ten months, once again shifting to the opposition after December 2009.[61] As the Great Recession exacerbated

---

[49] Pop-Eleches (2001; 2008); Popescu (2003).
[50] Gabor (2021); Gherghina (2014).
[51] Pop-Eleches (2008); Stevenson Murer (2002).
[52] By 10 percent and 4 percent, respectively.
[53] Ban (2016b: 90); Stevenson Murer (2002).
[54] Stevenson Murer (2002).
[55] From 57 percent in 2000 to 68 percent in 2004 (Pop-Eleches 2008).

[56] PNL was the largest surviving member of the coalition that had governed during the juncture.
[57] Appel and Orenstein (2016); Evans and Aligica (2008).
[58] Ban (2016b: 93–6).
[59] Downs (2009).
[60] Gherghina (2014); Pop-Eleches (2008).
[61] Borbáth (2018); Gabor (2021).

Romania's balance of payment crisis, leading to a GDP contraction that year, the Left simply "had no incentive to support a harsh fiscal adjustment."[62]

The austerity policies enacted by Boc's now explicitly rightist government after 2009 went above and beyond IMF bailout requirements.[63] The radical measures included an increase of the consumer value added tax (up to 24 percent), deep cuts in social spending, public sector employment, and salaries (by 25 percent), reduction of pensions and support benefits (by 15 percent), labor reforms weakening unions and collective bargaining, further privatization of government utilities, and an attempt to privatize healthcare. Such radicalism triggered intense anti-austerity protests and government collapse in early 2012.[64] It also gave the Social Democrats, now led by Victor Ponta, new opportunities to programmatically distance themselves from neoliberal radicals at a time when both politicians and journalists raised the ideological salience of "left versus right" discourses.[65]

Having harshly criticized the Right's austerity during the crisis,[66] PSD, once again in power between 2012 and 2015, shifted the economic policy paradigm by introducing counter-austerity measures meant to reduce poverty and inequality.[67] Specifically, the Social Democrats prioritized demand-side and neo-structuralist policies that included four waves of minimum wage increases, a reversal of the public sector wage cuts, a reduction of the value added tax on food, and the proposal of mortgage relief measures aimed at low- and medium-income households. Although the scale of this neo-developmentalist drift between 2012 and 2015 was admittedly limited – due to external and domestic constraints stemming from, respectively, Romania's commitment the EU's Stability and Growth Pact and the need to govern in a coalition with the National Liberals (2012–14) – PSD's tenure in government corresponded to a clear moderation of neoliberalism.[68] The party's left-leaning approach to economic governance was also reflected in its 2016 parliamentary election manifesto, which featured wage, financial, and sectoral policy proposals that signaled a commitment "to calibrate and even transgress neoliberalism."[69]

Returning to power in 2016 with a stunning 45.5 percent of the vote, PSD, now led by Liviu Dragnea, announced "national neo-developmentalist" plans to expand the state's involvement in industrial policy and to promote domestic firms. The Left then delivered demand-side policies between 2016 and 2019. For example, it increased minimum and public sector wages, ran current account and budget deficits, and cut the value added tax, with the commutative result being the improvement of labor's share of consumption relative to capital's share. Although the PSD-led government also continued neoliberal

[62] Ban (2016b: 222).

[63] Ban (2016b: 229–31).

[64] Bohle and Greskovits (2012); Borbáth (2018); King and Marian (2014).

[65] Gherghina (2014).

[66] Ban (2016a).

[67] Borbáth (2018); Gherghina (2015).

[68] Ban (2016b: 236–40).

[69] Ban et al. (2023).

practices – for example, by failing to reinstate collective bargaining and union rights and by further reducing the flat tax[70] – its overall approach to economic governance was both more socially sensitive and less dependent on foreign capital than the radical approach taken by the Right had been both during the Great Recession (2009–12) and before it (2004–8).[71] Having enacted generally left-leaning, if inconsistent, policies through the increase of government functions after 2016,[72] PSD achieved yet another, albeit more modest, electoral victory in 2000, despite experiencing serious problems due to corruption, popular protests, defections, and government instability.

In sum, after leading the parliamentary opposition during the postcommunist juncture, PSD distinguished itself as a credible skeptic (when in opposition) and moderator (when governing) of neoliberalism until the late 2010s. Although the Social Democrats' positions and policies were certainly far from radical, hardly ever crossing the limits of Romania's "disembedded neoliberal" model,[73] they nevertheless significantly constrained environmental opportunities for antiestablishment illiberal and post-neoliberal populist challengers,[74] whose electoral gains were either fleeting or rather limited during the 2000–20 period, as seen in Figure 6.1b. While neither the Left's vote share nor illiberal outcomes were static in the short term, Romania experienced general continuity over the long run. Since the Left was strong, electoral support for illiberal and post-neoliberal parties remained relatively weak and inconsistent – and certainly more so than in Slovakia and Poland. For example, Corneliu Vadim Tudor's anti-globalist Greater Romania Party (PRM)[75] declined steadily after its strong performance in the 2000 elections.[76] Other illiberal or post-neoliberal parties made even smaller ballot box gains in the 2010s, with only Dan Diaconescu's People's Party (PP-DD) achieving a double-digit election result once (14 percent in 2012), and the National Union for the Progress of Romania (UNPR), PRO Romania, and the Alliance of the Union of Romanians (AUR) drawing significantly less support.[77]

The key reason for this was PSD's ability to consistently attract a loyal core of rural, small-town, retired, less educated, and low-income Romanians,

---

[70] Ban et al. (2023); Feldman and Popa (2022).

[71] Ban (2016b; 2019); Feldman and Popa (2022).

[72] Feldman and Popa (2022).

[73] Ban (2016b); Bohle and Greskovits (2012).

[74] The five parties noted next fit both the illiberal and post-neoliberal populist categories, accounting for 85 percent of the overall illiberal vote and 100 percent of the post-neoliberal populist magnitude during the 2000–20 period. Electoral support for the ethnically based Democratic Alliance of Hungarians in Romania (UDMR), which only fits the illiberal category in 2016 and 2020 and had "its own, highly stable, electorate" (Gherghina and Jiglau 2011), constitutes just 15 percent of the overall illiberal vote during the 2000–20 period.

[75] Stevenson Murer (2002).

[76] PRM won 19.5 and 12.9 percent of the parliamentary election vote in 2000 and 2004, respectively, after which it continued to decline in every subsequent election, failing to gain representation after 2004.

[77] Respectively, 2.1 percent in 2012, 4.2 percent in 2020, and 9 percent in 2020.

many of whom were nostalgic for communism or lived in the country's poorer southern and eastern regions.[78] Indeed, with the sole exception of AUR, challengers of liberalism tended to target – rather unsuccessfully – precisely the kind of "economic and cultural losers of the transition" that constituted PSD's core base.[79] This was especially true for the two relatively more prominent anti-status quo parties – PRM, which in the early 2000s was disproportionately popular among older voters nostalgic for communism, industrial workers, the less educated, and the poor,[80] and PP-DD, which in 2012 found disproportionate support among rural constituents, the less educated, and those living in Romania's South and East.[81] Notably, while such voters chose antiestablishment alternatives in elections immediately following significant periods of neoliberal deepening – the postcommunist juncture and the Great Recession – they tended to be loyal to the Social Democrats in the long term. By consistently emphasizing the need for more just redistribution and less austerity – and delivering policies to that effect – PSD regularly drew many voters skeptical of economic liberalization.[82] As several waves of intense market reform weakened social protections in one of Europe's poorest countries,[83] where inequalities between rural and urban areas are "extreme," peasants, civil servants, and the low-income individuals typically supported the party that consistently advocated gradualism and state-led redistribution favoring the economically vulnerable.[84]

Importantly, PSD's ability to differentiate itself as a legitimate alternative to the Right does not mean that the party was genuinely progressive. Indeed, Romania's Social Democrats not only took on some economically liberal ideas, including on issues of government spending and taxation, and at times collaborated with rightist parties,[85] but also adopted socially conservative and nationalist positions aligned with those of electoral coalition partners.[86] While this may raise questions regarding the motivations of PSD's voters, there are two reasons why the Left's electoral stability had more to do with the party's relative positioning on economic, rather than social, issues. First, as political competition became increasingly focused on economic questions[87] – specifically, welfare and the state's role in the economy[88] – Romania's party system both stabilized and polarized around a clear economic left-right divide.[89] With the Right embracing a particularly radical neoliberal approach[90] during a period of increased

---

[78] Doiciar and Crețan (2021); Feșnic and Arneanu (2014); Mungiu-Pippidi (2001); Pickel (2007); Pop-Eleches (2008); Shafir (2001).

[79] Borbáth (2018: 138).

[80] Doiciar and Crețan (2021); Mungiu-Pippidi (2001); Pop-Eleches (2008); Sum (2010).

[81] Gherghina (2014).

[82] Ban (2016a); Pickel (2007: 100).

[83] Bohle and Greskovits (2012).

[84] Borbáth (2018); Mungiu-Pippidi (2001); Pickel (2007); Pop-Eleches (2008).

[85] Ban (2016b); Downs and Miller (2006); Gabor (2021); Gheorghiță (2023); Grzymała-Busse (2018); Pop-Eleches (2001); Tavits and Letki (2009); Tismaneanu and Kligman (2001).

[86] Ban (2016a); Borbáth (2018); Gabor (2021); Tismaneanu (2007).

[87] Borbáth (2018).

[88] Rohrschneider and Whitefield (2009).

[89] Gherghina (2014); Gherghina and Jiglau (2011); Pickel (2007).

[90] Ban (2016b).

popular skepticism of measures like the flat tax,[91] PSD clearly differentiated itself as Romania's "redistributive party."[92] As such, it consistently promoted spending on the retired, families in need of child benefits, government employees, and rural areas.[93] Second, although the Social Democrats adopted elements of social conservatism and nationalism, these were far from consistent,[94] with the party repeatedly distancing itself from xenophobia over the years.[95]

Overall, the main reasons for the Left's continued popularity, which in turn limited the appeal of liberalism's antiestablishment challengers, had to do with its rather nuanced, and often critical approach to neoliberalism – its calls for protectionism and egalitarianism[96] when in opposition and its willingness to moderate pro-market radicalism when in power. Of course, these were not the only reasons for the long-term electoral success of PSD, a party often associated with clientelist and corrupt practices.[97] Yet, as the Right benefited from targeted public spending no less than the Left[98] and as perceptions of PSD corruption and patronage declined,[99] such factors cannot explain why the Left did consistently well – and better than the Right – in elections during the 2000–20 period. Neither can popular dissatisfaction with Romania's poor economic performance, to which observers attributed PSD's electoral victory immediately after the postcommunist juncture.[100] Indeed, as the party's steady electoral support was independent of macroeconomic fluctuations, the ability to consistently differentiate itself from the Right accounted for both the Left's own long-term electoral success and the limited opportunities for liberalism's challengers in the two decades after the neoliberal juncture in Romania.

6.3 COMPARING THE CASES AND WEIGHING EXPLANATIONS

A comparison of the four Eastern European countries on which this chapter and Chapters 4 and 5 have focused not only confirms the hypothesized links between postcommunist junctures, the Left, and illiberalism but also affords an opportunity to reassess the central proposition relative to other explanations of illiberals' electoral viability. While I addressed rival accounts in Chapter 3 (and demonstrated empirically, in Appendix D, that they are unconvincing), the discussion in Part I of the book revolved around region-wide patterns. Next, I reconsider how alternative arguments measure up to the postcommunist juncture theory by comparing developments concretely in the countries analyzed in Part II.

---

[91] Gheorghiță (2023).
[92] Feldman and Popa (2022).
[93] Feldman and Popa (2022); Pickel (2007).
[94] Pop-Eleches (2010).
[95] Doiciar and Crețan (2021); Pop-Eleches (2001).
[96] Gherghina (2014).

[97] Ban (2016b); Volintiru and Stefan (2016).
[98] Pop-Eleches and Pop-Eleches (2012).
[99] Feldman and Popa (2022).
[100] Aligica (2001); Borbáth (2018); Mungiu-Poppidi (2001); Pop-Eleches (2001); Roper (2003).

6.3.1 Demand and Supply Side Factors

To begin, the intensity of liberalization and economic conditions do not account for divergent illiberal outcomes. All four countries continued adopting radical, or "avant-garde," market reforms throughout the 2000s. For example, while three of them implemented the flat tax, the only one that avoided it, Poland, also moved away from progressive taxation by "flattening" income taxes.[101] Because income inequality was highest in Romania and equally low in Slovakia and Czechia, while wealth inequality was highest in Poland yet lowest in Slovakia, inequality is unlikely to have affected long-term trends in illiberal outcomes. Another improbable culprit is inflation. Indeed, inflation, which declined significantly in Slovakia, Poland, and Romania in the early 2000s, was nearly as low, on average, in the two countries with highly viable illiberal outcomes (3.3 and 2.6 percent, respectively, in Slovakia and Poland) as it was in Czechia (2.3 percent), whereas it was highest in Romania (9.2 percent). As Slovakia's and Poland's average productivity growth (3.4 and 3.5 percent, respectively) – similar to that of Romania (3.7 percent) and somewhat higher than Czechia's (2.6 percent) – drove consistent employment gains in both countries during the 2000–20 period, such trends do not explain illiberal outcomes. Even if unemployment levels tended to be higher in the first two countries, trends in joblessness and illiberal voting actually diverged, with illiberalism and post-neoliberal populism gaining less ground when unemployment was at its highest (Slovakia in 2002; Poland in 2001) and more ground when joblessness was on the decline (e.g., Slovakia in 2006; Poland in 2005 and 2015).[102] Relatedly, while the Great Recession may have contributed to illiberal voting in Slovakia (in 2010 and 2012) and Romania (in 2012), the economic crisis was rather severe in Czechia,[103] where electoral support for illiberalism remained low in the subsequent two elections. Furthermore, as the Great Recession occurred after the most significant illiberal gains in Slovakia and was entirely avoided in Poland, it certainly did not drive trends in illiberal voting in either of these two countries.

The refugee influx does not explain persistent trends in ballot box support for illiberals either. Although it conditioned the electoral success of ethno-populist parties after 2015,[104] it did not produce a backlash in Romania, while in both Poland and Slovakia the main vehicles of illiberalism had already scored most of their impressive electoral victories well before it. Moreover, as support for Slovakia's SMER dropped considerably as soon as the party abandoned its hallmark bread-and-butter priorities,[105] yet still accounted for more than

---

[101] Appel and Orenstein (2018: 321–3).

[102] Outside of Central Europe, Albania, Croatia, and North Macedonia saw higher average unemployment in the 2000–20 period than Slovakia, Poland, Hungary, and Lithuania without, however, experiencing similar trends in illiberal voting.

[103] Kriesi and Pappas (2015).

[104] Buštíková and Guasti (2017); Vachudova (2020).

[105] Malová (2017); Marušiak (2021).

half (55 percent) of the overall illiberal vote share, xenophobia was certainly not the only factor explaining illiberal voting in Slovakia even at the height of the refugee influx. Other unsatisfactory explanations include perceptions of corruption, poor governance, and popular distrust of various institutions. For example, while perceived levels of public sector corruption were higher in Czechia than in Slovakia (and nearly as high as in Poland), Romania ranked lowest on government effectiveness between 2000 and 2020.[106] And while it is true that Romanians were most trusting of the EU, Czechs tended to be more distrustful than Slovaks and Poles of both the EU and national institutions.[107] As levels of distrust in such institutions were generally similar in the four countries during the 2000–20 period,[108] political demand does not account for long-term variation in illiberal voting. Neither does political supply. While the share and type of populist discourses in Czechia were comparable to those in Slovakia and Poland,[109] new antiestablishment parties that were especially reliant on leadership charisma were no fewer in Czechia and Romania than they were in Slovakia and Poland.[110] And although Slovakia and Poland saw more personalistic parties than Czechia, Romania had the largest number of such parties during the 2000–20 period.[111] In sum, the factors most commonly cited in the literature on illiberal voting do not explain developments in the case studies.

6.3.2 History Distant and Recent, Mainstream Parties Right and Left

Longue-durée history also fails to account for the persistent variation of illiberal voting in these four countries during the first two decades of the twenty-first century. Admittedly, the theory that Kitschelt and coauthors developed[112] does explain Czech and Romanian developments convincingly. For example, in Czechia the interlinked legacies of pre-communist formal rationalism and communist repression produced a stable postcommunist party system dominated by standard parties with clashing economic visions, which may have limited antiestablishment challengers with leftist economic positions. And in Romania, the dimension of competition, while also mostly focused on the economy, was somewhat more diffuse (and inclusive of social issues), as these authors correctly anticipated based on this country's patrimonial communist legacy. Thus, if Czech and Romanian Social Democrats prevented illiberal

---

[106] As documented in the World Bank's Government Effectiveness and Control of Corruption indices as well as Transparency International's Corruption Perceptions Index.

[107] Buštíková and Guasti (2017: 172).

[108] Slovaks were, on average, slightly less distrustful than citizens of Poland, Czechia, and Romania.

[109] Engler et al. (2019).

[110] See Haughton and Deegan-Krause (2020: 137). I operationalize charisma as higher than 0.8 based on these authors' scoring (on a scale from zero to one).

[111] See Lindberg et al. (2022). I count parties that achieved scores greater than two.

[112] Kitschelt (2002); Kitschelt et al. (1999).

challengers by remaining consistently popular, it is feasible that this popularity was due to the "correct" positioning of mainstream leftist parties based on pre-1989 histories.

And yet the longue-durée framework is less convincing regarding early twenty-first century developments in Slovakia and Poland. First, as shown by Kevin Deegan-Krause, the framework – which understates communist-era convergences between Slovakia and Czechia – is neither able to explain developments in Slovakia, especially those in the later periods of Kitschelt's sequential model, nor able to account for contemporary differences between Slovakia and Czechia.[113] Indeed, whether Slovakia's communist experience is described as rather patrimonial or national-accommodative,[114] the country's cleavage structure evolved between the 1990s and 2000s, when economic divides became central, as discussed in Chapter 5. As this shorter-term change, which indeed drove SMER's subsequent success, cannot be explained with reference to pre-communist or communist developments, longue-durée history did not shape early twenty-first century politics in Slovakia. Poland presents a similar challenge. While the legacy of national-accommodative communism there did produce a party system with a strong pro-market Left and dominated by sociocultural issues in the 1990s, as the theory focused on deep history correctly anticipated, this ended when economic issues gained salience by the early 2000s. As a result, PiS became a major party competing not just on social issues but also on economic ones – an unexpected outcome in Poland.

The reason why the nature of dominant cleavages underwent an evolution in Slovakia and Poland had, of course, much to do with the deepening of neoliberalism. While significant economic liberalization transformed cleavages in Poland slower after the juncture than in Slovakia – precisely due to the stronger legacy of national-accommodative communism in the first case – by the early 2000s the effects of continuous market reforms had altered the central axes of political competition in both countries, making cleavages there more similar to those in Czechia and Romania than had been the case in the 1990s. In all four countries, for example, the welfare dimension was most important by the early 2000s, as shown by Robert Rohrschneider and Stephen Whitefield. Indeed, as neoliberal reforms undermined welfare states throughout the region,[115] political competition in nearly all Eastern European party systems became mostly driven by issues of economic redistribution.[116]

This convergent trend, in turn, had implications in terms of illiberal outcomes because it created popular expectations of mainstream parties – expectations that could not always be fulfilled given the path-dependent legacies of postcommunist junctures. Notably, these legacies affected illiberal outcomes via dynamics on the Left much more than on the Right, as the quantitative

---

[113] Deegan-Krause (2006: 194–5).

[114] See Kitschelt (2002); Kitschelt et al. (1999).

[115] Bohle and Greskovits (2012).

[116] Rohrschneider and Whitefield (2009).

analysis in Chapter 3 showed and as the case studies confirmed. In Slovakia, as rightist parties performed well in elections before declining in 2012 (the Slovak Democratic and Christian Union) and 2016 (the Christian Democratic Movement), very few of their voters switched to SMER. While former voters of the larger and liberal (both economically and socially) Slovak Democratic and Christian Union had little reason to shift to the party's illiberal anti-pode, the smaller, economically liberal, and socially conservative Christian Democratic Movement remained stable for most of the period, losing less than 4 percent support in 2016. In Poland, deep polarization created similar disincentives for supporters of the mainstream Right, typically living in Poland A, to shift to illiberalism, which was predominantly associated with Poland B. Meanwhile, the consistent weakness of illiberalism in Czechia and Romania in the aftermath period was certainly not due to the strength of the mainstream Right. Indeed, in the 2000s and 2010s mainstream rightist parties in Czechia – namely, the Civic Democratic Party, the Civic Democratic Alliance, and the Christian Democrats – lost nearly 40 percent of the support they had enjoyed in the 1990s,[117] while their Romanian counterparts – the National Liberals and Christian Democrats – lost more than a quarter of their 1990s support.[118] As mainstream rightist parties dwindled most in Czechia and Romania, declined less in Slovakia, and gained strength Poland, electoral trajectories on the Right certainly did not shape illiberal voting in the long term.

If the rising importance of economic divides and distributive questions after postcommunist junctures made a difference in terms of illiberalism's electoral popularity, this was because it challenged the mainstream Left across the region to take up progressive – that is, statist and pro-distributive – positions on economic questions. Yet not all mainstream leftist parties were up to this challenge. Having failed to clearly differentiate themselves from rightist reformers during bait-and-switch junctures, Slovak and Polish Social Democrats proved unable to convince their constituencies that they could protect them from further neoliberal reforms – and lost electoral support as a result. As Chapter 5 showed, this inability then created environmental opportunities that adaptive populists consistently exploited with great electoral success in the first two decades of the twenty-first century. As discussed in the present chapter, the opposite dynamics unfolded in Czechia and Romania, where Social Democrats, having opposed rightist reformers during aligning junctures, were able to pro-grammatically distinguish themselves from the Right in the long term, thus

---

[117] From 45.2 percent, on average, in the 1990s to 27.6 percent, on average, in the 2000–20 period.

[118] From 26.5 percent, on average, in the 1990s to 19.7 percent, on average, in the 2000–20 period. Here, I only include the successors of the Romanian Democratic Convention

(CDR). Counting the Democratic Liberal Party (PDL), which used to be a center-left party, as part of the mainstream Right produces a similar result – that is, a 29 percent decline (from a 38 percent average in the 1990s to 27.7 percent average electoral support in the 2000–20 period).

sustaining considerable electoral support and limiting opportunities for illiberal adaptations and electoral success in the aftermath period. Crucially, while it is certainly true that transient electoral dynamics on the Left at times corresponded to short-term fluctuations of illiberal support in the opposite direction – as in Slovakia in 2002, Poland in 2005, Czechia in 2017, and Romania in 2016 and 2020 – this was not the case in most election cycles during the 2000–20 period. The case studies thus confirm what Chapter 3 (and Appendix D) demonstrated quantitatively. While short-term electoral fluctuations on the Left did play a role, it was the long-term trends engendered during postcommunist junctures that made the real difference in terms of political trajectories in Eastern Europe.

6.3.3 Economic and Social Positions after Postcommunist Junctures

What the case studies also conveyed is that constraining the forces of illiberalism required that the mainstream Left be able to take positions that were leftist in a relative, rather than absolute, sense. Although Czech and Romanian Social Democrats were hardly radicals and, as acknowledged above, did engage in some market reforms – as required by the European Commission, the European Central Bank, and the International Monetary Fund – they were nevertheless significantly more inclined than their rightist opponents to use the state for redistributive purposes. Indeed, a comparison of the average economic positions of the Left and Right in the four countries[119] confirms a key conclusion from the case studies. Thus, if Czechia's and Romania's Social Democrats were indeed significantly to the left of Poland's and Slovakia's Social Democrats[120] after postcommunist junctures, rightist parties varied far less in terms of their economic positioning in the four countries.[121] Thus, the degree of programmatic differentiation between the Left and Right had more to do with the economic positions of the former than with those of the latter. If the ideological divergence between mainstream leftist and rightist parties in Czechia and Romania tended to be greater, the reason for this was not that rightist parties

---

[119] Based on forty-eight Chapel Hill Expert Survey (CHES) scores, each being the average of all ratings assigned by experts participating in survey waves after post-communist junctures. See Bakker et al. (2015); Polk et al. (2017).

[120] According to the CHES data (scaled from zero to ten), the Left's average positioning on economic issues during the 2000–20 period was as follows. To the left relative to country medians – 2.5 points in Czechia, 3 points in Romania, and 0.1 points in Poland; to the left relative to regional medians – 2 points in Czechia, 1.8 points in Romania, 0.9 points in Poland. No expert survey data are available for the Slovak Party of the Democratic Left, which collapsed in 2002, but that party, like Poland's SLD, was unquestionably pro-market. See Fisher (2002); Grzymała-Busse (2002).

[121] For example, according to the CHES data (scaled from zero to ten), the Right's average positioning on economic issues was between 2 and 2.2 points to the right of the regional median in all four countries during the 2000–20 period.

there were any more neoliberal than their Polish and Slovak counterparts. The key reason, rather, was the relative positioning of the mainstream Left on economic issues. While they stayed clear of the ideological fringes,[122] Czech and Romanian Social Democrats nevertheless were able to distance themselves from the Right on the economic questions that sooner or later came to dominate national agendas after postcommunist junctures.

Finally, it can be argued that it was leftist parties' positioning on social, rather than economic, issues that constrained the electoral viability of liberalism's challengers in Romania and Czechia. Indeed, it is true that both Romania's Social Democrats and Czechia's Communists took positions that were not only economically leftist but also socially conservative, as seen, for instance, in the hardening of their anti-immigration stances following the refugee crisis.[123] While these parties' social conservatism likely played a marginal role in constraining new illiberal alternatives, two considerations suggest that their economic stances played the larger role. First, in both cases, these parties' social conservatism was less intense and salient than their economic leftism. As Czechia's Communists and Romania's Social Democrats were much further to the left on economic issues[124] than they were to the right on social matters,[125] and as economic issues were more salient than social ones for both parties (and countries),[126] these parties were consistently more economically "leftist" than socially conservative.

Second, although Czechia's Communists (gaining 12.4 percent of the vote, on average, after the juncture) were nearly three times smaller than Romania's Social Democrats (supported by over a third of the electorate, on average, in the aftermath period), challengers of liberalism were certainly not any more viable in Czechia than in Romania.[127] Crucially, the more electorally successful leftist party in Czechia – the Social Democrats (with an average 24 percent of the vote in the aftermath period) – consistently took economically progressive stances while veering clear of socially conservative ones.[128] And

---

[122] Both were well to the right of the Czech Communists.

[123] See the 2014 and 2019 waves of the Chapel Hill Expert Survey.

[124] Respectively, 4.4 and 3.0 points to the left of the Czech and Romanian medians. The corresponding distances from the regional median are 3.9 and 1.8. Based on data from the Chapel Hill Expert Survey. See Bakker et al. (2015); Polk et al. (2017).

[125] Respectively, 2.3 and 1.2 points to the right of the Czech and Romanian medians. The corresponding distances from the regional median are 1.4 and 1.0.

[126] As documented in the Chapel Hill Expert Survey. See Bakker et al. (2015); Polk et al. (2017).

[127] As a reminder, even if Czech Communists were to be counted not as a leftist party, but rather as an antiestablishment, illiberal, and post-neoliberal populist one, illiberal outcomes in Czechia would still be much less viable than in Slovakia and Poland. See note 1 in this chapter for more information.

[128] ČSSD scores to the left (that is, on the liberal side) of both the country and regional medians in the Chapel Hill Expert Survey waves during the 2000–20 period. Being split between conservative and liberal camps, ČSSD was most often liberal, at most centrist, and never truly conservative on social issues such as immigration or sexual minority rights.

in Romania, although the Social Democrats increasingly turned to traditionalist, authoritarian, and nationalist positions after 2010, they actually spent the first half of the aftermath period – when the viability of illiberal outcomes lessened – as a fairly moderate party on social questions.[129] Overall, because the social conservatism of Czechia's and Romania's leftist parties was always less intense and salient than their positions critical of neoliberalism, it was not the key reason why the electorally strong Left limited the viability of illiberalism in these two countries.

In the end, the key reason why social democratic parties constrained antiestablishment illiberalism in Czechia and Romania had to do with their sustained ability to take legitimately leftist economic positions – something that proved to be a great challenge for the ex-communists of Slovakia and Poland. As opposite types of postcommunist junctures left contrasting institutional legacies, the consolidation of neoliberalism – which either sustained (in Czechia) or raised (in Slovakia, Poland, and Romania) the salience of economic issues – corresponded to very different trajectories. Whereas the Left's systematic failure to differentiate itself from the neoliberal Right resulted in downward electoral trajectories in the aftermath of bait-and-switch junctures in Slovakia and Poland, the opposite processes unfolded in Czechia and Romania, where Social Democrats gained persistent popularity after voicing criticism of market reforms during aligning junctures. As these trajectories drove opposite trends in illiberal electoral outcomes – persistently viable in Slovakia and Poland and predominantly unviable in Czechia and Romania – the shadow of postcommunist junctures loomed large in these four countries.

6.3.4 Beyond the Four Cases

While I have examined how postcommunist junctures shaped divergent trajectories and outcomes in four countries, the insights from this chapter and Chapters 4 and 5 apply more broadly throughout Eastern Europe. First, postcommunist junctures of neoliberal deepening resulted in the growing salience of material divides across the region. Indeed, by the early 2000s, such divides were most dominant in the politics not only of Slovakia, Poland, Czechia, and Romania but also of Bulgaria, Estonia, Slovenia, Lithuania, and Moldova. Material issues were also salient elsewhere, structuring the second most significant political divide in Latvia and Hungary, and shaping the second and third most important cleavages in Ukraine.[130] And although different questions

---

[129] Their average TAN (traditional, authoritarian, and nationalist) positions on social issues were just less than 1 point (on a scale from zero to ten) to the right (that is, on the conservative side) of the country and regional medians in the 2002 and

2006 Chapel Hill Expert Survey waves and slightly to the left (that is, on the liberal side) of the country and regional medians in the 2010 survey wave.

[130] See Rohrschneider and Whitefield (2009). While the issue of welfare structured the

were more central in the Western Balkans, economic divides there either reinforced regional or political-social cleavages, as in, respectively, Albania and North Macedonia,[131] or were societally relevant despite insufficient political representation, as in Croatia.[132] In sum, while the nature and intensity of political conflicts across Eastern Europe varied, material questions generally gained salience after peak market reforms.

Second, this importance of material questions after postcommunist junctures was bad news for most mainstream parties. Although the mainstream Right tended, with few exceptions,[133] to lose steam across the region – most after aligning and least after bait-and-switch junctures – its electoral decline was generally not exploited for electoral success by liberalism's challengers, as shown in the quantitative analysis in Chapter 3. By contrast, such challengers tended to capitalize when the mainstream Left declined as a result specifically of adopting pro-market economic positions – a development least likely after aligning and most likely after bait-and-switch junctures.

Figure 6.2 categorizes the leading leftist party in each of the fifteen Eastern European countries analyzed in Chapter 3 by positions typically taken on economic and social issues during the 2000–20 period.[134] For each country, the figure also lists the variety of prior communist rule and type of postcommunist juncture experienced. To begin, neither the legacy of communist rule nor the type of postcommunist juncture appears to predict the Left's positioning on social issues. Leftist parties tended to be socially conservative in just four countries, all of which experienced patrimonial communism and three of which underwent aligning junctures. Yet, as these same legacies – of patrimonial communism and aligning junctures – also corresponded to many leftist parties adopting socially liberal positions, and as social liberalism was embraced by the Left quite widely across the region, historical experience – either distant or recent – did not affect the Left's positioning on social questions in the first two decades of the twenty-first century.

---

most important conflict in the first eight of these countries, the question of the balance between the market and the state was primary in Moldova. Conflicts over welfare were second most important in Latvia (where ethnicity was dominant) and Hungary (where nationalism was central), and third most important in Ukraine, where the role of the state versus the economy was the second most important issue (after democracy).

[131] Pickering (2009: 583–4); Ringdal and Starova (2010).

[132] Dolenec (2012).

[133] The exceptions were equally distributed across types of junctures: North Macedonia – aligning, Ukraine – ambiguous, and Poland – bait-and-switch.

[134] Most countries have just one leftist party. The exceptions, with two such parties, are Czechia, Latvia, and Ukraine. Since I focus here on leading leftist parties, I consider Czechia's Social Democrats, Latvia's Social Democratic Party "Harmony," and Ukraine's Communists, and I exclude Czechia's Communists, Latvia's Social Democratic Workers' Party, and Ukraine's Socialists. These secondary leftist parties are, however, included in the analysis in Chapter 3 and Appendix D.

Social issues

Tendency in positioning	Rather liberal	Rather conservative
Rather leftist	Albania: P, aligning Czechia: BA, aligning Estonia: NA, ambiguous Latvia: NA, ambiguous Slovenia: NA, ambiguous	Bulgaria: P, aligning Romania: P, aligning Moldova: P, aligning Ukraine: P, ambiguous
Rather pro-market	North Macedonia: P, aligning Croatia: NA, ambiguous Hungary: NA, bait-and-switch Lithuania: NA, bait-and-switch Poland: NA, bait-and-switch Slovakia: P, bait-and-switch	

(Economic issues appears as a row label on the left spanning both data rows.)

FIGURE 6.2 General positioning on economic and social issues of major leftist parties, with variety of communism and type of postcommunist juncture, 2000–20 (1) Tendency in positioning is based on data from the Chapel Hill Expert Survey. Scoring: "Rather leftist" = more than one point to the left of the country and regional medians on economic issues; "Rather pro-market" = positions to the right of "Rather leftist"; Rather liberal" = to the left of the country and regional medians on social issues; "Rather conservative" = to the right of the country and regional medians on social issues. (2) Varieties of communism (BA = bureaucratic-authoritarian; P = patrimonial; NA = national-accommodative) are drawn from Kitschelt et al. (1999: 39).

The picture changes when we turn to positioning on economic questions. Here, communist legacies seem to matter more, as correctly anticipated by Kitschelt and coauthors.[135] On the one hand, a majority of countries (six out of eight) that had experienced either patrimonial or bureaucratic-authoritarian communism could be said to have had a "true" mainstream Left – that is, a mainstream leftist party subscribing to statist, welfarist, and pro-distributive (or, "rather leftist") positions. On the other hand, most of the countries (four out of seven) with a national-accommodative communist experience featured a rather pro-market Left. Although these patterns substantiate Kitschelt's longue-durée historical theory, there are several mainstream leftist parties that do not fit as comfortably – particularly those of North Macedonia, Estonia, Latvia, Slovenia, and Slovakia.[136] Especially because communist rule mixed national-accommodation and either patrimonialism or bureaucratic

---

[135] Kitschelt et al. (1999).

[136] Although the Estonian and Slovenian Social Democrats are more ambiguously "rather leftist" on economic issues than other parties in the top left box of Figure 6.2 (and could fit Kitschelt's framework

more comfortably if coded as "rather pro-market"), they were still well to the left of their Hungarian, Polish, and Lithuanian counterparts, according to the Chapel Hill Expert Survey data.

authoritarianism in a number of countries (including not only Estonia, Latvia, and Slovakia[137] but also Lithuania and Poland), the theory focused on longue-durée historical legacies, although powerful, does not necessarily explain the Left's positioning on economic issues after the 1990s.

The reason, as I have argued in this and the previous two chapters, is that as postcommunist junctures tended to unsettle prior historical legacies, they also shaped the long-term economic positioning of mainstream leftist parties. Indeed, with just two exceptions – in North Macedonia and Croatia – aligning and ambiguous junctures incentivized such parties to adopt rather progressive stances. The opposite was true regarding bait-and-switch junctures, after which the mainstream Left tended to be pro-market. In turn, these positions were associated with divergent electoral trajectories – and thus with varying likelihood of illiberal voting in the long run.

Indeed, the persistent electoral strength of mainstream leftist parties limited illiberal reactions not only in Czechia and Romania, as discussed earlier, but also in the other four countries that experienced aligning junctures – Bulgaria, Moldova, Albania, and North Macedonia. This is because the challengers of liberalism typically thrived on the economic left-of-center space. Where this space was firmly occupied – because mainstream leftist parties usually gained momentum after distinguishing themselves as critics of neoliberalism during the juncture – illiberal challengers could hardly prosper. Notably, while some of these leftist parties did adopt socially conservative positions similar to those seen in Romania (especially in Moldova but also, and less consistently, in Bulgaria), others (for example, in Albania and North Macedonia) were socially liberal. More relevant in terms of limiting illiberal outcomes were, once again, leftist parties' positions on economic questions. As these positions were consistently distinguishable from the Right's, the Left sustained high electoral support – and constrained opportunities for illiberal challengers in the process. (Within the group of countries that experienced aligning junctures, illiberal outcomes were most viable in Bulgaria – the only case where the Left, although still remaining rather strong in the aftermath period, experienced a decline relative to the pre-juncture period.[138])

While also taking generally left-leaning stances on economic questions, leftist parties adopted more ambivalent positions in the long term in the majority of countries that had experienced ambiguous junctures. For example, having failed to clearly distinguish themselves as opponents of rightist neoliberal

---

[137] It could be argued that these three cases fit the longue-durée framework comfortably precisely because of their mixed nature. The counterargument would be that coding other cases (Lithuania and Poland) as mixed would further complicate the explanation focused on long-distance legacies.

[138] Bulgaria's Socialists gained an average of 22.5 percent of the vote in parliamentary elections during the 2000–20 period, which represents a 10.4-point drop relative to the pre-juncture period. This average vote share in the aftermath period is still higher than the average vote shares of leftist parties in two-thirds of the countries that did not experience aligning junctures.

reformers during the juncture, Social Democrats in Croatia, Estonia, and Slovenia took somewhat less progressive positions on economic questions than leftist parties did in Albania, Bulgaria, Czechia, Moldova, and Romania. The result, of course, was relatively weaker performances at the ballot box, which, in turn, meant better electoral opportunities for liberalism's challengers during the 2000–20 period. Indeed, a wide range of antiestablishment parties – for example, Croatia's Party of Rights and Human Blockade, Estonia's Center Party, Slovenia's Positive Slovenia and Levica, Latvia's Union of Greens and Farmers, and Ukraine's Fatherland – achieved moderately strong electoral results by adopting the type of economic positions that allowed them to compete for left-of-center voters, many of whom were routinely available for mobilization amid the Left's middling electoral performances after ambiguous junctures. Tellingly, just within the group of countries that had experienced such junctures, illiberal outcomes were least viable where the Left was electorally strongest (in Croatia) and most viable where it was electorally weakest (in Estonia and Ukraine) in the aftermath period.

Finally, illiberal outcomes were highly viable not only in Slovakia and Poland but also in Lithuania and Hungary, where the mainstream Left dwindled sooner or later following its decidedly reformist turn on economic issues after bait-and-switch junctures. In Lithuania, the "increasingly pro-market stance" and gradual decline of the Left – a merger of the ex-communists, who had been in charge during the juncture, and historical social democrats – created openings for "populist parties to appeal to the disgruntled voters from economic peripheries and of lower socioeconomic statuses."[139] Indeed, the three most successful illiberal or post-neoliberal populist challengers – Order and Justice, the Farmers and Greens Union, and the New Union – attracted many struggling voters and transformation "losers," including former supporters of the Left, by usually positioning themselves left-of-center on economic questions, which were consistently most important for the majority of voters.[140] As Lithuanians tended to be more left-leaning and pro-distribution than the mainstream parties representing them,[141] the same strategy was also pursued by less prominent antiestablishment parties – such as Frontas, the Way of Courage, and the Center Party – Nationalists – which also contributed to Lithuania's persistently high scores on illiberalism and post-neoliberal populist magnitude. Finally, although the Left's decline was somewhat delayed in Hungary, there, too, public disillusionment with the radical austerity program (known as the Bokros package) that the Socialists implemented during the juncture "contributed to Fidesz's electoral victory and lent some credibility to Viktor Orbán's later claim that his policies were superior to the left alternative, even in terms of social welfare."[142] Additionally, as the Socialists continued pursuing austerity

---

[139] Gudžinskas (2020: 219).
[140] Duvold and Jurkynas (2013); Jurkynas (2009; 2014); Ramonaitė (2020).
[141] Duvold and Jurkynas (2013).
[142] Bohle and Greskovits (2012: 177).

well after the juncture, they lost much support in low-income groups, which, in turn, defected to the highly illiberal Jobbik.[143] Overall, the Left's electoral decline may have followed somewhat different trajectories and occurred at varying speeds, but its pro-market positioning in all countries that experienced bait-and-switch junctures ultimately produced legacies opposite to those seen after aligning junctures.

6.4 CONCLUSION

In this chapter, I have completed the analysis of postcommunist juncture legacies in four Eastern European countries by, first, tracing developments after aligning junctures and, second, assessing illiberal outcomes from a broader comparative perspective. In the first half of the chapter, I discussed path dependencies in the otherwise very different Czechia and Romania, where political configurations during aligning junctures shaped the mainstream Left's long-term ability to act as a legitimate alternative to rightist reformers, retain strong electoral support, and constrain electoral opportunities for liberalism's challengers over time. While key social democratic parties in these two countries – pre-communist in Czechia and ex-communist in Romania – were neither identical to one another nor free from the occasional dabbling in neoliberal policy, their common ability to consistently differentiate themselves from the Right – even if mostly in relative, rather than absolute, terms – signaled a continued commitment to the economically leftist principles of statism, welfare, and redistribution. Although policy pressures associated with external requirements and economic crisis necessarily limited the efficacy of these commitments, Czech and Romanian mainstream leftist parties "owned" the material issues of the day, thereby successfully retaining many economically vulnerable voters in the long term. While such constituencies at times shifted to illiberal alternatives, the mainstream Left, having sustained electoral preeminence after aligning junctures, effectively constrained the electoral viability of such alternatives throughout most of the 2000–20 period.

Having traced the legacies of postcommunist junctures in Czechia and Romania, in the second half of the chapter I once again assessed alternative explanations of illiberal voting, this time by directly comparing the four cases in Eastern Europe. After reconsidering demand and supply side factors, as well as the legacies of longue-durée history, I demonstrated that postcommunist junctures constitute the strongest explanation of illiberal outcomes – because they shaped the positioning of the Left on the economic issues that neoliberal reforms made highly salient throughout the region. Indeed, as leftist parties' persistent stances on economic, rather than social, issues had long-term

---

[143] Lindner et al. (2021).

electoral consequences, postcommunist junctures generally left divergent legacies in the first two twenty-first century decades across Eastern Europe.

Finally, this chapter, like the previous one, showed that while the political configurations associated with early market reforms certainly shaped illiberal outcomes in the long term, they did not determine them. Indeed, although varying patterns generally defined the aftermath period, some countries – particularly Czechia and Slovakia – exhibited important fluctuations, especially toward the end of it. While it is possible that such developments signaled the conclusion of the historical cycle that began in the 1990s, it is also true that, as the critical juncture framework integrates human choice and fallibility, the explanation it can offer can only be probabilistic. Thus, while important choices made by Czechia's Bohuslav Sobotka in 2013 and Slovakia's Robert Fico in 2015–16 may in retrospect have been the "wrong" ones, key actors generally adapted in predictable ways to the environments shaped by postcommunist junctures. As political agents' adaptability to the path-dependent legacies of critical periods of neoliberal deepening was not unique to Eastern Europe, in the next two chapters I discuss intriguing parallels with developments in Latin America.

PART III

A CROSS-REGIONAL VIEW

7

Expanding the Analytical Framework

Dominant and Contestatory Varieties of Illiberalism in Eastern Europe and Latin America

If the critical juncture framework can explain illiberal voting in Eastern Europe in the early twenty-first century, can it also be deployed for making sense of differences between illiberal incumbents? As the cases explored in Chapter 5 showed, not all parties that rise to power on platforms combining economic statism and cultural conservatism govern identically. On the one hand, while some illiberal incumbents successfully dominate political systems for extended periods by winning multiple consecutive elections, as in Slovakia, others fail to do so, as in Poland. On the other hand, if Poland's prominent illiberals governed by contesting – and eroding – liberal democracy, Slovakia's were considerably more moderate, despite generally retaining their illiberal positioning on programmatic issues. As such differences are not adequately explained in the literature on illiberalism and populism, this chapter offers answers – by further elaborating the critical juncture framework and by justifying its cross-regional application.

I begin by drawing two lessons from the Slovak and Polish cases discussed earlier. The first is that contrary to conventional assumptions, illiberals' contestation of liberal democracy and their ability to be politically dominant are in fact empirically distinct phenomena. Second, I argue that these phenomena are best explained by unpacking the bait-and-switch junctures that generated illiberalism in the first place. By specifically focusing on two contingencies during junctures – (1) whether the political agent responsible for the bait-and-switch was a social democratic party or a polarizing personalist, and (2) whether the institutionalization of anti-neoliberal protest was viable or not – I develop, based on the Slovak and Polish experiences, a refined explanatory framework of path-dependent developments. As illiberal parties adapted to the political environments shaped by prior processes, the paths toward dominant illiberalism and contestatory illiberalism are best understood as legacies of concrete contingencies during prior junctures.

Having elaborated an explanation rooted in historical contingency, I then make the case for extending it to Latin America, where the populist reaction to neoliberalism, though ideologically very different, was for economic and political reasons generally parallel to that in Eastern Europe. Although scholarship has offered convincing accounts of region-wide patterns in Latin America, general frameworks have neither analyzed the contestatory character and dominant quality of illiberalism as two potentially separate dimensions in a case like Ecuador, nor accommodated an outlier like Peru, where populist moderation went hand in hand with failure to persist electorally. To address such lacunae, I make the case for tracing processes in Ecuador and Peru based on the explanatory framework derived from the Slovak and Polish experiences. I contend that as these four cases are comparable along key historical, regime, organizational, and ideological dimensions, they are crucial for a nuanced understanding of illiberal tendencies as phenomena with distinct roots in prior junctures. Concluding with a discussion of the insufficiency of standard explanations of illiberal tendencies, the chapter sets the stage for the comparative analysis of developments in Ecuador and Peru.

7.1 LESSONS FROM EASTERN EUROPE

As seen in Parts I and II of this book, illiberal outcomes after the period of most decisive neoliberal deepening in Eastern Europe are best understood as a post-neoliberal populist reaction with origins in postcommunist junctures. Specifically, when such junctures are characterized by bait-and-switch dynamics, high electoral support for illiberal parties persisted throughout the first two decades of the twenty-first century. However, while bait-and-switching during junctures explains the long-term electoral viability of subsequent populist critics of neoliberalism, it does not by itself illuminate two related but distinct questions – (1) whether such actors can become politically dominant over long periods, and (2) whether, once in power, they actually contest liberal democratic institutions.

7.1.1 Untangling the Concepts: The Different Illiberal Experiences of Slovakia and Poland

The scholarly literature has not shed much light on the above questions. The main reason for this is that authors often conflate illiberalism and populism with radicalism and even long-term domination. For example, if analysts of populism in the West have focused mostly on "populist radical right parties in Europe," the subject of Cas Mudde's influential book,[1] students of Latin America also saw as "radical" the left populism associated with the Hugo

---

[1] Mudde (2007).

Chávez-led pink tide in the early twenty-first century.[2] Accepting this link between populism and radicalism as a given, Takis Pappas, taking a cross-regional perspective, goes a step further and makes an argument about entrenchment in power. In his view, it is because of their radicalism that populist incumbents "display exceptionally strong electoral and political resilience" and "invariably establish an illiberal order."[3] The main reason for this, the argument goes, is charismatic leadership, which, when available, subsumes radicalism, undermines horizontal accountability, and leads to populist success.[4] Overall, if populism in power relies on charismatic leadership, it has a strong tendency toward both radicalism and long-term domination.

The supposed link between these concepts is indeed so strong that when populists moderate in power, they are typically considered to no longer be populist. Indeed, incumbency is seen as a major challenge for populists because it frequently compels them to moderate – due to either the logic of Downsian competition for the centrist voters often needed to win elections or governing responsibilities and coalition-building requirements.[5] Because they are suddenly forced to participate in "normal" institutional politics, the conventional wisdom holds, those who rise to power as populists but govern as moderates either fail because they break prior electoral promises or succeed by abandoning populism and illiberalism.[6]

To an extent, the theoretical affinity between populism and illiberalism, on the one hand, and radicalism, on the other, is a function of conceptualization. According to dominant "ideological" definitions, which view it either as a moralistic ideology[7] or as democratic illiberalism,[8] populism demands a radical break from the liberal status quo. There are two problems with this. First, and as shown by Daniele Albetrazzi and Duncan McDonnell, even if they are assumed to be ideological concepts, populism and illiberalism do not necessarily have to be radical, and indeed populists and illiberals in government can thrive while embracing moderation and without abandoning their populism and illiberalism.[9] Second, as explained by Kurt Weyland, because the term "radical" implies a "systematic assault on capitalist property relations" – which even Latin America's Bolivarian populists failed to deliver in the early twenty-first century – it does not reflect the ways in which populists actually govern.[10] For this reason, while I use the term "radical" generally when discussing smaller parties aspiring to subvert political and economic liberalism, I reserve Weyland's term "contestatory" for something more specific (and

---

[2] See Levitsky and Roberts (2011: 12, 19); Weyland (2009).
[3] Pappas (2019: 82).
[4] Pappas (2016b).
[5] Akkerman et al. (2016); Schwörer (2021); Tepe (2019).

[6] Canovan (1999); Heinisch (2003); Spáč and Havlík (2015).
[7] Mudde (2004).
[8] Pappas (2016a).
[9] Albertazzi and McDonnell (2015: 7, 26).
[10] Weyland (2010: 3).

approximating Pappas' notion).[11] Concretely, *contestatory illiberalism* seeks to concentrate power by altering the established political framework of liberal democracy, with the goal of undermining institutional protections of the opposition.[12] Crucially, however, contestatory illiberalism does not necessarily lead to entrenchment in power, as seen in Poland. Meanwhile, moderate illiberalism in power – under which attempts to undermine liberal democratic institutions are not predominant – can go hand in hand with long-term domination without the abandonment of illiberal policy positions, as seen in Slovakia. Overall, while Poland and Slovakia consistently saw high electoral support for illiberals after bait-and-switch junctures, as discussed previously, their experiences with illiberalism in power were far from identical.

To begin, whereas the main illiberal party dominated politics in Slovakia during the 2000–20 period, the same did not happen in Poland. Although Slovakia's SMER did not win all national elections during this period,[13] it won four consecutive parliamentary elections (2006, 2010, 2012, and 2016), while its candidates were top vote getters in the first round of two presidential elections (2009 and 2014) and second round of one presidential election (2009). Meanwhile, although Poland's PiS also came on top in a number of national polls,[14] it failed to do so in the 2001, 2007, and 2011 parliamentary elections, the first round of the 2005 and 2010 presidential elections, and the second round of the 2010 presidential election. Of particular note is the difference between the two parties' *election winning rates* – defined here as the number of national elections in which they won the most votes divided by the total number of national elections – when they were in government and in opposition. If SMER's election winning rate as an incumbent (71.4 percent) was significantly higher than as a challenger (40 percent), the opposite was true of PiS, whose winning rate as an incumbent (50 percent) was lower than as a challenger (62.5 percent) and, notably, significantly lower than SMER's rate as an incumbent. More capable of winning elections as an incumbent, SMER spent most of the 2000–20 period, particularly after 2006, governing Slovakia, either alone (2012–16) or by heading coalitions (2006–10, 2016–20). Although PiS also governed, both in a coalition (2005–7) and alone (after 2015), its lower election winning rate as an incumbent required the party to spend most of the period after 2000 in opposition.[15] Whereas SMER dominated national politics in Slovakia for more than a decade, PiS did not accomplish such a feat in Poland.

---

[11] See also Pugh (2009: 2).

[12] Madrid et al. (2010: 141).

[13] Namely, the 2002 and 2020 parliamentary elections, the first round of the 2019 presidential election, and both rounds of the 2014 and 2019 presidential elections.

[14] The 2005, 2015, and 2019 parliamentary elections, the first round of the 2015 and 2020 presidential elections, and the second round of the 2005, 2015, and 2020 presidential elections.

[15] The last parliamentary elections as of the time of this writing – in 2023 for parliament in both countries – confirmed these overall trends, with SMER returning to power in Slovakia and PiS losing power in Poland.

Moreover, although neither party was fully consistent over time in terms of its rhetoric and actions, as recognized by experts,[16] SMER and PiS, having both emerged as centrist antiestablishment parties at the turn of the twenty-first century, embraced opposite overall strategies vis-à-vis liberal democracy. As it did not systematically seek to alter liberal democratic institutions when in power, and indeed became less interested in conflict over time,[17] SMER adopted a general strategy of moderation. By contrast, PiS contested liberal democracy by repeatedly seeking to reconstitute Poland's institutional framework when in power, the reason why it has been consistently referred to as "radical" ever since it first governed in the mid 2000s. These differences had important implications in terms of the quality of liberal democracy, as revealed by a quantitative comparison of results obtained by averaging Freedom House's *Nations in Transit* indicators, which measure the health of liberal democratic institutions on a scale from one to seven.[18] For example, although SMER (2006–10) and PiS (2005–7) first governed by heading very similar coalitions with more extreme parties, Slovakia's average indicator deteriorated by 0.16 points relative to the previous period of liberal-led governments (1998–2006) while Poland's deteriorated by 0.49 points relative to the previous period of socialist-led government (2001–5). In turn, if the period of SMER's single-party majority government (2012–16) resulted in a decline of just 0.09 points, the period of PiS's single party majority government (2015–23) led to a considerable deterioration of 0.74 points and a transition from a consolidated to semi-consolidated democracy.

Three conclusions emerge from these comparisons. First, although democracy did not improve under any of the SMER-led governments,[19] SMER governed more in line with liberal democratic norms during its second period in power, after shedding its more extreme coalition partners. Second, while liberal democracy deteriorated more in Poland during both of the periods when PiS was in charge, it worsened especially in the second period, when PiS governed alone. If Slovakia's most successful illiberal project was moderate vis-à-vis liberal democracy, Poland's was contestatory. Third, because dominant illiberalism and contestatory illiberalism did not coincide in Slovakia and Poland, they must be understood as separate phenomena with possibly distinct origins.

7.1.2 Unpacking Bait-and-Switch Junctures: Shape and Mood of the Anti-Neoliberal Reaction

What explains the difference between Slovakia's more dominant yet moderate illiberalism and Poland's less dominant yet contestatory illiberalism? While

---

[16] Interviews POL-28; SVK-02.
[17] Interviews SVK-07; SVK-15; SVK-16.
[18] Namely, national democratic governance, electoral process, civil society, independent media, local democratic governance, judicial framework and independence, and corruption.
[19] Including SMER's second coalition government (2016–20), when the deterioration was 0.04 points.

the main purpose of Chapter 5 was to trace processes linking bait-and-switch junctures and the electoral viability of illiberalism in these two countries, the evidence presented there also suggests a theoretically informed answer to this question. This answer is not only consistent with the overall argument of this book, which links postcommunist junctures to *quantitatively* measured illiberal outcomes, but also considers how nuanced differences between otherwise similar junctures produced *qualitatively* different illiberal tendencies. Indeed, if bait-and-switch junctures triggered similar electoral reactions to neoliberalism, these reactions still varied depending on two factors. First, the *type of political agent breaking electoral promises during the juncture* molded the relative extensiveness – or shape – of the electoral coalition that carried subsequent illiberals to power, which, in turn, had implications for their ability to dominate in the long term. Second, *whether the advent of partisan channels for militant opposition to neoliberalism was viable or not during the juncture* made a difference in terms of the mood of the electoral reaction to which subsequent illiberals had to adapt – by adopting either contestatory or moderate strategies vis-à-vis liberal democracy – as they emerged and competed for votes. I next develop these two theoretical propositions based on the empirical evidence from Slovakia and Poland.

7.1.3 Agency, Coalition Extensiveness, and Dominant Illiberalism

The critical juncture framework underscores the centrality of agency. There are two types of political agents that can facilitate the deepening of neoliberalism by bait-and-switching – an institutionalized left-leaning, or social democratic, party like Slovakia's Party of the Democratic Left (SDĽ), or a personalist leader without such a party, such as Poland's Lech Wałęsa. As discussed in Chapter 5, these agents had risen to power by using different appeals. Taking advantage of their high level of institutionalization, which entailed organizational presence across the country, Slovakia's Left had attracted, through traditional programmatic appeals, a highly extensive coalition – in fact, the most nationalized (that is, evenly distributed geographically) in 1990s Slovakia – before the juncture. In contrast, lacking a standard partisan organization with branches across Poland, personalist Wałęsa had prioritized identity-priming appeals, thereby politicizing historically based cleavages that had been inactive under communism. Consequently, although bait-and-switch junctures produced quantitatively similar illiberal reactions at the ballot box in both countries, the core electoral coalitions embodying these reactions differed in terms of relative extensiveness. Following the social democratic bait-and-switch in Slovakia, SMER took advantage of a highly extensive electoral coalition centered around the former voters of a well-institutionalized party that had had a balanced presence across the country. Following the personalist bait-and-switch in Poland, PiS both benefitted from and was constrained by a more segmented coalition with a core in Poland B, which had been originally politicized via Wałęsa's identity-priming appeals and then disproportionately hurt by the neoliberal reforms.[20]

Crucially, as these reactive electoral coalitions, themselves legacies of bait-and-switch junctures, took shape *before* illiberals' rise to power, their relative extensiveness, or "nationalization" – defined as the degree to which electoral support is uniformly spread throughout the country[21] – made a difference in terms of SMER's and PiS's ability to dominate in the long term. Notably, these parties behaved consistently with theories predicting that party nationalization "has a prominent effect" in terms of electoral linkages, legislative unity, and, ultimately, public policies.[22] Specifically, parties with geographically extensive electoral coalitions have three advantages over ones with more segmented electorates. First, relatively nationalized parties connect with voters based on national – as opposed to local – issues, a linkage that is additionally reinforced by local proxies who, by acting on behalf of the party's center, help to shift voters' attention to national issues. Second, as such parties prioritize organizational unity and robustness based on common national agendas, they are likely to foster legislative cohesion. Third, the public policies such cohesive parties supply when in power tend to be of universal scope rather than targeting specific geographical units.[23]

These advantages were particularly relevant in contexts such as Slovakia's and Poland's, where both economic issues and populist parties gained national salience in the early twenty-first century. On the one hand, as relatively high nationalization facilitates the provision of public goods of national scope – such as generous material benefits that ease the economic pressure for much of the population – it solidifies the bonds between the incumbents supplying and the constituencies benefitting from them. On the other hand, as populist parties are focused precisely on fostering electoral linkages – that is, the top-down mobilization of votes[24] – their ability to supply nationally relevant material benefits as incumbents matters greatly for their future cohesion and electoral prospects. Finally, it is worth reiterating that whereas nationally relevant public policies can sustain, and even strengthen, the electoral linkages between illiberal incumbents and their electorates, the shape of the coalitions that brought illiberals to power is theoretically prior to the public policies, as it congealed as a reaction to earlier market reforms.

Indeed, having constructed the most nationalized electoral coalition of any party in modern Slovakia even before rising to power, SMER focused on economic questions, which were the most important national issue at the time of the party's appearance. The party also maintained impressive cohesion, which

---

[20] Binev (2024b).
[21] Bochsler (2010); Morgenstern (2017).
[22] Jones and Mainwaring (2003).
[23] Alemán and Kellam (2008: 193–4); Jones and Mainwaring (2003: 143–4); Morgenstern (2017: 20–1).
[24] Barr (2009: 35).

was further reinforced as it prioritized organizational unity – for example, by restricting membership only to those approved by the party presidium. As a result of delivering nationally relevant public goods, SMER solidified its bonds with voters and dominated in the long term. Indeed, as noted by both its critics and supporters, the party's recipe for long-term electoral success was precisely in its ability to deliver tangible material benefits consistently, which became synonymous with governing the country effectively.[25] SMER's broad appeal also made it attractive to ambitious local leaders across Slovakia, who, by prioritizing electoral self-interest, reinforced the party's national image as a generous provider.[26] In short, endowed with a nationwide electorate from the beginning, SMER emerged as a highly cohesive technocratic machine able to legislate for popular material benefits satisfactory to its various constituencies. This was all the more impressive considering that the party contained conflicting oligarchic and ideological wings, of which the social democratically minded were hardly the strongest.[27]

By contrast, having consistently attracted a more segmented electoral coalition, Poland's PiS remained non-cohesive for a long time, despite the centralizing proclivities of its leadership. The party not only had insufficient organizational presence across Poland, possessed the weakest membership among major parties,[28] and, as activists lamented, featured little connection between the national and local levels,[29] but also continued struggling with factionalism,[30] expulsions, and splinters a full decade after its foundation.[31] Unlike the cohesive SMER, which during its first term in power (2006–10) focused on highly salient economic questions and supplied nationally relevant material benefits, PiS not only failed to focus on such issues during its first term in office (2005–7) but also subsequently lost important high-level politicians and many members[32] – a symptom of its poor cohesion. As discussed in Chapter 5, the lack of a common legislative vision was an important (although not the only) factor behind PiS's problems of governance – including failures to facilitate coalition discipline and policymaking – in the mid 2000s. Such failures, in turn, dogged the party, which became associated with poor governance, for most of the following decade, as PiS politicians and activists complained.[33] Whereas Slovakia's SMER, seen as generous and competent, convincingly fostered electoral linkages – and dominated for most of the

---

[25] Interviews SVK-03; SVK-06.
[26] Interview SVK-20.
[27] Interviews SVK-06; SVK-07; SVK-08; SVK-14; SVK-18.
[28] Moreover, as one PiS district treasurer complained, many members did not pay dues and remained inactive (Interview POL-13).
[29] Interviews POL-12; POL-13.

[30] Interview POL-27. One PiS youth leader (who would later become a Sejm representative) identified five conflicting factions in 2015 (Interview POL-22).
[31] Szczerbiak (2013: 486); Tworzecki (2012: 618).
[32] Interviews POL-04; POL-06; POL-07; POL-08; POL-09.
[33] Interviews POL-04; POL-07.

2000–20 period, Poland's PiS, enjoying a more limited appeal and cohesion, certainly did not project comparable dominance.[34]

7.1.4 From Viability of Protest Institutionalization to Contestatory Illiberalism or Moderation

If bait-and-switching occurred through the agency of dissimilar political protagonists, it also triggered, already during the juncture, societal responses that differed in terms of the viability of anti-neoliberal protest institutionalization. In Poland, where constituencies were particularly aggrieved at the bait-and-switch – because they had been disproportionately hurt by reforms promulgated by the same political agent, Wałęsa, they had previously supported – the institutionalization of highly contentious counteraction was viable. Here, the anti-neoliberal backlash that materialized during the juncture (1990–93) included a key institutional dimension embodied by the militantly anti-neoliberal party Self-Defense (SO). Founded soon after the 1991 farmer protests – a constituency especially hard hit by shock therapy – SO justified its advent specifically by arguing that the agrarian branch of Solidarity had failed to force the government to deliver on prior promises. Despite its electoral marginality throughout the 1990s, SO "took an increasingly radical turn," organizing disruptive and violent action specifically on socioeconomic grounds.[35] In early 1999, for example, SO was the key protagonist behind the farmer protests – Poland's most significant anti-neoliberal contentious action after the juncture.[36] This immediately destabilized, and indeed spelled the beginning of the end of, the government of Solidarity Electoral Action (AWS) and Freedom Union (UW).[37] As both AWS and UD lost representation by 2001, and the ex-communist Democratic Left Alliance (SLD) collapsed amid further SO-led protests thereafter, by 2005 the party systems of the 1990s had entirely collapsed, with a meager 17 percent of Sejm seats going to parties from the previous decade. With deepening neoliberalism transforming institutionalized anti-neoliberal protest into increasingly salient anti-systemic radicalism, party system upheaval benefitted two protest parties – the larger and militantly anti-neoliberal SO and the newer and smaller ethno-nationalist League of Polish Families (LPR) – which controlled one-fifth of Sejm seats after both the 2001 and 2005 parliamentary elections.

In Slovakia, by contrast, anti-neoliberal protest was not institutionalized during or soon after the juncture, as the bait-and-switching agent – the Party of the Democratic Left – had not mobilized and then disproportionately hurt

---

[34] Although these tendencies were eventually disrupted in both countries in 2015–6, as discussed in Chapter 5, they certainly shaped illiberal experiences in the two countries for most of the period after 2000.

[35] Stanley (2015b: 192–4).

[36] See Foryś and Gorlach (2002); Pellen (2009).

[37] Szczerbiak (2002: 43).

any one particular constituency through the reforms it spearheaded from the Ministry of Finance. Moreover, as the juncture (1998–2002) occurred following the disgraceful end of Mečiarism, radical parties, which had been Mečiar's coalition partners,[38] were weakened – to the point of losing all parliamentary representation by the juncture's end. As radicalism dwindled, the following parliamentary elections produced legislatures in which established parties from the 1990s gained, respectively, 66 (in 2002) and 52 (in 2006) percent of seats[39] – notable stability compared to Poland's party system upheaval. While anti-neoliberal protests rose soon after 2002, they were not organized by parties or unions.[40] And although the reunified Slovak National Party (SNS) returned to the National Council and even to the government by 2006, "the potency of its rhetoric waned"[41] as SNS moderated its identity over time.[42] Unlike in Poland, where anti-neoliberal contention morphed into surging anti-systemic radicalism amid party system meltdown by the early 2000s, the environmental context of Slovakia during the same period featured relative party system continuity and the diminished salience of radical parties and agendas.[43]

These differences had profound implications in terms of the strategies of leading illiberals vis-à-vis liberal democracy. First, party system collapse signaled a much more serious crisis of liberal democratic institutions in Poland than in relatively more stable Slovakia. Indeed, as substantially more Poles than Slovaks had "no trust" in their parties, parliament, legal system, politicians, and government in the early 2000s,[44] Poland's PiS had stronger incentives to adopt an anti-systemic posture than Slovakia's SMER. Second, and relatedly, because radical contenders – which scholars view as "transformative forces" that radicalize the mainstream[45] – varied in terms of electoral relevance, major illiberal parties in Poland and Slovakia had to adapt to different political environments.[46] Whereas the relevance of radical contenders further incentivized Poland's main illiberal party to adjust by embracing a more anti-systemic agenda in its quest for new voters, as recognized by both political observers

---

[38] The far-left Union of the Workers of Slovakia and far-right nationalists, who temporarily split between the original Slovak National Party and the True Slovak National Party.

[39] SDKÚ-DS, SMK-MKP, KDH, and HZDS.

[40] Specifically, protests by healthcare workers demanding higher salaries (Interviews SVK-12; SVK-20) and protests in Eastern Slovakia after state subsidies for large families were cut (Interviews SVK-11; SVK-13). See also Bohle and Greskovits (2004).

[41] Haughton et al. (2021: 331).

[42] Interviews SVK-12; SVK-14.

[43] Interview SVK-09; Binev (2015).

[44] Based on data from the 2004 European Social Survey, the shares of respondents expressing "no trust" of various institutions were as follows: parties – 32.6 in Poland versus 19.0 percent in Slovakia; parliament – 26.8 in Poland versus 17.4 percent in Slovakia; legal system – 18.1 in Poland versus 11.8 percent in Slovakia; politicians – 32.7 in Poland versus 22.3 percent in Slovakia; and the government – 23.1 in Poland versus 16.1 percent in Slovakia.

[45] Minkenberg (2015; 2017: 121).

[46] Burgess and Levitsky (2003).

and PiS functionaries,[47] the insignificance of environmental radicalism encouraged Slovakia's SMER to moderate.

Indeed, while both SMER and PiS began in the early 2000s as centrist and mainstream parties, and then led similarly composed governments that included more extreme coalition partners (SNS and HZDS in 2006–10 in Slovakia; SO and LPR in 2005–7 in Poland), only SMER adopted an overall strategy of moderation.[48] Although SMER retained its illiberal positioning on programmatic issues, this moderate strategy was reflected in the lesser deterioration of Slovakia's liberal democracy. PiS, by contrast, turned to contesting liberal democracy as it sought to attract – after its dissatisfying inaugural performance in the 2001 parliamentary election – voters from the radical competition in an electoral environment characterized by a party system in serious crisis. After overtaking many former LPR supporters by embracing harsh ethno-nationalism in 2005, it drew former voters of the even more radical SO in 2007 – that is, after proving its fidelity to a clearly antidemocratic agenda during the 2005–7 government. Having fully embraced contestatory illiberalism, PiS then eroded liberal democracy in Poland after returning to power in 2015.[49]

7.1.5 From Bait-and-Switch Junctures to Different Illiberal Tendencies

Figure 7.1 sketches these two theoretically grounded explanations – (1) of dominant versus nondominant illiberalism and (2) of contestatory versus moderate illiberalism – derived from the empirical records of Slovakia and Poland by using the conceptual building blocks of the critical juncture analytical framework. On the one hand, as it is perpetrated by one of two types of agents, bait-and-switching during the juncture stimulates the formation of electoral coalitions of different shape – or relative extensiveness – which subsequently channel popular reactions to neoliberalism. As illiberals rise to power on the shoulders of these electoral coalitions, they differ in terms of their ability to dominate in the long term. Those ascending based on extensive electoral coalitions, after a social democratic bait-and-switch, develop impressive organizational cohesion and supply the kinds of material benefits that are highly valued by their national constituencies – a virtuous cycle that only reinforces their unity and popularity, thus facilitating their dominance in the long term. By contrast, those rising with support from more segmented electorates, after a personalist bait-and-switch, are less organizationally cohesive and thus more

---

[47] Interviews POL-12; POL-24; POL-25; POL-26; POL-27; POL-28.

[48] I focus here on illiberalism as a strategy of contestation (in Poland) or moderation (in Slovakia) relative specifically to liberal democracy. For a comparison of PiS's and SMER's illiberalism from the perspective of analyzing economic policies, see Scheiring (2021b).

[49] Tworzecki (2019).

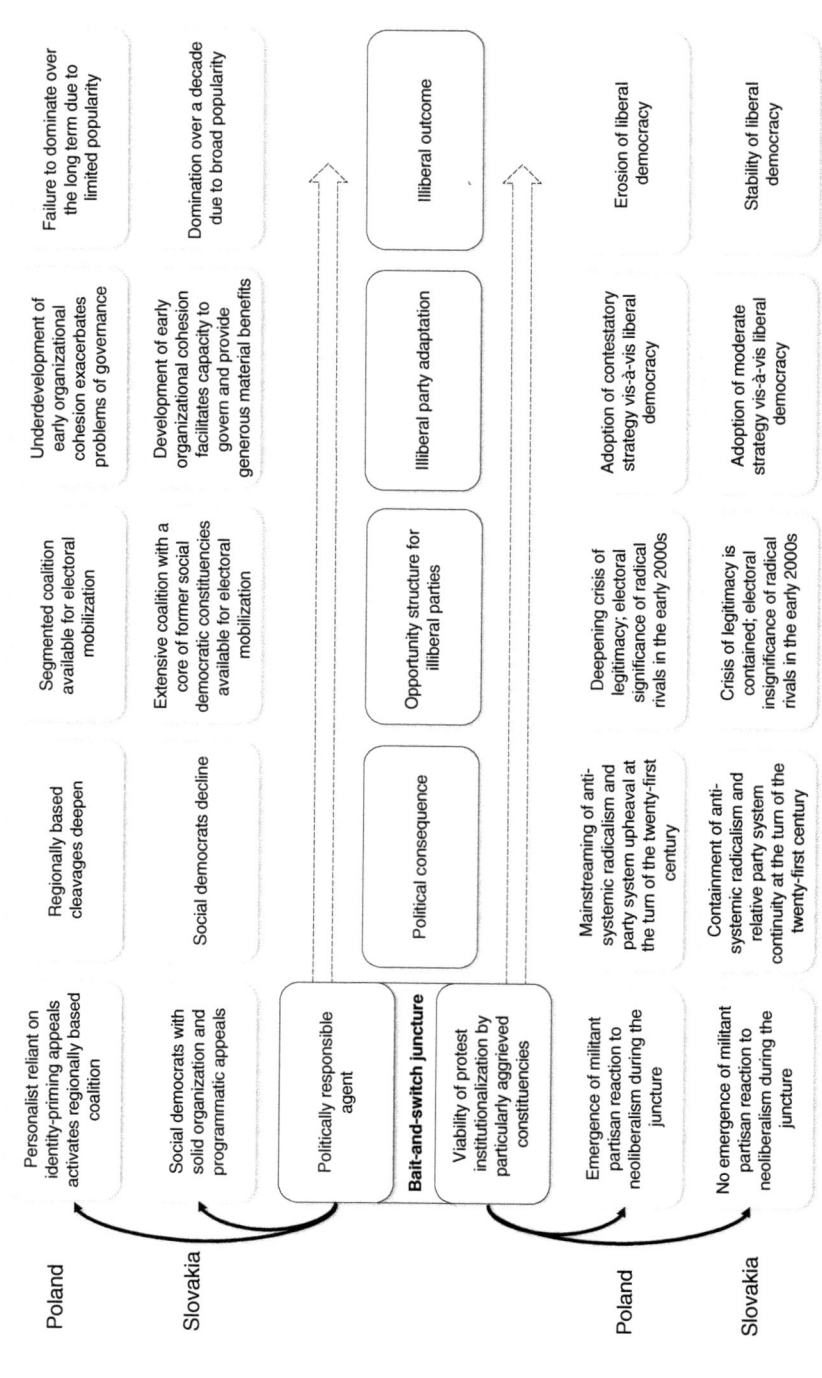

FIGURE 7.1 Legacies of bait-and-switch junctures

associated with significant problems of governance – a vicious cycle that limits their popularity and ability to dominate.

On the other hand, as bait-and-switching proceeds, the institutionaliza-tion of anti-neoliberal protest through the advent of militant parties is espe-cially viable when particular constituencies – such as Poland's farmers – are especially aggrieved at the reforms during the juncture. Where viable, protest institutionalization facilitates, as the neoliberal consensus deepens, the main-streaming of anti-systemic radicalism and party system upheaval, thus shap-ing an electoral environment characterized by a serious crisis of legitimacy. It is this environment that incentivizes leading illiberals to adopt contestatory strategies – and ultimately erode liberal democracy when in power. By con-trast, where anti-neoliberal protest institutionalization is nonviable during the juncture, the subsequent containment of party systemic crisis and anti-systemic radicalism conditions an electoral environment that predisposes illiberals toward moderation.

Finally, explaining different illiberal tendencies as a function of nuanced divergences with origins in contingencies during bait-and-switch junctures certainly does not suggest that leaders of illiberal parties possess no agency. Indeed, as discussed in the case studies in Part II, such leaders exercise enor-mous influence over the priorities of their parties. However, and consistent with this book's overall framework, their choices – for example, what public policies to prioritize or whether to adopt a contestatory or moderate strategy vis-à-vis liberal democracy – are molded by the political environments they encounter, which in turn stem from prior contingencies during junctures. While illiberal party leaders did not always make the most fitting choices given the contextual opportunities (as SMER's Robert Fico did by abandoning bread-and-butter issues during the 2015–16 migrant influx into Europe) and could even sometimes overcome their own limitations (as PiS's Jarosław Kaczyński did by prioritizing material benefits after 2015), their decisions and actions tended to be strongly conditioned by the historical legacies of junctures.

7.2 EXTENDING THE FRAMEWORK TO LATIN AMERICA

Having offered a theoretically grounded explanation of varying illiberal tendencies based on postcommunist experiences, I next extend the analyti-cal framework cross-regionally. Indeed, since this book began by applying insights from the Latin American experience to the postcommunist context, it is fair to ask whether lessons from Eastern Europe can, in turn, challenge previous thinking regarding developments in Latin America. My answer to this question – in the affirmative – suggests that regardless of the undeniable differences between countries in these two distinct world regions, societal opposition to neoliberalism was channeled via strikingly similar mechanisms linking illiberal experiences to comparable origins during prior bait-and-switch junctures.

Incorporating Latin American cases into a common framework with Eastern European ones can facilitate a more nuanced understanding of trajectories after neoliberal junctures, for reasons having to do with both economic and political developments. Indeed, after Latin American and Eastern European countries transitioned from state-led development, economic reformers in both regions often relied on similar political tactics[50] when enacting neoliberal policies.[51] The neoliberal revolution, in turn, provoked strong political reactions that channeled popular discontent with historically unprecedented market reforms in both regions. As I have argued elsewhere, there reactions, though not identical, are best understood with reference to the family resemblance concept of post-neoliberal populism. Crucially, this category is both historically grounded – because it captures developments after the peak of economic reforms – and reflective of regional particularisms, such as the more specific ideological content of political responses in the two regions.[52]

Given that post-neoliberal populism represents a reaction to similarly fundamental neoliberal transformations, during which many labor-based parties acted as key agents of market reform in both regions, it is not surprising that its magnitude at the ballot box was negatively – and similarly – correlated with the decline of the traditional Left in Latin America and Eastern Europe.[53] Indeed, if one way to make sense of the electoral viability of Eastern European illiberalism is to think of it as a post-neoliberal populist reaction rooted in earlier periods of building capitalism, as I have argued in this book, this response was generally parallel to post-neoliberal populist reactions in Latin America. As in Eastern Europe, some Latin American countries were affected more than others.[54]

While a number of scholars have explored the post-neoliberal populist reaction in Latin America,[55] and have explained it *generally* in region-wide studies emphasizing either economic[56] or political factors,[57] there are *particular* cases – such as Peru – that do not fit comfortably in general frameworks. The Peruvian case is an especially intriguing outlier because, although the backlash to neoliberalism was electorally strong there, it did not lead to a populist hegemony or the contestation of liberal democracy, as in Venezuela, Ecuador, and Bolivia. Differently from these paradigmatic cases, Peru's main post-neoliberal populist project both moderated and failed over time. While important books by Gustavo Flores-Macías, Kenneth Roberts, and Noam Lupu do not include this country as a case, separate works by Eduardo Silva and Maxwell Cameron discuss developments before Peru's most prominent post-neoliberal populist agent actually rose to power.[58] More recent work has been more attentive to the Peruvian exception, but it still does not explain this case convincingly. For

---

[50] Weyland (1999).
[51] Greskovits (1998); Weyland (1999).
[52] Binev (2024a).
[53] Binev (2024a).
[54] Binev (2024a).

[55] For example, Levitsky and Roberts (2011).
[56] For example, Roberts (2014); Silva (2009).
[57] For example, Handlin (2017).
[58] Cameron (2011); Flores-Macías (2012); Lupu (2016); Roberts (2014); Silva (2009).

example, Samuel Handlin includes Peru in his study of polarization but qualifies it as "a partially aberrant case."[59] Alberto Vergara and Daniel Encinas, meanwhile, identify the moderation of Peru's post-neoliberal populist project as rooted in the constitutionalization of the state's techno-bureaucracy. Yet, because this explanation explicitly rejects the significance of elections,[60] it neither accounts for post-neoliberal populism's failure to remain electorally relevant over time nor considers possible societal factors.

Although the Latin American experience appears to bear out the generally held notion that illiberalism's contestatory proclivity and the tendency toward domination likely share the same roots, a comparative exploration of path-dependent processes illuminates that the story of their origins is somewhat more nuanced. This, in turn, has important implications for understanding populist rule in early twenty-first century Latin America not as a function of either economic or political factors, but rather as a consequence of the historical interplay between both. To demonstrate this, I engage in a paired comparison of the cases of Peru and Ecuador based on the explanatory framework derived from Slovakia and Poland. Importantly, the function of these case studies, developed in Chapter 8, is not to represent larger universes of cases but rather, following Harry Eckstein and Sidney Tarrow, to facilitate a comparison aiming at two related goals – (1) to assess, from a cross-regional perspective, outcomes via process tracing and (2) to demonstrate a theory, in this case one prioritizing neoliberal junctures, that problematizes standard explanations through the exploration of "crucial cases."[61] As I discuss next, whereas the two Andean cases are crucial due to both their uniqueness within Latin America and their comparability with the Eastern European ones, all four cases are pivotal for making sense of how those who challenged the liberal establishment via initially new parties and illiberal appeals evolved under conditions where authoritarianism did not consolidate.

7.3 INCORPORATING ECUADOR AND PERU: COMMONALITIES AND OUTCOMES

Ecuador and Peru are not only uniquely comparable to one another but are also comparable to Slovakia and Poland along four dimensions of development after junctures of market reform, as summarized in Table 7.1. First, and as further detailed in Chapter 8, these two Andean countries are historically similar along a number of political, economic, and societal dimensions. As two rare cases of Latin American countries that had experimented with left-leaning dictatorial rule in the 1970s, Ecuador and Peru, like Slovakia and Poland, experienced bait-and-switch junctures of neoliberal reform that entailed high party

---

[59] Handlin (2017: 7n2).
[60] Vergara and Encinas (2016: 161).
[61] See Eckstein (1975); Tarrow (2010: 248–9).

TABLE 7.1 *Comparability of illiberal developments after neoliberal junctures featuring bait-and-switch dynamics in Ecuador, Peru, Poland, and Slovakia*

Dimension	Commonalities
Historical	Bait-and-switch junctures of neoliberal deepening trigger high party system instability
Regime	Powerful electoral reactions bring challengers of neoliberalism to power without leading to authoritarian consolidation
Organizational	Most important political challenges to neoliberalism are associated with top-down parties that initially compete as brand-new organizations
Ideological	Leading post-neoliberal populists mix economic statism with cultural conservatism representative of predominantly conservative societies

system instability. If these two Andean countries tended to have more unstable party system than the other bait-and-switch cases in Latin America (namely, Argentina, Costa Rica, Bolivia, and Venezuela),[62] Poland and Slovakia exited the juncture with higher electoral volatility than the other bait-and-switch cases in Eastern Europe (Hungary and Lithuania).[63]

Second, given the high magnitude of preexistent political instability, the four countries saw particularly powerful post-neoliberal populist reactions in the early twenty-first century. Being stronger and materializing earlier than in other bait-and-switch cases such as Costa Rica and Lithuania, this backlash shaped politics during most of the 2000–20 period in Ecuador, Peru, Slovakia, and Poland. Yet in none of the four countries did the populist reactions lead to authoritarian consolidation. Indeed, although democratic erosion certainly occurred in Ecuador[64] and Poland, illiberal heads of government there either voluntarily stepped down (Ecuador) or left power after elections (Poland) – a scenario unlike in Venezuela, Hungary, and even Bolivia.

Third, post-neoliberal populist reactions in Ecuador, Peru, Slovakia, and Poland had organizational features that made them both similar to one another and unlike other prominent cases in the two regions. Unlike in Bolivia, where the backlash against neoliberalism began as a bottom-up grassroots movement, leading populists in Ecuador and Peru mobilized publics from the top down,[65] as in Slovakia and Poland. And unlike in Argentina and Hungary,

---

[62] Roberts (2014: 109, 113–4).

[63] Author's dataset. Slovakia's party system volatility is not to be confused with the continuity in the early 2000s discussed earlier. Party systems can be volatile even as established parties retain large shares of the vote (see Powell and Tucker 2014).

[64] For example, whereas Ecuador's Freedom House score for political rights did not decline under Correa, the civil liberties score declined only minimally in 2016 before recovering in 2017.

[65] Levitsky and Roberts (2011); Roberts (2007).

where the populist reaction was predominantly organized via already established parties – the Peronist Justicialist Party and Fidesz – the parties channeling it in Ecuador, Peru, Slovakia, and Poland were founded by unambiguously personalistic leaders as brand-new organizations during or after the peak of market reforms.

Fourth, the most significant Ecuadorian and Peruvian post-neoliberal populist parties were similar to the Slovak and Polish ones in terms of the scope of their illiberalism, which – due to its culturally conservative dimension[66] – was more comprehensive than that of their "pink tide" counterparts in Latin America. Indeed, leading challengers of neoliberalism in Ecuador and Peru gained salience not only by critiquing economic liberalism and portraying as corrupt the political establishment advancing it, but also by emphasizing Christian-based opposition to abortion and sexual minority rights (and in the Peruvian case, anti-Chilean nationalism).[67] This "dualism between public progressivism and private conservatism"[68] is the reason why many interviewees in Ecuador and Peru adamantly rejected designating the main post-neoliberal populist projects of these countries as "leftist."[69] As they were certainly more conservative than their counterparts in Argentina, Bolivia, and Venezuela, who enacted socially progressive reforms despite the comparable Catholicism of their countries, Ecuador's and Peru's leading post-neoliberal populists were often perceived – like their Eastern European counterparts – as highly organic representatives of their conservative societies.[70]

Finally, just as illiberal populists rose to initial electoral prominence in the mid 2000s in Poland and Slovakia by gaining over 20 percent electoral support, so did they in Peru and Ecuador. Indeed, by winning 30.6 and 22.8 percent in the first round of the 2006 presidential elections in Peru and Ecuador, respectively, illiberals Ollanta Humala and Rafael Correa qualified for the second round. This initial similarity, however, was followed by a divergence. In Ecuador, Correa won the second round, after which he contested liberal democracy by rewriting the constitution[71] and dominated politics for a decade through his party, the Proud and Sovereign Fatherland Alliance (the PAÍS Alliance). (Notably, a number of Ecuadorian experts, journalists, politicians, and activists that I interviewed argued, in line with Weyland, that Correa's contestation of liberal democracy should be understood as separate from his "radical" economic policies, which included the

---

[66] While the Catholic leanings of Poland's PiS are well-known, Slovakia's SMER carefully adapted itself to the Catholic Church (Interviews SVK-02; SVK-06; SVK-07).

[67] McClintock (2013); Viteri (2020).

[68] Interview ECU-18.

[69] Interviews ECU-03; ECU-05; ECU-17; ECU-19; ECU-20; ECU-21; ECU-24, PER-01;

PER-05; PER-14; PER-15; PER-18; PER-19; PER-20; PER-21.

[70] That is, seen as "natural" and reflective of their countries' conservative societies (Interviews ECU-06; ECU-14; PER-18; PER-23; PER-25; POL-01; POL-08; POL-09; POL-17; POL-19; SVK-03; SVK-10; SVK-11; SVK-13; SVK-14).

[71] Madrid et al. (2010).

privatization of natural resources.[72] As one critic stated mockingly, "One day Correa sings 'Comandante Che Guevara,' the next day he signs a petroleum contract."[73])

In Peru, meanwhile, Humala lost the second round of the presidential election in 2006. Although he ultimately won both rounds as a presidential candidate in the following general election of 2011, he not only adopted a strategy of moderation but also failed to prevent his Peruvian Nationalist Party (PNP) from collapsing during his term in office. These outcomes are especially puzzling considering that, when they initially rose to prominence, Humala (with nearly a third of the first-round vote in 2006) had in fact been more popular in Peru than Correa in Ecuador (with less than a quarter of the first-round vote that same year) and had been generally perceived as more antidemocratic. For example, whereas Correa, a former academic and finance minister, was originally seen by many as a liberal emphasizing individual rights,[74] Humala, who had spent his career in the military and engaged in a failed coup attempt, caused widespread concern with his open disrespect for liberal democracy and his "quasi-fascist" ethnocacerist ideology.[75]

Overall, then, the Ecuadorian and Peruvian cases are an ideal pairing for understanding divergent outcomes from a comparative perspective. On the one hand, these cases are both comparable to one another and unlike others in Latin America in terms of the historical, regime, institutional, and ideological dimensions discussed earlier. On the other hand, they share much along these same dimensions with the Slovak and Polish cases. Indeed, as bait-and-switch junctures of market reform further destabilized already unstable party systems in all four countries, political projects that had begun as brand-new organizations during or after these junctures eventually rose to executive power after mobilizing, from the top down, considerable electoral support based on illiberal – that is, economically statist and culturally conservative – positions. Despite the rise of illiberal actors to power, however, none of the four countries descended into Venezuelan or Hungarian style electoral autocracies. Ecuador and Peru, like Slovakia and Poland, are thus comparable (and rare) cases of political forces that rose to prominence as illiberals critical of neoliberalism and then governed without consolidating authoritarian rule. Finally, these cases represent parallel divergences in terms of overall illiberal tendencies, as shown in Figure 7.2. Whereas illiberal incumbents were electorally and politically dominant for over a decade in Ecuador and Slovakia, their "staying power" was certainly more limited in Peru and intermittent in Poland. And if these same illiberals contested liberal democracy in Ecuador and Poland, they moderated in Peru and Slovakia.

---

[72] Interviews ECU-11; ECU-12; ECU-13; ECU-17; ECU-19; ECU-20; ECU-24.
[73] Interview ECU-21.
[74] Becker (2011a: 48).
[75] McClintock (2013).

Illiberal tendency	Contestatory	Moderate
Dominant	Ecuador	Slovakia
Unstable or intermittent	Poland	Peru

FIGURE 7.2 Main illiberal tendencies in Ecuador, Peru, Poland, and Slovakia in the early twenty-first century

These parallelly divergent outcomes require two clarifications. First, the parallelism certainly does not imply sameness across regions. If Ecuador's illiberal project was more electorally successful, and thus relatively more dominant, than Slovakia's, Peru's was overall less successful and more fragile than Poland's. Likewise, it is undeniable that Ecuador's Correa, who was able to write a new constitution in 2008, contested liberal democracy more successfully than PiS, unable to change the fundamental rules of the game, did in Poland. While such *differences in degree* undeniably exist as a function of numerous factors at country, regional (e.g., EU membership), and institutional (e.g., presidential versus parliamentary systems) levels, my interest, following other analysts of populism,[76] is a cross-regional comparison of general *similarities in kind* – specifically, the kind of illiberal tendencies – in these four countries in the early twenty-first century.

Second, and as also seen in Figure 7.2, as illiberal tendencies correlated differently in Eastern Europe and the Andes, each of the four cases represents a unique combination. Whereas illiberalism was both dominant and contestatory in Ecuador, these tendencies corresponded to different cases in postcommunist Europe. This, however, is not a concern because, rather than examining dominant and contestatory types of illiberalism (and their opposites) as necessarily coalescent, I analyze them as conceptually different products of concrete processes. While I have proposed that the drivers of such illiberal tendencies are distinct and rooted in different aspects of bait-and-switch junctures based on the Slovak and Polish experiences, in the following chapter I assess whether analogous mechanisms were at work in Ecuador and Peru, despite overall different configurations. In short, by disaggregating illiberal tendencies and the processes shaping them, I next test the cross-regional validity of the explanatory framework developed earlier in this chapter.

Finally, it should be clear from the above that if extending the comparative framework from Slovakia and Poland to Ecuador and Peru aims at a cross-regional generalization, this generalization is only limited to these four crucial cases, which share a number of relevant similarities, as discussed earlier. Indeed, rather than generalize more broadly, my purpose here is to assess

---

[76] See Mudde and Rovira Kaltwasser (2012; 2013); Rovira Kaltwasser and Taggart (2016).

divergent illiberal tendencies via an analytical framework rooted in (1) the conceptual differentiation between dominant and contestatory illiberalism and (2) the unpacking of prior neoliberal junctures. While previous scholarship and prior chapters of this book have demonstrated that bait-and-switching during neoliberal junctures conditioned illiberal electoral viability in these two regions, much less is known about how more specific contingencies during junctures may have shaped subsequent developments. For example, although the central role of agency during neoliberal junctures has been acknowledged, students of Latin American politics have been mostly interested in the long-term effects of bait-and-switching under institutionalized parties (as in Ecuador), without addressing the possibly different effects of bait-and-switching under a personalist agent, as was the case in Peru.[77] And while it is well-known that a powerful anti-neoliberal movement materialized in Ecuador, but not in Peru, during the peak neoliberal reform years, the long-term effects of such developments have not been analyzed from a comparative perspective that draws insights cross-regionally. In sum, incorporating Ecuador and Peru into a comparative framework informed by the Slovak and Polish experiences is theoretically valuable. By focusing on potentially parallel mechanisms, this comparison not only contributes to a more nuanced understanding of the effects of neoliberal junctures but also facilitates making sense of illiberalism in the early twenty-first century from a perspective attentive to both cross-regional similarities and contextual specificities.

7.4 THE INSUFFICIENCY OF STANDARD EXPLANATIONS OF DOMINANT AND CONTESTATORY VARIETIES OF ILLIBERALISM

Having argued that dominant and contestatory types of illiberalism are distinct phenomena, identified the paths toward each in Slovakia and Poland, and made the case for adding Ecuador and Peru to the comparative analysis, I close this chapter by discussing why standard explanations of these phenomena are individually unsatisfactory when explaining variation in these four cases.

7.4.1 Dominant Illiberalism or Not

The literature identifies four reasons why only some illiberal populists might benefit electorally as incumbents and are thus more likely to dominate politically in the long term.[78] The first explanation emphasizes access to material resources that generous incumbents can use to buy popular support. For example, if Latin American left-populists gained sustained popularity through social spending during oil "boom cycles,"[79] Eastern European populist incumbents

---

[77] See Lupu (2016); Roberts (2014).   [79] Weyland (2009).
[78] Based on Binev (2024b: 4–7).

benefitted from financial support from the European Union (EU). Yet this explanation faces challenges. Whereas some populists elected on leftist platforms in the Andes remained in power despite low commodity prices,[80] others, such as Ecuador's Lucio Gutiérrez, lost power as they kept social spending low despite improved oil rents. And although Poland has received more EU funding than any other Eastern European country, illiberals there tended to be less dominant than in Slovakia.

The second argument focuses on populists' proclivity to establish competitive authoritarian regimes, thus maximizing their chances of winning consecutive elections by creating institutional disadvantages for their opponents.[81] Although this argument certainly explains important developments in the Andes,[82] Humala's presidency in Peru is evidence that not all incumbents elected as populists attempt to govern as authoritarians.[83] And even those who try do not necessarily succeed, as the Polish experience in the mid 2000s shows. As discussed earlier, dominant illiberalism, which is predicated on the ability to win consecutive elections, and contestatory illiberalism, which is closely associated with a tendency toward democratic erosion, are two distinct concepts.

Third, scholars have highlighted the relevance of organizational advantages such as civil society support from indigenous movements or labor unions, party institutionalization, charismatic leadership, and the ability to manipulate voters via antiestablishment and anti-immigrant discourses. To begin, while it is true that the indigenous movement has been much stronger in Ecuador than in Peru, its relationship with illiberal Correa was adversarial during most of the dominant president's tenure. Moreover, because labor unions have been comparably weak in both the Andes and Eastern Europe, they are not the type of resource populists can mobilize for long-term domination. Neither is party institutionalization, as understood in terms of membership, professionalism, and centralization.[84] On the one hand, populist parties tend to be highly centralized regardless of how dominant they are.[85] On the other hand, whereas more and less successful populist parties are similarly under-institutionalized in the Andes,[86] they are comparably well-organized in the two postcommunist countries under analysis.[87] In turn, as charismatic authority was comparably prevalent in the Ecuadorian, Peruvian, Slovak, and Polish illiberal parties analyzed here,[88] it cannot account for differences among the four countries. Finally, because neither antiestablishment discourses – more consistent in Poland than Slovakia[89] – nor anti-immigrant rhetoric, which escalated in Europe in the mid

---

[80] Levitsky and Loxton (2013: 109).
[81] Levitsky and Way (2010).
[82] Levitsky and Loxton (2013).
[83] Cameron (2011: 396n6); Madrid (2012).
[84] Grzymała-Busse (2002); Tavits (2013).
[85] Mudde (2007).
[86] Levitsky and Roberts (2011); Madrid (2012).
[87] See Rybář and Deegan-Krause (2008); Tavits (2013).
[88] See Kitschelt (2013).
[89] Engler et al. (2019).

2010s, correlate with illiberal outcomes, such "internal supply" factors are not satisfactory explanations of long-term domination.

The fourth explanation centers on illiberal presidents, whose personal prestige facilitates the ability of their otherwise less popular parties to command highly nationalized electorates and thus legislative majorities supportive of the president's agenda. This "presidential coattails" argument locates Correa's ability to dominate in Ecuador after 2013 as rooted in an electorate transcending historically salient regional divides,[90] but it ignores the prior circumstances – for example, policies or conditions – from which his high popularity across the country stemmed. Indeed, as Correa's popularity increased over time in Ecuador, while Humala's steadily declined in Peru, the true sources of these presidents' divergent ability to dominate through legislative majorities remain unclear. Additionally, because illiberal incumbents in Poland, where the presidency is stronger, were less electorally dominant than in Slovakia, where it is weaker, the explanation emphasizing presidential coattails remains unconvincing.

7.4.2 Contestatory Illiberalism or Moderation

Scholars have also made four arguments regarding why illiberals might contest liberal democracy or moderate by accepting its institutional norms. First, according to the inclusion-moderation thesis, illiberal populists who transition from opposition to government tend to moderate if demands for coalition building are high[91] – either at the societal level, where they compete for centrist voters before assuming power,[92] or at the government level, where they become more restrained due to possible pressure from coalition partners.[93] Although this argument accounts for developments in Peru, where Humala moderated due to the need to appeal to centrist voters,[94] it does not explain why such voters were more politically consequential there than in Ecuador. Additionally, as the inclusion-moderation thesis implies that governing either with more extreme parties or alone incentivizes illiberals to pursue contestatory agendas, it does not account for developments in Eastern Europe either. Indeed, although both Slovakia's SMER and Poland's PiS governed in similar coalitions with more extreme parties in the 2000s, only PiS actively sought to subvert liberal democracy. And while PiS became even more contestatory vis-à-vis liberal democracy when governing alone after 2015, SMER moderated during its single-party majority government between 2012 and 2016, as discussed earlier.

The second explanation emphasizes party organization. In particular, whereas new populist parties with authority concentrated in personalist leaders

---

[90] Polga-Hecimovich (2014).   [93] Schwörer (2021).
[91] See Thomeczek (2023).   [94] Lupu (2012).
[92] Tepe (2019).

are likely to contest liberal democracy because their institutional limitations encourage anti-systemic agendas, those that invest in "normal" organization building are likely to moderate.[95] This argument is not convincing either. Although organizational characteristics can possibly account for contestatory illiberalism in Ecuador[96] and moderate illiberalism in Slovakia,[97] they do not explain developments in Peru, where Humala moderated despite his neglect of party building, as well as in Poland, where PiS kept contesting liberal democracy well after it ceased to be a new and poorly organized party.

Third, scholars of Latin America have argued that when neoliberalism is institutionalized, specifically through constitutionally sanctioned agencies empowering technocrats within state institutions, even the most ardent populist campaigners are eventually compelled to embrace liberal democracy as a regime most conducive to neoliberal policy. Although this argument has been used convincingly to explain Humala's moderation in Peru,[98] constitutions can be rewritten given sufficient popular support, as seen twice in Ecuador between 1998 and 2008. The "constitutional straitjacket" explanation is also unconvincing for Slovakia and Poland. On the one hand, Slovakia's SMER moderated despite the absence of a "neoliberal" constitution. On the other hand, well-staffed and prestigious pro-market bureaucracies in Poland[99] have enjoyed a status as privileged as Peru's powerful INDECOPI,[100] and Poland's 1997 constitution certainly contributed toward neoliberal institutionalization – not only by securing Central Bank independence and a focus on price stability[101] but also by eliminating previously guaranteed social rights. Yet this did not prevent PiS from contesting liberal democracy,[102] and neither did the primacy of European Union law, to which Poland is subject on economic matters.

Centering on the availability of relevant competitors in the electoral environment, the final explanation posits that the presence of leftist (in Latin America) or radical right (in Eastern Europe) alternatives incentivizes mainstream parties, including illiberal or populist ones, to pursue more revisionist agendas.[103] Although such arguments are not wrong – because environmental factors certainly play a role, as discussed earlier based on the Slovak and Polish cases – their focus on contemporaneous or immediate effects renders them insufficiently precise. For example, whereas more extreme contenders performed almost identically in elections immediately preceding illiberals' single-party majority governments in Slovakia (2012) and Poland (2015),[104]

---

[95] See Hegedüs (2019: 409); Levitsky and Roberts (2011).

[96] See Conaghan (2011).

[97] Spáč and Havlik (2015).

[98] Vergara and Encinas (2016).

[99] Especially Poland's Ministry of Privatization (Bugarič 2016: 317) and the Office of Competition and Consumer Protection.

[100] National Institute for the Defense of Competition and the Protection of Intellectual Property.

[101] Bohle and Greskovits (2012: 175).

[102] See Krajewski (2023).

[103] Burgess and Levitsky (2003); Minkenberg (2017).

[104] Slovakia's Nationalists and Poland's KORWiN gained, respectively, 4.6 and 4.8 percent.

a contestatory strategy was pursued only in the second case. And although rising illiberals in Ecuador and Peru co-opted more radical parties into their electoral alliances, they, too, governed very differently from one another. Indeed, illiberal incumbents can pursue contestatory agendas years after more extreme competitors have been eliminated, as they did in Poland and Ecuador, because environmental effects can be lagged. Thus, while environmental forces do matter, their causes and effects require further specification. As shown in Figure 7.1, such factors are best understood as a building block of the critical juncture framework.

Overall, the above review shows not that standard arguments are irrelevant but rather that each of them individually fails to offer a sufficiently convincing explanation of developments in the four crucial cases under study. Indeed, it is true that natural and organizational resources made a difference in terms of illiberals' capacity for long-term domination in, respectively, Ecuador and Slovakia, that the neoliberal constitution helped moderate illiberalism in Peru, and that environmental factors contributed toward PiS's contestatory approach in Poland. Yet, as these individual arguments miss crucial historically grounded and sequential perspectives, they fail to link the different elements of the puzzle of divergent illiberal tendencies into a complete, and thus more convincing, explanation. By contrast, incorporating the two Andean cases into a cross-regional comparison with Slovakia and Poland not only demonstrates the limits of standard explanations but also, and more importantly, helps to illuminate how neoliberal juncture contingencies shaped in analogous ways path-dependent legacies in very different political systems. As it shows how adaptive illiberals interacted with societal forces molded by the contingencies of historically unprecedented neoliberal junctures, the analytical framework expanded in this chapter and further tested in the next is sensitive to both historical developments and political agents' capacities for adaptation.

7.5 CONCLUSION

This chapter has expanded the critical juncture framework advanced in this book in two ways – theoretically and cross-regionally. It began with the simple observation that while bait-and-switching during postcommunist junctures explains the high salience of illiberal voting in the Eastern Europe of the early twenty-first century, it alone cannot account for more fine-grained differences of illiberal experiences. Indeed, the reality of such differences, as observed in Eastern Europe, challenges a central scholarly assumption – that illiberals' ability to dominate in the long term is necessarily the product of their subversion of liberal democracy. Having discussed why illiberals' contestation of liberal democracy and domination over time are best understood as distinct phenomena, I used the cases of Slovakia and Poland, both of which experienced bait-and-switch junctures, to develop an explanation of divergent illiberal tendencies – (1) toward either a decade-long illiberal hegemony or failure to dominate in the long term and (2) toward either contestatory illiberalism or moderation. As this explanation problematizes nuanced contingencies during prior bait-and-switch junctures – specifically, the agency of those politically responsible for deepening market reforms and the viability of institutionalizing anti-neoliberal protest – it is both consistent with the book's overall theoretical framework and suggestive of a need for increased analytical precision when studying the effects of critical junctures.

Having extended the analytical framework conceptually, I then made the case for also extending it cross-regionally. Returning to the book's original theme – that post-neoliberal populist experiences in Eastern Europe and Latin America are broadly comparable and even parallel – I identified developments in Peru, where the most prominent post-neoliberal populist project both moderated and failed to persist electorally, as insufficiently explained by prior scholarship, and I problematized the taken-for-granted equivalency between dominant and contestatory (vis-à-vis liberal democracy) populism in Ecuador. I then argued that as Peru and Ecuador are comparable to Slovakia and Poland along several key dimensions, these four countries are crucial cases for making sense of varying illiberal tendencies after bait-and-switch junctures and under conditions where authoritarianism did not consolidate. Indeed, a comparison of these cases not only shows that standard explanations of illiberal domination and contestatory illiberalism are individually insufficient; it also has the potential to illuminate possible parallelisms during the post-neoliberal era in the very different contexts of Eastern Europe and Latin America.

In sum, this chapter has challenged standard assumptions about general illiberal trends and offered an original analytical framework for making sense of these tendencies from a cross-regional perspective. Because this framework links different factors into a historically grounded explanation of institutional path dependencies, it is both reflective of how societal forces are shaped by contingencies during neoliberal junctures and sensitive to how subsequent illiberal agents adapt to these forces. As shown in the following chapter, while post-neoliberal developments in the Andes occurred under very different circumstances, the linkages between neoliberal juncture contingencies, societal responses to marketization, and illiberal tendencies were strikingly parallel to the ones seen in Eastern Europe.

8

Parallel Paths in the Eastern European Mirror

Reinterpreting Developments in Ecuador and Peru

Having refined the theoretical framework based on Eastern European experiences, made the case for comparability with Latin American countries, and discussed the insufficiency of standard explanations of varying illiberal tendencies, in this chapter I assess developments in Ecuador and Peru. This paired comparison is instructive for two reasons. On the one hand, by unpacking neoliberal junctures, analyzing concrete patterns in the evolution of electoral dynamics, and distinguishing between the sources of contestatory illiberalism and dominant illiberalism in these two comparable systems, I contribute to prior research on the consequences of crucial periods of market reform in Latin America.[1] On the other hand, by offering a historically informed explanation of divergent patterns, I illuminate intriguing parallels with the Eastern European experience. As I show, the trajectories culminating in varying illiberal tendencies in Ecuador and Peru involved patterns remarkably parallel to those seen in Slovakia and Poland, despite undeniable cross-regional differences.

The chapter is organized following the conventions of critical juncture analysis.[2] After briefly discussing relevant antecedent conditions, cleavages, and crises before crucial market reforms, I explore neoliberal junctures in Ecuador and Peru by highlighting the agency responsible for bait-and-switch reforms and whether or not the institutionalization of anti-neoliberal contention was viable. Having established variation in terms of both of these aspects, I next trace divergent path dependencies after junctures. As I ultimately show that in Ecuador and Peru the contingencies of bait-and-switch junctures molded historical legacies in ways analogous to the Slovak and

---

[1] See Roberts (2014).

[2] See Collier and Collier (1991); Collier and Munck (2022).

Polish experiences, I conclude that contestatory and dominant varieties of illiberalism, although sometimes concurrent, are best understood as two distinct political adaptations to societal reactions with different origins in neoliberal junctures. By offering a nuanced, comparative, and historically grounded account of illiberal tendencies, the chapter invites a new way of thinking about developments after the peak of neoliberalism in Latin America.

8.1 ANTECEDENT CONDITIONS, CLEAVAGES, AND CRISES BEFORE NEOLIBERAL JUNCTURES

Ecuador and Peru are two similar Andean countries in terms of overall historical development as well as political, economic, societal, and demographic conditions,[3] including mestizo majorities and important indigenous minorities[4] – a key constituency mobilized by illiberal populism, as discussed later. In both, the first century after independence from Spanish colonialism was a period of oligarchic rule featuring high political instability borne out of competition among various *caudillos*, regional rivalries between conservative landholders dominating the highlands and their liberal opponents in coastal cities, and the rise and fall of modernizing liberal regimes – Peru's Aristocratic Republic and Ecuador's governments under Eloy Alfaro – by the 1920s. Despite these major transformations, however, regionally based oligarchs continued benefitting disproportionately from export-oriented and highly unequal agricultural economies dependent on indigenous labor exploitation, particularly in highland areas.[5] While between the 1930s and 1960s oligarchic power in both countries was challenged by the popular sectors that rose as a result of urbanization, the willingness of ideologically flexible populist beneficiaries – Peru's American Popular Revolutionary Alliance (APRA) and Ecuador's José María Velasco Ibarra – to compromise by engaging in conservative coalition-making limited the political incorporation of labor, prevented considerable agrarian reform, and contributed to turbulence featuring multiple transitions between democratic and authoritarian governments.[6]

---

[3] See Collier and Collier (1991) on Peru; Roberts (2014) on Ecuador; and Conaghan and Malloy (1994) on both. For studies of indigenous politics, see Madrid (2012); Van Cott (2005); Yashar (2005).

[4] As reported by Madrid (2012: 79, 119), in the first decade of the twenty-first century about 78 percent of Ecuadorians and 58 percent of Peruvians self-identified as mestizo, while about 6 percent of Ecuadorians and 27 percent of Peruvians self-identified as indigenous.

Less than 11 and 5 percent, respectively, self-identified as white in Ecuador and Peru.

[5] Alexander (2007: 155–6); Coatsworth (1998); Collier and Collier (1991: 130–1, 138–45); Conaghan and Malloy (1994); Engerman and Sokoloff (2000); Lauderbaugh (2012); Levitt (2012).

[6] Collier and Collier (1991: 149–57, 316–9, 469–74, 477–82, 695–706, 710–14, 719–20); Conaghan (1988); Conaghan and Malloy (1994); de la Torre (2010); Lauderbaugh (2012).

The political instability, in turn, was used as a justification for the military dictatorships in charge of both countries by the early 1970s. Differently from elsewhere in Latin America, Peruvian and Ecuadorian generals ruled first by implementing economically nationalist strategies of state-led development – under Peru's Velasco Alvarado (1968–75) and Ecuador's Rodríguez Lara (1972–76) – and then by paving the way, after conservative coups (in 1975 in Peru and 1976 in Ecuador), to initial economic liberalization and negotiated democratic transitions by the end of the decade.[7] Yet, as democracy opened up new spaces for ideological divides between neoliberals and state interventionists in political and civil society, market-friendly governments – under presidents Fernando Belaúnde (1980–85) in Peru and León Febres-Cordero (1984–88) in Ecuador – failed to sustain significant reforms.[8] As a result, their economic policies did not constitute neoliberal junctures.

These macro-historical similarities notwithstanding, key twentieth-century experiences with populism differed considerably. If Peruvian populism was associated with a major labor mobilizing party, APRA, which was excluded from power before the 1980s, the Ecuadorian brand – epitomized by Velasco Ibarra's five elections to the presidency – was defined by elitist domination through patrimonial and clientelist practices.[9] Consequently, although military statism in both countries sought to build a "historical alliance" with organized labor and the predominantly indigenous peasantry via import substituting industrialization and agrarian reform,[10] this was more successful in Peru, where channels of popular mobilization were better institutionalized, than in Ecuador, where persistent elitism continued frustrating major social change.[11]

As in Eastern Europe, historical antecedents shaped the crises that emerged in the two countries soon after the end of state-led development under dictatorial rule. In Peru, the legacy of powerful labor mobilization before and during the military dictatorship strengthened the radical United Left (IU) in the early 1980s. This created pressures for the once again prolabor APRA, finally in power during Alan García's presidency (1985–90), to enact heterodox economic policies, which led to catastrophic hyperinflation that caused state-interventionist parties to either become seriously discredited (APRA) or diminished due to the rise of the informal economy (IU).[12] In Ecuador, by contrast, the legacy of party system elitism facilitated the entrenchment of patrimonial and clientelist practices, which hindered both labor mobilization – even under the popular and left-leaning Jaime Roldós, the first democratically elected president after military rule – and the development of a comparably powerful radical

---

[7] Conaghan (1988: 41–7); Conaghan and Malloy (1994); Levitt (2012).

[8] Conaghan and Malloy (1994).

[9] Collier and Collier (1991); de la Torre (2010).

[10] Interview ECU-18.

[11] Alexander (2007); Conaghan and Malloy (1994); Yashar (2005).

[12] Burgess and Levitsky (2003); Conaghan and Malloy (1994); Levitt (2012); Pop-Eleches (2009); Roberts (1996); Seawright (2012).

partisan Left.[13] With considerably less environmental pressure for heterodox policies, the governments of Roldós (1979–81), Osvaldo Hurtado (1981–84) and Febres-Cordero (1984–88) were able to adopt limited economic reforms that prevented the declining economy – almost entirely dependent on petroleum exports and in trouble amid falling oil prices in the early 1980s – from collapsing.[14] As Ecuador faced an economic crisis that was significantly milder than in Peru, its main center-left party – the social democratic Democratic Left (ID) – not only avoided the ill fate of the Peruvian Left but also found itself in a position of relative strength by the late 1980s.[15]

Overall, while the historical similarities ultimately shaped central political cleavages as Peru and Ecuador exited state-led development, the contrasting legacies of labor mobilization and elitism conditioned different political environments by the late 1980s as well as the economic crises that subsequent neoliberal junctures would resolve. In both countries, the historic conflict between export-orientated oligarchs and popular majorities was ultimately reproduced as the central political divide of the 1980s – that between leading partisans of neoliberalism (Peru's conservative PPC and liberal AP; Ecuador's conservative PSC and liberal PLRE)[16] and their state interventionist opponents (Peru's leftist IU and labor-based populist APRA; Ecuador's Marxist MPD and social democratic ID).[17] Yet, if state interventionists were weakened amid a hyperinflationary crisis in Peru, the social democratic Left was relatively stronger amid a milder economic crisis on the eve of the neoliberal juncture in Ecuador.

8.2 NEOLIBERAL JUNCTURE CONTINGENCIES: AGENCY OF BAIT-AND-SWITCH AND VIABILITY OF INSTITUTIONALIZING ANTI-NEOLIBERAL PROTEST

8.2.1 Ecuador

Ecuador experienced several waves of market reforms between the late 1970s and early 2000s, but the "the beginning of conventional neoliberalism"[18] occurred under the watch of social democratic president Rodrigo Borja (1988–92),[19] when his ID headed a congressional coalition of leftist

---

[13] Whereas in Peru radical leftist parties gained an average of 20.4 percent of the vote in presidential, congressional, and municipal elections in the period between the fall of the military dictatorship and the neoliberal juncture (1980–90), in Ecuador such parties gained an average of 8.8 percent during the equivalent period (1978–88). (Author's dataset.)

[14] Interview ECU-03.

[15] Alexander (2007); Conaghan and Malloy (1994); Freidenberg and Alcántara

Sáez (2001); Lauderbaugh (2012); Vos (2002).

[16] Christian People's Party (PPC); Popular Action (AP); Social Christian Party (PSC); Ecuadorian Radical Liberal Party (PLRE).

[17] United Left (IU); American Popular Revolutionary Alliance (APRA); Democratic People's Movement (MPD); United Left (ID).

[18] Interview ECU-12.

[19] Roberts (2014).

and centrist parties.[20] Confronted with not only inflation reaching over 80 percent and serious fiscal deficit amid newly falling oil prices but also persistently high external debt,[21] the social democrats, following IMF advice, initiated and sustained throughout the entire term a stabilization program featuring major trade, price, and wage liberalization, agricultural price controls deregulation, social spending cuts, and sharp increases of energy prices.[22] Although more austerity measures were implemented under future presidents, subsequent reforms were relatively more modest due to either lack of party cohesiveness, as under conservative president Sixto Durán Ballén (1992–96), or extreme political instability leading to the ousters of presidents, as in the cases of Abdalá Bucaram (1996–97), Jamil Mahuad (1998–2000), and Lucio Gutiérrez (2003–5).[23] Indeed, economic liberalization was steeper under Borja's than under any other administration, including that of relatively successful reformer Gustavo Noboa (2000–3).

The neoliberal juncture featured clear bait-and-switching on the part of the social democratic ID,[24] which had been Ecuador's best organized political party in the 1970s and 1980s.[25] During this period, ID had consistently emphasized its programmatic adherence to the "just distribution of income, economic security, and the rejection of foreign dependency," thus distinguishing itself as a champion of "social change and the modification of social injustice through a commitment to the humble, the poor, the peasants, [and] the marginalized."[26] While in the decade preceding the juncture these leftist positions had resonated widely across Ecuador – the reason why ID was no weaker than other major parties even in the more prosperous coastal provinces – they had especially struck a chord in provinces with large indigenous populations, predominantly found in the highlands.[27] Indeed, the mostly poor indigenous population, enfranchised during the democratic transition in the late 1970s, had consistently rewarded with disproportionate electoral support "the only major party to recruit a number of indigenous leaders"[28] and consider indigenous concerns,[29] making ID by far the strongest performer in the highlands, where it "gained most of its votes."[30] As the social democrats had also headed a progressive bloc in congress "with the

---

[20] Friedenberg and Alcántara Sáez (2001).

[21] Vos (2002: 269–70).

[22] Silva (2009: 155); Yashar (2005: 136).

[23] Conaghan and Malloy (1994: 228–9); de la Torre and Ortiz Lemos (2016: 4); Roberts (2014: 158–9, 267); Silva (2009: 161–2, 170–1, 175–88); Vos (2002: 271–4).

[24] Launderbaugh (2012: 140).

[25] Interview ECU-21; Friedenberg and Alcántara Sáez (2001).

[26] Friedenberg and Alcántara Sáez (2001: 131, 138).

[27] Based on author's calculations comparing the six coastal – and indigenous-poor – provinces and the eight provinces with the highest shares of indigenous population. Whereas indigenous people averaged less than 2 percent of the population in the indigenous-poor coastal provinces, they accounted for more than 20 percent in the indigenous-rich provinces. See Van Cott (2005: 101).

[28] Madrid (2012: 82).

[29] Madrid (2012: 82); Mijeski and Beck (2011: 16).

[30] Madrid (2012: 83); Van Cott (2005: 105, 111).

express purpose of opposing neoliberalism" during the presidency of Borja's predecessor, the conservative Febres-Cordero,[31] they had ascended to power as a legitimately anti-neoliberal alternative supported by both the indigenous rural sector and the main body of organized labor, the United Workers' Front.[32]

The social democrats' realization that "the market should be the distributor of wealth"[33] disappointed many leftists, who saw this as *"Febres-Borjismo."*[34] This, in turn, induced the institutionalization of a militant anti-neoliberal reaction no sooner than the effects of Borja's economic policies were felt. As organized labor remained weak, it was the indigenous movement – organizing since the 1970s and now led by the Confederation of Indigenous Nationalities of Ecuador (CONAIE)[35] – that led the struggle against neoliberalism.[36] CONAIE may have been originally focused on cultural issues but, as one of its former activists stated, Borja's reforms "represented the culmination of economic injustice."[37] Less than two years into Borja's term, in 1990, CONAIE thus started arguing that previously discriminated against peasants and indigenous nationalities were "most affected by ... the government's social policies."[38] Organizing a massive national uprising, which featured roadblocks, the occupation of properties, and seizure of offices,[39] the organization specifically focused on issues of economic citizenship and class.[40] Indeed, CONAIE's central demand – for land reform – "originated in the economic dislocation caused by neoliberal reforms ... which depressed sources of income..., increased poverty and turned attention back to land as a principle source of income."[41] As the social democrats' austerity program produced continuous declines in real income and the minimal wage, which fell to a third of what they had been a decade prior,[42] its immediate effect was to propel CONAIE's transformation into the organizational backbone of militant protest against market reforms.[43] With Borja's government refraining from using repressive measures against this "opening wave of anti-neoliberal contention,"[44] indigenous-based protest was quickly becoming institutionalized, gaining "a very significant social presence."[45]

8.2.2 Peru

Without a doubt, Peru's neoliberal juncture occurred during the first term of the decade-long presidency of Alberto Fujimori,[46] who enacted some of the most comprehensive market liberalization in Latin America.[47] Confronted

---

[31] Conaghan and Malloy (1994: 135–6, 147).
[32] Silva (2009: 155); Van Cott (2005: 110–1).
[33] Interview ECU-21.
[34] Interview ECU-03.
[35] Silva (2009: 156); Yashar (2005: 139).
[36] Becker (2011b: 27); Yashar (2005: 144).
[37] Interview ECU-09.
[38] Becker (2011b: 30–2).
[39] Zamosc (2007: 9).

[40] Silva (2009: 157–8); Yashar (2005: 145).
[41] Silva (2009: 156–7).
[42] Vos (2002: 271, 290).
[43] Interviews ECU-05; ECU-20.
[44] Silva (2009: 160–9).
[45] Interview ECU-07.
[46] Roberts (2014: 114).
[47] Crabtree and Thomas (1998); José Díaz et al. (2002).

with a dire economic situation, including hyperinflation and 800,000 jobs lost in 1988–89 alone,[48] between 1990 and 1995 Fujimori implemented aggressive shock therapy that not only featured deep structural reforms and stabilization efforts[49] but also institutionalized a neoliberal citizenship regime.[50] These reforms came "by surprise,"[51] however, as they fundamentally contradicted the central message of his 1990 campaign, during which he had adopted "aggressive and classist" rhetoric championing the poor against the rich[52] and rejecting shock therapy.[53] As the fracturing of the party system amid economic crisis[54] had entailed the collapse of state interventionist parties,[55] Fujimori had positioned himself as a left-leaning alternative to famed novelist Mario Vargas Llosa, a shock therapy advocate backed by an alliance of the right-of-center AP and PPC.[56] Consequently, in the first round Fujimori successfully drew "much of Peru's left and center-left" electorate,[57] including formal and informal workers "frightened" by Vargas Llosa's plans.[58] Having qualified for the second round, Fujimori – who had previously tried "to obtain a position on the senatorial list of the ... Socialist Left"[59] – was then endorsed as a legitimate anti-neoliberal candidate by major labor federations and the Left.[60] Additionally, "everyone from APRA was told to vote for him."[61] Given Fujimori's credibility as a left-leaning candidate endorsed by labor-based parties and civil society organizations, and supported by left-leaning voters,[62] the subsequent *Fujishock* was a clear case of bait-and-switch.[63]

With poverty and indigeneity overlapping in Peru, Fujimori's campaign also emphasized ethnicity as he sought to distinguish himself from Vargas Llosa, the white-skinned representative of coastal elites.[64] Lacking a standard party,[65] Fujimori relied on personalism and ethno-populism – a mixture of outsider, antiestablishment, classist, and ethnic appeals[66] – that allowed him to dominate electorally Peru's lower classes, comprising largely of the discriminated against indigenous population.[67] Although this population had been previously

[48] Roberts (1995: 96).

[49] See Arce (2006: 37–8); Silva (2009: 237–8).

[50] Vergara and Encinas (2016); Yashar (2005: 239).

[51] Seawright (2012: 66).

[52] Boas (2016: 140).

[53] Cameron (1994: 112–3, 118, 121); Roberts (1995: 95).

[54] Weyland (1999).

[55] Cameron (1994); Roberts (1998).

[56] Cameron (1994: 59–74).

[57] Roberts (1998: 10, 264). Also, Collier and Collier (1991).

[58] Cameron (1994: 121); McClintock (2013).

[59] Roberts (1995: 95).

[60] Cameron (1994: 137); Roberts (1995: 99); Seawright (2012: 141, 166).

[61] Interview PER-05.

[62] Cameron (1994: 140); Roberts (1998: 266).

[63] Roberts (1995; 2014).

[64] Boas (2016: 138–40); Madrid (2012: 122, 269).

[65] Levitsky (1999: 82); Roberts (1998).

[66] Madrid (2012: 8); Roberts (1995: 88, 92–3).

[67] Madrid (2011: 269–70; 2012: 120); Thorp and Paredes (2010: 22–31). For the links between Peru's subaltern sectors, lower classes, and indigenous population, see Madrid (2012: 95); Roberts (1995: 88, 92–3, 95).

activated – socially under Velasco and politically with the enfranchisement of illiterates in the late 1970s – its mobilization had not been a priority for major parties in the 1980s.[68] While the United Left had been the only party to overperform in indigenous-rich provinces,[69] predominantly located in the highlands, even there it was usually eclipsed by APRA, which certainly did not prioritize ethnic appeals. By contrast, as Fujimori disproportionately attracted indigenous voters, he "took advantage of the profound cultural cleavage" separating them from nonindigenous Peruvians.[70] In the second round of the 1990 election, the personalist contender did especially well in indigenous-rich provinces, where he overperformed by 14.6 points relative to his impressive overall result of 62.4 percent – the largest differential in Peru's democratic history to date.[71] By using "cleavage-priming appeals,"[72] Fujimori pioneered the politicization of ethnicity[73] and activated electorally the regionally based divide between highland and coastal Peru.

The lower classes may have placed their trust in Fujimori, but the social costs of his reforms were "extremely high" for them.[74] Although the economy recovered,[75] the end of industrial protectionism produced the growth of unemployment, underemployment, and informal employment, and thus rising inequality and poverty, which now engulfed more than half the population.[76] Especially vulnerable were two groups – the urban poor and the indigenous public. Although urban poverty declined somewhat by 1997, the economic downturn thereafter reversed improvements, and by the year 2000, 45 percent of Lima residents lived in poverty or extreme poverty – more than in 1993.[77] Meanwhile, unemployment in the capital remained higher than regional averages in the 1990s, with a high share of people working informally against their preferences.[78] As migration from the provinces intensified in the 1990s,[79] with many new city residents subsisting by begging, being poor in Lima was still a "matter of survival."[80] In turn, indigenous communities not only failed to gain from growth[81] but were also affected in uniquely pernicious ways. If they had once benefited from Velasco's agrarian reforms,[82] Fujimori's liberalization of land markets, elimination of agricultural subsidies,[83] and opening of mining to foreign direct investment[84] represented a clear reversal. As the indigenous population now experienced

---

[68] Madrid (2012: 121–2); Van Cott (2005: 150–2).

[69] Defined as having an indigenous population of over 20 percent and based on Van Cott's measure (2005: 142), which is also used by Madrid (2012).

[70] Madrid (2012: 124).

[71] Author's dataset.

[72] Boas (2016: 140).

[73] Madrid (2012: 122–5, 132–4).

[74] Crabtree (1998: 16).

[75] McClintock (2013: 220).

[76] Abugattas (1998: 72–8); Crabtree and Thomas (1998: 269); Roberts (1995: 97).

[77] Peters and Skop (2007: 153).

[78] Leonard (2000: 439); Sheahan (2006: 190).

[79] Interview PER-18.

[80] Interviews PER-05; PER-19; PER-27.

[81] Thorp and Paredes (2010: 177).

[82] Interview PER-04.

[83] Yashar (2005: 237).

[84] Arce (2014: 47); Thorp and Paredes (2010: 177).

heightened extreme poverty rates, neoliberal reforms left it "worse off by any measure."[85] Having pioneered cleavage-priming appeals,[86] Fujimori deepened the divide between the "official Peru" of the coast and the "deep Peru where indigenous people live"[87] through economic policy.

Unlike in Ecuador, however, these circumstances did not produce the institutionalization of anti-neoliberal militancy. While the reasons for this are complex and partially have to do with developments in the 1980s – particularly the violence of the Maoist Shining Path and the hyperinflationary crisis[88] – Fujimori's presidency certainly obstructed the development of protest infrastructure. On the one hand, Fujimori sapped the collective action capacities of the indigenous population in three ways – (1) by increasing indigenous dependency on his government by means of clientelist spending;[89] (2) by using state violence in indigenous areas in response to the Shining Path;[90] and (3) by targeting Peru's Indians with particularly repressive measures, including the forced sterilization of hundreds of thousands of indigenous women.[91] On the other hand, by deregulating the market through legislative decrees, Fujimori destroyed unions,[92] thus further fragmenting organized labor, which had been a critical social base of the radical United Left. Indeed, if what had been the radical Left declined significantly (by 11.7 points, or down to 13 percent[93]) between its national peak in 1985 and 1990 due to events before Fujimori, its total collapse (by another 12.4 points, or down to 0.6 percent) between 1990 and 1995 was due to developments during the juncture.[94] As it was precisely the radical Left that had previously mobilized Peru's indigenous vote and urban poor, its complete decimation under Fujimori would have profound consequences in the future. Overall, by the juncture's end, both the indigenous population and the urban poor were left with no meaningful institutional infrastructure for organizing against neoliberalism.

8.3 FROM AGENCY OF BAIT-AND-SWITCH TO DOMINANT ILLIBERALISM OR NOT

8.3.1 Ecuador

The social democrats' bait-and-switch immediately led to a hemorrhage of voters, many of whom now became available for an initial wave of post-neoliberal populist mobilization lasting from 1996 to 2002. In contrast to the other major

---

[85] Yashar (2005: 239).
[86] Boas (2016: 140).
[87] Arce (2014: 71).
[88] Roberts (1996).
[89] Interviews PER-09; PER-25; Crabtree and Thomas (1998: 269).

[90] Yashar (2005).
[91] Lizarzaburu (2015); Schmidt (2006: 170); Yashar (2005).
[92] Interview PER-10.
[93] Results from presidential elections.
[94] Roberts (1996).

parties, which tended to grow,[95] ID experienced a precipitous electoral decline in the decade after the juncture (1992–2002) relative to the decade prior to it (1978–88) – by 55.8 and 44.1 percent, respectively, in first-round presidential and legislative elections.[96] Specifically, the Left's electoral decline during and immediately after the bait-and-switch juncture – from over 20 percent in 1988 to 13 percent in 1990 to less than 10 percent in 1992 and 1994[97] – opened space for a new ethnic party to be formed in 1995.[98] As this party, Pachakutik, was particularly successful in indigenous-rich provinces[99] – where between 1996 and 2002 it replicated ID's previous dominance of a third of the vote[100] and where it won, on average, three times more support than on the more prosperous coast[101] – it capitalized specifically on the Left's decline. Indeed, Pachakutik's strength was certainly not due to electoral losses of the coast based Roldosist Party or Popular Democracy, both of which made gains in indigenous-rich and coastal provinces in the decade after the juncture relative to the prior decade. Neither was it due to losses of PSC, which before the juncture had been twice (in 1984) and thrice (in 1988) less popular in indigenous-rich provinces than ID and which after the juncture saw relatively less erosion there.[102] It was thus concretely ID's decline following the bait-and-switch that fueled the transformation of the indigenous vote from the social democrats' main support base before the juncture into a backbone of ethnically based post-neoliberal populist mobilization thereafter.

Indeed, although it absorbed many ID voters as well as "a good share of the left's human and financial resources,"[103] Pachakutik is best understood not as a standard leftist party but rather as a post-neoliberal populist reaction, for two reasons. First, rejecting neoliberalism from the beginning, Pachakutik was formed as a multi-class coalition of indigenous groups,[104] organized and informal labor, and Christian communities.[105] Second, having originated as a brand new antiestablishment organization, it supported two personalist outsiders as presidential candidates[106] – the television personality

---

[95] The Social Christian Party, the Roldosist Party, and Popular Democracy improved their average performance in legislative elections, and two of them also gained ground in presidential elections. PSC declined in presidential elections (from 21.9 to 16.1 percent), although less precipitously than ID.

[96] Respectively, from 21.7 to 9.6 percent in first-round presidential elections and from 18 to 10.6 percent in elections for provincial deputies.

[97] Presidential and legislative elections in 1998 and 1992; legislative elections only in 1990 and 1994.

[98] Van Cott (2005: 114).

[99] Madrid (2012).

[100] While ID averaged 33.8 percent of the vote in the 1984 and 1988 first-round presidential elections in the eight indigenous-rich provinces, Pachakutik averaged 32.1 percent in 1996, 1998, and 2002. (Author's dataset.)

[101] Author's dataset.

[102] Author's dataset.

[103] Van Cott (2005: 124).

[104] Interview ECU-09; Becker (2011b).

[105] See Madrid (2012: 83–6); Mijeski and Beck (2011: 36–47); Van Cott (2005: 113–23); Yashar (2005: 149n120).

[106] Carreras (2012).

Freddy Ehlers in 1996 and 1998 and "military putschist" Lucio Gutiérrez in 2002.[107] Since both were not only backed by broader and more centrist electoral constituencies than Pachakutik's[108] but were also perceived by the indigenous movement as opportunistic and insufficiently leftist (and in Ehlers' case, possibly racist),[109] the relationship between these candidates and the ethnic party was always based on strategic calculation. Indeed, as its personalist candidates averaged significantly higher results (18.6 percent) in presidential elections between 1996 and 2002 than the party did in legislative elections (6.8 and 10.4 percent, respectively, for provincial and national deputies) during the same period, Pachakutik's electoral successes were the product of both repudiating neoliberalism and personalism – that is, of post-neoliberal populism.

While Ehlers failed to even make it to the second round of the 1996 and 1998 presidential election, Gutiérrez won both rounds in 2002 by leading a coalition between Pachakutik and his own Patriotic Society Party (PSP). Although this election once again reproduced the persistent divide between the more conservative coast, now electorally dominated by the rightist runner-up Álvaro Noboa, and the indigenous-rich highlands, where Gutiérrez overperformed significantly,[110] the importance of indigenous voting based on narrow ethnic appeals had gradually subsided since 1996 and, by 2002, given way to regional voting based on broader populist appeals.[111] By the early twenty-first century, then, Ecuador's regional divide persisted while populist appeals were becoming less ethnically based. Indeed, ethnic appeals became even less attractive after Pachakutik collaborated, in 2003, with the conservative PSC against Gutiérrez – the very president it had helped elect.

As the salience of ethnicity declined at the expense of broader populist appeals, Ecuador's next, and most successful, post-neoliberal populist experiment – led by the illiberal Rafael Correa – finally overcame the historically persistent regional divide. By attracting both his primary support base from the coast[112] and many voters in the highlands through a mix of economically leftist and Christian rhetoric,[113] in 2006 Correa constructed an extensive electoral coalition. For example, while his first-round nationalization score was higher than his rivals' and much higher than Ehlers' and Gutiérrez's had been in 1996, 1998, and 2002, his second-round nationalization score was the second highest to date after the democratic transition

---

[107] Levitsky and Loxton (2013: 120); Madrid (2012: 95).

[108] Madrid (2012: 94–9).

[109] Becker (2011b: 53).

[110] For example, by winning 45.7 and 77.9 percent of the vote in the first and second rounds, respectively, in the eight indigenous-rich provinces. By contrast, in

the first round, Noboa received 56 percent along the coast and 28.4 percent in the *sierra*. (Author's dataset.)

[111] Madrid (2012); Mijeski and Beck (2011: 59–61, 84–7).

[112] Polga-Hecimovich (2014).

[113] Interviews ECU-03; ECU-05; ECU-24; Becker (2011b: 104); Conaghan (2011); Silva (2009).

in the late 1970s.[114] Crucially, and in line with theoretical expectations, this coalition was assembled "mainly with support from the Democratic Left,"[115] many of whose cadres migrated to Correa's new party, the PAÍS Alliance (AP),[116] and whose electorate Correa mostly inherited, especially in the highlands.[117] Having mobilized a geographically extensive electoral coalition early on, Correa next invested in building an organizational structure for AP by holding Ecuador's first internal party primaries in which members chose candidates for the presidency and legislature.[118] As a result, AP successfully incorporated a number of local notables across the country[119] into a pragmatic and "nationally focused elite party" with a strong visibility across Ecuador.[120] By the 2009 election, *correísmo* further improved the extensiveness of its electoral coalition, with both Correa and AP receiving much more balanced electoral support throughout the country than their rivals.[121] While critics and supporters agree that it never developed into a "real" party,[122] and its own national secretary of territorial organization described it as a "movement", AP built strong bonds with voters as it remained focused on the most pressing national issue – the economy.[123]

Endowed with a solid electoral anchoring throughout Ecuador, AP emerged as a cohesive technocratic organization capable of delivering public policies that undeniably benefited its broad constituency.[124] With its focus on nationally salient economic questions, which its local proxies helped sharpen, AP developed the exceptionally strong legislative cohesion "required to implement its post-neoliberal policy agenda."[125] Importantly, while this agenda, known as the Citizens' Revolution, was to a large extent bankrolled with the help of high commodity prices, other factors – particularly cohesion – certainly played a role. For example, legislative cohesion was crucial during the 2008–9 financial crisis, which hit Ecuador particularly hard as oil prices collapsed, and during the 2009–13 term, when AP did not have legislative majority. Indeed, it was precisely cohesion that in 2009 enabled AP to pass key legislation – ending Central Bank independence, doubling taxes on capital flight, and requiring banks to bring a substantial part of their liquid assets into the country – that

---

[114] Namely, Correa's PNSw of 0.833 in the first round, as compared to Ehlers' 0.640 (1996) and 0.718 (1998), and Gutiérrez's 0.693 (2002). Correa's nationalization score was the sixth highest of all fifty-six candidates who gained more than 2 percent of the vote in first-round presidential elections between 1978 and 2006. Correa's 2006 second-round PNSw of 0.939 was, until then, surpassed only by Jaime Roldós' 1979 second-round PNSw of 0.942. (Author's dataset.)

[115] Interview ECU-03; Jameson (2011: 69).

[116] Interview ECU-21.

[117] Interviews ECU-12; ECU-23; ECU-24.

[118] Interview ECU-14; Bowen (2015: 103).

[119] Interview ECU-18; Clark and García (2019: 231).

[120] Poertner (2018: 86, 89).

[121] Correa's PNSw was 0.904; AP's were 0.832 (provincial deputies) and 0.856 (national deputies). (Author's dataset.)

[122] Interviews ECU-13; ECU-14.

[123] Interviews ECU-11; ECU-22.

[124] Interviews ECU-06; ECU-15; ECU-16.

[125] Clark and García (2019: 231–6); Vera Rojas and Llanos-Escobar (2016).

made Correa's large fiscal stimulus and government spending highly effective during the global financial crisis.[126] These financial and regulatory reforms cushioned Ecuadorians from the Great Recession and facilitated a quick recovery thereafter. Moreover, in a move very different from Venezuela's nationalization of private industries, AP successfully modernized the tax collection system and increased levies on mining corporations, oil companies, and financial institutions, which, in turn, allowed the government to significantly expand social welfare programs.[127] As AP "deepened the Citizens' Revolution without a legislative majority,"[128] these policies challenging neoliberalism would have been impossible without legislative cohesion.

In the end, as the post-neoliberal policy agenda centered on the doubling of public spending – particularly on social welfare, employment, healthcare, urban development, education, and housing – Ecuador saw a drastic reduction of poverty and inequality.[129] As substantiated in multiple interviews, it was such improvements that over time boosted *correísmo*'s popularity among the urban poor, including those in coastal provinces[130] – new constituents that AP took over from the Right by combining socially conservative rhetoric and the supply of material benefits.[131] This, in turn, paved the way to more electoral victories – not only in 2013, when Correa again led the ticket, but also in 2017, even after oil prices fell again and when the charismatic leader no longer ran as the party's presidential candidate. Indeed, with or without Correa at the helm, with or without oil revenues, the Citizens' Revolution remained highly popular even after the party split in 2017.[132] Crucially, if material benefits enabled *correísmo* to dominate for a decade, it was not just the commodity boom but also AP's cohesion that made a difference – especially when oil prices fell, as in 2008–9 and after 2014. As this cohesion was rooted in a focus on the economic questions most relevant to Correa's highly extensive electoral coalition – which had first become available for electoral mobilization after the juncture and then embraced broader populist appeals over time – dominant illiberalism in Ecuador was a legacy of the neoliberal juncture.

8.3.2 Peru

As Fujimori's reforms created winners, especially the coastal middle and upper classes benefitting from now booming business and finance-dependent sectors, and losers, particularly in the highlands,[133] they redefined the lines of

---

[126] Acosta et al. (2009: 122); Weisbrot et al. (2017).

[127] Clark and García (2019: 236–7).

[128] Interview ECU-23.

[129] Weisbrot et al. (2017: 11).

[130] Interviews ECU-01; ECU-02; ECU-04; ECU-11.

[131] Interviews ECU-18; ECU-20; ECU-23.

[132] The party representing the de facto continuation of Correa's wing of AP gained the most votes in the presidential and legislative elections of 2021 and 2023.

[133] Abugattas (1998: 61–87); Carrión (2006: 130–1); Crabtree and Thomas (1998: 268); Figueroa (1998: 127–49).

electoral competition in Peru. Having risen to power with disproportionate indigenous support, by 2000 Fujimori had alienated indigenous voters – now more likely to vote against him[134] – to such a degree that "he could no longer win a majority without resorting to corruption."[135] While the immediate heir to the indigenous constituency, Alejandro Toledo, received significant backing in indigenous-rich regions, in the second round of the 2001 presidential election he drew less support there than Fujimori had attracted in 1990.[136] The likely reason for this was that, although Toledo also emphasized ethnic appeals,[137] his promises to address what was by now "shocking poverty" did not entail a challenge to Fujimori's economic model.[138] As his refusal to confront neoliberalism led to the continuation of structural adjustment and expansion of mining – which created more social conflict than employment[139] – during his presidency (2001–6) Toledo experienced a dramatic loss of popularity.[140]

The unlikely beneficiary was APRA, the party blamed for the economic crisis of the late 1980s, which now fashioned itself as an "ideologically evolved" social democratic option.[141] As one Aprista put it, "The Socialist International changed, and so did APRA; we learned from Europe's socialists."[142] After its head, former president García, lost the 2001 presidential election as a critic of market radicalism,[143] APRA distinguished itself as both the leader of the congressional opposition to Toledo's "savage neoliberalism"[144] and "the only national-level party with important presence across" Peru.[145] With such infrastructure and now criticizing free trade with the United States,[146] García ultimately won the 2006 presidential election. Yet, and in line with APRA's new understanding that "you have to run on the Left but govern on the Right,"[147] between 2006 and 2011 he also deepened neoliberalism,[148] once again advantaging coastal business and middle classes.[149] This, however, precipitated another decline for APRA – a party that not only lacked stable grounding in society following the abandonment of its historic labor base[150] but had also become increasingly out of step with indigenous Peruvians.[151] Indeed, if

---

[134] Madrid (2012: 124).

[135] Interview PER-20.

[136] Specifically, in the second round. (Author's dataset.)

[137] Boas (2016: 148–9); Madrid (2012: 125–7, 134–6); Raymond and Arce (2013: 562).

[138] Silva (2009: 246). Toledo's economic positions were right-of-center, as documented by Baker and Greene (2011).

[139] Interview PER-08.

[140] Silva (2009: 246–7); St John (2010: 40–3).

[141] Interviews PER-01; PER-03; PER-04; PER-06; PER-17; PER-24.

[142] Interview PER-05.

[143] Interview PER-11. See also Boas (2016: 166); Levitt (2012: 136); Roberts (2007: 7).

[144] Interview PER-18. See also Levitt (2012: 142–4).

[145] Arce (2014: 55).

[146] McClintock (2013); Vergara and Encinas (2016: 162).

[147] Interview PER-07.

[148] Cameron (2011: 376–7); Levitsky and Roberts (2011: 18); Vergara and Encinas (2016).

[149] Interview PER-02; Cameron (2011: 395).

[150] Interviews PER-03; PER-29.

[151] See Arce (2014: 33).

APRA's presidential candidate had won in 1985 with considerable support in indigenous-rich regions, this support declined significantly by 2001 and then dwindled even more by 2006, when he received even fewer votes there than immediately after his disastrous first presidency.[152] With Peru's mainstream parties becoming more distanced from indigenous voters, the divide between the coast and highlands was only growing.

Consequently, by 2006 the indigenous constituency was largely mobilized by illiberal ethno-populist Humala, whose nationalist agenda favoring economic statism, social equality through wealth redistribution, and the end of foreign dominated extractivism was supplemented with culturally conservative appeals.[153] Widely seen as an antidemocratic leader similar to the military ruler Velasco,[154] Humala lost the second round of the 2006 presidential election. (See below for a discussion.) Nevertheless, *nacionalismo* – represented that year by him and Union for Peru (UPP) – gained pluralities in the first round of the general election. Remarkably, by rejecting neoliberalism, *nacionalismo* significantly overperformed in the highlands and indigenous-rich areas[155] – in fact, to an even greater extent than Fujimori back in 1990.[156] As it retained the indigenous constituency[157] while also attracting some middle-class supporters after moderating its message,[158] in 2011 *nacionalismo* not only won the presidency but also gained more seats in the legislature.

Despite this victory, however, and unlike Ecuador's *correísmo*, Peru's *nacionalismo* did not gain power by bridging the deep divide – initially activated for electoral gain by Fujimori and then sustained through neoliberal policies – between the indigenous highlands and the coast. Indeed, between 2006 and 2011, Humala may have improved his electoral showing in coastal regions, but he also improved in highland and indigenous-rich areas.[159] Although the electoral gaps narrowed somewhat during this period, *nacionalismo*'s electoral base remained very poorly nationalized.[160] Supported by a highly segmented electoral coalition, Humala's party failed to achieve any organizational coherence. Indeed, this party was a "disaster" amid the chaos caused by congressional candidates living outside of the provinces where they competed.[161] Plagued by infighting,[162] the nationalists neither did well in local elections[163] nor incorporated many local notables that could have helped them

---

[152] 47.5 percent in 1985, 24.5 percent in 2001, and 18.4 percent in 2006. The same trend generally applies for APRA in legislative elections. (Author's dataset.)

[153] Cameron (2011); Levitsky and Roberts (2011); Madrid (2012: 130–1); McClintock (2013: 225–33).

[154] Interviews PER-04; PER-05; PER-20; PER-28.

[155] Madrid (2012: 129–30).

[156] Author's dataset.

[157] Madrid (2012: 142–4).

[158] Boas (2016: 170–2); McClintock (2013: 233–7).

[159] Madrid (2012).

[160] PNSw values were indeed quite low – 0.779 (Humala) and 0.740 (Union for Peru) in 2006, and 0.777 (Humala) and 0.814 (Peru Wins) in 2011. (Author's dataset.)

[161] Cameron (2011).

[162] Interview PER-17.

[163] Interview PER-09.

connect better with voters.[164] Equally problematic was their 2011 alliance, Peru Wins (GP), whose congressional candidates largely ignored grassroots activists and whose local cells were disbanded soon after the election.[165] As one former activist complained, "Humala did not unify the social force supporting him."[166]

Lack of organizational unity, in turn, corresponded to an unusually high number – even by Peruvian standards – of defections from the Peru Wins congressional delegation during Humala's presidency (2011–6).[167] (Although it did not have a congressional majority, the delegation controlled enough seats to build a majority coalition, which, however, thinned mostly due to defections from Humala's Peruvian Nationalist Party.[168]) While this disintegration has been attributed to Humala's ultimately pro-market economic policies, this was not always the only problem,[169] as defections began very early in his administration, before Humala's neoliberal turn took clear shape and amid the implementation of social programs that "reversed some of the most negative effects of neoliberalism."[170] Moreover, if Humala antagonized social movements by expanding mining in Peru – the key reason for early defections from his party in congress[171] – Correa did the same by continuing extractivism in Ecuador without, however, destroying the cohesion of his party in congress. A key difference was that while Correa's party remained focused, even when lacking a congressional majority, on the economic issues important to its highly extensive electoral coalition, Humala's party, lacking such a coalition, never developed as a coherent and unified organization, as multiple party activists complained.[172] Unlike Correa, Humala certainly was not in charge of a cohesive party capable of technocratic governance, as one political scientist differentiated.[173] This, in turn, led to loss of legislative control, considerable government instability, and significant decline of popular approval.[174] As crime and "tremendous citizen insecurity" remained serious problems for many Peruvians, what was generally perceived as bad governance alienated former supporters of *nacionalismo*.[175]

Humala's presidency thus proved highly ineffectual. Having lost its popular base as a result, *nacionalismo* not only failed to produce a presidential successor in 2016, as AP did in Ecuador after Correa bowed out in 2017, but also effectively disappeared as a political factor. Overall, if the electoral feats of Peru's most important challenger of neoliberalism traced their roots to the most critical period of market reforms,[176] so did *nacionalismo's* failure to

---

[164] Interview PER-13.
[165] Interviews PER-26; PER-27.
[166] Interview PER-15.
[167] Interview PER-12.
[168] Carrión and Zárate (2023: 19); Jaramillo (2023: 652).
[169] Interviews PER-19; PER-23.
[170] Interview PER-22.

[171] Interviews PER-22; PER-29.
[172] Interviews PER-14; PER-23; PER-25; PER-26; PER-27; PER-28.
[173] Interview PER-09.
[174] Muñoz and Dargent (2016: 324, 334).
[175] Interview PER-04; PER-13; PER-18; PER-19; PER-24; PER-25; PER-27.
[176] Roberts (2014).

persist at the ballot box. As personalist Fujimori raised the electoral and economic salience of regionally based cleavages, the segmented electoral coalition that emerged as a result of the juncture both enabled illiberalism's subsequent successes at the ballot box and constrained its capacity for continued relevance through cohesive and effective governance.

8.4 FROM VIABILITY OF INSTITUTIONALIZING ANTI-NEOLIBERAL CONTENTION TO CONTESTATORY ILLIBERALISM OR MODERATION

8.4.1 Ecuador

If the social democrats' neoliberal turn triggered the sprouting of organizationally based militancy through CONAIE in 1990, the following fifteen years saw the further institutionalization of anti-neoliberal protest in Ecuador. Indeed, as subsequent governments kept shaping the country's deepening neoliberal consensus, CONAIE organized a series of contentious actions against all popularly elected presidents. These included an Amazon march forcing President Borja to legalize indigenous lands in 1992; an uprising against President Durán-Ballén's capitalist agriculture and water privatization plans in 1994; anti-austerity demonstrations, which helped force President Bucaram out of office in 1997 and spurred a new constitution that recognized indigenous rights in 1998; three large mobilizations against austerity and dollarization in 1998 and 1999, which led to a CONAIE-supported coup that removed President Mahuad in 2000; and, finally, protests against the neoliberal turn of President Gutiérrez in 2004. Along the way, CONAIE also founded, in 1995–6, Pachakutik as an ethnic protest party, thus further institutionalizing anti-systemic contention.[177] In the words of one journalist, "beginning with Borja, the indigenous movement started to have more presence, and this presence became more intense, combative, and radical."[178]

Although Pachakutik certainly featured democratic tendencies in its party structures and is generally understood to be a "democratizing force,"[179] its long-standing connections with the military,[180] its "ambiguousness regarding the law,"[181] and its "lack of belief in institutions"[182] certainly played a destabilizing role in terms of *liberal* democratic norms and institutions at the national level.[183] Having been involved in a coup, supported military putschist Gutiérrez's run for the presidency, and then broken with him in 2003, Pachakutik contributed toward party system collapse. While public

---

[177] Becker (2011b); Zamosc (2007: 1–15).
[178] Interview ECU-13.
[179] Interviews ECU-07; ECU-21.
[180] Interview ECU-18.

[181] Interview ECU-12.
[182] Interview ECU-21.
[183] Interview ECU-13; Zamosc (2007).

confidence in liberal democratic institutions was already low following the 2000 coup, it declined precipitously during Pachakutik's 2003 confrontation with Gutiérrez.[184] For example, if in the first round of the 2002 presidential election more than 60 percent of voters chose candidates representing parties that had not existed in the 1990s, by the 2006 election more than two-thirds of voters supported such candidates. By the early to mid 2000s, then, the party system of Ecuador's "poorly practiced pseudo-democracy"[185] had collapsed.

It was in such an environment characterized by a "profound crisis of institutional legitimacy and social mobilization"[186] that illiberal Correa, whose supporters viewed the 2000 coup as understandable and necessary,[187] adopted an electorally successful strategy of contesting liberal democracy. This strategy was additionally fueled by the demands of the radical Pachakutik, which, though having lost much of its credibility after 2003,[188] still remained an electorally relevant factor in the 2006 election. As Correa sought Pachakutik's endorsement, he credibly committed to its central demands for root and branch institutional transformation, thus ensuring, even before entering office, that as president he could not have possibly governed according to liberal democratic norms.

To begin, despite Correa's strong antiestablishment and anti-neoliberal credentials, he was initially viewed by the indigenous movement and radical leftist sectors more generally with suspicion and even antagonism due to his base in technocratic and coastal elites, Catholic leanings, and Keynesian, rather than Marxist, critique of markets.[189] Some even saw him as a "neoliberal wolf in sheep's clothing" similar to Peru's Fujimori.[190] On his part, when Correa, initially agnostic to indigenous demands, "came to support … the holding of a constituent assembly, he did so in an opportunistic fashion that coopted a key issue for the indigenous movement."[191] Crucially, as an alliance with Pachakutik failed,[192] Correa strategically competed in 2006 as a presidential candidate without a congressional list – that is, as someone unable to govern, if elected president, barring a constituent assembly. As this extreme personalism[193] also represented a credible commitment to the indigenous movement's central demand, many of those who had voted for Pachakutik previously chose Correa rather than the ethnic party's own candidate.[194] Despite this, Correa drew only a minority of indigenous voters – 16 percent – in the first round of

---

[184] According to Latinobarómetro, between 2002 and 2003, the share of those with "no confidence" in parliament and parties rose, respectively, from 59 to 71.6 percent and from 62.2 to 70.8 percent.

[185] Interview ECU-17.

[186] Interview ECU-07.

[187] Interviews ECU-09; ECU-14.

[188] Becker (2011b: 83–94).

[189] Interviews ECU-10; ECU-11; Conaghan (2011: 264–71); Levitsky and Loxton (2013: 120); Madrid (2012: 107); Montúfar (2013); Roberts (2014: 268).

[190] Interview ECU-03.

[191] Becker (2011b: 104–5).

[192] Madrid (2012: 103); Mijeski and Beck (2011: 104–5).

[193] Roberts (2014: 268).

[194] Madrid (2012: 104).

the 2006 election,[195] a reason why he intensified efforts to attract more indigenous support in the second round.[196] Indeed, he escalated his antiestablishment rhetoric between the first and second rounds in the hopes of attracting Pachakutik's endorsement.[197] As Correa now promised a "radical restructuring of the government," which finally earned him Pachakutik's "unconditional support,"[198] he won 74 percent of the vote in majority indigenous counties in the second round of the election[199] – and thus the presidency in 2006. Crucially, Correa would not have won without such high support from the indigenous constituency,[200] which he captured by means of his strategy of contesting liberal democratic norms even before being elected.

Since Correa became president without a party, his election generated what one sociologist described as "the worst antagonism imaginable in a presidential system."[201] Indeed, facing a congress controlled by the opposition, Correa had to urgently fulfill his promise to convoke a constituent assembly if he had any hopes of actually governing. Since this required a congressionally approved referendum, however, Correa orchestrated a series of confrontations, which, being "without any credible basis in law,"[202] immediately undermined liberal democratic institutions. Indeed, the referendum was approved after both the expulsion of congressional opponents to it by the electoral tribunal and the sacking of constitutional tribunal judges opposed to this by the new pro-Correa congressional majority. Having cleared legal obstacles and in control of key institutions, Correa easily won the 2007 constitutional referendum. After his newly created AP then gained a majority of seats in the constitutional assembly election that year, it rewrote the constitution by 2008, significantly strengthening the presidency at the expense of congress.[203] This centralization of power, in turn, undermined pluralism, civil rights,[204] and the freedom of speech, a main concern of journalists and human rights activists.[205]

Overall, the erosion of liberal democracy in Ecuador was the culmination of a historically contingent process. As Correa encountered a profound political crisis amid party system collapse and made a credible commitment to reconstitute the battered political system when he sought to attract the much-needed former voters of the radical Pachakutik, his contestatory strategy vis-à-vis liberal democracy was not incidental. While opponents and advocates of

---

[195] Clientelist networks targeting the poor allowed Gutiérrez's right-leaning brother, Gilmar, to gain 45 percent of the indigenous vote. See Madrid (2012: 105); Mijeski and Beck (2011: 110).

[196] Madrid (2012: 106).

[197] Interviews ECU-05; ECU-19.

[198] Becker (2011b: 111).

[199] Madrid (2012: 106).

[200] Báez Rivera and Solo de Zaldívar (2006: 22–3); Madrid (2012: 105–7); Mijeski and Beck (2011: 106–11).

[201] Interview ECU-07.

[202] Puddington (2008: 224).

[203] Conaghan (2011).

[204] de la Torre (2013).

[205] Specifically, through the 2013 Communication Law (Interviews ECU-05; ECU-13; ECU-19; ECU-20).

correísmo contest whether he cynically "used" Pachakutik[206] or was genuinely influenced by its radicalism,[207] few disagree that Correa adjusted his strategy in response to the institutional context this party had helped to shape. Since this strategy was an adaptation to an environment conditioned by party system collapse and the salience of anti-systemic radicalism – which became progressively destabilizing following its origins during the juncture – contestatory illiberalism in Ecuador was the result of path-dependent developments.

8.4.2 Peru

Although Peru re-democratized following Fujimori's resignation amid evidence of widespread corruption in 2000,[208] the personalist style underpinning his authoritarianism destroyed, to an unparalleled degree, the capacity of political parties to function as institutional channels of representation.[209] As his policies helped to decimate what had been "the strongest Left on the continent" and sabotage ethnic-based organizing, they left both the urban poor and indigenous groups without the resources necessary to politicize neoliberalism.[210] The indigenous movement failed to form key organizations – the National Confederation of Communities Affected by Mining (CONACAMI) and Permanent Coordinator of Indigenous Peoples of Peru (COPPIP) – until the late 1990s, or several years after the juncture. Even later, activists could not establish a viable ethnic party.[211] Without its own political vehicle to articulate demands in a unified manner, the indigenous movement remained regionally fragmented and ineffectual well into the twenty-first century.[212]

This is not to say that contentious action based on indigenous grievances was absent in the post-Fujimori era, during which the neoliberal consensus solidified. Indeed, as the growth of mining at the expense of indigenous regions aggravated highland poverty and indigence[213] – which by 2006 stood at 69 and 47 percent, respectively[214] – President Toledo (2001–6) faced four waves of indigenous-led anti-neoliberal protest in highland areas affected by mining.[215] In turn, the expansion of free trade under García's second presidency (2006–11) resulted in new peaks of indigenous protest in the late 2000s.[216] While these two presidents handled anti-neoliberal contention differently – Toledo by assuming a pro-indigenous rhetorical posture; García by using state violence – they both successfully outmaneuvered indigenous protestors, whose divisions and lack of party organization rendered their otherwise considerable mobilization less

---

[206] Interviews ECU-02; ECU-03; ECU-05; ECU-19; ECU-24.
[207] Interviews ECU-09; ECU-10; ECU-11; ECU-23.
[208] Levitsky and Way (2010); St John (2010: 34).
[209] Levitsky (1999); Roberts (2006b: 81).
[210] Interview PER-10.

[211] Van Cott (2005: 140).
[212] Arce (2008); Madrid (2012: 117–8); Van Cott (2005: 163–70).
[213] Arce (2014: 49); Silva (2009: 256).
[214] McClintock (2013: 227).
[215] Arce (2008).
[216] Arce (2014: 31–41).

visible.[217] Whereas the institutionalized indigenous movement of Ecuador routinely brought down presidents by militant action, its fragmented counterpart to the south consistently failed to influence heads of state in Peru.

Although the electoral rise of illiberalism in 2006 represented a major challenge to the status quo, its figurehead – Ollanta Humala – ultimately switched from a contestatory electoral strategy to moderation vis-à-vis liberal democracy. While scholars have explained this outcome as a product of Peru's booming economy, which benefitted the urban middle classes that Humala ended up appeasing, and the straitjacket of the Fujimori constitution, which empowered a neoliberal state technocracy, they have paid less attention to the non-viability of institutionalizing anti-neoliberal protest on behalf of Peru's popular classes. Yet, as Peruvian political scientists accept that such mechanisms of neoliberal reproduction had not been fully established by the "crucial" general election in 2006,[218] I argue that this non-viability was a key factor behind Humala's eventual moderation, for two reasons.

First, a comparison with Ecuador is instructive regarding the linkages between the institutionalization of protest and liberal democratic legitimacy. Although overall developments during the 1990s and early 2000s were different in the two countries, three relevant similarities stand out. First, while the Peruvian economy grew significantly in the late 2000s, the five years before the critical 2006 elections in the two countries saw very similar growth rates.[219] Indeed, with comparable unemployment, poverty, and inequality metrics, Peru's economy was not particularly stronger than Ecuador's in the early 2000s.[220] Second, just like Ecuador had its attempted coup d'état moment – in early 2000 amid a financial crisis, so did Peru – when Humala led a military uprising in late 2000 amid the political crisis that ended Fujimori's presidency. Third, in the early 2000s, presidents Gutiérrez and Toledo deepened neoliberalism in both countries, thus antagonizing the very indigenous voters that had elevated them to power.

Despite these similarities, Ecuador and Peru diverged in terms of overall political stability in the early 2000s. This divergence had much to do with the viability of institutionalizing radicalism. In Ecuador, the well-coordinated indigenous movement, headed by CONAIE and Pachakutik, helped both to remove President Mahuad via the 2000 coup and to destabilize Gutiérrez's presidency thereafter. By contrast, the lack of such coordination corresponded to relative political stability in Peru,[221] where the 2000 uprising failed and where militant

---

[217] Arce (2014: 34–7).
[218] Interviews PER-09; PER-16.
[219] In 2001–5, GDP per capita grew on average by 3.1 percent in Ecuador and 3 percent in Peru.
[220] In 2001–5, the average rates for Peru and Ecuador, respectively, were as follows: unemployment – 8.3 versus 9.4 percent;

absolute poverty – 18.1 versus 14.3 percent; and Gini index – 54.9 versus 52.5. Peru did have, on average, lower inflation during this period, but Ecuador averaged even lower inflation in the two years before 2006. (Data from the IMF and World Bank.)
[221] Interviews PER-21; PER-29.

actors did not unsettle Toledo's presidency. Furthermore, if in 2002 and 2006 the great majority of Ecuadorian voters supported the presidential candidates of parties that had not existed in the 1990s, in 2001 and 2006 the great majority of Peruvian voters supported the presidential candidates of parties that had existed in the previous decade. Although this does not mean that the Peruvian party system was stable, it does suggest that in 2006 Humala encountered an environment where democracy had been significantly less delegitimated. As Peruvians were twice more likely than Ecuadorians to express "a lot of confidence in democracy" in 2006,[222] Humala's antidemocratic discourse that year was, according to one political scientist, a whole separate issue from his anti-neoliberalism – and the real dealbreaker for most Peruvians.[223] Indeed, in the first round of the 2006 election in Peru, 55 percent of voters had chosen candidates – Humala and García – associated with anti-neoliberal positions, which at the time were no less popular in Peru than in Ecuador.[224] While Humala called for the nationalization of industries, former president García, having led Peru into the hyperinflationary crisis of the late 1980s, had an actual track record of nationalization and "irresponsible" economic governance. The real difference was that, unlike Humala, García was viewed as – in the words of supporters, opponents, and independent analysists alike – the democratic option.[225] Ultimately, Humala's loss of the 2006 runoff had to do less with popular aversion to his anti-neoliberalism and more with the perception that he was an actual threat to democracy.

Second, the lack of institutionalization of leftist radicalism limited Humala's appeal among constituents desiring systemic change. More speculatively, an endorsement and grassroots mobilization effort from a radical ethnic party similar to Ecuador's Pachakutik could have possibly secured even more indigenous support for Humala in the tight second round of the 2006 election. In the runoff, Humala, who was generally popular among Peru's indigenous public, received as much indigenous support as Correa,[226] whom Ecuador's indigenous community distrusted. Meanwhile, Humala was relatively less appealing among indigenous constituents and voters who had attended protests than Evo Morales was in Bolivia, a country with which Peru is comparable specifically in terms of demographic profile and the larger size of indigenous populations.[227] An important difference was that in Bolivia a powerful ethnic party prioritized indigenous demands, organized protests, and electorally mobilized indigenous supporters and those who protested. By contrast, the lack of such a party in Peru suggests that Humala – who neither made indigenous demands

---

[222] 12.8 versus 6.3 percent (2006 Latinobarómetro survey).

[223] Interview PER-11.

[224] According to the latest survey results obtained before the 2006 election, 24.9 percent of Peruvians and 23.6 percent of Ecuadorians disagreed that the

market economy was the optimal system for development (2005 Latinobarómetro survey).

[225] Interviews PER-06; PER-09; PER-10; PER-24; PER-29.

[226] Madrid (2012: 106, 123).

[227] Madrid (2012: 22–3, 69, 141).

central to his 2006 campaign nor collaborated meaningfully with social move-ments[228] – likely failed to maximize his full electoral potential in the indige-nous highlands.[229]

Less speculatively, the decimation of the radical Left in the early 1990s meant that there was no partisan infrastructure available to rally the urban poor to vote for Humala in 2006. While the radical Left had dominated this constituency, even capturing Lima's mayorship, in the 1980s,[230] in the 2006 runoff Humala failed to win a majority of the vote in any Lima districts.[231] The problem, of course, was less lack of poverty – in which a quarter of Lima still lived in 2006[232] – and more lack of an institutionalized framework for leftist mobilization. Especially because "the Nationalist Party was weak and the movement was not enough," as one Lima district secretary of the party lamented,[233] the lack of preexisting organization on the Left certainly hindered Humala's ability to mobilize the urban poor.[234] Or, as one former nationalist congressman explained, echoing a common frustration among activists with the "lack of capacity,"[235] "the party did not play its role, and no one organized the social sectors that supported us."[236] Finally, as argued convincingly by Maxwell Cameron, there were no structural reasons preventing Humala from winning the presidency in 2006, and indeed he came very close to taking Peru in an Ecuadorian direction.[237] (This notion was shared by multiple interview-ees who speculated that if in the runoff Humala had faced the rightist Lourdes Flores – who fell half a percentage point short of qualifying – he would have "no doubt" won.[238]) Moreover, as several prominent Peruvian social scientists argued, had Humala won in 2006 – that is, before the subsequent economic boom – he would have likely been able to quickly mount popular support, dis-band congress, and change the constitution, similarly to Correa in Ecuador.[239]

---

[228] Handlin (2017: 237); Madrid (2012: 53–68, 128). As Madrid shows in his case study of Bolivia's MAS, making indigenous demands central to the campaign does not imply abandonment of "inclusive" appeals (and thus alienation of non-indigenous voters).

[229] This is supported by the finding that the party whose candidate Humala was in 2006, Union for Peru, was less sup-ported among indigenous people than the Peruvian Nationalist Party, which he had failed to register in time for the election. See Raymond and Arce (2013).

[230] Roberts (1996).

[231] Cameron (2011: 387).

[232] Interview PER-12; de Olarte et al. (2011).

[233] Interviews PER-18; PER-27.

[234] Attracting both the rural and urban poor does not necessarily mean that Humala's

party nationalization scores would have been high, as evidenced by the relatively low scores of the United Left, which drew support from both constituencies in the 1980s. Thus, the arguments about Humala's failure to build party cohesion and about his moderation remain separate.

[235] Interviews PER-23; PER-25; PER-26; PER-27; PER-28; PER-29.

[236] Interview PER-22.

[237] Cameron 2011.

[238] Interviews PER-22; PER-25; PER-26; PER-27; PER-28; PER-29. The usual argument was that the more left-oriented supporters of APRA would not have, before the economic boom, voted for Lourdes Flores in the sec-ond round.

[239] Interviews PER-09; PER-11; PER-16; PER-21.

While the causes of his failure to win the narrow 2006 election as a contestatory illiberal are multiple and complex, the weakness of institutionalized channels for rallying more supporters on his behalf was not an insignificant factor.

Having failed in 2006 and once again facing the same limitations, but this time in more prosperous times, Humala then moderated significantly. Now seeking support from the urban middle classes, he formally promised not only to respect property rights and disavow nationalization but also to not centralize power or seek reelection. Consequently, although many liberals still saw the 2011 presidential contest – between Humala, who sustained his socially conservative and economically leftist (although now less radical) positions,[240] and Keiko Fujimori, the staunchly pro-market daughter of the former autocrat – as a lose-lose situation, Humala won narrowly. Even if much had changed since 2006, a majority of voters still prioritized preserving democracy over neoliberal continuity, with the main cleavage in Peruvian politics remaining democracy versus authoritarianism.[241] Having become president in 2011, Humala then governed as a liberal democrat. Notably, this moderation took place amid renewed protests,[242] which, however – and as usual – no institutionalized body coordinated in a truly organized manner.

Overall, while the reasons for Humala's moderation remain contested, the evidence from the Peruvian case problematizes standard accounts, which ignore the linkages between the prior availability of institutionalized channels for anti-systemic contention and the viability of contestatory strategies vis-à-vis liberal democracy. Whether the weakness of such channels meant that the environment Humala encountered in 2006 did not feature a sufficiently delegitimated party system, as in Ecuador, or it meant that Humala could not maximize his potential to attract the poor (either in the highlands or cities), it constrained his ability to win as a contestatory illiberal. While other factors, including the growing economy in the late 2000s and technocratic entrenchment in state institutions, also played a role for Humala's subsequent moderation, his unsuccessful contestatory strategy in 2006 – what a number of Peruvian analysts consider the major learning experience that incentivized this moderation[243] – is not explained by such factors. Instead, it was the lack of institutionalized contention – in the form of either an anti-neoliberal ethnic party or a radical leftist one – that conditioned a political context in which it was significantly harder, though not impossible, for contestatory illiberalism to be a winning electoral strategy in 2006. Because this lack was largely a legacy of the juncture, during which organized channels for anti-neoliberal protest were seriously compromised, the moderation of illiberalism in Peru was rooted in historical contingency.

---

[240] See Baker and Greene (2011); Binev (2024a).
[241] Interview PER-12.
[242] Burron (2012: 136).

[243] Interviews PER-08; PER-09; PER-11; PER-13; PER-20.

8.5 THE NUANCED LEGACIES OF BAIT-AND-SWITCH JUNCTURES

By paying close attention to dynamics before leading illiberals rose to executive power, the earlier discussion invites new ways of thinking about the political reactions to neoliberalism in Ecuador and Peru. While these reactions can be traced back to generally similar bait-and-switch tactics during neoliberal junctures,[244] the two countries experienced them in fundamentally different ways. These experiences, I have argued, hinged on developments rooted in the nuanced contingencies of bait-and-switch junctures – particularly, the agency of bait-and-switch reforms and the viability of institutionalizing anti-neoliberal protest. Since such nuances shaped subsequent paths in ways similar to those seen in Slovakia and Poland, as I discuss next, illiberal trajectories and tendencies in the Andes had much in common with those experienced in the very different contexts of postcommunist Europe.

Beginning with the agency of bait-and-switch, Ecuador's experience was much like Slovakia's. In both cases, those in charge of neoliberal deepening during the juncture were social democratic parties whose extensive organizations and programmatic appeals had previously underpinned their ability to draw voters widely across the country. As social democrats declined following their neoliberal turn, subsequent illiberals successfully mobilized their former constituencies as they assembled highly extensive popular coalitions during formative electoral experiences. Indeed, both Ecuador's *correísmo* and Slovakia's SMER enjoyed electoral coalition extensiveness that surpassed their political rivals', beginning with the very first elections they contested and before rising to power.[245] Their better nationalized electorates, in turn, incentivized party cohesion early on, which then facilitated illiberals' ability to legislate for nationally relevant public goods as incumbents. As they supplied generous material benefits that reinforced their popularity over time, illiberals in Ecuador and Slovakia won multiple consecutive elections and dominated politically for at least a decade starting in 2006.

By contrast, as the agent politically responsible for the bait-and-switch during the juncture in Peru was a personalist leader, the trajectory this Andean country followed was more similar to the Polish experience, characterized by the inability of the main illiberal actor to subsequently dominate in the long term. Lacking standard party organizations, personalists Alberto Fujimori and Lech Wałęsa used identity-priming, rather than programmatic, appeals, thereby politicizing historically based regional cleavages and disproportionately mobilizing less economically developed constituencies – namely, "deep

---

[244] Roberts (2014).
[245] For how the extensiveness of Slovakia's SMER, Poland's PiS, Ecuador's *correísmo*, and Peru's *nacionalismo* evolved over time and compared to the extensiveness of other parties in their respective party systems, see Binev (2024b).

Peru" and "Poland B" – on their way to executive power. Yet, since the neoliberal reforms they championed also hurt these constituencies disproportionately, the solidified regionally based polarization would be reproduced, with consequences for the future.

As seen in Table 8.1, in the 1990 election Fujimori disproportionately dominated the indigenous-rich "deep Peru," in a way similar to Wałęsa's mobilization of "Poland B" that same year. When these "neoliberal populist" presidents[246] eventually passed from the scene after alienating what had been their core voters – faster in democratic Poland, slower in authoritarian Peru – "Poland B" and "deep Peru" became again available for populist electoral mobilization. Although these constituencies were soon drawn to different political projects – especially Solidarity Electoral Action (AWS) in 1997 in Poland and Toledo in 2001 in Peru – regional polarization at first remained less pronounced than what it had been when Wałęsa and Fujimori first politicized cleavages, as seen in the smaller absolute and relative differences in the table.[247] Yet, as neoliberal reforms continued negatively impacting less developed regions in both countries, illiberal nationalists PiS and Humala captured "Poland B" and "deep Peru" so disproportionately that regionally based electoral polarization surpassed even what it had been in 1990.

Indeed, as Peruvian and Polish illiberals rose to power with support from highly segmented constituencies, their electoral coalitions were less extensive than their political rivals', both when they first contested elections and more generally over time.[248] Entering the political arena without relatively uniform support across the country[249] and failing to achieve sustainably high nationalization relative to their political rivals, Peruvian and Polish illiberals certainly did not develop party cohesion early on. Consequently, they could not govern as effectively as their Ecuadorian and Slovak counterparts when they initially assumed power. While Polish and Peruvian illiberals struggled with problems of governance, their Slovak and Ecuadorian counterparts governed better, taxed more effectively, and spent significantly more on social programs.[250] These differences, in turn, corresponded to differential outcomes in terms of societal well-being. For example, although Ecuador's economy grew less under

---

[246] Weyland (1999).

[247] The relative differences were larger in the case of the Polish People's Party (PSL), which, however, commanded less support in "Poland B."

[248] Poland's PiS improved its coalition extensiveness relative to its competitors only briefly, in 2005–7. (Author's dataset.)

[249] Whereas the PNSw of Peru's *nacionalismo* averaged 0.760 in 2006, the PNSw of Poland's PiS was only 0.700 in 2001. (Author's dataset.)

[250] While social spending as a share of GDP rose by 8 percent in Correa's Ecuador, it rose by only 1.2 percent in Peru under Humala. And if it rose by 2.9 percent during the first SMER-led government (even under EU budgetary restrictions), it declined by 2.8 percent during the first PiS-led government. (Author's calculations based on data from Economic Commission for Latin America and the Caribbean and the Organization for Economic Co-operation and Development.)

TABLE 8.1 Mobilizing "Poland B" and "Deep Peru"

Poland

Political project	Mobilizing power					
	Wałęsa, 1990	PSL, 1991–3	AWS, 1997	PSL, 2001	PiS, 2001–7	PiS, 2011–19
Concentration of electoral support						
Vote share in "Poland B"	45.0	15.6	38.6	14.1	25.7	46.4
Absolute difference from "Poland A"	12.2	5.0	9.8	6.9	7.6	15.1
Relative difference from "Poland A"	1.37	1.43	1.34	1.94	1.38	1.51

Peru

Political project	Mobilizing power					
	Fujimori, 1990	Fujimori, 1995	Fujimori, 2000	Toledo, 2001	Humala, 2006	Humala, 2011
Concentration of electoral support						
Presidential elections, first round						
Vote share in "Deep Peru"	31.9	66.7	46.2	44.6	50.1	52.2
Absolute difference from rest of country	8.8	0.9	–6.3	8.6	21.1	20.6
Relative difference from rest of country	1.38	1.01	0.88	1.24	1.73	1.65
Presidential elections, second round						
Vote share in "Deep Peru"	77.0	–	68.1	61.4	66.1	69.9
Absolute difference from rest of country	15.9	–	–7.1	10.9	18.6	18.9
Relative difference from rest of country	1.26	–	0.91	1.22	1.39	1.37

Author's calculations based on subnational election data at the level of *powiat* in Poland (parliamentary elections) and *provincia* in Peru (presidential elections). For brevity, I have averaged PiS's scores for two periods – an earlier period in the 2000s and a later period in the 2010s. "Poland B" corresponds to regions of the former Russian and Austrian empires, whereas "Deep Peru" corresponds to regions where the indigenous population is more than 20 percent of the total.

Correa's presidency than the Peruvian economy under Humala's administration,[251] Ecuador made significantly more progress in terms of inequality reduction. If by the end of Correa's presidency Ecuador's bottom half earned 22 percent more and were 8.5 percent wealthier than the last year before Correa assumed power, by the end of Humala's term the bottom half earned just 3 percent more and had 3 percent less wealth than the last year before his presidency.[252] And although Ecuador's Human Development Index before Correa assumed power had been lower than Peru's before Humala's term in office, by the end of their presidencies the situation was reversed.

Similarly, Slovakia's economy under the first SMER-led government (2006–10) may have underperformed relative to Poland's under the first, and generally similar, PiS-led government (2005–7),[253] but social indicators improved. In Slovakia, inequality declined by the end of the first SMER-led government, with the top 1 percent earning 11 percent less and the bottom half earning 8 percent more relative to the year before Fico's first premiership began. In Poland, inequality worsened, with the top 1 percent earning 15 percent more and the bottom half earning 5 percent less as a result of the first PiS-led government. And while Slovakia's Human Development Index before the first SMER-led government had been lower than Poland's before the first PiS-led government, the situation was reversed by the end of these governments.

The bottom line is that whereas Ecuadorian and Slovak illiberals developed reputations as providers of nationally relevant material benefits and guarantors of improved prospects for popular majorities, their Peruvian and Polish counterparts not only failed to develop such reputations but also became known for legislative disfunction and ineffective governance driven by poor party cohesion. As a result, the latter could not turn incumbency into an electoral advantage and were thus less politically dominant in the early twenty-first century.[254]

If the agency of bait-and-switch shaped illiberals' ability to dominate or not in the long run, the viability of institutionalizing anti-neoliberal protest during the juncture molded strategies of contestation or moderation vis-à-vis liberal

---

[251] During Correa's presidency (2007–17), Ecuador's GDP per capita grew on average by 3.4 percent per year, being, on average, $10,008 (PPP, current prices). Peru's annual averages during Humala's presidency (2011–16) were 4.7 percent growth and $11,129 GDP per capita. (Author's calculations based on IMF data.)

[252] Similarly, Ecuador's top 1 percent earned 20 percent less and was 11 percent less wealthy. Peru's top 1 percent earned 4 percent more and was 6 percent wealthier. The income and wealth of the top 10 percent also declined in Ecuador, while they persisted at stable levels in Peru. (Data from the World Inequality Database.)

[253] During the first SMER-led government, Slovakia's GDP per capita grew on average by 5.1 percent per year, being, on average, $18,748 (PPP, current prices). Poland's annual averages during the first PiS-led government were 9.7 percent growth and $21,384 GDP per capita. (Author's calculations based on IMF data.)

[254] Although Poland's PiS was certainly more successful than Peru's *nacionalismo*, eventually overcoming this trend by providing material benefits after 2015, it still spent most of the 2000–20 period in opposition.

democracy. From this perspective, Ecuador was similar to Poland, where anti-neoliberal protest gained an institutional expression during the juncture. Whereas in Poland this was the farmer-based Self-Defense, in Ecuador it was the peasant-based CONAIE, which soon founded Pachakutik as an indigenous party demanding radical change. Self-Defense and Pachakutik may have been very different from one another but, with the neoliberal consensus only deepening in Poland and Ecuador throughout the 1990s, both parties escalated militant action as they rejected liberal democratic norms. With their anti-neoliberal contention morphing into anti-systemic radicalism, these parties not only gained significant electoral relevance but also contributed to party system upheaval by the turn of the twenty-first century. As leading illiberals emerged in contexts of deep legitimacy crises, which required them to compete for radical parties' constituencies, they adapted by embracing contestatory strategies vis-à-vis liberal democracy, which would sooner or later lead to liberal democratic erosion in Ecuador and Poland.

By contrast, as anti-neoliberal protest failed to find an organizational vehicle during the juncture in Peru, subsequent developments toward illiberal moderation there resembled the pattern seen in Slovakia. The circumstances foreclosing the institutionalization of anti-neoliberal contention may have been very different, but they nevertheless limited the efficacy of anti-systemic radicalism in both cases. As a result, party systems were much less delegitimated, and radical parties did not play important mobilizing roles by the time leading illiberals entered politics in Peru and Slovakia. As the political environments in which they competed entailed both the mobilizational weakness of radical parties and a sense of greater systemic legitimacy, illiberals here adopted strategies of moderation more amenable to liberal democratic governance.

Overall, then, illiberal tendencies during the 2000–20 period in Ecuador and Peru, as in Slovakia and Poland, are best understood as political adaptations to societal path dependencies with origins in the nuanced contingencies of bait-and-switch junctures. Indeed, since none of these four countries followed the Venezuelan and Hungarian autocratic paths, their illiberal tendencies were less the products of illiberal incumbents' authoritarian proclivities and more shaped by prior developments in the political environment. As bait-and-switch juncture contingencies molded electoral reactions to neoliberalism in parallel ways in the Andes and Eastern Europe, illiberals adapted to societal pressures in generally similar manners. To reiterate a point from Chapter 7, cross-regional parallelism does not suggest that processes, actors, and outcomes were identical in the significantly different contexts of these two world regions. Rather, parallelism implies analogousness. Notwithstanding the obvious cross-regional differences, the agency of bait-and-switch and the viability of institutionalizing anti-neoliberal contention during junctures shaped in analogous ways subsequent illiberal tendencies, as shown in Figure 8.1. Whether illiberalism in these four countries tended to be contestatory or moderate, whether it was dominant or not, its social bases had historically contingent origins.

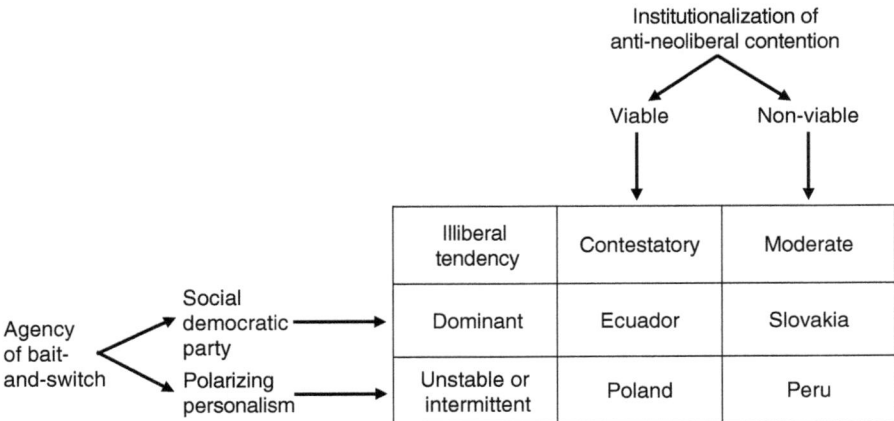

FIGURE 8.1 Bait-and-switch juncture contingencies and their illiberal legacies

Finally, this historically grounded perspective on developments in these crucial cases has two theoretically relevant implications. First, while they do not dispute the role of the alternative factors discussed in Chapter 7, the cross-regional comparisons demonstrate that such factors are individually insufficient for understanding illiberal tendencies. Indeed, social spending and organizational resources made a difference for illiberals' ability to dominate, and environmental factors mattered in terms of their contestatory or moderate strategies vis-à-vis liberal democracy. Yet, because the argument offered here links such factors into a framework sensitive to the interactions between historical contingency and illiberals' adaptive capacities, it offers a more exhaustive and compelling account of post-neoliberal trajectories in postcommunist European and Andean countries that eschewed authoritarian consolidation. It is based on the framework's ability to accommodate both path dependency and cross-regional parallelism that we can make better sense of developments in these countries.

Second, by highlighting their different origins and evolution, my argument lends support to the idea, developed in Chapter 7, that dominant illiberalism and contestatory illiberalism are best understood as conceptually distinct phenomena – not only in Eastern Europe but also in the Andes. Although it is true that the populist challenge to neoliberalism resulted in both an assault on liberal democracy and long-term political domination in Ecuador (as well as Venezuela and Bolivia), the hegemony of *correísmo* cannot be explained simply as a function of democratic erosion. Whereas Ecuador's liberal democracy experienced limited backsliding during Correa's presidency, the impact that the Citizens' Revolution made by delivering nationally relevant material benefits was much less limited, thereby underpinning *correísmo*'s long-term popularity. And while it is true that these benefits were certainly enabled by the profitable exploitation of natural resources in Ecuador, the Slovak case is a reminder that oil rents alone cannot explain the capacity to deliver them. Indeed, Ecuadorian president Lucio Gutiérrez also had access to oil rents, yet he did not deliver.[255] A key factor was that Gutiérrez – elected with a highly segmented coalition – could not have taken advantage of legislative cohesion and thus had to bow to the Washington Consensus. By contrast, Correa – elected with a much more inclusive electoral coalition – had at his disposal the legislative cohesion necessary for the passage of laws that made possible the countercyclical policies that eased public spending and shielded Ecuador from the worst effects of the 2008 economic crisis. Overall, if *correísmo*'s contestatory approach to liberal democracy originated as an adaptation to an environment characterized by deep political crisis and the salience of anti-systemic radicalism, its long-term domination stemmed from its capacity to deliver nationally relevant public goods, itself rooted in the ability to mobilize an extensive electoral coalition after the juncture. Although it is impossible to fully decouple *correísmo*'s hegemony from the erosion of liberal democracy, illiberal domination in Ecuador was predominantly conditioned by different historical developments.

The nuanced contingencies of bait-and-switch junctures mattered just as much in Peru, where they also shaped illiberal tendencies, but in opposite ways. Here, the destruction of institutional channels for anti-neoliberal protest during the juncture eventually conditioned Humala's moderation, while the regional polarization politicized and deepened by personalist Fujimori ultimately constrained *nacionalismo*'s capacity to govern and persist – much less dominate – as a political project. In the end, *nacionalismo* failed not because its moderate leader was unable to change the institutional rules in his favor, but rather because it lacked the organizational capacity – above all, legislative cohesion – to govern effectively. If illiberalism's contestatory tendency and ability to dominate had distinct sources in Ecuador, so did their opposites in Peru, where moderation and failure did not necessarily have to go hand in hand.

Indeed, as the agency politically responsible for reforms and the viability of institutionalizing anti-neoliberal protest were two separate aspects of bait-and-switch junctures, which could be combined in different ways, as seen in Eastern Europe (and Figure 8.1), they are best understood as contingencies charting their own historical trajectories. Put differently, if Ecuador's illiberalism was both contestatory and dominant, while the opposite tendencies concurred in Peru, these conjunctions were more the product of contingency than determinism. Indeed, had Ecuador's social democratic reformers repressed protest (as both their conservative predecessor had done[256] and as Fujimori did in Peru[257]), and had Peru's Fujimori refrained from authoritarianism (as Brazil's similarly personalist neoliberal reformer, Fernando Collor,[258] did), the overall illiberal experiences of these Andean countries would have likely been quite different.

---

[255] Interview ECU-21.
[256] Interviews ECU-03; ECU-13; ECU-08; ECU-24.
[257] Becker (2011b: 32).
[258] Weyland (1999).

8.6 CONCLUSION

By tracing the trajectories culminating in various illiberal tendencies in two Andean countries, this chapter has offered a new way of thinking about the challenge to neoliberalism in Latin America. Having briefly discussed historical antecedents, cleavages, and crisis before critical periods of market reform in Ecuador and Peru, I examined neoliberal junctures featuring bait-and-switch tactics with an eye to two aspects – the agency responsible for deepening neoliberalism and the viability of institutionalizing anti-neoliberal protest. As I traced the path dependencies rooted in these contingencies, I found that the processes culminating in varying illiberal tendencies – toward domination or not, and toward contestation or moderation vis-à-vis liberal democracy – featured patterns strikingly parallel to those seen in Slovakia and Poland. Although Andean and Eastern European contexts are significantly different, and relevant actors and trajectories were not identical, illiberal tendencies in these four crucial cases free of authoritarian consolidation were political adaptations to societal forces reflected in electoral dynamics and analogously rooted in historical contingency.

If unpacking bait-and-switch junctures builds on prior research[259] in order to facilitate a more complete historically grounded account, it also helps to clarify that, while democratic backsliding sometimes goes hand in hand with illiberals' ability to dominate, as in Ecuador, such tendencies rooted in contingency neither must necessarily coexist, as the postcommunist European cases showed, nor share the same origins, as the Andean cases confirmed. Indeed, whereas illiberals' ability to become politically dominant hinged on the provision of material goods, itself facilitated via institutional capacities built on the bases of broad electoral coalitions, their attacks on democracy stemmed from competition for the voters of radical alternatives in the electoral environment. As illiberal tendencies in the four Andean and Eastern European cases originated in the subtle contingencies of otherwise similar bait-and-switch junctures, they embodied nuanced historical legacies.

---

[259] Roberts (2014).

9

Illiberalism, Democracy, and the Left after the Neoliberal Revolution

Concluding Reflections

The dual passage from state-led development under dictatorship to market liberalism under democracy had profound and durable consequences for politics and societies across the world. As this study has shown, the momentous changes that took place in Eastern Europe soon after the end of the Cold War not only shaped political trajectories in the long term but also did so in ways resonant with experiences in Latin America. This concluding chapter briefly summarizes the book's main arguments and findings, notes its key contribution toward understanding patterns of institutional continuity and change from a perspective that integrates agency and the legacy of recent history, and highlights some of its main implications. These include insights regarding scholarship in the Polanyian tradition, the legacies of the dual transition to democracy and the market in Eastern Europe, and the relationship between neoliberalism, illiberalism, and leftist politics.

By reiterating some of the study's central themes, I emphasize several key takeaways. First, while developments in the southern and eastern peripheries of global capitalism were far from identical,[1] and overall experiences with neoliberal reform, societal adjustments, and political counterreactions reflected contextual peculiarities, the roads Eastern European and Latin American countries travelled betrayed a similar historical embeddedness in the long shadow of the leap into economic and political liberalism. Second, as the legacies of the transition years conditioned institutional environments to which political agents subsequently adapted to the best of their imperfect abilities, the historical path dependencies they charted were always probabilistic rather than deterministic. Third, although the shadow of recent history loomed large on developments throughout the first two decades of the twenty-first century, the voluntarist

---

[1] Appel and Orenstein (2018); Madariaga (2020: 8).

capacity for learning and action nevertheless holds the promise of countering contemporary populism's most unsavory facets.

9.1 MAIN ARGUMENTS AND FINDINGS

The study advanced two main arguments, both drawing causal arrows from contingent political configurations during critical periods of major economic reform soon after the end of dictatorships to highly probabilistic institutional outcomes in the aftermath period (2000–20). Specific to Eastern Europe yet illuminated by developments in and scholarship on Latin America, particularly Kenneth Roberts' work on party systems in the neoliberal era,[2] my primary contention involved two steps. First, *postcommunist junctures* – the earliest periods of decisive market reform sometime after second competitive elections – conditioned mainstream leftist parties' ideological and electoral tendencies in the long run. Developments on the Left, in turn, shaped contexts to which ensuring antiestablishment parties – typically driven by incentives for proving contrarian legitimacy and distinguished by their capacity for leadership autonomy – adapted strategically in ways most likely to be electorally rewarding. Whether illiberal and post-neoliberal populist projects, which typically positioned themselves as critics of liberal economics, were likely to be persistently viable at the ballot box thus depended on the path-dependent status of the Left, itself shaped by prior juncture contingencies.

Having advanced this argument in Chapter 2, I presented empirical findings that substantiate it. First, the quantitative perspective developed in Chapter 3 demonstrated that the hypothesized programmatic and electoral tendencies on the Left both originated in postcommunist junctures and predicted, better than other factors (as seen in Appendix D), illiberal outcomes at the ballot box in Eastern Europe. Where leftist parties had led the parliamentary opposition to rightist reformers during the juncture, their persistently progressive positioning on economic issues resulted in relative electoral strength, which, in turn, constrained opportunities for illiberalism in the long run. Where, by contrast, leftist or other labor-based actors had championed neoliberal deepening during the juncture, the Left's clearly pro-market positions on economic issues corresponded to electoral weakening, thus persistently enhancing opportunities for illiberalism's electoral viability. As neither the crises that provoked postcommunist junctures nor the political roles that major mainstream parties played at the time were determined by historical antecedents, as shown in Chapter 4, postcommunist junctures constituted real turning points in the history of Eastern European countries. Whereas the processes they engendered in Slovakia and Poland illustrated how bait-and-switch dynamics during the juncture ultimately produced, albeit in contextually specific ways, high illiberal viability (Chapter 5), developments that took place in Czechia and Romania

---

[2] Roberts (2014).

following a generally more predictable pattern of alignment during the juncture had the opposite long-term effect (Chapter 6).

As my findings show, even if the postcommunist juncture theory does not anticipate the positioning on economic issues and electoral performance of all leftist and antiestablishment parties in the Eastern Europe of the first two decades of the twenty-first century, it is highly predictive – and indeed far more predictive of such parties' programmatic and electoral long-term tendencies than alternative explanations, including those focused on demand side factors, supply side dynamics, political institutions, international influences, or longue-durée history. As periods of considerable institutional disruption and innovation, postcommunist junctures deepened neoliberalism and triggered, in contexts that featured increasingly salient economic questions, varying political responses to its problems. Whether these responses were likely to be channeled via the establishment Left, which tended to moderate neoliberalism after leading the opposition during the key period of market reform, or via illiberal or post-neoliberal parties, which were usually most viable where the Left distanced itself from its historic commitment to economic progressivism, depended on historical contingency during the juncture.

If the intuition behind my primary argument was that the linkage between critical junctures of neoliberal deepening and subsequent illiberal viability is pertinent beyond Latin America, while the programmatic and electoral status of the mainstream Left defines a causal "mechanism of production"[3] specific to Eastern Europe, my secondary argument was both grounded in rethinking juncture contingency and explicitly tested in terms of cross-regional validity. Developed in Chapter 7 based on the quantitatively similar yet qualitatively different illiberal experiences of Slovakia and Poland, this argument treated, against conventional wisdom, illiberalism's dominant and antiliberal democratic tendencies as distinct outcomes of reactive sequences with origins in nuanced juncture contingencies – namely, (1) whether the bait-and-switching agents in charge of market reforms were social democrats or polarizing populists and (2) whether anti-neoliberal protest was institutionalized or not. Having also contended that Slovakia, Poland, Ecuador, and Peru are comparable on a number of relevant dimensions and discussed the insufficiency of standard explanations of illiberals' ability to dominate politics in the long run as well as of their proclivity to contest liberal democracy, I then engaged in a comparative analysis of processes in the two Andean cases.

The findings, detailed in Chapter 8, demonstrate the validity of the refined theory prioritizing prior juncture contingencies. First, in Ecuador, as in Slovakia, the bait-and-switching agent in charge during the juncture had been a social democratic party reliant on programmatic appeals and an extensive organization. As a result, ensuing illiberals were able to mobilize highly

---

[3] See Collier and Munck (2017: 6).

nationalized electorates with a core of former social democratic supporters, based on which they built strong legislative cohesion and delivered popular material benefits that reinforced their long-term popularity – and thus their ability to dominate executive power for over a decade. By contrast, in Peru, as in Poland, the bait-and-switching agent had been a polarizing populist who had risen to power by using identify priming appeals – and thus politicizing long-standing historical divides – prior to promoting policies that hurt core constituencies in economically less developed regions. Subsequently, important illiberal parties were able to mobilize relatively segmented coalitions, based on which they built less cohesive organizations and provided insufficient material benefits – the reason why they remained relatively less popular and hegemonic in the aftermath period.

Second, in both Poland and Ecuador, the institutionalization of protest on behalf of constituencies particularly aggrieved at neoliberal reforms during the juncture ultimately contributed to subsequent party system breakdown and the electoral relevance of radical competitors – developments to which key illiberals competing for votes adjusted by adopting a contestatory strategy vis-à-vis liberal democracy. In Slovakia and Peru, by contrast, the lack of similar anti-neoliberal protest institutionalization resulted in relative party system stability and the weakness of radical contenders – a political environment that contributed to illiberals' greater toleration of liberal democratic norms and institutions.

Crucially, even if these parallel reactive sequences unfolded in particularistic ways – and developments in the Eastern European and Latin American cases were thus far from identical – they nevertheless featured equivalent building blocks. Thus, while the cross-regional comparisons did not reject the relevance of the more contextually specific factors that other scholars emphasize as crucial for understanding contemporary populism, they added much needed nuance by emphasizing similar patterns of historical embeddedness. Although the social reaction to market liberalism typically occurred under different, even opposite, ideological banners – "socialism of the twenty-first century" in Latin America, national conservatism in Eastern Europe – it nevertheless materialized in highly analogous ways and for similar reasons after the neoliberal revolutions at the capitalist periphery.

9.2 HISTORY AND AGENCY SHAPING EACH OTHER

The above set of findings are the product of an innovative research design, which emphasized the causal centrality of juncture contingency by grounding case-oriented research into a probabilistic mode of analysis.[4] By deploying qualitative and quantitative methods and data (e.g., qualitative process tracing and interviews, quantitative statistical techniques and party nationalization

---

[4] Dunning (2017: 41).

scores) for the analysis of the effects of junctures of neoliberal deepening, the book makes a distinctive contribution to debates regarding the roles of legacy and agency in terms of historical continuity and change[5] in postcommunist Europe and beyond after the Cold War.

While scholars are unlikely to reach a consensus regarding how much temporal leverage is sufficient for critical junctures to be recognized,[6] this book has suggested that relatively early periods of neoliberal reform in Eastern Europe indeed constituted critical junctures, as they shaped institutional legacies whose duration far outlasted them.[7] Although these were not the earliest market liberalization advances in a transformation that had already been underway, postcommunist junctures certainly represented the first time when considerable neoliberal deepening coincided with genuine political debate on important economic questions. In hindsight, it was precisely this combination of significant market reform and democratic sanction that truly transformed Eastern Europe, where postcommunist citizenship now meant – for the first time and finally – the ability to engage in politically consequential ways with questions of both economics and democracy. Because this context not only materialized as a result of massive transformations with effects uniformly felt in countries exiting state-led development but also set the stage for subsequent institutional trajectories and outcomes, the developments embedded in it reflected profound historical change. As the transformative turn to the market economy, embraced more enthusiastically in postcommunist Europe than anywhere else,[8] went hand in hand with the recently (re)discovered concept of democratic choice, the societal reaction it provoked was always bound to elicit, as Karl Polanyi discerned long ago, a range of possible political responses.[9]

If the emergence of economic and political liberalism generally defined the historical context at the capitalist periphery, the political means of channeling societal reactions were products of contingent configurations that materialized during junctures of market reform. As the political actors that happened to structure these configurations at the time campaigned, made choices, and acted in newly democratic settings – either as enablers or detractors of neoliberalism – they shaped the general historical context in particular ways, thus molding environments to which liberalism's challengers would have to adapt strategically. Yet, while these adaptations reflected the historical continuities originating in prior junctures – the reason why this study was able to identify durable trends across countries – they were also products of human agency prone to both error and learning. In the end, whether the result was illiberal viability at the ballot box or assault on liberal democracy, the interactive dynamics between the historical legacies of contingency, which resulted from junctures triggered by major change, and the agency of adaptive yet imperfect

---

[5] See Collier and Munck (2022).
[6] Collier and Munck (2017).
[7] See Capoccia and Kelemen (2007: 360–3).

[8] Appel and Orenstein (2016; 2018).
[9] Polanyi ([1944] 2001).

political actors meant that even in contexts where illiberalism tended to be highly salient or pernicious, such outcomes were never truly inevitable.

9.3 IMPLICATIONS

The arguments and findings of this book have implications regarding (1) comparative Polanyian perspectives on the effects of the market economy; (2) discussions about illiberal regimes' social bases and adaptiveness to evolving neoliberalism; (3) interpretations of the legacies of the dual transition in Eastern Europe; and (4) debates on liberalism and leftist politics more generally.

9.3.1 Extending the Polanyian Perspective

The study extends research in the Polanyian tradition on the relationship between neoliberalism and illiberalism in Eastern Europe, as advanced predominantly by anthropologists, especially Chris Hann and Don Kalb, and political economists, including Dorothee Bohle, Béla Greskovits, and Gábor Scheiring, among others.[10] These authors have offered important insights regarding how the liberation of markets from state control produced a double movement, with technocratically minded elites actively pushing societies deeper into the neoliberal frontier and populist countermovements reacting to the dislocating effects of marketization. Central in this scholarship has been the problem of economic dependency on Western capital, with postcommunist Europe feeling tensions among key societal segments and business interests, and illiberal populists offering statist resurrection as a way to cope with the pressures of globalization.

This study complements such work by explicitly focusing from a comparative perspective on the domestic institutional mechanisms and political dynamics that underpin the movements for marketization and societal protection. Indeed, as critical scholarship on the Eastern European reactions to global capitalism has emphasized the pre-1989 origins of neoliberal thinking and practices in the region,[11] researchers in the Polanyian tradition have devoted less attention to the particular and intricate ways in which postcommunist illiberalism not only came to be but also came to characterize a historically peculiar period in the region. This book has addressed such gaps by explaining how the uniquely intense market reforms, economic dislocations, and political competition after communism corresponded to a distinctive era shaped during especially consequential moments of building capitalism in Eastern Europe. By identifying how concrete political agents acted during such watershed periods, how their actions conditioned parties and party systems in the long term, and how populist forces adapted to contextual opportunities and constraints,

---

[10] See Chapter 2 for an extended discussion.

[11] For example, Fabry (2019); Gagyi (2016; 2021).

the study has added needed nuance regarding the political forces driving and opposing marketization in the three decades after 1989.

As a result, we now know not only that the illiberal seed was planted early in the transition years but also why the political agents who bear the main historical responsibility for it acted in the ways they did. We can acknowledge that although consequential choices during the turbulent and unpredictable transformation were mostly the result of contingency, the long-term strategies and development of the Left remained the most important predictor of illiberal viability during the first two decades of the twenty-first century. And we can understand that rather than a simple product of either supply or demand side factors, the populist challenge was driven by both political elites and societal forces, with leftist parties supplying visions and policies, social coalitions demanding protection from neoliberal dislocations, and populist parties opportunistically maneuvering the political terrain. As the core argument explains varying outcomes across a wide range of countries in postcommunist Europe and the secondary arguments are also valid for Latin American cases, I have offered a more general perspective than prior scholarship on the links between neoliberalism and illiberalism. Grounded in quantitative and qualitative data and methods and including cross-regional comparisons, the historical-institutionalist framework developed here thus contributes both theoretical refinements and methodological novelty to research on the double movement of marketization and societal protection.

While the Polanyian countermovement was embodied by populist projects whose economic and social stances reflected the desire to limit individual liberty in both domains, this study made clear that it was parties' positioning on economic questions that especially mattered for political trajectories following the neoliberal revolutions of the 1990s. For this reason, long-term illiberal outcomes in Eastern Europe are best understood as post-neoliberal populist reactions to developments with prior origins. The book also showed how, as economic concerns increasingly gained salience with the solidification of the neoliberal consensus, developments after communism shared similarities with dynamics seen in the Global South. As in Latin America, post-neoliberal populist countermovements in Eastern Europe were driven less by momentary outbursts of protest against particular policies or the governments enacting them and more by pent-up disappointments accumulated over several decades.

Because these analogous reactions to marketization came, for historical and geopolitical reasons, from opposite sides of the ideological spectrum,[12] the illiberal experiences of Latin America and Eastern Europe are best understood as mirror images that reflect largely similar societal adjustments to market reform. Indeed, if illiberalism tended to attach itself to opposite ideologies – the left-wing nationalism of Bolivarian socialists in Latin America and more traditional ethnic nationalism in Eastern Europe – it was nevertheless grounded

---

[12] Binev (2024a).

in a common critique of economic globalization as a driver of marketization in both regions. These ideologically distinct yet causally parallel developments suggest not only that the intensified struggle between the forces of nationalism and globalism has fundamentally restructured divides across the world in comparable ways but also that the political effects of the transnational cleavage[13] have been especially unique and perverse after communism. After all, while in Latin America economic statism was revived in ways echoing previous historical experiences, along familiar ideological lines, and for the material benefit of popular majorities, in Eastern Europe it became unprecedentedly associated with anti-socialist conservatives who used the public's trust to advance rather different goals. As the relentless expansion of the market left many postcommunist voters no less frustrated than their counterparts in the Global South, those to whom they turned for defense were hardly interested in shielding them.

9.3.2 Illiberalism's Social Bases and Neoliberal Adaptation

The book's societally sensitive perspective helped dispel some misconceptions about political phenomena that rise to prominence and even power by questioning the liberal status quo. Contrary to standard analyses, which tend both to conflate the hegemonic and antidemocratic potential of populist projects and to judge them mostly with reference to the institutional standards of modern liberalism, this study showed that the antiliberal democratic and popular sides of populism after the peak of neoliberalism are best understood as distinct from one another. Indeed, although these two aspects sometimes coincided, as for example in Ecuador, they in fact had different origins and separate societal bases. While the contestation of liberal democracy was rooted in the intense radicalism of particular constituencies that had been especially hurt by market reforms, populists' ability to dominate stemmed from the capacity to sustain broad electoral coalitions by delivering palpable material benefits. Thus, if illiberalism's transgressions of liberal democratic norms rose to satisfy intensely radical yet relatively narrow societal sectors, its capacity to dominate politically resulted from broad and rather moderate coalitions seeking respite from the demands of the neoliberal consensus. The populist proclivity for authoritarian slippage is thus not necessarily the same as the capacity to be politically dominant. The two phenomena can have different social bases.

Did illiberals deliver for the social bases that elevated them to power, and how convincingly did they challenge neoliberalism, as they had promised? Predominantly driven by opportunistic rather than democratic impulses, illiberal incumbents related to their social bases rather pragmatically, never fully abandoning practices of neoliberal exclusion and marginalization. This was the case even in Ecuador, where the Polanyian reaction was among the strongest. Taking advantage of oil rents, a unified anti-globalization movement across Latin

---

[13] Hoogle and Marks (2018).

America, and broad popular support, Rafael Correa declared much of the country's debt illegitimate, redistributed generously, and openly contested neoliberalism. At the same time, however, he turned against the core progressive movement that had initially supported him, using authoritarian methods to suppress indigenous opposition to mining and oil extraction the government deemed necessary for development. As Correa's regime was highly technocratic, involved with private industry, and seeking "to disembed the economic from the social and the political," it did not completely dismantle neoliberal governance in Ecuador.[14]

Illiberal incumbents were less able and willing to act against the status quo in Eastern Europe, where the legacies of communism and priorities of transnational integration incentivized them to embrace and modify neoliberalism for their purposes rather than challenge it in practice. Thus, where they captured power, postcommunist illiberals offered only minimal material concessions to popular majorities, as they preferred to accumulate political and economic power for themselves and their cronies while adjusting to realities shaped by foreign capital and financialization.[15] The most prominent example has been Hungary under Fidesz. Here, the government of Viktor Orbán modified and intensified neoliberalism by authoritarian means, creating a national bourgeoisie, transferring wealth from "unproductive" to "productive" citizens, dismantling trade unions and curtailing labor rights for the benefit of capitalists, and forcing the "deserving" poor into clientelist relationships. As transnational capital remained key in important sectors of the economy, the government engaged in a careful balancing act between domestic and foreign business,[16] creating new incentives for the loyalty of beneficiaries and reinforcing an exclusionary neoliberal regime for the rest.[17] With poverty and inequality increasing, the illiberal regime tamed popular anger by developing paternalist workfare programs.[18] These initiatives resonated with vulnerable groups, creating a sense of social embeddedness and stability, and even legitimating authoritarianism.[19]

Although it was less embedded in economic elites than Hungary's Fidesz, the other prominent example of contestatory illiberalism in East Central Europe, Poland's Law and Justice (PiS), also reproduced neoliberalism. Notably, as PiS's coalition involved large segments of blue-collar and agricultural workers disillusioned with the social disintegration wrought by neoliberalism, its modification of the status quo was less anti-social, resulting in the introduction of a generous welfare program and the reduction of poverty. As a strong national capitalist class already existed in Poland due to earlier industrial policies, PiS's welfare chauvinist government could afford implementing more inclusive policies than in Hungary.[20] Nevertheless, Poland's illiberals ended up sustaining neoliberalism

---

[14] Riofrancos (2020).
[15] Matiolli (2018; 2020); Rogers (2020b).
[16] Scheiring (2021a).
[17] Rogers (2020a; 2024); Scheiring (2020b); Scheiring and Szombati (2020).
[18] Scheiring and Szombati (2020); Szombati (2021).
[19] Hann (2018; 2019b; 2021b); Szombati (2021).
[20] Scheiring (2021b).

by coopting resistance to it, deepening divisions through various arenas of social reproduction, and ultimately reinforcing the logic of market competition.[21]

Finally, illiberal incumbents that abstained from democratic backsliding neither significantly modified neoliberalism nor empowered its victims. On the one hand, if such projects lacked extensive social coalitions and solid organizational foundations, as in Peru, they could all too easily embrace market reformism, which was contrary to broad societal demands for the opposite. On the other hand, even if such projects were somewhat more successful as moderators of neoliberalism, as in Slovakia, the public goods they offered to their broad electorates were far less substantive and universal than instrumental, purely for mobilizing electoral support. Indeed, in both countries those who came to power as challengers of neoliberalism ended up only entrenching it further.[22] Typically organized from the top down and lacking grassroots-based accountability, illiberalism failed to deepen democracy even where it did not necessarily undermine it.

9.3.3 The Illiberal Legacies of Postcommunist Europe's Dual Transition

The arguments made in this study resonate with voices critical of the triumphalist narrative regarding the dual transition to political and economic liberalism after communism.[23] Although the transformation had produced an initial recession, by the mid 1990s the seemingly triumphant march toward free markets and democracy in East Central European countries convinced influential observers that there was a natural affinity between the two.[24] Accordingly, they set out to show in various ways that Adam Przeworski's famously pessimistic take on the feasibility of radical market reform under political democracy[25] was exaggerated. Joel Hellman demonstrated that further neoliberal reforms were opposed not by popular majorities but rather by corrupt elites who had benefited from initial liberalization.[26] M. Steven Fish argued not only that democratization and market reforms are compatible[27] but also that "economic liberalization advances rather than undermines democracy."[28] Anders Åslund contended that the faster the economic transformation, the more successful the democratic consolidation, a view shared by Michael McFaul.[29] Regarding more concrete political dynamics, while Fish saw the reformation of the ex-communist parties as a key determinant of economic reform,[30] Anna

[21] Baranowski (2023); Shields (2015; 2021).
[22] Scheiring (2021b); Vergara and Watanabe (2019).
[23] See, for example, Appel and Orenstein (2018), Ghodsee and Orenstein (2021), and the scholarship in the Polanyian tradition discussed in Chapter 2.
[24] See Appel and Orenstein (2018: 177).
[25] Przeworski (1991).
[26] Hellman (1998).
[27] Fish (1998).
[28] Fish and Choudhry (2007).
[29] Åslund (2001); McFaul (2002: 221).
[30] Fish (1998: 61).

Grzymała-Busse concluded that when such parties quickly broke with the communist past – which entailed, among other things, embracing neoliberalism – they were able to develop responsive appeals and be electorally successful in democracy.[31] Analyzing the ideological distance between the executive and the opposition, Timothy Frye argued that when polarization is low, liberal democracy and economic reform go hand in hand.[32]

Such optimistic assessments about the complementarities between economic and political liberalism are understandable, especially considering the historical context during which they were formulated. Having lived under "shortage economies"[33] for a long time and generally tolerating economic pain as a supposed requisite for a brighter future, hopeful Eastern European publics proved remarkably patient during the first postcommunist decade.[34] With competitive elections being a novelty, the contention between center-left and center-right parties throughout the 1990s seemed like "normal" democratic politics,[35] even if partisan rivals often enough did not differ much on economic policy. Indeed, having lost the Cold War, leftist parties seemed to have little choice but to substantiate their divorce from socialism.[36] And even though by the early 2000s illiberalism had started gaining ground in an exemplary reformer like Poland, the priorities associated with the prospects of a European Union future still inspired hopefulness regarding the assumed symmetry between neoliberal reform and democratic consolidation. Given such circumstances, it is no surprise that publics, scholars, and political practitioners alike optimistically viewed free markets and democracy as necessarily related and mutually reinforcing.

This book has offered a corrective to such assessments by taking advantage of an extended historical perspective and showing that the political legacies of the dual transition to democracy and the market truly crystallized in the second and third postcommunist decades. Indeed, as illiberalism was especially salient in some of the countries that followed the neoliberal script most faithfully, it is now clear that the long-term prospects of democracy were not necessarily best where market reform was most advanced. Indeed, whether radical marketization was implemented immediately after 1989 (Poland), later in the 1990s (Hungary), or more than a decade after communism (Slovakia), illiberal outcomes were consistently viable in the aftermath. And although the challenge to liberalism was somewhat less pronounced in other postcommunist countries in the neoliberal avant-garde – particularly Estonia, Latvia, and Lithuania – they, too, saw routinely high levels of popular support for illiberalism during the 2000–20 period. Even in Czechia – a country where advanced market reform did not lead to persistent backlash at the ballot box – illiberalism gained salience by the end of the second twenty-first century decade.

---

[31] Grzymała-Busse (2002: 265–6).

[32] Frye (2010).

[33] Kornai (1992).

[34] Greskovits (1998).

[35] See Pop-Eleches (2010).

[36] Tavits and Letki (2009).

Overall, even if long-term illiberal viability did not always follow exemplary neoliberal reformism,[37] the Eastern European experience of the first three postcommunist decades challenges conventional assumptions about the self-reinforcing sustainability and democratic potential of free markets. As the durable effects of the dual transition were shaped by contingent political configurations and agency, it is now clear that comprehensive market reforms could well produce legacies that were neither economically nor politically liberal. Leaving the many at the mercy of markets and requiring, when necessary, the suspension of political responsiveness on the part of the Left, neoliberalism failed to produce democratic durability precisely where it had presumably fostered democratization. Because such path-dependent dynamics originated in the early transition years, the first postcommunist decade remains crucial for understanding the uneasy relationship between markets and democracy in Eastern Europe.

9.3.4 Liberalism and the Left

Although this study advanced specific arguments about the legacies of the transition from state-led development under dictatorship to democracy and the market, its findings are relevant to broader debates about the exhaustion of mainstream liberalism and the status of the political Left. Indeed, the liberal democratic order that emerged after World War II is clearly in trouble, and, as Jan-Werner Müller observed, not just the ultrarich but also the economically vulnerable no longer feel invested in its institutions.[38] Since the second category for a long time constituted the core of social democratic parties, the delegitimation of liberalism and the crisis of the Left are two related aspects of the current political predicament.

Beginning with liberalism, leading scholars of various ideological persuasions and analytical approaches have identified aspects of the philosophical doctrine centered on individualism as driving the current crisis in the West. Not surprisingly, criticism from progressive corners has focused on the neoliberal dimension of contemporary liberalism. In Chantal Mouffe's neo-Gramscian reading, because neoliberal hegemony prioritized technocratic solutions and abandoned political contestation, it directly led to "post-democracy"[39] – which Colin Crouch understood as domination by insular business and political elites[40] – and even techno-authoritarianism.[41] Also invoking Gramsci, Nancy Fraser has argued that as the progressive-neoliberal bloc – which had for a long time balanced the recognition of rights and distribution of income – abandoned blue collar workers, it ultimately suffered defeat by hyper-reactionary neoliberal forces.[42] In Wendy Brown's Foucauldian

---

[37] The example of Ukraine before 2012 also suggests this but in a way opposite to the Czech case.
[38] Müller (2021).

[39] Mouffe (2018).
[40] Crouch (2020).
[41] Mouffe (2022).
[42] Fraser (2019).

perspective, it was neoliberal rationality that "undid the demos" and unintentionally strengthened authoritarian purveyors of traditional morality.[43] For historian Quinn Slobodian, the fusion between free-market absolutism, nationalism, and racism was the design of ideologues who intentionally distorted Friedrich Hayek's economic philosophy in their quest to protect markets from democracy after the Cold War.[44] Because the intense wave of marketization that began in the 1970s and intensified after 1989 produced declining growth, rising inequality, and escalating debt, sociologist Wolfgang Streeck argued, the legitimacy of neoliberalism has been severely compromised.[45] Historian Gary Gerstle and social theorists Paolo Gebraudo and Vivek Chibber agree that the neoliberal consensus in the West is over.[46]

While other critics of contemporary liberalism are less focused on neoliberalism per se, they, too, acknowledge the societally noxious effects of key neoliberal priorities such as elevating individualism and denigrating collectivism at all costs. In Samuel Moyn's view, for example, liberalism was crippled during the Cold War – an era during which leading Western intellectuals single-mindedly prioritized individual liberty, defended neoliberalism, and abandoned progressive Enlightenment principles of equality and popular democracy.[47] James Traube explained that liberalism lost its grip on the American public because it aligned itself with the forces of globalization, abandoning its progressive vision of community and nationalism.[48] Josiah Ober argued that as liberalism has obscured the positive value of collective self-government, democracy without liberalism can potentially restore – through citizen participation – the security and prosperity needed for human flourishing.[49] Offering a social conservative perspective, Patrick Deneen attributed liberalism's failure to a hard cultural shift toward individualism.[50] As such changes were accelerated by a political Left that prioritized cultural struggles at the expense of the economic concerns of the masses, Richard Rorty's prediction that "at some point, something will crack" seems to have come true.[51] Indeed, as this "brahmin" Left embraced highly educated elites instead of working classes and contributed, in Thomas Piketty's account, to rising inequality across the West,[52] angry and frustrated voters wishful for an end of the neoliberal "dispensation" turned, as liberal historian Mark Lilla showed, for solutions to illiberal autocrats.[53]

This book has affirmed the connections between the hegemony of neoliberalism, the failures of the mainstream Left, and the crisis of liberal democracy during the era of post-Cold War hyper-individualism. It also offered two contributions to the above debates. First, contrary to the tendency of many liberal

---

[43] Brown (2015; 2019).
[44] Slobodian (2025).
[45] Streeck (2016; 2024).
[46] Chibber (2022a); Gebraudo (2021); Gerstle (2022).
[47] Moyn (2023).
[48] Traub (2019).
[49] Ober (2017).
[50] Deneen (2018).
[51] Rorty (1998: 90).
[52] Piketty (2020).
[53] Lilla (2017).

commentators to conflate illiberalism with authoritarianism and cultural chauvinism while downplaying its economic aspects, the case studies conveyed that illiberalism's various dimensions, while sharing certain affinities, do not always travel together. Put simply, parties and governments can be economically or culturally illiberal, or both, without necessarily being autocratic in their politics. Because it is specifically the popular call for egalitarianism that drives important political trends in many countries, illiberalism often reflects a widespread demand not for autocracy but rather for redistributive justice. Accordingly, the study of populism would benefit from an increased focus on the substantive, rather than formal institutional, aspects of democracy.

Second, while this study identified the defeat of leftist parties as particularly relevant for the salience of illiberalism, its critical juncture framework suggested that the Left's ideological abdication was grounded in a concrete historical period characterized not only by intense crises and neoliberal shocks but also by elements of contingency and unpredictability. Indeed, leftist parties may have generally transformed, but not all of them responded to the post-Cold War requirement for uncompromising marketization in uniform ways. While some accelerated neoliberalism, others moderated it, at least temporarily, with the difference implying divergent prospects for illiberals in the long run. As the Left's adaptations and path-dependent trajectories were primarily driven by exogenous factors and contingent political configurations during consequential moments of reform, they were certainly not predetermined. It follows, then, that although significantly compromised, leftist parties need not be ineffectual or incapable of change. Especially as liberalism has faltered and political options have expanded in the decades after the neoliberal revolution, the Left stands at a crossroads.

Following its failures during the neoliberal era, the Left is currently engaged in intense internal debates. Piketty's transnational social federalism,[54] Streeck's return to national sovereignty,[55] Mouffe's advocacy of affective populist appeals,[56] Chibber's insistence on reviving materialism[57] – these are some of the strategies that leading progressive voices propose as a way forward. Even more urgently, although neoliberalism appears weakened and some have even announced its surrender to modern forms of feudalism,[58] the Left must recognize that capitalism has an uncommon capacity for adaptability, dynamism, and reinvention.[59] And as not all capitalist configurations are uniformly adversarial to those most affected by neoliberal marketization,[60] leftist parties' revitalization hinges on the capacity to both use existing templates and devise novel ones aimed at re-embedding parts of the economy in social life under the evolving conditions. Investing in the development of solidaristic relations

---

[54] Piketty (2020).
[55] Streeck (2024).
[56] Mouffe (2018; 2022).
[57] Chibber (2022b)

[58] Dean (2025); Varoufakis (2023).
[59] Fraser (2022); Milanovic (2019); Slobodian (2023).
[60] Bohle and Greskovits (2012); Thelen (2014).

within occupational communities[61] and pushing to deinstitutionalize the imperative toward infinite growth[62] are examples of such priorities that can be politically energizing. Yet such steps would be unlikely if leftist parties kept subscribing to old notions of partisanship conducive to transactional negotiation in the political arena – a practice that led to the neoliberal compromises in the first place. As Jonathan White and Lea Ypi explained a decade ago, partisanship can indeed be reimagined as a principled activity of politically committed agents who subject themselves to mutual obligations, politically justify their ends in ways that enlist adherents to conscionable causes, and advance general, rather than particular, interests. While a reinvigorated Left guided by such ethical standards can be responsive to change, its grounding in principled commitment and mutual obligation implies that it does not have to give up its integrity.[63]

Even if the task at hand is exacting, it is neither unimaginable nor unattainable. Considering the opportunities afforded by the crisis of neoliberalism and with the hindsight of the comparative historical perspective offered in this book, it should be clear that, though the illiberal challenge is an understandable development, its future reproduction is by no means inevitable. As the legacies of the neoliberal revolution shaped political behavior without inhibiting choice, progressive agents of change are certainly capable of mobilizing support behind new projects of deepening democracy. While constructing such works demands both imaginative theorizing and committed pursuit, it should be clear that the task at minimum requires partisans who prioritize the economic concerns of the broad social sectors for whom democracy must deliver if it is to be endowed with substance. As such political projects have performed important functions in support of advancing popular sovereignty in countries such as Uruguay, Bolivia,[64] Chile, and Mexico, Eastern Europeans – and others – can once again take a page from developments in the Global South. Of course, this does not suggest copying and pasting; these examples have been anything but error-free. Rather, it means taking a cue and creatively applying useful lessons to new contexts. It is only through such learning based on both our own experiences from the past and the experiences of those seemingly very different from us, that we can make sense of our present political dilemmas and fortify our democracies.

---

[61] Dukes and Streeck (2023).
[62] Fraser (2022).
[63] See White and Ypi (2016).
[64] Anria (2018).

Appendices

APPENDIX A. MEASURING ILLIBERALISM IN
POSTCOMMUNIST EUROPE, 2000–20

The following rules are used in order to identify parties taking stances against economic and cultural liberalism and to measure illiberalism by aggregating these parties' vote shares. First, parties' overall illiberalism scores are based on their positions on economic and cultural issues relative to country-specific and regional medians calculated based on data from the Chapel Hill Expert Survey (CHES, 2002–19)[1] and the Democratic Accountability and Linkages Project (DALP, 2008–9).[2] For each parliamentary election, parties' economic and cultural positions are assigned scores ranging from zero to three, mostly based on the CHES *lrecon*[3] and *gal-tan*[4] variables. Thus, the score for a party's economic position can be zero – indicating "center-right" (to the right of both country *and* regional medians); one – "somewhat leftist" (*between* country and regional medians); two – "explicitly leftist" (to the left of both country *and* regional medians); or three – "exceptionally leftist" (more than one standard deviation to the left of the regional median). Similarly, the score for a party's cultural position can be zero – indicating "GAL" (to the left of both country *and* regional medians); one – "somewhat TAN" (*between* country and regional medians); two – "explicitly TAN" (to the right of both country *and* regional medians); or three – "exceptionally TAN" (more than one standard deviation to the right of the regional median).

[1] Bakker et al. (2015); Polk et al. (2017).

[2] Kitschelt (2013).

[3] Measuring general left versus right economic positioning.

[4] Measuring green, alternative, and libertarian versus traditional, authoritarian, and nationalist positioning.

Second, for a party to be coded as illiberal, the sum of scores for its positions on economic and cultural issues must be greater than two. The sum of scores is used to measure illiberalism for all parties that gained at least 1 percent electoral support in parliamentary elections after postcommunist junctures. Because scores are based on multiple expert survey waves, parties can be illiberal in some elections and not in other. Third, for Moldova, Albania before 2013, and Ukraine before 2012, I use DALP data to construct a mean based on three variables – *social spending (d1)*, *state role in the economy (d2)*, *and public spending (d3)* – as a proxy for economic positions, and another mean based on two variables – *national identity (d4) and traditional authority, institutions, and customs (d5)* – as a proxy for positions on social issues. DALP-based scores were normalized on a scale from zero to ten for comparability with CHES-based scores.

The following parties gained at least 1 percent of the vote and received an overall illiberalism score of three or above in parliamentary elections from 2000 to 2020. They are thus coded as illiberal for the indicated parliamentary election years.

Albania

Socialist Movement for Integration (LSI): 2005, 2009

Bulgaria

Movement for Rights and Freedoms (DPS): 2001, 2005, 2009, 2013, 2014
Ataka: 2005, 2009, 2013, 2014
Order, Law, and Justice (RZS): 2009
Lider: 2009, 2013
Bulgaria Without Censorship (BBT): 2014
National Front for the Salvation of Bulgaria (NFSB): 2013, 2014
Internal Macedonian Revolutionary Organization (VMRO): 2013, 2014, 2017
Volya: 2017
Revival: 2017

Croatia

Croatian Party of Pensioners (HSU): 2000, 2003, 2007
Croatian Democratic Assembly of Slavonia and Baranja (HDSSB): 2007, 2011, 2015, 2016
Croatian Peasant Party (HSS): 2000, 2003, 2007, 2011
Croatian Party of Rights (HSP): 2000, 2003, 2007, 2011
Croatian Party of Rights Dr. Ante Starčević (HSP-AS): 2011
Croatian Laborists – Labor Party (HL-SR): 2011
Bridge of Independent Lists (Most): 2015, 2016, 2020

Independent Democratic Serbian Party (SDSS): 2015, 2016, 2020
Human Blocade (ZZ): 2015, 2016, 2020
Bandić Milan 365 – Labor and Solidarity Party (MB 365): 2015, 2016
Homeland Movement (DP): 2020

Czechia

Rally for the Republic – Republican Party of Czechoslovakia (SPR-RSČ): 2002
Action of Dissatisfied Citizens (ANO 2011): 2017
Freedom and Direct Democracy (SPD): 2017

Estonia

Estonian United People's Party (EUR)/Constitution Party (KP): 2003, 2007
Estonian Country People's Party (EME)/People's Union of Estonia (ER): 2003, 2007, 2011
Estonian Center Party (EK): 2007, 2011, 2015
Conservative People's Party (EKRE): 2015, 2019

Hungary

Christian Democratic People's Party (KDNP): 2002, 2006
Hungarian Justice and Life Party (MIEP): 2002
Hungarian Justice and Life Party (MIEP)/Movement for a Better Hungary (JOBBIK): 2006
Movement for a Better Hungary (JOBBIK) 2010, 2014, 2018
Fidesz: 2010, 2014, 2018

Latvia

Latvia's First Party (LPP): 2002
For Fatherland and Freedom – LNNK (TB-LNNK): 2002, 2006
Union of Greens and Farmers (ZZS): 2002, 2010, 2011, 2014, 2018
For Human Rights in a United Latvia (PCTVL)/Latvian Russian Union (LKS): 2006, 2010, 2014, 2018
National Alliance (NA): 2010, 2011, 2014, 2018
Latvian Association of Regions (LRA): 2014
From Latvia from the Heart (NSL): 2014

Lithuania

New Union (NS): 2000
Electoral Action of Poles in Lithuania (LLRA): 2000, 2004, 2008, 2012, 2016, 2020

New Democratic Party (NDP): 2000

Young Lithuanians – New Nationalists and Political Prisoners' Union (JL-PKS): 2000

Liberal Union of Lithuania (LLS): 2000

Lithuanian Russian Union (LRS): 2000

Lithuanian Peasant Party (LVP)/Peasant Popular Union (LVLS)/Peasant and Greens Union (LVZS): 2000, 2004, 2008, 2012, 2016, 2020

Order and Justice (TT): 2004, 2008, 2012, 2016

Front Party (FRONT)/Socialist People's Front (SPF): 2008, 2012

Way of Courage (DK): 2012, 2020

Lithuanian Center Party (LCP)/Center Party – Nationalists (CPT): 2016, 2020

Moldova

Motherland/Party of Socialists of the Republic of Moldova (PSRM): 2001, 2005, 2014, 2019

Equality/Șor Party (ȘOR): 2005

Communist Reformist Party (PCR): 2014

Democratic Party of Moldova (PDM): 2014, 2019

Our Party (PN): 2019

North Macedonia

Internal Macedonian Revolutionary Organization – People's Party (VMRO-NP): 2006

Democratic Party of Albanians (DPA): 2011, 2014, 2016, 2020

Democratic Union for Integration (DUI): 2011, 2014, 2016, 2020

Poland

Law and Justice (PiS): 2001, 2005, 2007, 2011, 2015, 2019

Labor Union (UP): 2001

League of Polish Families (LPR): 2001, 2005, 2007

Self-Defense of the Republic of Poland (SO): 2001, 2005, 2007

Polish People's Party (PSL): 2001, 2007, 2011, 2015, 2019

Congress of the New Right (KNP)/KORWiN/Confederation: 2005, 2011, 2015, 2019

Together (R): 2015

Romania

Greater Romania Party (PRM): 2000, 2004, 2008, 2012, 2016

Romanian Humanist Party/Conservative Party (PUR/PC): 2004, 2008, 2012

People's Party – Dan Diaconescu (PP-DD): 2012
National Union for the Progress of Romania (UNPR): 2012
Democratic Alliance of Hungarians in Romania (UDMR): 2016, 2020
PRO Romania (PRO): 2020
Alliance for the Union of Romanians (AUR): 2020

Slovakia

People's Party – Movement for a Democratic Slovakia (ĽS-HZDS): 2002, 2010
Movement for Democracy (HZD): 2002
Slovak National Party (SNS): 2002, 2006, 2010, 2012, 2016, 2020
True Slovak National Party (PSNS): 2002
Communist Party of Slovakia (KSS): 2002, 2006
Direction (SMER): 2006, 2010, 2012, 2016, 2020
We Are Family (SR): 2016, 2020
People's Party – Our Slovakia (ĽSNS): 2010, 2012, 2016, 2020

Slovenia

Democratic Party of Pensioners of Slovenia (DeSUS): 2000, 2004, 2008, 2011, 2014
New Slovenia – Christian Democrats (NSi): 2000, 2004, 2008, 2011, 2014
Slovenian National Party (SNS): 2000, 2004, 2008, 2011, 2014, 2018
Slovenian Democratic Party (SDS): 2014, 2018
United Left (ZL)/Levica: 2014, 2018

Ukraine

Communist Party of Ukraine (renewed) ((KPU(o)): 2002
Progressive Socialist Party of Ukraine (PSPU): 2002, 2006, 2007
Fatherland: 2002, 2006, 2007, 2012
Freedom: 2012
Party of Regions (PR): 2012

APPENDIX B. INTERVIEWS FROM FIELDWORK, 2015–16

Poland. Krakow (March 2015) and Warsaw (April 2015)

POL-01. Professor of sociology and district council chairman from PiS, March 12

POL-02. Wojciech Kolarski, bureau chief for Member of European Parliament (and future Polish president) Andrzej Duda, March 13

POL-03. Elżbieta Duda, district council chairwoman and future Sejm deputy from PiS, March 15

POL-04. City councilor from PiS, March 18

POL-05. Assistant to high-ranking PiS politician, March 18

POL-06. City councilor expelled from PiS, March 18

POL-07. City councilor collaborating with PiS, March 19

POL-08. District council treasurer from PiS, March 24

POL-09. District council chairman from PiS, March 24

POL-10. Krzysztof Szczerski, Sejm deputy from PiS and future Polish ambassador to the United Nations, March 25

POL-11. City councilor from PiS, March 26

POL-12. City councilor from PiS, March 26

POL-13. District council treasurer who resigned from PiS, March 27

POL-14. Former district council chairwoman expelled from PiS, March 28

POL-15. District council chairman from PiS, March 28

POL-16. PiS activist, March 28

POL-17. District council chairman from PiS, March 29

POL-18. Peter Boron, former senator from PiS, March 30

POL-19. Assistant to future Polish president Andrzej Duda, April 1

POL-20. PiS activist, April 4

POL-21. PiS youth activist, April 7

POL-22. PiS youth leader, April 9

POL-23. PiS youth activist, April 12

POL-24. Social scientist at the Polish Academy of Sciences, April 13

POL-25. City councilor from PiS, April 14

POL-26. Journalist at Gazeta Wyborcza, April 16

POL-27. Journalist at Gazeta Wyborcza, April 16

POL-28. Director of a leading NGO, April 16

Slovakia. Bratislava (April–May 2015)

SVK-01. Civil society activist opposed to SMER, April 21

SVK-02. Researcher at the Slovak Academy of Sciences, April 22

SVK-03. Former SMER politician, April 23

SVK-04. Political scientist at Comenius University, April 23

SVK-05. Conservative political consultant, April 23

SVK-06. Milan Ftáčnik, former Minister of Education and Mayor of Bratislava, April 27

SVK-07. Juraj Droba, member of the National Council from Freedom and Solidarity and future governor of the Bratislava region, April 29

SVK-08. President of a research institute, April 30

SVK-09. Social scientist at a research institute, April 30

SVK-10. Robert Žanony, campaign manager for SMER and prime minister Robert Fico, April 30

SVK-11. Katarína Neveďalová, director of SMER's foreign office and former member of the European Parliament, May 4

SVK-12. Martin Muránsky, political theorist and director of the Institute "Analyses, Strategies, Alternatives," May 6

SVK-13. Miroslav Číž, SMER's Deputy Speaker of the National Council, May 6, 2015

SVK-14. Luboš Blaha, SMER member of the National Council, May 6

SVK-15. Director of an NGO, May 7

SVK-16. Magdaléna Vášáryová, member of the National Council from SDKÚ-DS and former presidential candidate, May 12

SVK-17. Senior advisor at the Ministry of Finance, May 13

SVK-18. Andrej Kolesik, SMER member of the National Council, May 13

SVK-19. Sociologist at Comenius University, May 13

SVK-20. Senior advisor at the Ministry of Finance, May 13

Peru. Lima (October 2015–January 2016)

PER-01. Activist of the American Popular Revolutionary Alliance (APRA), October 28

PER-02. APRA activist, October 30

PER-03. Long-term APRA activist, November 4

PER-04. Former supporter of the Peruvian Nationalist Party (PNP), November 5

PER-05. Former APRA functionary, November 7

PER-06. Long-term APRA activist, November 17

PER-07. APRA activist, November 24

PER-08. Journalist at La República, November 27

PER-09. Professor at Pontificia Universidad Católica del Perú, November 30

PER-10. High-level PNP functionary, November 30

PER-11. Professor at Universidad del Pacífico, December 1

PER-12. Group interview with three political scientists, December 1

PER-13. Lecturer at Pontificia Universidad Católica del Perú, December 2

PER-14. High-level political functionary of PNP, December 2

PER-15. Former PNP activist, December 3

PER-16. Social scientist and leading commentator on national politics, December 3

PER-17. APRA activist, December 3

PER-18. PNP activist, December 4

PER-19. Group discussion with two PNP youth leaders, December 5

PER-20. Luis Enrique Gálvez, former candidate for mayor of Lima, December 7

PER-21. Sociologist at Pontificia Universidad Católica del Perú, December 10

PER-22. Serjio Tejada, congressman who left PNP, December 11

PER-23. PNP activist, December 12

PER-24. Long-term APRA activist, December 14

PER-25. Former PNP activist, January 9

PER-26. Former district governor and PNP activist, January 11
PER-27. Former PNP member and activist, January 12
PER-28. Former PNP functionary, January 13
PER-29. Professor and long-term leftist activist, January 14

Ecuador. Quito (June–August 2016)

ECU-01. Blue collar worker supportive of *correísmo*, June 15
ECU-02. Group interview with an anti-*correísta* small business owner and a low-wage worker supportive of *correísmo*, July 1
ECU-03. Diego Delgado Jara, 2009 presidential candidate and former congressman, July 8
ECU-04. Activist of Alliance "Proud and Sovereign Fatherland" (PAÍS), July 10, 2016
ECU-05. Radio journalist, July 18
ECU-06. PAÍS functionary employed at the National Assembly, July 26
ECU-07. Sociologist at FLACSO, July 26
ECU-08. Long-term activist of the Democratic Left, July 27
ECU-09. Pachakutik founder who left the party, July 29
ECU-10. Analyst at the Ministry of Justice and Human Rights, August 2
ECU-11. Analyst at the Ministry of Justice and Human Rights, August 2
ECU-12. Economist at the Ministry of Finance, August 3
ECU-13. Leading journalist and author, August 4
ECU-14. PAÍS youth leader, August 4
ECU-15. Analyst at the PAÍS Institute for Political Thought, August 8
ECU-16. Analyst at the PAÍS Institute for Political Thought, August 14
ECU-17. Pamela Troya, LGBTQ and human rights activist, August 15
ECU-18. Sociologist at FLACSO, August 17
ECU-19. Human rights and women's rights activist, August 18
ECU-20. Executive director of a leading NGO, August 18
ECU-21. Political functionary of the Democratic Left, August 19
ECU-22. Luis Monge, PAÍS National Secretary of Territorial Organization, August 19
ECU-23. Sociologist at FLACSO, August 23
ECU-24. Martha Roldós, 2009 presidential candidate, August 24

APPENDIX C. THE LEFT AND RIGHT IN POSTCOMMUNIST EUROPE, 2000–20

Leftist Parties

Albania: Socialist Party of Albania (PSS)
Bulgaria: Bulgarian Socialist Party (BSP)

Croatia: Social Democratic Party of Croatia (SPH)

Czechia: Czech Social Democratic Party (ČSSD); Communist Party of Bohemia and Moravia (KSČM)

Estonia: Social Democratic Party (SDE) (formerly Moderates)

Hungary: Hungarian Socialist Party (MSZP)

Latvia: Social Democratic Party "Harmony" (SDPS) (formerly People's Harmony and Harmony Center); Latvian Social Democratic Workers' Party (LSDSP)

Lithuania: Democratic Labor Party (LDDP); Social Democratic Party of Lithuania (LSDP)

Moldova: Party of Communists of the Republic of Moldova (PCRM)

North Macedonia: Social Democratic Union (SDSM)

Poland: Democratic Left Alliance (SLD)

Romania: Social Democratic Party (PSD)

Slovakia: Party of the Democratic Left (SDĽ)

Slovenia: Social Democrats (SD)

Ukraine: Socialist Party of Ukraine (SPU); Communist Party of Ukraine (KPU)

Rightist Parties

Albania: Democratic Party of Albania (PDSH); Republican Party of Albania (PRSH)

Bulgaria: Union of Democratic Forces (SDS)/United Democratic Forces (ODS), later Democrats for a Strong Bulgaria (DSB); Blue Coalition (SK); Reformist Bloc (RB)

Croatia: Croatian Democratic Union (HDZ)

Czechia: Civic Democratic Party (ODS); Civic Democratic Alliance (ODA); Christian Democratic Union – People's Party (KDU-ČSL)

Estonia: Pro Patria (Fatherland); Estonian National Independence Party (ERSP); Estonian Reform Party (ER)

Hungary: Hungarian Democratic Forum (MDF); Alliance of Free Democrats (SZDSZ); Fidesz – Hungarian Civic Union (before 2010)

Latvia: Latvian Way/Latvia's First Party (LC/LPP); Christian Democratic Union (KDS)

Lithuania: Sajudis; Homeland Union (TS); Lithuanian Christian Democratic Party (LKDP); Homeland Union – Lithuanian Christian Democrats (TS-LKD)

Moldova: Christian Democratic People's Party (PPCD); Reform Party (PR)/ Liberal Party (PL); Party of Democratic Forces (PFD); Party of Rebirth and Conciliation (PRCM)

North Macedonia: Internal Macedonian Revolutionary Organization – Democratic Party for Macedonian National Union (VMRO-DPMNE);

Liberal Party (LP); Democratic Party (DP); Liberal Democratic Party (LDP)

Poland: Liberal Democratic Congress (KLD); Democratic Union (UD)/ Freedom Union (UW)/Democratic Party (PD); Solidarity Electoral Action (AWS); Civic Platform (PO)

Romania: National Liberal Party (PNL); Christian Democratic National Peasants' Party (PNŢCD); Romanian Democratic Convention (CDR)

Slovakia: Christian Democratic Movement (KDH); Democratic Union of Slovakia (DEÚS); Slovak Democratic Coalition (SDK); Slovak Democratic and Christian Union – Democratic Party (SDKÚ-DS)

Slovenia: Liberal Democracy of Slovenia (LDS); Slovenian People's Party (SLS); Slovenian Christian Democrats (SKD)

Ukraine: Rukh – People's Movement of Ukraine (NRU); Our Ukraine (NU)

APPENDIX D. STATISTICAL TESTS

Analytical Strategy

I assess the postcommunist juncture theory relative to rival explanations of illiberal electoral outcomes in postcommunist Europe by conducting a number of statistical tests. Here, I present my overall strategy for empirical evaluation and then turn to operationalization, data sources, and regression analysis results. To facilitate the discussion, I organize my assessment in five categories, which correspond to the discussion of competing explanations in Chapter 3.

Importantly, the multiple regression analysis I conduct is at the aggregate-country, rather than individual, level. There are several reasons for this. First, I am interested in why illiberal electoral outcomes are more probable in some countries than others, rather than whether individual attributes or opinions make people more likely to vote for illiberal or post-neoliberal populist parties. As discussed by Baker and Greene, individual-level relationships between explanatory variables and vote choice (which is the basis for my dependent variables) can remain the same across elections, even in the presence of aggregate shifts in both, which, in turn, can miss causally important factors.[5] Second, individual-level analysis based on cross-sectional surveys can lead to endogeneity problems and thus potentially biased conclusions about retrospective voting. By contrast, aggregate time series evidence "is most likely to yield valid inferences about underlying individual-level effects."[6] Indeed, aggregate-level analysis is more appropriate when making causal claims connecting

---

[5] Baker and Greene (2011: 56).

[6] Baker and Greene (2011: 56–7); Doyle (2011); Kramer (1983: 93).

"institutions or systemic phenomena and populist movements, all of which are more than the sum of individual attitudes and behaviors."[7]

To test alternative hypotheses systematically, I ran regressions with two dependent variables – the vote share for illiberal parties and post-neoliberal populist magnitude. While below I present results from the regressions with the illiberal vote share, running models with post-neoliberal populist magnitude as the outcome variable does not change the main findings. Additionally, my models include the two sets of key independent variables that specifically compare the electoral performance of the Left and Right, as explained in Chapter 3. The first set of key independent variables consists of the concurrent proportional measures for the Left and the Right. Specifically for the Left, the concurrent proportional measure is not only highly correlated with the actual vote share but also captures persistent and divergent tendencies after junctures, as discussed. The second set of independent variables consists of the lagged proportional measures for the Left and the Right. The lagged proportional measures are both conducive for studying long-term electoral effects relative to pre-juncture periods, which they capture, and especially useful for comparisons with the effects of short-term electoral shifts between elections, which they do not capture.[8] Notably, my two sets of key independent variables are weakly correlated ($r = 0.57$ for the Left; $r = 0.24$ for the Right), which makes sense as they are based on successive elections.[9] Overall, while the two sets of key independent variables capture somewhat different concepts and nuances, as explained in Chapter 3, they both focus on the long-term electoral tendencies and effects central to my theory.

For all empirical tests, I use two types of regressions. First, I primarily rely on standard ordinary least squares (OLS) regressions with robust standard errors clustered by country in order to account for potential unobserved heterogeneity in the standard errors within countries. This approach is appropriate given the nature of my data, which includes at most 87 observations (or 82 when I use the lagged proportional measures[10]) as well as some variables that are either time-invariant or do not vary much within countries.[11] Second, as a

---

[7] Hawkins (2010: 131).

[8] In the regressions with lagged proportional measures, I use standardized Z-scores for direct comparability of coefficients because the measures capturing long- and short-term effects are scaled differently. This is not a problem, as Z-scores do not affect significance levels.

[9] For the concurrent measures – elections concurrent to the ones used for the construction of the dependent variables; for the lagged measures – elections preceding the ones used for the construction of the dependent variables.

[10] Because I study illiberal outcomes beginning with the year 2000, my lagged proportional measure is not analytically meaningful for the five countries where first post-juncture elections took place in the early 2000s – Bulgaria in 2001, Moldova in 2001, North Macedonia in 2002, Romania in 2000, and Slovakia in 2002. As the lagged measure would have to be based entirely on data before junctures in these cases, it would fail to capture the effect of junctures.

[11] For a similar approach, see Powell and Tucker (2014).

robustness check, I also conducted random- and fixed-effects estimations with panel-corrected standard errors robust to potential problems of heteroskedasticity, which deal specifically with issues of temporal variation within and unobserved heterogeneity across countries.[12] While random-effects estimations are generally preferable given the nature of the data,[13] the results from the fixed-effects estimations are very similar to the results from the random-effects estimations, as seen below. Finally, I test all regression models for multicollinearity[14] and avoid overfitting them by assessing alternative hypotheses based on the category of rival explanations.

Economic Demand

I evaluate economic demand factors by relying on several measures. While I use the overall scores issued by the Heritage Foundation (in the regressions) and the Fraser Institute (as a robustness check) as a measure of the depth of market liberalization,[15] I study economic performance in two ways – (1) as a long-term trend, which I measure as a country's gross domestic product (GDP) per capita as a percentage of transition levels (in 1989 or, where 1989 data are unavailable, in 1990) and for which I use data from the United Nations and (2) and as a short-term factor, which I operationalize as the annual percent change of real GDP growth, as recorded by the International Monetary Fund (IMF). To further study the effect of short-term economic voting, I use IMF data and also consider the unemployment rate and two-year average inflation rate. Finally, to investigate the effect of inequality, I rely on data from the World Inequality Database and develop two measures[16] – (1) income inequality, operationalized as the proportion that the top 10 percent earn in pretax national income relative to the bottom 50 percent[17] and (2) wealth inequality, measured as the proportion that the top 10 percent have in net personal wealth relative to the bottom

---

[12] As these panel data techniques use different assumptions about whether time-invariant and unobserved differences specific to countries are systematically correlated with the predictors (fixed effects) or not (random effects), here I use both as robustness checks.

[13] There are several reasons why random-effects models are preferable here. First, fixed-effects models cannot be used to study variation between countries, which is my main interest, and are inappropriate for the analysis of factors that display no or little variability over time, such as critical juncture types or most institutional supply variables. Second, fixed-effects models reduce

the degrees of freedom, which, given my relatively limited number of observations, can become a problem. Third, unobserved country characteristics tend to be uncorrelated with the predictors, as reflected in Hausman test results obtained from comparing the two types of models.

[14] All reported models include variables with variance inflation factors of less than four.

[15] The two are strongly correlated ($r = 0.82$).

[16] Weakly correlated ($r = 0.39$).

[17] Highly correlated with the income of the top 1 percent ($r = 0.81$), top 10 percent ($r = 0.91$), bottom 50 percent ($r = -0.75$), and the proportion of income of the top 10 percent to bottom 50 percent ($r = 0.91$).

50 percent.[18] All economic demand measures are for the year preceding the election under study.

As Table D.1 shows, the Left's long-term electoral performance is the strongest predictor of illiberal voting, and this remains the case even when short-term electoral shifts gain significance in the models with the lagged measures for key variables. Indeed, liberalization, long- and short-term economic performance, and unemployment are not reliable predictors across models. While income inequality appears as significant in several models, it is wrongly signed. Notably, wealth inequality is significant and correctly signed in multiple models, suggesting that it possibly plays at least some role in illiberal voting. Yet, as this variable does not perform consistently across models, it still remains a less reliable predictor of outcomes than the electoral performance of the Left.

Political Demand

To evaluate the possible effects of political demand, I rely on data from three sources. First, I use Transparency International's Corruption Perceptions Index, which focuses specifically on the public sector and is based on surveys of experts and businesspeople. Second, I consider the World Bank's Worldwide Governance Indicators, which combine a wider range of surveys that also include citizens who are not experts or businesspeople. In particular, the Government Effectiveness estimate captures perceptions of the quality of public services, civil service independence from political pressures, the quality of policies, and the credibility of governments. For my dataset, this estimate is highly correlated with the World Bank's Control of Corruption estimate ($r = 0.92$), which measures corruption in the public and private sectors and assesses perceptions of unethical use of public power as well as of state capture by elites and private interests. Third, to focus even more specifically on popular attitudes regarding the legitimacy of institutions, I also aggregate public opinion data from the Eurobarometer surveys. In particular, for each year when a country is surveyed, I calculate the mean share of respondents who distrust (1) the European Union, (2) the national government, and (3) democratic institutions, including the parliament and political parties.[19] As the latter two variables are highly correlated, I include government distrust in the regressions and use institutional distrust as a robustness check. Finally, as the latter variables

---

[18] Moderately correlated with the wealth of the top 1 percent ($r = 0.59$), top 10 percent ($r = 0.58$), and bottom 50 percent ($r = -0.63$), and strongly correlated with the proportion of wealth of the top 10 percent to bottom 50 percent ($r = 0.99$).

[19] I measure distrust in democratic institutions by averaging the share of respondents distrusting the parliament and the share of

respondents distrusting political parties. The Eurobarometer-based variables offer fewer observations (sixty-three for distrust in the national government and institutions and sixty-five for distrust in the EU) as the surveys did not cover all fifteen countries in all years from 2000 to 2020. Nevertheless, Eurobarometer covers more countries and years for these variables than the European Social Survey.

TABLE D.1 *The illiberal vote share and postcommunist juncture electoral dynamics, with controls for economic demand (OLS, random-effects, and fixed-effects estimations)*

Variables	(1) OLS	(2) RE	(3) FE	(4) OLS	(5) RE	(6) FE	(7) OLS	(8) RE	(9) FE
Leftist vote	-0.80*** (0.14)	-0.91*** (0.17)	-0.99*** (0.24)						
Rightist vote	-0.47*** (0.11)	-0.54*** (0.12)	-0.57*** (0.19)						
Left/juncture				-16.78*** (3.53)	-18.39*** (4.67)	-18.35** (6.33)			
Right/juncture				-4.59 (2.90)	-8.47*** (2.66)	-10.76*** (2.76)			
Left/juncture, lag (std)							-11.99*** (2.54)	-12.51*** (2.55)	-16.16*** (3.88)
Right/juncture, lag (std)							-2.20 (2.43)	-2.29 (2.52)	-5.89* (2.98)
Left short-term change	0.12 (0.14)	0.22* (0.12)	0.28* (0.14)	-0.05 (0.17)	0.10 (0.11)	0.13 (0.13)			
Right short-term change	-0.03 (0.16)	0.02 (0.13)	0.03 (0.13)	-0.05 (0.16)	-0.01 (0.16)	0.02 (0.18)			
L short-term change (std)							-8.90*** (1.39)	-8.86*** (1.46)	-8.80*** (1.73)
R short-term change (std)							-4.01* (1.99)	-3.99** (1.99)	-5.13** (1.94)
Liberalization	-0.59** (0.25)	-0.14 (0.38)	0.10 (0.50)	-0.66* (0.32)	-0.15 (0.48)	0.19 (0.43)	-0.58* (0.28)	-0.59 (0.34)	0.07 (0.57)
Income inequality	-6.86* (3.43)	-5.45* (2.88)	-4.67 (2.96)	-6.39** (2.84)	-5.28** (2.61)	-4.80 (2.94)	-5.63* (2.76)	-5.47** (2.35)	-4.42 (2.75)

	(1)	(2)	(3)	(4)	(5)	(6)	(7)	(8)	(9)
Wealth inequality	0.11*	0.07	0.04	0.19***	0.13**	0.09	0.18***	0.17***	0.04
	(0.06)	(0.07)	(0.08)	(0.05)	(0.06)	(0.09)	(0.05)	(0.05)	(0.11)
GDP per capita	-0.00**	-0.00**	-0.00	0.00	-0.00	-0.00	0.00	0.00	0.00
	(0.00)	(0.00)	(0.00)	(0.00)	(0.00)	(0.00)	(0.00)	(0.00)	(0.00)
GDP per capita v. 1989	0.06***	0.05***	0.05	0.04*	0.03*	0.04	0.03	0.03	0.01
	(0.01)	(0.02)	(0.04)	(0.02)	(0.02)	(0.02)	(0.02)	(0.02)	(0.02)
GDP growth	-0.34	-0.25	-0.21	-0.70*	-0.32	-0.24	-0.67*	-0.51	-0.16
	(0.33)	(0.33)	(0.35)	(0.37)	(0.33)	(0.35)	(0.37)	(0.36)	(0.39)
Inflation	-0.04	-0.04	-0.02	0.06	0.05	0.08	0.34	0.14	-0.26
	(0.15)	(0.13)	(0.13)	(0.16)	(0.10)	(0.13)	(0.41)	(0.40)	(0.53)
Unemployment	-0.11	0.04	0.19	-0.34	0.11	0.43	-0.22	-0.20	0.26
	(0.17)	(0.24)	(0.35)	(0.23)	(0.35)	(0.44)	(0.27)	(0.27)	(0.47)
Constant	93.17***	70.71***	56.98*	91.33***	59.16**	35.22	62.47***	63.06***	20.65
	(13.60)	(20.78)	(28.35)	(22.01)	(25.38)	(20.11)	(19.75)	(22.30)	(33.48)
Observations	87	87	87	87	87	87	82	82	82
R-squared	0.69	0.70	0.63	0.57	0.39	0.57	0.59	0.64	0.60
Number of countries	15	15	15	15	15	15	15	15	15

Robust standard errors in parentheses. "Between" R-squared for the RE models.

*** $p < 0.01$, ** $p < 0.05$, * $p < 0.1$

are only available for a limited number of years, my estimations here include relatively fewer observations. All political demand measures use data for the year preceding the election under study or, in several cases, for the latest year prior to an election for which data are available.

Table D.2 shows that the measure of long-term electoral path-dependency on the Left is, once again, the most powerful predictor of illiberal outcomes. Worsening public opinion regarding the quality of governance, as measured by perceptions of government effectiveness and corruption or popular distrust of national government and institutions or the EU, does not predict illiberal outcomes. Even as the Left's short-term shifts gain significance in the last three models, they remain less substantively important than the proportional measure of leftist parties' electoral resilience. Notably, the Left's long-term electoral performance relative to the pre-juncture period becomes a relatively more substantial predictor when country-specific characteristics are accounted for in the random-effects and fixed-effects estimations.

Cultural Demand

I assess cultural demand hypotheses by drawing data from several sources. First, I study mass society by collecting data from the World Bank's Development Indicators on media exposure, operationalized as the percent of individuals using the internet, as well as information from the Quality of Government dataset on education, operationalized as the gross percent of those enrolled in tertiary education. In turn, my measure of mass society is represented by the residuals from a regression of internet use on education.[20] Second, I assess the strength of civil society by using data from the Varieties of Democracy (V-Dem) main dataset.[21] Specifically, I use the Core Civil Society Index, which provides annual data on the robustness of civil society, "understood as one that enjoys autonomy from the state and in which citizens freely and actively pursue their political and civic goals."[22] For robustness tests, I additionally collected data on civil society participation from the Bertelsmann Foundation's Transformation Index (BTI) and constructed a measure, based on World Values Survey (WVS) data on organizational membership, by replicating Marc Howard's approach in his study of the weakness of civil society in postcommunist Europe.[23] Third, while I also collected WVS data on post-materialism – namely the four-point and twelve-point scale indices, which are highly correlated in my dataset – these data are not sufficient to conclusively test the effect of post-materialist values

---

[20] For a very similar approach that focuses on percent of households with a television set, see Hawkins (2010: 137–41). I prefer internet exposure due to its relevance in the twenty-first century.

[21] Coppedge et al. (2021).

[22] Coppedge et al. (2021: 305).

[23] See Howard (2003). While using the BTI data results in seventy-one observations, the WVS data results only in twenty-one observations due to uneven coverage.

TABLE D.2 *The illiberal vote share and postcommunist juncture electoral dynamics, with controls for political demand (OLS, random-effects, and fixed-effects estimations)*

Variables	(1) OLS	(2) RE	(3) FE	(4) OLS	(5) RE	(6) FE	(7) OLS	(8) RE	(9) FE
Leftist vote	-0.83***	-0.72***	-0.82**						
	(0.20)	(0.16)	(0.31)						
Rightist vote	-0.23	-0.54***	-0.70***						
	(0.18)	(0.20)	(0.20)						
Left/juncture				-15.15***	-15.51***	-14.85*			
				(4.14)	(5.09)	(7.81)			
Right/juncture				-2.48	-11.90	-19.40*			
				(7.12)	(8.47)	(10.70)			
Left/juncture, lag (std)							-10.94***	-12.54***	-13.21**
							(2.94)	(3.46)	(4.57)
Right/juncture, lag (std)							-1.98	-8.35	-12.55*
							(4.96)	(5.94)	(6.96)
Left short-term change				-0.09	-0.00	0.01			
				(0.17)	(0.16)	(0.21)			
Right short-term change				-0.28	-0.10	-0.02			
				(0.24)	(0.19)	(0.21)			
L short-term change (std)							-8.73***	-8.41***	-8.48***
							(2.26)	(1.81)	(2.09)
R short-term change (std)							-3.99	-4.82	-6.02*
							(3.44)	(3.17)	(3.07)
Corruption perception	-0.11	0.08	0.01	-0.07	0.11	0.07	-0.09	0.11	0.08
	(0.33)	(0.25)	(0.28)	(0.31)	(0.24)	(0.28)	(0.33)	(0.26)	(0.31)

(continued)

TABLE D.2 (continued)

Variables	(1) OLS	(2) RE	(3) FE	(4) OLS	(5) RE	(6) FE	(7) OLS	(8) RE	(9) FE
Government effectiveness	1.72	4.80	13.71	9.04	8.46	11.79	8.65	8.91	13.84
	(5.26)	(6.05)	(11.32)	(5.92)	(6.96)	(13.31)	(6.60)	(7.52)	(11.97)
Government distrust	-0.01	0.04	0.06	-0.04	0.09	0.15	-0.11	0.01	0.04
	(0.26)	(0.13)	(0.14)	(0.24)	(0.13)	(0.15)	(0.23)	(0.10)	(0.09)
EU distrust	0.11	0.01	-0.11	0.17	0.02	-0.09	0.24	0.08	-0.04
	(0.14)	(0.15)	(0.19)	(0.20)	(0.16)	(0.22)	(0.20)	(0.15)	(0.15)
Constant	50.44*	45.08**	52.49**	38.67	34.14*	39.81*	23.56	10.74	11.43
	(26.50)	(18.03)	(17.38)	(27.07)	(20.16)	(20.43)	(23.01)	(13.20)	(12.11)
Observations	63	63	63	63	63	63	62	62	62
R-squared	0.53	0.55	0.57	0.47	0.48	0.45	0.50	0.52	0.52
Number of countries		13	13		13	13		13	13

Robust standard errors in parentheses. "Between" R-squared for the RE models.
*** $p < 0.01$, ** $p < 0.05$, * $p < 0.1$

due to the few observations (twenty-one) available based on the small number of Eastern European countries covered in WVS waves. Such effects, as well as the effects of a possible reaction against post-materialism, are perhaps better examined by considering two other factors – the number of refugees seeking asylum, which I take from the World Bank's Development Indicators,[24] and women's empowerment. Because women's empowerment is a multifaceted concept, I operationalize it in three distinct ways – (1) as political empowerment, which I measure by relying on V-Dem's women political empowerment index, (2) as economic empowerment, which I operationalize as the pretax female labor income share, as recorded in the World Inequality Database, and (3) as legislative representation, as reflected in the Quality of Government data on the share of women in the lower house of parliament. All of these data are for the year preceding the election under study or for the latest year prior to an election for which data are available.

A look at a simple correlation matrix reveals that only some of these variables appear as significantly, albeit weakly, correlated with the outcome variables. This is particularly the case for mass society, post-materialism (twelve-point scale), women's empowerment (which is highly correlated with post-materialism in my dataset, $r = 0.74$), and women's income. Yet none of the cultural factors is a highly significant predictor of illiberal voting in the multivariate regression models, as seen in Table D.3. On the one hand, the interaction between internet use and education, the weakness of civil society, and the number of refugees appear as insignificant. One the other hand, although aspects of the status of women in society – particularly degree of representation in parliament and income – appear as significant in some regression models, they are not consistent predictors across models. What does remain significant is the electoral performance of the Left, which, especially when analyzed as a long-term trend, is once again the most substantively important predictor in all models.

Finally, as relatively few of the variables discussed earlier rely on public opinion data, I developed measurements based on such data to additionally probe the cultural backlash thesis. Concretely, I assess the hypotheses tested by Inglehart and Norris in their influential 2016 paper, which advanced the thesis based on data from the European Social Survey (ESS). Specifically, by also using ESS data and focusing on many of the same variables analyzed by these authors, I study public opinion regarding economic conditions,[25]

---

[24] These data originate from the United Nations High Commissioner for Refugees (UNHCR).

[25] I operationalize opinion regarding economic conditions as the average of values aggregated at the country level for three variables: (1) sum of shares of respondents who reported receiving unemployment/ redundancy or other social benefits or grants, multiplied by ten; (2) sum of shares of respondents who reported difficulties living on household income (answered "Difficult" or "Very difficult"); and (3) share of respondents who reported experience of unemployment lasting longer than three months.

TABLE D.3 *The illiberal vote share and postcommunist juncture electoral dynamics, with controls for cultural demand (OLS, random-effects, and fixed-effects estimations)*

Variables	(1) OLS	(2) RE	(3) FE	(4) OLS	(5) RE	(6) FE	(7) OLS	(8) RE	(9) FE
Leftist vote	-0.88***	-0.98***	-1.19***						
	(0.11)	(0.14)	(0.18)						
Rightist vote	-0.29**	-0.42***	-0.42**						
	(0.13)	(0.11)	(0.16)						
Left/juncture				-15.24***	-19.03***	-19.38**			
				(4.44)	(4.96)	(6.86)			
Right/juncture				-2.88	-7.54***	-11.02***			
				(3.32)	(2.26)	(2.61)			
Left/juncture, lag (std)							-10.99***	-15.76***	-18.71***
							(3.19)	(3.23)	(3.05)
Right/juncture, lag (std)							-0.36	-2.90	-4.31
							(2.65)	(2.42)	(2.57)
Left short-term change	0.03	0.18	0.35**	-0.08	0.07	0.10			
	(0.14)	(0.12)	(0.12)	(0.17)	(0.12)	(0.13)			
Right short-term change	-0.15	-0.15	-0.17	-0.17	-0.17	-0.15			
	(0.16)	(0.14)	(0.15)	(0.15)	(0.14)	(0.16)			
L short-term change (std)							-8.45***	-9.47***	-10.17***
							(1.91)	(1.49)	(1.32)
R short-term change (std)							-4.13*	-5.50***	-6.33***
							(2.20)	(1.62)	(1.41)
Mass society	-0.03	-0.06	-0.06	0.18	0.09	-0.04	0.10	0.07	-0.01
	(0.14)	(0.14)	(0.14)	(0.17)	(0.14)	(0.13)	(0.15)	(0.15)	(0.14)
Civil society	-1.39	-0.27	0.66	-1.11	-0.83	0.20	-1.19	-0.60	0.51
	(2.32)	(2.44)	(2.09)	(3.70)	(4.14)	(3.79)	(3.86)	(3.84)	(3.01)

Refugees	0.00	-0.00	-0.00**	0.00	-0.00	-0.00	0.00	-0.00	-0.00**
	(0.00)	(0.00)	(0.00)	(0.00)	(0.00)	(0.00)	(0.00)	(0.00)	(0.00)
Women's empowerment	-0.48	-5.38	-10.88***	1.76	-6.83	-15.72**	4.02	-6.89	-16.73***
	(3.98)	(4.02)	(3.09)	(4.68)	(5.44)	(6.64)	(4.41)	(5.54)	(4.72)
Women's income	2.59	5.05	9.34	8.56	12.33	8.14	8.39	12.93**	11.82*
	(5.29)	(5.45)	(8.37)	(7.19)	(7.64)	(11.08)	(7.70)	(6.04)	(5.70)
Women in parliament	0.09	0.50**	0.82***	-0.12	0.51**	1.08***	-0.22	0.41	0.89***
	(0.22)	(0.20)	(0.17)	(0.29)	(0.24)	(0.22)	(0.37)	(0.29)	(0.18)
Constant	54.83*	79.85***	103.68***	-5.88	54.98	141.47**	-37.03	28.34	106.83***
	(26.48)	(27.78)	(33.47)	(42.05)	(47.58)	(56.26)	(39.48)	(43.70)	(30.74)
Observations	87	87	87	87	87	87	82	82	82
R-squared	0.59	0.51	0.65	0.49	0.28	0.61	0.53	0.37	0.66
Number of countries	15	15	15	15	15	15	15	15	15

Robust standard errors in parentheses. "Between" R-squared for the RE models.

*** $p < 0.01$, ** $p < 0.05$, * $p < 0.1$

anti-immigrant attitudes,[26] anti-globalist attitudes,[27] distrust of national governance,[28] authoritarian values,[29] and right-wing ideology.[30] Because the ESS does not cover all countries consistently in all of the ten survey waves in the 2000–20 period, my dataset of country-level public opinion aggregates can be applied to forty-nine of the eighty-seven Eastern European elections under analysis.[31] Nevertheless, this is a sufficient number of observations for multiple regression analysis involving relatively few predictors.

As the results of this analysis, reported in Table D.4, demonstrate, neither economic grievances nor cultural backlash, as measured through public opinion, make a difference in terms of outcomes. Although the cultural backlash thesis may uncover the attributes or opinions of individual citizens who

---

[26] I operationalize anti-immigrant attitudes as the average of values aggregated at the country level for three variables: (1) sum of shares of respondents who tend to think immigrants are rather bad for the country's economy (answered zero, one, two, three, or four on a scale from zero to ten); (2) sum of shares of respondents who tend to think immigrants undermine the country's cultural life (answered zero, one, two, three, or four on a scale from zero to ten); and (3) sum of shares of respondents who tend to think immigrants make the country a worse place to live (answered zero, one, two, three, or four on a scale from zero to ten).

[27] I operationalize anti-globalist attitudes as the average of values aggregated at the country level for two variables: (1) sum of shares of respondents who tend not to trust the United Nations (answered zero, one, two, three, or four on a scale from zero to ten) and (2) sum of shares of respondents who tend not to trust the European Parliament (answered zero, one, two, three, or four on a scale from zero to ten).

[28] I operationalize distrust of national governance as the average of values aggregated at the country level for three variables: (1) sum of shares of respondents who tend not to trust politicians (answered zero, one, two, three, or four on a scale from zero to ten); (2) sum of shares of respondents who tend not to trust the national government (answered zero, one, two, three, or four on a scale from zero to ten); and (3) sum of shares of respondents who tend to not be satisfied with democracy (answered zero,

one, two, three, or four on a scale from zero to ten).

[29] I operationalize authoritarian values as the average of values aggregated at the country level for five variables: (1) sum of shares of respondents who tend to think it is important to live in secure and safe surroundings (answered "Very much like me," "Like me," or "Somewhat like me"); (2) sum of shares of respondents who tend to think it is important for one to do what one is told and follow rules (answered "Very much like me," "Like me," or "Somewhat like me"); (3) sum of shares of respondents who tend to think it is important to behave properly (answered "Very much like me," "Like me," or "Somewhat like me"); (4) sum of shares of respondents who tend to think it is important that the government is strong and ensures safety (answered "Very much like me," "Like me," or "Somewhat like me"); and (5) sum of shares of respondents who tend to think it is important to follow traditions and customs (answered "Very much like me," "Like me," or "Somewhat like me").

[30] I operationalize right-wing ideology as the sum of shares of respondents who tend to place themselves on the ideological right (answered six, seven, eight, nine, or ten on a scale from zero to ten).

[31] While for forty-two of these elections I use survey data collected for the last two years before elections, for seven of the elections I use data from surveys administered shortly after the election. Regression results based on forty-two observations are not meaningfully different from results based on forty-nine observations.

TABLE D.4 *The illiberal vote share and postcommunist juncture electoral dynamics, with controls for aggregate public opinion (OLS, random-effects, and fixed-effects estimations)*

Variables	(1) OLS	(2) RE	(3) FE	(4) OLS	(5) RE	(6) FE	(7) OLS	(8) RE	(9) FE
Leftist vote	-0.86*** (0.22)	-0.86*** (0.19)	-1.12*** (0.34)						
Rightist vote	-0.30 (0.26)	-0.67*** (0.21)	-0.87*** (0.20)						
Left/juncture				-19.19*** (5.08)	-19.74*** (5.76)	-18.75** (7.77)			
Right/juncture				-3.20 (4.61)	-11.00*** (3.74)	-18.79*** (3.70)			
Left/juncture, lag (std)							-14.46*** (3.30)	-16.91*** (3.92)	-18.19*** (3.97)
Right/juncture, lag (std)							0.33 (2.81)	-5.19 (3.26)	-12.33*** (4.07)
Left short-term change	0.05 (0.25)	0.21 (0.19)	0.41* (0.21)	0.08 (0.28)	0.13 (0.24)	0.13 (0.19)			
Right short-term change	-0.21 (0.22)	0.03 (0.18)	0.13 (0.19)	-0.29 (0.26)	-0.09 (0.22)	0.02 (0.25)			
L short-term change (std)							-8.63*** (2.25)	-8.96*** (2.17)	-9.31*** (2.37)
R short-term change (std)							-3.50 (3.42)	-3.92 (2.80)	-5.62* (2.94)
Economic difficulty	0.03 (0.31)	-0.06 (0.29)	-0.10 (0.38)	-0.07 (0.35)	0.03 (0.29)	0.14 (0.40)	-0.02 (0.35)	0.16 (0.28)	0.30 (0.30)

(continued)

TABLE D.4 (*continued*)

Variables	(1) OLS	(2) RE	(3) FE	(4) OLS	(5) RE	(6) FE	(7) OLS	(8) RE	(9) FE
Anti-immigrant attitudes	-0.05	-0.12	-0.21	-0.00	-0.16	-0.39	0.03	-0.09	-0.16
	(0.23)	(0.29)	(0.41)	(0.20)	(0.23)	(0.44)	(0.21)	(0.23)	(0.36)
Anti-globalist attitudes	-0.28	-0.23	-0.26	-0.15	0.03	-0.13	-0.04	0.14	0.06
	(0.33)	(0.27)	(0.32)	(0.34)	(0.28)	(0.27)	(0.30)	(0.28)	(0.33)
Distrust of nat'l governance	0.24	0.29	0.31	0.10	0.07	0.20	0.03	-0.08	-0.22
	(0.31)	(0.19)	(0.18)	(0.38)	(0.22)	(0.21)	(0.35)	(0.20)	(0.22)
Authoritarian values	0.28	0.06	-0.41	-0.03	-0.02	0.36	-0.13	-0.26	-0.25
	(0.33)	(0.42)	(0.78)	(0.52)	(0.60)	(0.78)	(0.54)	(0.68)	(0.82)
Right-wing ideology	0.35	-0.07	-0.49	0.30	0.03	0.37	0.31	-0.13	-0.35
	(0.41)	(0.37)	(0.36)	(0.37)	(0.45)	(0.52)	(0.30)	(0.36)	(0.38)
Constant	17.08	55.94	121.00*	46.42	57.58	26.12	30.91	51.33	67.40
	(28.12)	(34.99)	(61.86)	(47.63)	(51.74)	(63.58)	(48.22)	(57.41)	(62.24)
Observations	49	49	49	49	49	49	49	49	49
R-squared	0.50	0.51	0.68	0.44	0.32	0.61	0.50	0.39	0.62
Number of countries	14	14	14	14	14	14	14	14	14

Robust standard errors in parentheses. "Between" R-squared for the RE models.
*** $p < 0.01$, ** $p < 0.05$, * $p < 0.1$

support populist parties, it does not appear to explain developments at the systemic level. What best accounts for illiberal voting in Eastern Europe is, once again, the electoral performance of the Left, especially when it is analyzed as a long-term trend in the aftermath of postcommunist junctures.

Institutional Supply

To test institutional supply side propositions, I rely on several data sources. First, I use party system scores from the Bertelsmann Foundation's Transformation Index. While these scores do not cover elections prior to 2004, they nevertheless cover seventy-one elections and are thus a comprehensive and uniform measure of party system institutionalization in Eastern Europe. Second, I assess personalism by using data on party personalization from the Varieties of Democracy's V-Party Dataset.[32] Specifically, for each election under analysis, I calculated the average of all parties covered by the V-Party data. Finally, I collected data on average district magnitudes from the Quality of Government dataset and developed my own data, which include electoral thresholds and register whether, at the time of each parliamentary election under analysis, countries had directly elected presidents and fully proportional representation systems (as opposed to electoral systems with majoritarian elements). With the exception of the party systems scores, which are for the year prior to analyzed elections, all scores for these institutional variables correspond to the election year under analysis.

The results are shown in Table D.5, which reports findings from OLS and random-effects estimations. (Here, I do not estimate fixed-effects models due to the time-invariant nature of most institutional supply variables.) While several institutional variables are significantly, albeit weakly ($r < 0.3$), associated with illiberal voting when examined independently, party system institutionalization and personalism are the two that appear as significant across the multiple regression models. Not surprisingly, party system institutionalization is strongly and negatively correlated with illiberal voting. Importantly, since this factor is heavily conditioned by the programmatic positions and electoral performance of leftist parties, as explained in Chapter 2, variation in party system institutionalization is best understood as a function of dynamics on the Left. In other words, the institutionalization of party systems makes a difference for illiberal outcomes precisely because of the importance of leftist parties. Somewhat more surprisingly, as the personalization of party systems, itself negatively and weakly correlated with party system institutionalization ($r = -0.33$), is significantly and negatively associated with illiberal voting in the regressions, it appears that postcommunist publics actually prefer to channel their preferences for illiberal solutions via non-personalistic parties. And

---

[32] Lindberg et al. (2022).

TABLE D.5 *The illiberal vote and postcommunist juncture electoral dynamics, with controls for institutional supply (OLS and random-effects estimations)*

Variables	(1) OLS	(2) RE	(3) OLS	(4) RE	(5) OLS	(6) RE
Leftist vote	-0.94***	-0.90***				
	(0.14)	(0.17)				
Rightist vote	-0.07	-0.43***				
	(0.13)	(0.11)				
Left/juncture			-19.88***	-18.51***		
			(4.76)	(5.57)		
Right/juncture			-1.47	-12.10***		
			(3.96)	(3.37)		
Left/juncture, lag (std)					-13.36***	-13.26***
					(2.88)	(3.48)
Right/juncture, lag (std)					0.96	-3.04
					(2.55)	(3.79)
Left short-term change	0.11	0.15*	0.16	0.13		
	(0.07)	(0.08)	(0.14)	(0.10)		
Right short-term change	-0.48**	-0.24*	-0.58***	-0.35***		
	(0.19)	(0.13)	(0.19)	(0.13)		
L short-term change (std)					-8.06***	-8.32***
					(1.43)	(1.70)
R short-term change (std)					-6.38**	-6.28***
					(2.30)	(2.09)
Party system	-4.71***	-3.98***	-3.82**	-4.25***	-4.00**	-5.13***
	(1.20)	(1.20)	(1.76)	(1.40)	(1.81)	(1.94)
Personalism	-5.98**	-7.87***	-9.82***	-11.59***	-9.82***	-10.82***
	(2.34)	(2.36)	(2.76)	(2.28)	(2.98)	(2.57)

	(1)	(2)	(3)	(4)	(5)	(6)
Directly elected president	-0.19	0.58	-3.43	2.19	-4.13	0.84
	(4.66)	(5.18)	(5.67)	(5.90)	(5.47)	(5.63)
Proportional representation	-13.43*	-11.20**	-11.71	-12.31**	-10.51	-11.19*
	(7.31)	(4.90)	(7.01)	(5.02)	(7.55)	(6.23)
District magnitude	-0.02*	-0.03***	-0.00	0.03	-0.01	-0.00
	(0.01)	(0.01)	(0.02)	(0.03)	(0.02)	(0.03)
Electoral threshold	-0.32	-2.50***	-0.12	-1.88**	-0.16	-1.64*
	(1.30)	(0.55)	(1.43)	(0.91)	(1.38)	(0.95)
Constant	97.44***	108.10***	90.98***	104.90***	69.94***	82.07***
	(15.51)	(12.36)	(17.97)	(15.16)	(18.54)	(18.81)
Observations	66	66	66	66	66	66
R-squared	0.73	0.67	0.64	0.55	0.65	0.58
Number of countries	15	15	15	15	15	15

Robust standard errors in parentheses. "Between" R-squared for the RE models.

*** $p < 0.01$, ** $p < 0.05$, * $p < 0.1$

although elements of the electoral systems – particularly, the availability of proportional representation and high electoral thresholds – appear statistically significant in several estimations, the first of these variables is not correctly signed, and neither of these two factors is consistently significant across models. Finally, as none of these variables outperforms the measure of post-juncture trends on the Left, which once again remains overall the strongest predictor, institutional supply does not alter the basic relationship between leftist electoral dynamics and illiberal outcomes.

International Factors

I test hypotheses based on international factors by using data from the IMF and my own dataset. First, to study Western leverage through EU conditionality, I consider whether countries were EU applicants, candidates, or members in the year prior to each studied election. Second, to analyze Western linkage through trade, I follow Levitsky and Way and, by using the United Nations' Direction of Trade statistics, calculate the sum of total imports and exports, as a share of GDP, with Western European EU members[33] and the United States for the year prior to elections under study. Third, to test for illiberal diffusion, I develop two sets of variables, each containing measures corresponding to my dependent variables. While one set takes the *mean* of the illiberal vote share, another set takes the *highest* illiberal vote share, as obtained in the most recent legislative elections, in neighboring postcommunist countries under study. Thus, I not only analyze the potential effects of Western leverage and linkage by relying on standard metrics but also conceptualize illiberal diffusion from neighboring countries in two different ways.

None of these measures is a significant predictor of illiberal voting, as seen in Table D.6. While diffusion from neighboring countries gains significance in some estimations, this variable does not perform strongly or consistently across models.[34] Meanwhile, neither countries' status relative to the EU nor trade with the West appears to be significantly associated with illiberal voting. What remains the most important predictor is the electoral dynamics on the Left, with long-term post-juncture trends being, once again, the most dominant factor.

The above empirical tests confirm that the postcommunist juncture theory offers a superior explanation of illiberal voting in contemporary Eastern Europe than factors associated with economic, political, and cultural demand, as well as with institutional supply and international dynamics. Moreover,

---

[33] As I collected trade data through 2020, this also includes the United Kingdom, which exited the EU in 2020.

[34] While here I present results based on the average illiberal vote shares in neighboring countries, the results are nearly identical when diffusion is measured by using the highest illiberal vote shares.

TABLE D.6 *The illiberal vote share and postcommunist juncture electoral dynamics, with controls for international factors (OLS, random-effects, and fixed-effects estimations)*

Variables	(1) OLS	(2) RE	(3) FE	(4) OLS	(5) RE	(6) FE	(7) OLS	(8) RE	(9) FE
Leftist vote	-0.82*** (0.18)	-0.93*** (0.18)	-1.09*** (0.26)						
Rightist vote	-0.24 (0.14)	-0.42*** (0.11)	-0.50** (0.19)						
Left/juncture				-16.29*** (4.19)	-18.44*** (4.77)	-18.10** (7.50)			
Right/juncture				-1.72 (2.45)	-7.10*** (1.97)	-10.91*** (2.35)			
Left/juncture, lag (std)							-11.35*** (2.83)	-14.50*** (2.98)	-16.46*** (3.57)
Right/juncture, lag (std)							-0.06 (1.76)	-3.11 (2.05)	-5.71* (2.98)
Left short-term change	0.08 (0.17)	0.20 (0.13)	0.32* (0.15)	0.01 (0.18)	0.09 (0.12)	0.09 (0.14)			
Right short-term change	-0.19 (0.20)	-0.07 (0.17)	-0.03 (0.19)	-0.30 (0.20)	-0.11 (0.19)	-0.04 (0.20)			
L short-term change (std)							-7.23*** (1.70)	-8.08*** (1.72)	-8.68*** (1.71)
R short-term change (std)							-5.50** (1.91)	-5.29*** (2.00)	-5.80** (2.11)
EU applicant or candidate	-4.02 (3.30)	-2.03 (4.27)	-0.26 (6.30)	-6.72 (5.84)	-4.37 (5.31)	1.09 (5.02)	-8.15 (5.90)	-10.60* (6.11)	-7.71 (4.94)

(continued)

TABLE D.6 (*continued*)

Variables	(1) OLS	(2) RE	(3) FE	(4) OLS	(5) RE	(6) FE	(7) OLS	(8) RE	(9) FE
EU member	1.70	0.59	1.55	3.44	1.50	6.60	1.03	-7.11	-5.77
	(4.64)	(4.68)	(7.51)	(7.87)	(6.37)	(6.47)	(8.05)	(7.11)	(6.13)
Trade with the West	-0.00	0.01	0.01	-0.01	0.01	0.06	-0.01	0.05	0.13
	(0.17)	(0.13)	(0.24)	(0.16)	(0.13)	(0.20)	(0.16)	(0.12)	(0.15)
Diffusion	0.09	0.13	0.13	0.22**	0.17*	0.09	0.23**	0.29***	0.25**
	(0.10)	(0.08)	(0.11)	(0.09)	(0.09)	(0.11)	(0.09)	(0.10)	(0.10)
Constant	46.63***	51.87***	57.01***	37.82***	45.65***	43.84**	20.79***	21.24***	17.23*
	(8.32)	(8.59)	(18.95)	(8.86)	(10.20)	(16.46)	(5.01)	(5.85)	(8.10)
Observations	83	83	83	83	83	83	79	79	79
R-squared	0.58	0.58	0.60	0.51	0.40	0.54	0.55	0.49	0.61
Number of countries	15	15	15	15	15	15	15	15	15

Robust standard errors in parentheses. "Between" R-squared for the RE models.
*** $p < 0.01$, ** $p < 0.05$, * $p < 0.1$

these results are confirmed when the illiberal vote share is replaced with post-neoliberal populist magnitude as the dependent variable. Overall, as long-term trends on the Left were shaped by postcommunist junctures, they drove varying illiberal electoral outcomes in the region during the 2020–20 period. As the statistical tests demonstrate, while the specific conceptualization of "long-term electoral trends" does make a difference – with short-term electoral shifts on the Left undeniably gaining significance when the lagged measures of the key independent variables are used – long-term electoral dynamics always remain the strongest and most significant predictor of outcomes, regardless of the controls introduced in the models. Notably, this finding is based on both OLS and panel data analyses. Indeed, as random- and fixed-effects models – both of which account for unobserved country-specific factors and address the time series nature of the data – invariably produce lower negative coefficients for the variables measuring long-term effects than for those measuring short-term effects, the negative correlations between illiberal electoral outcomes and key independent variables are mostly driven by persistent, rather than transient, dynamics on the Left.

References

Abugattas, Luis. 1998. "The Impact of Structural Adjustment on Agricultural Performance." In *Fujimori's Peru: The Political Economy*, edited by John Crabtree and Jim Thomas, 61–87. London: Institute of Latin American Studies, University of London.

Acemoglu, Daron, Georgy Egorov, and Konstantin Sonin. 2013. "A Political Theory of Populism." *The Quarterly Journal of Economics* 128(2): 771–805.

Acosta, Alberto, Hugo Jácome, Guillaume Long, Fernando Martín-Mayoral, Franklin Ramírez, María Cristina Vallejo, Marcelo Varela, and Alison Vásconez. 2009. *Análisis de Coyuntura: Una Lectura de Los Principales Componentes Económicos, Políticos y Sociales de Ecuador Durante el Año 2009.* Ecuador: Flacso and Friedrich Ebert Stiftung.

Akkerman, Tjitske, Sarah de Lange, and Matthijs Rooduijn. 2016. "Inclusion and Mainstreaming? Radical Right-Wing Populist Parties in the New Millennium." In *Radical Right-Wing Populist Parties in Western Europe: Into the Mainstream?*, edited by Tjitske Akkerman, Sarah de Lange, and Matthijs Rooduijn, 1–28. London: Routledge.

Albertazzi, Daniele, and Duncan McDonnell. 2015. *Populists in Power.* New York: Routledge.

Alemán, Eduardo, and Marisa Kellam. 2008. "The Nationalization of Electoral Change in the Americas." *Electoral Studies* 27(2): 193–212.

Alexander, Robert Jackson. 2007. *A History of Organized Labor in Peru and Ecuador.* Westport: Praeger Publishers.

Aligica, Paul Dragos. 2001. "Romania's Economic Policy: Before and after the Elections." *East European Constitutional Review* 92(1): 92–96.

Anria, Santiago. 2018. *When Movements Become Parties: The Bolivian MAS in Comparative Perspective.* New York: Cambridge University Press.

Appel, Hilary, and Mitchell A. Orenstein. 2016. "Why Did Neoliberalism Triumph and Endure in the Post-Communist World?" *Comparative Politics* 48(3): 313–31.

2018. *From Triumph to Crisis: Neoliberal Economic Reform in Postcommunist Countries.* New York: Cambridge University Press.

Arce, Moisés. 2006. "The Societal Consequences of Market Reform in Peru." *Latin American Politics and Society* 48(1): 27–54.

2008. "The Repoliticization of Collective Action after Neoliberalism in Peru." *Latin American Politics and Society* 50(3): 37–62.

2014. *Resource Extraction and Protest in Peru*. Pittsburgh: University of Pittsburgh Press.

Armingeon, Klaus, and Besir Ceka. 2014. "The Loss of Trust in the European Union during the Great Recession since 2007: The Role of Heuristics from the National Political System." *European Union Politics* 15(1): 82–107.

Åslund, Anders. 2001. *Building Capitalism: The Transformation of the Former Soviet Bloc*. Cambridge: Cambridge University Press.

Báez Rivera, Sara, and Víctor Bretón Solo de Zaldívar. 2006. "El Enigma del Voto Étnico o las Tribulaciones del Movimiento Indígena: Reflexiones sobre los Resultados de la Primera Vuelta Electoral (2006) en las Provincias de la Sierra." *Ecuador Debate* 69(December): 19–36.

Bagashka, Tanya, Cristina Bodea, and Sung Min Han. 2022. "Populism's Rise in Post-Communist Countries: Breaking Electoral Promises and Incumbent Left Parties' Vote Losses." *European Journal of Political Research* 61(1): 134–53.

Baka, Władysław. 2005. "The Economic Agenda of the Polish Round Table 15 Years Later: Lessons for the Future." In *The Polish Miracle: Lessons for the Emerging Markets*, edited by Grzegorz W. Kołodko, 49–62. Burlington: Ashgate Publishing Company.

Baker, Andy, and Kenneth F. Greene. 2011. "The Latin American Left's Mandate: Free-Market Policies and Issue Voting in New Democracies." *World Politics* 63(1): 43–77.

Bakke, Elisabeth, and Nick Sitter. 2021. "Each Unhappy in Its Own Way? The Rise and Fall of Social Democracy in the Visegrád Countries since 1989." In *Social Democracy in the 21st Century*, edited by Nik Brandal, Øivind Bratberg, and Dag Einar Thorsen, 37–68. Bingley: Emerald Publishing Limited.

Bakker, Ryan, Catherine de Vries, Erica Edwards, Liesbet Hooghe, Seth Jolly, Gary Marks, Jonathan Polk, Jan Rovny, Marco Steenbergen, and Milada Vachudova. 2015. "Measuring Party Positions in Europe: The Chapel Hill Expert Survey Trend File, 1999–2010." *Party Politics* 21(1): 143–52.

Balcerowicz, Leszek. 1995. *Socialism, Capitalism, Transformation*. Budapest: Central European University Press.

Ban, Cornel. 2016a. "Romania: A Social Democratic Anomaly in Eastern Europe?" openDemocracy, December 12. Accessed June 15, 2023. www.opendemocracy.net/en/can-europe-make-it/romania-social-democratic-anomaly-in-eastern-europe/.

2016b. *Ruling Ideas: How Global Neoliberalism Goes Local*. New York: Oxford University Press.

2019. "Dependent Development at a Crossroads? Romanian Capitalism and Its Contradictions." *West European Politics* 42(5): 1041–68.

Ban, Cornel, Gábor Scheiring, and Mihai Vasile. 2023. "The Political Economy of National-Neoliberalism." *European Politics and Society* 24(1): 96–114.

Bański, Jerzy. 2003. "Transforming the Functional Structure of Poland's Rural Areas." *Rural Areas and Development* 1: 19–37.

Baranowski, Mariusz. 2023. "The Illiberal Turn in Politics and Ideology through the Commodified Social Policy of the 'Family 500+' Programme." *Forum for Social Economics* 52(3): 270–81.

Barany, Zoltan, and Ivan Volgyes, eds. 1995. *The Legacies of Communism in Eastern Europe*. Baltimore: Johns Hopkins University Press.

Barber, Benjamin. 2011. "As President Lech Wałęsa Said to President Lula Da Silva." *The Huffington Post*, October 3. Accessed March 15, 2024. www.huffpost.com/entry/as-president-lech-walesa_b_992913.

Barr, Robert R. 2009. "Populists, Outsiders and Anti-establishment Politics." *Party Politics* 15(1): 29–48.

Bartha, Eszter. 2011. "'It Can't Make Me Happy that Audi Is Prospering': Working-Class Nationalism in Hungary after 1989." In *Headlines of Nation, Subtexts of Class: Working Class Populism and the Return of the Repressed in Neoliberal Europe*, edited by Don Kalb and Gábor Halmai, 92–112. New York: Berghahn Books.

2013. *Alienating Labour: Workers on the Road from Socialism to Capitalism in East Germany and Hungary*. New York: Berghahn Books.

Bartha, Eszter, and András Tóth. 2021. "The Emasculation of Trade Unions and Workers' Drift to Neonationalism in Hungary." *Europe-Asia Studies* 73(9): 1726–47.

Becker, Marc. 2011a. "Correa, Indigenous Movements, and the Writing of a New Constitution in Ecuador." *Latin American Perspectives* 38(1): 47–62.

2011b. *Pachakutik: Indigenous Movements and Electoral Politics in Ecuador*. Lanham: Rowman & Littlefield.

Beissinger, Mark, and Stephen Kotkin, eds. 2014. *Historical Legacies of Communism in Russia and Eastern Europe*. Cambridge: Cambridge University Press.

Bell, Janice. 1997. "Unemployment Matters: Voting Patterns during the Economic Transition in Poland, 1990–1995." *Europe-Asia Studies* 49(7): 1263–91.

2001. *The Political Economy of Reform in Post-Communist Poland*. Cheltenham: Edward Elgar Publishing.

Beloshitzkaya, Vera. 2021. "Affirmative Gender Equality Policies in Central and Eastern Europe: Moving beyond the EU Requirements." *Party Politics* 27(5): 953–64.

Berman, Sheri, and Maria Snegovaya. 2019. "Populism and the Decline of Social Democracy." *Journal of Democracy* 30(3): 5–19.

Bernhard, Michael, and Krzysztof Jasiewicz. 2015. "Whither Eastern Europe? Changing Approaches and Perspectives on the Region in Political Science." *East European Politics and Societies* 29(2): 311–22.

Bertelsmann Foundation. 2023. BTI Transformation Index. Accessed January 10, 2024. https://bti-project.org/en/?&cb=00000.

Betz, Hans-Georg. 1994. *Radical Right-Wing Populism in Western Europe*. New York: St. Martin's Press.

Bill, Stanley, and Ben Stanley. 2020. "Whose Poland Is It to Be? PiS and the Struggle between Monism and Pluralism." *East European Politics* 36(3): 378–94.

Binev, Binio S. 2015. "Mainstream Populism in Post-Communist Europe: Ideological Variation, Adaptation, and Success in the Twenty-First Century." *Perspectives on Europe* 45(1): 76–81.

2023. "Post-Communist Junctures, the Left, and Illiberalism: Theory with Evidence from Central and Eastern Europe." *Comparative Political Studies* 56(4): 465–502.

2024a. "Post-Neoliberal Populism in Latin America and Eastern Europe: Recognizing Family Resemblance." *Studies in Comparative International Development* 59(3): 517–81.

2024b. "The Social Bases of Populist Domination: Market Reforms and Popular Reactions in Latin America and Post-Communist Europe." *Government and Opposition* 59(1): 23–46.

Birch, Sarah. 2001. "Electoral System and Party System Stability in Post-Communist Europe." Paper prepared for the 98th annual meeting of the American Political Science Association, San Francisco, August 26–29.

Bláha, Petr, Jakub Charvát, and Pavel Maškarinec. 2022. "Explaining the Rise of Populist Parties in the 2013 and 2017 Czech Parliamentary Elections: Economic Grievances and Political Protest?" In *The Rise of Populism in Central and Eastern Europe*, edited by Simona Kuković and Petr Just, 39–52. Northampton: Edward Elgar Publishing.

Bleich, Erik, and Robert Pekkanen. 2013. "How to Report Interview Data." In *Interview Research in Political Science*, edited by Layna Mosley, 84–105. Ithaca: Cornell University Press.

Block, Fred, and Margaret Somers. 1984. "Beyond the Economistic Fallacy: The Holistic Social Science of Karl Polanyi." In *Vision and Methods in Historical Sociology*, edited by Theda Skocpol, 47–84. New York: Cambridge University Press.

Boas, Taylor C. 2016. *Presidential Campaigns in Latin America: Electoral Strategies and Success Contagion.* New York: Cambridge University Press.

Bochsler, Daniel. 2010. "Measuring Party Nationalization: A New Gini-Based Indicator That Corrects for the Number of Units." *Electoral Studies* 29(1): 155–68.

Bockman, Johanna. 2011. *Markets in the Name of Socialism: The Left-Wing Origins of Neoliberalism.* Stanford: Stanford University Press.

Bogumił, Piotr. 2009. "Regional Disparities in Poland." *Economic Analysis from the Directorate-General for Economic and Financial Affairs of the European Commission* 6(4): 1–7.

Bohle, Dorothee, and Béla Greskovits. 2004. "Capital, Labor, and the Prospects of the European Social Model in the East." Central and Eastern Europe Working Paper 58. Cambridge: Minda de Gunzburg Center for European Studies, Harvard University.
2012. *Capitalist Diversity on Europe's Periphery.* Ithaca: Cornell University Press.

Borbáth, Endre. 2018. "When the Post-Communist Left Succeeds: The 2016 Romanian Parliamentary Election." In *2017: Europe's Bumper Year of Elections*, edited by Brigid Laffan and Lorenzo Cicchi, 133–50. San Domenico di Fiesole: European University Institute.

Borelli, Caterina, and Fabio Mattioli. 2013. "The Social Lives of Postsocialism." *Laboratorium: Russian Review of Social Research* 5(1): 4–13.

Bowen, James David. 2015. "Rethinking Democratic Governance: State Building, Autonomy, and Accountability in Correa's Ecuador." *Journal of Politics in Latin America* 7(1): 83–110.

Bozóki, András, and John T. Ishiyama. 2002. "Introduction and Theoretical Framework." In *The Communist Successor Parties of Central and Eastern Europe*, edited by András Bozóki and John T. Ishiyama, 3–13. Armonk: M.E. Sharpe.

Brinks, Daniel, and Michael Coppedge. 2006. "Diffusion Is No Illusion: Neighbor Emulation in the Third Wave of Democracy." *Comparative Political Studies* 39(4): 463–89.

Brown, Wendy. 2015. *Undoing the Demos: Neoliberalism's Stealth Revolution.* Brooklyn: Zone Books.

2019. *In the Ruins of Neoliberalism: The Rise of Antidemocratic Politics in the West.* New York: Columbia University Press.

Bugaric, Bojan. 2016. "Neoliberalism, Post-Communism, and the Law." *Annual Review of Law and Social Science* 12: 313–29.

Bukowski, Paweł, and Filip Novokmet. 2021. "Between Communism and Capitalism: Long–Term Inequality in Poland, 1892–2015." *Journal of Economic Growth* 26(2): 187–239.

Bunce, Valerie. 1999. "Peaceful versus Violent State Dismemberment: A Comparison of the Soviet Union, Yugoslavia, and Czechoslovakia." *Politics and Society* 27(2): 217–37.

2003. "Rethinking Recent Democratization: Lessons from the Postcommunist Experience." *World Politics* 55(2): 167–92.

2005. "The National Idea: Imperial Legacies and Post-Communist Pathways in Eastern Europe." *East European Politics and Societies* 19(3): 406–42.

Burawoy, Michael. 2003. "For a Sociological Marxism: The Complementary Convergence of Antonio Gramsci and Karl Polanyi." *Politics and Society* 31(2): 193–261.

2010. "From Polanyi to Pollyanna: The False Optimism of Global Labor Studies." *Global Labour Journal* 1(2): 301–13.

2013. "Marxism after Polanyi." In *Marxisms in the 21st Century: Crisis, Critique and Struggle*, edited by Michelle Williams and Vishwas Satgar. 34–52. Johanesburg: Wits University Press.

2019. "Afterword: Resolving Polanyi's Paradox." In *Karl Polanyi's Political and Economic Thought: A Critical Guide*, edited by Christopher Holmes, Gareth Dale, and Maria Markantonatou, 213–24. New Castle: Agenda Publishing.

Burgess, Katrina, and Steven Levitsky. 2003. "Explaining Populist Party Adaptation in Latin America: Environmental and Organizational Determinants of Party Change in Argentina, Mexico, Peru, and Venezuela." *Comparative Political Studies* 36(8): 881–911.

Burron, Neil. 2012. "Ollanta Humala and the Peruvian Conjuncture: Democratic Expansion or 'Inclusive' Neoliberal Redux?" *Latin American Perspectives* 39(1): 133–39.

Buštíková, Lenka. 2014. "Revenge of the Radical Right." *Comparative Political Studies* 47(12): 1738–65.

Buštíková, Lenka, and Petra Guasti. 2017. "The Illiberal Turn or Swerve in Central Europe?" *Politics and Governance* 5(4): 166–76.

Buzalka, Juraj. 2007. *Nation and Religion: The Politics of Commemoration in South-East Poland.* Berlin: LIT Verlag.

2018. "Post-Peasant Memories: Populist or Communist Nostalgia." *East European Politics and Societies* 32(4): 988–1006.

2021a. *The Cultural Economy of Protest in Post-Socialist European Union: Village Fascists and Their Rivals.* Abington and New York: Routledge.

2021b. "Village Fascists and Progressive Populists: Two Faces of the Countermovement in Slovakia." *Europe-Asia Studies* 73(9): 1658–82.

Cameron, Maxwell A. 1994. *Democracy and Authoritarianism in Peru: Political Coalitions and Social Change.* New York: St. Martin's Press.

2011. "Peru: The Left Turn That Wasn't." In *The Resurgence of the Latin American Left*, edited by Steven Levitsky and Kenneth Roberts, 375–98. Baltimore: The Johns Hopkins University Press.

Canovan, Margaret. 1999. "Trust the People! Populism and the Two Faces of Democracy." *Political Studies* 47(1): 2–16.

Capoccia, Giovanni, and R. Daniel Kelemen. 2007. "The Study of Critical Junctures: Theory, Narrative, and Counterfactuals in Historical Institutionalism." *World Politics* 59(3): 341–69.

Cardoso, Fernando Henrique, and Enzo Faletto. 1979. *Dependency and Development in Latin America*. Berkeley: University of California Press.

Carreras, Miguel. 2012. "The Rise of Outsiders in Latin America, 1980–2010: An Institutionalist Perspective." *Comparative Political Studies* 45(12): 1451–82.

Carrión, Julio F. 2006. "Public Opinion, Market Reforms, and Democracy in Fujimori's Peru." In *The Fujimori Legacy: The Rise of Electoral Authoritarianism in Peru*, edited by Julio F. Carrión, 126–47. University Park: The Pennsylvania State University Press.

Carrión, Julio, and Patricia Zárate. 2023. "Peru: Deep Political Dissatisfaction Weakens Support for Democracy." *Revista Latinoamericana de Opinión Pública* 12(2): 25–54.

Casal Bértoa, Fernando. 2014. "Party Systems and Cleavage Structures Revisited: A Sociological Explanation of Party System Institutionalization in East Central Europe." *Party Politics* 20(1): 16–36.

Castle, Marjorie, and Ray Taras. 2002. *Democracy in Poland*. 2nd ed. Boulder: Westview Press.

Cheibub, José Antonio, Jennifer Gandhi, and James Raymond Vreeland. 2010. "Democracy and Dictatorship Revisited." *Public Choice* 143(1): 67–101.

Chibber, Vivek. 2022a. *Confronting Capitalism: How the World Works and How to Change It*. Brooklyn: Verso.

2022b. *The Class Matrix: Social Theory after the Cultural Turn*. Cambridge: Harvard University Press.

Clark, Patrick, and Jacobo García. 2019. "Left Populism, State Building, Class Compromise, and Social Conflict in Ecuador's Citizens' Revolution." *Latin American Perspectives* 46(1): 230–46.

Coatsworth, John H. 1998. "Economic and Institutional Trajectories in Nineteenth-Century Latin America." In *Latin America and the World Economy since 1800*, edited by John H. Coatsworth and Alan M. Taylor, 23–54. Cambridge: Harvard University Press.

Collier, David, and Gerardo L. Munck. 2017. "Building Blocks and Methodological Challenges: A Framework for Studying Critical Junctures." *Qualitative and Multi-Method Research* 15(1): 2–9.

2022. "Introduction: Tradition and Innovation in Critical Juncture Research." In *Critical Junctures and Historical Legacies: Insights and Methods for Comparative Social Science*, edited by David Collier and Gerardo L. Munck, 1–29. Lanham: Rowman & Littlefield.

Collier, Ruth Berins, and David Collier. 1991. *Shaping the Political Arena: Critical Junctures, the Labor Movement, and Regime Dynamics in Latin America*. Princeton: Princeton University Press.

Conaghan, Catherine M. 1988. *Restructuring Domination: Industrialists and the State in Ecuador*. Pittsburgh: University of Pittsburgh Press.

2011. "Ecuador: Rafael Correa and the Citizens' Revolution." In *The Resurgence of the Latin American Left*, edited by Steven Levitsky and Kenneth Roberts, 260–82. Baltimore: The Johns Hopkins University Press.

Conaghan, Catherine M., and James M. Malloy. 1994. *Unsettling Statecraft: Democracy and Neoliberalism in the Central Andes.* Pittsburgh: University of Pittsburgh Press.

Concejo Nacional Electoral (CNE) del Ecuador. 2023. Bases de Datos. Accessed December 23, 2023. www.cne.gob.ec/estadisticas/bases-de-datos/.

Conniff, Michael L., ed. 1999. *Populism in Latin America.* Tuscaloosa: University of Alabama Press.

Connor, Walter, and Piotr Ploszajski. 1992. "Introduction: Background to Crisis." In *The Polish Road from Socialism: The Economics, Sociology and Politics of Transition*, edited by Walter Connor and Piotr Ploszajski, 15–27. Armonk: M.E. Sharpe.

Cook, Linda, and Mitchell A. Orenstein. 1999. "The Return of the Left and Its Impact on the Welfare State in Poland, Hungary, and Russia." In *Left Parties and Social Policy in Postcommunist Europe*, edited by Linda Cook, Mitchell A. Orenstein, and Marilyn Rueschemeyer, 47–108. Boulder: Westview Press.

Coppedge, Michael, John Gerring, Carl Henrik Knutsen, Staffan Lindberg, Jan Teorell, David Altman, Michael Bernhard, et al. 2021. "'V-Dem Codebook V11.1' Varieties of Democracy (V-Dem) Project."

Corrales, Javier. 2007. "*Leftism and Populism in Today's Latin America: Is Chavismo Contagious?*" Washington: Center for Latin American Studies, Hudson Institute.

Crabtree, John. 1998. "Neo-Populism and the Fujimori Phenomenon." In *Fujimori's Peru: The Political Economy*, edited by John Crabtree and Jim Thomas, 7–23. London: Institute of Latin American Studies, University of London.

Crabtree, John, and Jim Thomas. 1998. "Neoliberalism, Democracy, and Exclusion." In *Fujimori's Peru: The Political Economy*, edited by John Crabtree and Jim Thomas, 265–72. London: Institute of Latin American Studies, University of London.

Crouch, Colin. 2020. *Post-Democracy after the Crises.* Cambridge: Polity Press.

Crowley, Stephen. 2004. "Explaining Labor Weakness in Post-Communist Europe: Historical Legacies and Comparative Perspective." *East European Politics and Societies* 18(3): 394–429.

Cyr, Jennifer. 2017. *The Fates of Political Parties: Institutional Crisis, Continuity, and Change in Latin America.* New York: Cambridge University Press.

Dangerfield, Martin. 1997. "Ideology and the Czech Transformation: Neoliberal Rhetoric or Neoliberal Reality?" *East European Politics and Societies* 11(3): 436–69.

De la Torre, Carlos. 2010. *Populist Seduction in Latin America.* 2nd ed. Athens: Ohio University Press.

——— 2013. "Latin America's Authoritarian Drift: Technocratic Populism in Ecuador." *Journal of Democracy* 24(3): 33–46.

De la Torre, Carlos, and Andrés Ortiz Lemos. 2016. "Populist Polarization and the Slow Death of Democracy in Ecuador." *Democratization* 23(2): 221–41.

De Olarte, Efraín Gonzales, Vhal del Solar Rizo Patrón, Juan Manuel del Pozo, Carlos de Mattos, and Wiley Ludeña. 2011. "Lima Metropolitana después de las Reformas Neoliberales: Transformaciones Económicas Urbanas." In *Lima-Santiago: Reestructuración y Cambio Metropolitano*, edited by Carlos de Mattos, Wiley Ludeña, and Luis Fuentes, 135–5. Lima and Santiago: Centro de Investigación de la Arquitectura y la Ciudad, Pontificia Universidad Católica del Perú, and Instituto de Estudios Urbanos y Territoriales, Pontificia Universidad Católica de Chile.

Dean, Jodi. 2025. *Capital's Grave: Neofeudalism and the New Class Struggle*. New York: Verso.

Deegan-Krause, Kevin. 2000. "Public Opinion and Party Choice in Slovakia and the Czech Republic." *Party Politics* 6(1): 23–46.

2006. *Elected Affinities: Democracy and Party Competition in Slovakia and the Czech Republic*. Stanford: Stanford University Press.

Deneen, Patrick J. 2018. *Why Liberalism Failed*. New Haven: Yale University Press.

Di Tella, Torcuato. 1965. "Populism and Reform and Latin America." In *Obstacles to Change in Latin America*, edited by Claudio Véliz. London: Oxford University Press.

Doiciar, Claudia, and Remus Crețan. 2021. "Pandemic Populism: COVID-19 and the Rise of the Nationalist AUR Party in Romania." *Geographica Pannonica* 25(4): 243–59.

Dolenec, Danijela. 2012. "The Absent Socioeconomic Cleavage in Croatia: A Failure of Representative Democracy?" *Politička Misao* 49(5): 69–88.

Downs, William M. 2009. "The 2008 Parliamentary Election in Romania." *Electoral Studies* 28(3): 510–13.

Downs, William M., and Raluca V. Miller. 2006. "The 2004 Presidential and Parliamentary Elections in Romania." *Electoral Studies* 25(2): 409–15.

Doyle, David. 2011. "The Legitimacy of Political Institutions: Explaining Contemporary Populism in Latin America." *Comparative Political Studies* 44(11): 1447–73.

Dukes, Ruth, and Wolfgang Streeck. 2023. *Democracy at Work: Contract, Status, and Post-Industrial Justice*. Cambridge: Polity Press.

Dunning, Thad. 2017. "Contingency and Determinism in Research on Critical Junctures: Avoiding the 'Inevitability Framework.'" *Qualitative and Multi-Method Research* 15(1): 41–47.

Duvold, Kjetil, and Mindaugas Jurkynas. 2013. "Lithuania." In *The Handbook of Political Change in Eastern Europe*, edited by Sten Berglund, Joakim Ekman, Kevin Deegan-Krause, and Terje Knutsen, 125–66. Northampton: Edward Elgar Publishing.

Economic Commission for Latin America and the Caribbean (ECLAC). 2023. Statistics. Accessed June 16, 2023. www.cepal.org/en/work-areas/statistics.

Eckstein, Harry. 1975. "Case Study and Theory in Political Science." In *Handbook of Political Science: Strategies of Inquiry*, edited by Fred I. Greenstein and Nelson W. Polsby, 79–138. Reading: Addison-Wesley.

Ekiert, Grzegorz. 1997. "Rebellious Poles: Political Crises and Popular Protest under State Socialism, 1945–89." *East European Politics and Societies* 11(2): 299–338.

1998. "Legacies of Struggle and Defeat." In *Transition to Democracy in Poland*, edited by Richard F. Staar, 15–45. New York: St. Martin's Press.

Ekiert, Grzegorz, and Jan Kubik. 1998. "Contentious Politics in New Democracies: East Germany, Hungary, Poland, and Slovakia, 1989–93." *World Politics* 50(4): 547–81.

Ekiert, Grzegorz, Jan Kubik, and Michal Wenzel. 2017. "Civil Society and Three Dimensions of Inequality in Post-1989 Poland." *Comparative Politics* 49(3): 331–50.

Engerman, Stanley L., and Kenneth L. Sokoloff. 2000. "Factor Endowments: Institutions, and Differential Paths of Growth among New World Economies: A View from

Economic Historians of the United States." In *Modern Political Economy and Latin America: Theory and Policy*, edited by Jeffry Frieden, Manuel Pastor Jr., and Michael Tomz, 122–33. Boulder: Westview Press.

Engler, Sarah. 2020. "'Fighting Corruption' or 'Fighting the Corrupt Elite'? Politicizing Corruption within and beyond the Populist Divide." *Democratization* 27(4): 643–61.

Engler, Sarah, Bartek Pytlas, and Kevin Deegan-Krause. 2019. "Assessing the Diversity of Anti-Establishment and Populist Politics in Central and Eastern Europe." *West European Politics* 42(6): 1310–36.

Enyedi, Zsolt. 2016. "Populist Polarization and Party System Institutionalization." *Problems of Post-Communism* 63(4): 210–20.

Enyedi, Zsolt, and Fernando Casal Bértoa. 2018. "Institutionalization and De-Institutionalization in Post-Communist Party Systems." *East European Politics and Societies* 32(3): 422–50.

Epstein, Rachel A. 2020. "The Economic Successes and Sources of Discontent in East Central Europe." *Canadian Journal of European and Russian Studies* 13(2): 1–19.

Eurobarometer. 2023. All Surveys. Accessed July 7, 2023. https://europa.eu/eurobarometer/surveys/browse/all.

European Bank for Reconstruction and Development (EBRD). 2023. Transition Indicators (1989–2014). Accessed January 11, 2024. www.ebrd.com/home/what-we-do/office-of-the-chief-economist.html.

European Social Survey (ESS). 2023. ESS Data Portal. Accessed December 12, 2023. www.europeansocialsurvey.org/data-portal.

Evans, Anthony John, and Paul Dragos Aligica. 2008. "The Spread of the Flat Tax in Eastern Europe: A Comparative Study." *Eastern European Economics* 46(3): 49–67.

Evans, Geoffrey, and Stephen Whitefield. 1998. "The Structuring of Political Cleavages in Post-Communist Societies: The Case of the Czech Republic and Slovakia." *Political Studies* 46(1): 115–39.

Eyal, Gil, Iván Szelényi, and Eleanor Townsley. 1997. "The Theory of Post-Communist Managerialism." *New Left Review* (I/222): 60–92.

1998. *Making Capitalism without Capitalists: Class Formation and Elite Struggles in Post-Communist Central Europe*. New York: Verso.

Fabry, Adam. 2019. *The Political Economy of Hungary: From State Capitalism to Authoritarian Neoliberalism*. New York: Palgrave Macmillan.

Faletti, Tulia G., and Julia F. Lynch. 2009. "Context and Causal Mechanisms in Political Analysis." *Comparative Political Studies* 42(9): 1143–66.

Feldmann, Magnus, and Mircea Popa. 2022. "Populism and Economic Policy: Lessons from Central and Eastern Europe." *Post-Communist Economies* 34(2): 219–45.

Feșnic, Florin, and Oana Arneanu. 2014. "Does Education Make Voters More Leftist or More Rightist? A West vs. East Cross-Regional Analysis." *Studia Politica. Romanian Political Science Review*, (1): 29–46.

Figueroa, Adolfo. 1998. "Income Distribution and Poverty in Peru." In *Fujimori's Peru: The Political Economy*, edited by John Crabtree and Jim Thomas, 127–49. London: Institute of Latin American Studies, University of London.

Filippov, Mikhail G., Peter C. Ordeshook, and Olga V. Shvetsova. 1999. "Party Fragmentation and Presidential Elections in Post-Communist Democracies." *Constitutional Political Economy* 10(1): 3–26.

Fish, M. Steven. 1998. "The Determinants of Economic Reform in the Post-Communist World." *East European Politics and Societies* 12(1): 31–78.

Fish, M. Steven, and Omar Choudhry. 2007. "Democratization and Economic Liberalization in the Postcommunist World." *Comparative Political Studies* 40(3): 254–82.

Fisher, Sharon. 2002. "The Troubled Evolution of Slovakia's Ex-Communists." In *The Communist Successor Parties of Central and Eastern Europe*, edited by András Bozóki and John T. Ishiyama, 116–40. Armonk: M.E. Sharpe.

    2006. *Political Change in Post-Communist Slovakia and Croatia: From Nationalist to Europeanist*. New York: Palgrave Macmillan.

Fisher, Sharon, John Gould, and Tim Haughton. 2007. "Slovakia's Neoliberal Turn." *Europe-Asia Studies* 59(6): 977–98.

Fitzmaurice, John. 1996. "The 1996 Czech Elections." *Electoral Studies* 15(4): 575–80.

Flores-Macías, Gustavo A. 2012. *After Neoliberalism? The Left and Economic Reforms in Latin America*. New York: Oxford University Press.

Foley, Paul, Jo Hutchinson, Andrzej Kondej, and Jim Mueller. 1996. "Economic Development in Poland: A Local Perspective." *European Business Review* 96(2): 23–31.

Foryś, Grzegorz, and Krzysztof Gorlach. 2002. "The Dynamics of Polish Peasant Protests under Post-Communism." *Eastern European Countryside* 8: 47–65.

Fraser Institute. 2023. Economic Freedom. Accessed June 6, 2023. https://efotw .org/?geozone=world&page=map.

Fraser, Nancy. 2019. *The Old Is Dying and the New Cannot Be Born: From Progressive Neoliberalism to Trump and Beyond*. Brooklyn: Verso.

    2022. *Cannibal Capitalism: How Our System Is Devouring Democracy, Care, and the Planet – and What We Can Do about It*. Brooklyn, NY: Verso.

Freedom House. 2023. Nations in Transit. Accessed March 17, 2024. https://freedom house.org/report/nations-transit.

Freidenberg, Flavia, and Manuel Alcántara Sáez. 2001. *Los Dueños del Poder: Los Partidos Políticos en Ecuador (1978–2000)*. Quito: Flacso.

Frye, Timothy. 2010. *Building States and Markets after Communism: The Perils of Polarized Democracy*. New York: Cambridge University Press.

Gabor, Eugen. 2021. "The Romanian Social Democratic Party (PSD) as Part of The European Socialist Family: Ideological and Organizational Influences (2004–2019)." *Perspective Politice* 14(1–2): 25–41.

Gagyi, Agnes. 2016. "'Coloniality of Power' in East Central Europe: External Penetration as Internal Force in Post-Socialist Hungarian Politics." *Journal of World-Systems Research* 22(2): 349–72.

    2021. *The Political Economy of Middle Class Politics and the Global Crisis in Eastern Europe: The Case of Hungary and Romania*. New York: Palgrave Macmillan.

Gawlicz, Katarzyna, and Marcin Starnawski. 2018. "Educational Policies in Central and Eastern Europe: Legacies of State Socialism, Modernization Aspirations and Challenges of Semi-Peripheral Contexts." *Policy Futures in Education* 16(4): 385–97.

Gerbaudo, Paolo. 2021. *The Great Recoil: Politics after Populism and Pandemic*. Brooklyn: Verso.

Germani, Gino. 1978. *Authoritarianism, National Populism and Fascism*. New Brunswick: Routledge.

Gerstle, Gary. 2022. *The Rise and Fall of the Neoliberal Order: America and the World in the Free Market Era*. New York: Oxford University Press.

Gheorghiță, Andrei. 2023. "Understanding Public Support for the Flat-Rate Personal Income Tax in a Post-Communist Context: The Case of Romania." *Sustainability* 15(9): 7576.

Gherghina, Sergiu. 2014. "Ideological Disagreement in the 2014 European Election." *Studia Politica. Romanian Political Science Review* 24(3): 407–22.

2015. "The Romanian Presidential Election, November 2014." *Electoral Studies* 38(2): 109–14.

Gherghina, Sergiu, and George Jiglau. 2011. "The Ideological Institutionalization of the Romanian Party System." *Romanian Journal of Political Science* 11(1): 71–90.

Gherghina, Sergiu, and Sergiu Miscoiu. 2014. "A Rising Populist Star: The Emergence and Development of the PPDD in Romania." *Debatte: Journal of Contemporary Central and Eastern Europe* 22(2): 181–97.

Ghodsee, Kristen, and Mitchell A. Orenstein. 2021. *Taking Stock of Shock: Social Consequences of the 1989 Revolutions*. New York: Oxford University Press.

Glenny, Misha. 2012. *The Balkans, 1804–2012: Nationalism, War and the Great Powers*. New York: Penguin Books.

Gorlach, Krzysztof. 2000. "Freedom for Credit: Polish Peasants Protests in the Era of Communism and Post-Communism." *Polish Sociological Review* 129(1): 57–85.

Gould, John. 2009. "Slovakia's Neoliberal Churn: The Political Economy of the Fico Government, 2006–8." Working Papers Issue No. 01/2009. Bratislava: Institute of European Studies and International Relations, Comenius University.

Greskovits, Béla. 1998. *The Political Economy of Protest and Patience: Eastern European and Latin American Transformations Compared*. Budapest: Central European University Press.

Grosfeld, Irena, and Ekaterina Zhuravskaya. 2013. "Persistent Effects of Empires: Evidence from the Partitions of Poland." Working Paper 2013–05. Paris: Paris School of Economics.

Grzebalska, Weronika, and Andrea Pető. 2018. "The Gendered Modus Operandi of the Illiberal Transformation in Hungary and Poland." *Women's Studies International Forum* 68(May–June): 164–72.

Grzymała-Busse, Anna. 2002. *Redeeming the Communist Past: The Regeneration of Communist Parties in East Central Europe*. New York: Cambridge University Press.

2007. *Rebuilding Leviathan: Party Competition and State Exploitation in Post-Communist Democracies*. New York: Cambridge University Press.

2008. "Beyond Clientelism: Incumbent State Capture and State Formation." *Comparative Political Studies* 41(4–5): 638–73.

2018. "Victims of Their Own Success: The Paradoxical Fate of the Communist Successor Parties." In *Life after Dictatorship: Authoritarian Successor Parties Worldwide*, edited by James Loxton and Scott Mainwaring, 145–74. New York: Cambridge University Press.

Guasti, Petra. 2020. "Populism in Power and Democracy: Democratic Decay and Resilience in the Czech Republic (2013–2020)." *Politics and Governance* 8(4): 473–84.

Guasti, Petra, and Zdenka Mansfeldová. 2018. "Democracy in Crisis? The Czech Republic in Post-Accession and Economic Turmoil." In *Democracy under Stress: Changing Perspectives on Democracy, Governance, and Their Measurement*, edited by Petra Guasti and Zdenka Mansfeldová, 71–94. Prague: Institute of Sociology of the Czech Academy of Sciences.

Gudžinskas, Liutauras. 2020. "Trajectories of Social Democracy in the Baltic Countries: Choices and Constraints." *Politics in Central Europe* 16(1): 211–30.

Gwiazda, Anna. 2008. "The Parliamentary Election in Poland, October 2007." *Electoral Studies* 27(4): 740–73.

Halász, Gábor. 2015. "Education and Social Transformation in Central and Eastern Europe." *European Journal of Education* 50(3): 350–71.

Handlin, Samuel. 2017. *State Crisis in Fragile Democracies: Polarization and Political Regimes in South America*. New York: Cambridge University Press.

Hanley, Seán. 2002. "The Communist Party of Bohemia and Moravia after 1989: 'Subcultural Party' to Neocommunist Force?" In *The Communist Successor Parties of Central and Eastern Europe*, edited by András Bozóki and John T. Ishiyama, 141–65. Armonk: M.E. Sharpe.

2004. "Getting the Right Right: Redefining the Centre-Right in Post-Communist Europe." *Journal of Communist Studies and Transition Politics* 20(3): 2–27.

Hanley, Seán, and Allan Sikk. 2016. "Economy, Corruption or Floating Voters? Explaining the Breakthroughs of Anti-Establishment Reform Parties in Eastern Europe." *Party Politics* 22(4): 522–33.

Hanley, Seán, and Aleks Szczerbiak, eds. 2006. *Centre-Right Parties in Post-Communist East-Central Europe*. New York: Routledge.

Hann, Chris. 2011. "Moral Dispossession." *InterDisciplines* 2(2): 11–37.

2018. "Moral(ity and) Economy: Work, Workfare, and Fairness in Provincial Hungary." *European Journal of Sociology* 59(2): 225–54.

2019a. *Repatriating Polanyi: Market Society in the Visegrád States*. Budapest: Central European University Press.

2019b. "Resilience and Transformation in Provincial Political Economy: From Market Socialism to Market Populism in Hungary, 1970s–2010s." *Cargo Journal* 17(1–2): 1–23.

2021a. "Introduction: Work and Ethics in Anthropology." In *Work, Society, and the Ethical Self: Chimeras of Freedom in the Neoliberal Era*, edited by Chris Hann, 1–25. New York: Berghahn Books.

2021b. "The Dialectics of Disembedding and Civil Society in Provincial Hungary." *Europe-Asia Studies* 73(9): 1596–1621.

Hann, Chris, and Gábor Scheiring. 2021. "Neoliberal Capitalism and Visegrád Countermovements." *Europe-Asia Studies* 73(9): 1555–68.

Hanson, Stephen E. 1995. "The Leninist Legacy and Institutional Change." *Comparative Political Studies* 28(2): 306–14.

1998. "Analyzing Post-Communist Economic Change: A Review Essay." *East European Politics and Societies* 12(1): 145–70.

Harvey, David. 2005. *A Brief History of Neoliberalism*. New York: Oxford University Press.

Haughton, Tim. 2001. "HZDS: The Ideology, Organization and Support Base of Slovakia's Most Successful Party." *Europe-Asia Studies* 53(5): 745–69.

2003. "'We'll Finish What We've Started': The 2002 Slovak Parliamentary Elections." *Journal of Communist Studies and Transition Politics* 19(4): 65–90.

2004. "Explaining the Limited Success of the Communist-Successor Left in Slovakia: The Case of the Party of the Democratic Left (SDL')." *Party Politics* 10(2): 177–91.

Haughton, Tim, and Kevin Deegan-Krause. 2015. "Hurricane Season: Systems of Instability in Central and East European Party Politics." *East European Politics and Societies* 29(1): 61–80.

Haughton, Tim, and Kevin Deegan-Krause. 2020. *The New Party Challenge: Changing Cycles of Party Birth and Death in Central Europe and Beyond*. Oxford: Oxford University Press.

Haughton, Tim, Marek Rybář, and Kevin Deegan-Krause. 2021. "Leading the Way, but Also Following the Trend: The Slovak National Party." *Politics and Governance* 9(4): 329–39.

Havlík, Vlastimil, and Petr Voda. 2018. "Cleavages, Protest or Voting for Hope? The Rise of Centrist Populist Parties in the Czech Republic." *Swiss Political Science Review* 24(2): 161–86.

Hawkins, Kirk A. 2009. "Is Chávez Populist? Measuring Populist Discourse in Comparative Perspective." *Comparative Political Studies* 42(8): 1040–67.

2010. *Venezuela's Chavismo and Populism in Comparative Perspective*. New York: Cambridge University Press.

Hawkins, Kirk, Madeleine Read, and Teun Pauwels. 2017. "Populism and Its Causes." In *The Oxford Handbook of Populism*, edited by Cristóbal Rovira Kaltwasser, Paul Taggart, Paulina Ochoa Espejo, and Pierre Ostiguy. New York: Oxford University Press.

Hegedüs, Daniel. 2019. "Rethinking the Incumbency Effect. Radicalization of Governing Populist Parties in East-Central-Europe. A Case Study of Hungary." *European Politics and Society* 20(4): 406–30.

Heinisch, Reinhard. 2003. "Success in Opposition – Failure in Government: Explaining the Performance of Right-Wing Populist Parties in Public Office." *West European Politics* 26(3): 91–130.

Hellman, Joel S. 1998. "Winners Take All: The Politics of Partial Reform in Postcommunist Transitions." *World Politics* 50(2): 203–34.

Henderson, Karen. 1995. "Czechoslovakia: The Failure of Consensus Politics and the Break-up of the Federation." *Regional and Federal Studies* 5(2): 111–33.

2002. *Slovakia: The Escape from Invisibility*. New York: Routledge.

2004. "The Slovak Republic: Explaining Defects in Democracy." *Democratization* 11(5): 133–55.

Heritage Foundation. 2023. Index of Economic Freedom. Accessed January 22, 2024. www.heritage.org/index/.

Hirschman, Albert O. 1970. *Exit, Voice, and Loyalty: Responses to Decline in Firms, Organizations, and States*. Cambridge: Harvard University Press.

Hix, Simon, and Andreas Follesdal. 2006. "Why Is There a Democratic Deficit in the EU? A Response to Majone and Moravcsik." *Journal of Common Market Studies* 44(3): 533–62.

Holmes, Leslie. 2013. "Postcommunist Transitions and Corruption: Mapping Patterns." *Social Research* 80(4): 1163–86.

Hooghe, Liesbet, and Gary Marks. 2018. "Cleavage Theory Meets Europe's Crises: Lipset, Rokkan, and the Transnational Cleavage." *Journal of European Public Policy* 25(1): 109–35.

Howard, Marc Morjé. 2003. *The Weakness of Civil Society in Post-Communist Europe*. New York: Cambridge University Press.

Huntington, Samuel P. 1968. *Political Order in Changing Societies*. New Haven: Yale University Press.

Inglehart, Ronald. 1990. *Culture Shift in Advanced Industrial Society*. Princeton: Princeton University Press.

Inglehart, Ronald, and Pippa Norris. 2016. "Trump, Brexit, and the Rise of Populism: Economic Have-Nots and Cultural Backlash." HKS Working Paper RWP16-026. Faculty Research Working Paper Series. Cambridge: Harvard Kennedy School.

Innes, Abby. 2001. *Czechoslovakia: The Short Goodbye*. New Haven: Yale University Press.

2002. "Party Competition in Postcommunist Europe: The Great Electoral Lottery." *Comparative Politics* 35(1): 85–104.

International Monetary Fund (IMF). 2023. IMF Data. Accessed November 22, 2023. www.imf.org/en/Data.

Jackman, Robert W., and Karin Volpert. 1996. "Conditions Favouring Parties of the Extreme Right in Western Europe." *British Journal of Political Science* 26(4): 501–21.

Jameson, Kenneth P. 2011. "The Indigenous Movement in Ecuador: The Struggle for a Plurinational State." *Latin American Perspectives* 38(1): 63–73.

Jańczak, Jarosław. 2015. "Phantom Borders and Electoral Behavior in Poland: Historical Legacies, Political Culture and Their Influence on Contemporary Poland." *Erdkunde* 69(2): 125–37.

Janos, Andrew C. 1994. "Continuity and Change in Eastern Europe: Strategies of Post-Communist Politics." *East European Politics and Societies* 8(1): 1–31.

2000. *East Central Europe in the Modern World: The Politics of the Borderlands from Pre- to Postcommunism*. Stanford: Stanford University Press.

Jaramillo, Cristhian. 2023. "The Impossibility of Party Unity in Peru: Party Affiliation, Subnational Electoral Competition and Party Discipline (2011–2019). *Bulletin of Latin American Research* 42(5): 649–62.

Jasiewicz, Krzysztof. 1992. "Polish Elections of 1990: Beyond the 'Pospolite Ruszenie.'" In *The Polish Road from Socialism: The Economics, Sociology and Politics of Transition*, edited by Walter Connor and Piotr Ploszajski, 181–98. Armonk: M.E. Sharpe.

Jeannet, Anne-Marie. 2020. "Immigration and Political Distrust in Europe: A Comparative Longitudinal Study." *European Societies* 22(2): 211–30.

Johnson, Juliet. 2001. "Path Contingency in Postcommunist Transformations." *Comparative Politics* 33(3): 253–74.

Johnson, Juliet, and Andrew Barnes. 2015. "Financial Nationalism and Its International Enablers: The Hungarian Experience." *Review of International Political Economy* 22(3): 535–69.

Jones, Mark P., and Scott Mainwaring. 2003. "The Nationalization of Parties and Party Systems: An Empirical Measure and an Application to the Americas." *Party Politics* 9(2): 139–66.

José Díaz, Juan, Jaime Saavedra, and Máximo Torero. 2002. "Peru: Stabilization, Liberalization and Inequality." In *Economic Liberalization, Distribution, and Poverty: Latin America in the 1990s*, edited by Rob Vos, Lance Taylor, and Ricardo Paes de Barros, 390–430. Northampton: Edward Elgar Publishing.

Jowitt, Ken. 1992. *New World Disorder*. Berkeley: University of California Press.

Judis, John. B. 2016. *The Populist Explosion: How the Great Recession Transformed American and European Politics*. New York: Columbia Global Reports.

Jurkynas, Mindaugas. 2009. "The Parliamentary Election in Lithuania, October 2008." *Electoral Studies* 28(2): 329–33.

2014. "The Parliamentary Election in Lithuania, October 2012." *Electoral Studies* 34(2): 334–38.

Kalb, Don. 2009. "Conversations with a Polish Populist: Tracing Hidden Histories of Globalization, Class, and Dispossession in Postsocialism (and Beyond)." *American Ethnologist* 36(2): 207–23.

2018. "Upscaling Illiberalism: Class, Contradiction, and the Rise of the Populist Right in Post-Socialist Central Europe." *Fudan Journal of the Humanities and Social Sciences* 11(3): 303–21.

2019. "Post-Socialist Contradictions: The Social Question in Central and Eastern Europe and the Making of the Illiberal Right." In *The Social Question in the Twenty-First Century: A Global View*, edited by Jan Breman, Kevan Harris, Ching Kwan Lee, and Marcel van der Linden, 208–26. Oakland: University of California Press.

Kalb, Don Kalb, and Gábor Halmai, eds. 2011. *Headlines of Nation, Subtexts of Class: Working Class Populism and the Return of the Repressed in Neoliberal Europe*. New York: Berghahn Books.

Kapiszewski, Diana, Lauren M. MacLean, and Benjamin L. Read. 2015. *Field Research in Political Science: Practices and Principles*. Cambridge: Cambridge University Press.

Kaufman, Robert, and Barbara Stallings. 1991. "The Political Economy of Latin American Populism." In *The Macroeconomics of Populism in Latin America*, edited by Rudiger Dornbusch and Sebastian Edwards, 15–43. Chicago: The University of Chicago Press.

King, Ronald, and Cosmin Marian. 2014. "Antagonism and Austerity: The December 2012 Romanian Parliamentary Elections." *Electoral Studies* 34(August): 310–15.

Kishishita, Daiki, and Atsushi Yamagishi. 2021. "Contagion of Populist Extremism." *Journal of Public Economics* 193(C): 104–24.

Kitschelt, Herbert P. 1992. "The Formation of Party Systems in East Central Europe:" *Politics and Society* 20(1): 7–50.

Kitschelt, Herbert P. 2000. "Linkages between Citizens and Politicians in Democratic Polities." *Comparative Political Studies* 33(6–7): 845–79.

2002. "Constraints and Opportunities in the Strategic Conduct of Postcommunist Successor Parties: Regime Legacies as Causal Argument?" In *The Communist Successor Parties of Central and Eastern Europe*, edited by András Bozóki and John T. Ishiyama, 14–40. Armonk: M.E. Sharpe.

2003. "Party Competition in Latin America and Post-Communist Eastern Europe. Divergence of Patterns, Similarity of Explanatory Variables." Paper prepared for the 100th annual meeting of the American Political Science Association, Philadelphia, August 27–31.

2013. Democratic Accountability and Linkages Project (DALP). Durham: Duke University.

2015. "Analyzing the Dynamics of Post-Communist Party Systems: Some 'Final Thoughts' on the EEPS Special Section." *East European Politics and Societies* 29(1): 81–91.

Kitschelt, Herbert P., Zdenka Mansfeldová, Radosław Markowski, and Gábor Tóka. 1999. *Post-Communist Party Systems: Competition, Representation, and Inter-Party Cooperation*. New York: Cambridge University Press.

Kitschelt, Herbert P., and Anthony J. McGann. 1995. *The Radical Right in Western Europe: A Comparative Analysis*. Ann Arbor: The University of Michigan Press.

Klašnja, Marko, Joshua A. Tucker, and Kevin Deegan-Krause. 2016. "Pocketbook vs. Sociotropic Corruption Voting." *British Journal of Political Science* 46(1): 67–94.

Klaus, Vaclav. 2014. "Czechoslovakia and the Czech Republic: The Spirit and Main Contours of the Postcommunist Transformation." In *The Great Rebirth: Lessons from the Victory of Capitalism over Communism*, edited by Anders Åslund and Simeon Djankov, 53–72. Washington: Peterson Institute for International Economics.

Kollman, Ken, Allen Hicken, Daniele Caramani, David Backer, and David Lublin. 2024. Constituency-Level Election Archive (CLEA). Accessed April 17, 2024. www.electiondataarchive.org.

Kołodko, Grzegorz. 1991. "Polish Hyperinflation and Stabilization 1989–1990." *Economic Journal on Eastern Europe and the Soviet Union* (1): 9–36.

Kopeček, Lubomir. 2002. "The Slovak Party of the Democratic Left: A Successful Post-Communist Party?" *German Policy Studies/Politikfeldanalyse* 2(2): 241–58.

Kopeček, Lubomír, and Pavel Pšeja. 2008. "Czech Social Democracy and Its 'Cohabitation' with the Communist Party: The Story of a Neglected Affair." *Communist and Post-Communist Studies* 41(3): 317–38.

Kopecký, Petr, and Cas Mudde. 1999. "The 1998 Parliamentary and Senate Elections in the Czech Republic." *Electoral Studies* 18(3): 415–24.

Kopstein, Jeffrey S., and David A. Reilly. 2000. "Geographic Diffusion and the Transformation of the Postcommunist World." *World Politics* 53(1): 1–37.

Kopstein, Jeffrey S., and Michael Bernhard. 2015. "Post-Communism, the Civilizing Process, and the Mixed Impact of Leninist Violence." *East European Politics and Societies* 29(2): 379–90.

Kornai, János. 1992. *The Socialist System: The Political Economy of Communism.* Princeton: Princeton University Press.

Kowalski, Mariusz. 2000. *The Electoral Geography of Poland: Spatial Differences in Electoral Behavior, 1989–1998.* Warsaw: Polish Academy of Sciences.

Krajewski, Michał. 2023. "The Constitutional Quandary of Social Rights: Questions in Times of the Polish Illiberal Turn." *International Journal of Constitutional Law* 21(1): 156–86.

Kramer, Gerald H. 1983. "The Ecological Fallacy Revisited: Aggregate- versus Individual-Level Findings on Economics and Elections, and Sociotropic Voting." *The American Political Science Review* 77(1): 92–111.

Krastev, Ivan. 2007. "The Strange Death of the Liberal Consensus." *Journal of Democracy* 18(4): 56–63.

Krekó, Péter, and Zsolt Enyedi. 2018. "Explaining Eastern Europe: Orbán's Laboratory of Illiberalism." *Journal of Democracy* 29(3): 39–51.

Kriesi, Hanspeter. 2014. "The Populist Challenge." *West European Politics* 37(2): 361–78.

Kriesi, Hanspeter, Edgar Grande, Martin Dolezal, Marc Helbling, Dominic Höglinger, Swen Hutter, and Bruno Wüest. 2012. *Political Conflict in Western Europe.* New York: Cambridge University Press.

Kriesi, Hanspeter, and Takis S. Pappas, eds. 2015. *European Populism in the Shadow of the Great Recession.* Colchester: ECPR Press.

Krivý, Vladimír. 1995. "The Parliamentary Elections 1994: The Profile of Supporters of the Political Parties, the Profile of Regions." In *Slovakia – Parliamentary Elections 1994: Causes, Consequences, Prospects*, edited by Soňa Szomolányi and Grigorij

Mesežnikov, 114–35. Bratislava: Slovak Political Science Association – Friedrich Ebert Association.

Kubik, Jan. 2015. "Between Conceptualization and Comparison." *East European Politics and Societies* 29(2): 352–65.

Ladányi, János, and Iván Szelényi. 2002. "Prospects and Limits of New Social Democracy in the Transitional Societies of Central Europe." In *The Communist Successor Parties of Central and Eastern Europe*, edited by András Bozóki and John T. Ishiyama, 41–48. Armon: M.E. Sharpe.

LaPorte, Jody, and Danielle N. Lussier. 2011. "What Is the Leninist Legacy? Assessing Twenty Years of Scholarship." *Slavic Review* 70(3): 637–54.

Latin American Electoral Data (LAEDA). 2010. Electronic Data Archive. Accessed May 15, 2023. http://lanic.utexas.edu/laeda/.

Latinobarómetro. 2023. Online Analysis Platform. Accessed November 11, 2023. www.latinobarometro.org/online-analysis.

Lauderbaugh, George M. 2012. *The History of Ecuador*. Santa Barbara: Greenwood.

Leonard, John B. 2000. "City Profile: Lima." *Cities* 17(6): 433–45.

Levitsky, Steven. 1999. "Fujimori and Post-Party Politics in Peru." *Journal of Democracy* 10(3): 78–92.

Levitsky, Steven, and James Loxton. 2013. "Populism and Competitive Authoritarianism in the Andes." *Democratization* 20(1): 107–36.

Levitsky, Steven, and Kenneth M. Roberts. 2011. "Latin America's 'Left Turn': A Framework for Analysis." In *The Resurgence of the Latin American Left*, edited by Steven Levitsky and Kenneth M. Roberts, 1–28. Baltimore: The Johns Hopkins University Press.

Levitsky, Steven, and Lucan A. Way. 2005. "International Linkage and Democratization." *Journal of Democracy* 16(3): 20–34.

2010. *Competitive Authoritarianism: Hybrid Regimes after the Cold War*. New York: Cambridge University Press.

Levitt, Barry Steven. 2012. *Power in the Balance: Presidents, Parties, and Legislatures in Peru and Beyond*. Notre Dame: University of Notre Dame Press.

Lieberman, Evan S. 2005. "Nested Analysis as a Mixed-Method Strategy for Comparative Research." *American Political Science Review* 99(3): 435–52.

Lilla, Mark. 2017. *The Once and Future Liberal: After Identity Politics*. New York: Harper.

Lindberg, Staffan, Nils Düpont, Masaaki Higashijima, Yaman Berker Kavasoglu, Kyle Marquardt, Michael Bernhard, Holger Döring, et al. 2022. "Codebook Varieties of Party Identity and Organization (V-Party), V2." V-Dem.

Lindner, Attila, Filip Novokmet, Thomas Piketty, and Tom Zawisza. 2021. "Political Conflict, Social Inequality, and Electoral Cleavages in the Czech Republic, Hungary, and Poland, 1990–2018." In *Political Cleavages and Social Inequalities: A Study of Fifty Democracies, 1948–2020*, edited by Amory Gethin, Clara Martínez-Toledano, and Thomas Piketty, 287–310. Cambridge: Harvard University Press.

Linz, Juan J., and Alfred Stepan. 1996. *Problems of Democratic Transition and Consolidation: Southern Europe, South America, and Post-Communist Europe*. Baltimore: The Johns Hopkins University Press.

Lipset, Seymor Martin. 1960. *Political Man: The Social Bases of Politics*. New York: Doubleday & Company.

Lizarzaburu, Javier. 2015. "Forced Sterilization Haunts Peruvian Women Decades On." *BBC News*, December 2, sec. Latin America and Caribbean. Accessed November 28, 2023. www.bbc.com/news/world-latin-america-34855804.

Lupu, Noam. 2012. "The 2011 General Elections in Peru." *Electoral Studies* 31(3): 621–24.

2013. "Party Brands and Partisanship: Theory with Evidence from a Survey Experiment in Argentina." *American Journal of Political Science* 57(1): 49–64.

2016. *Party Brands in Crisis: Partisanship, Brand Dilution, and the Breakdown of Political Parties in Latin America.* New York: Cambridge University Press.

Lussier, Danielle N., and Jody LaPorte. 2022. "Leninist Extinction?: Critical Junctures, Legacies, and the Study of Post-Communism." In *Critical Junctures and Historical Legacies: Insights and Methods for Comparative Social Science*, edited by David Collier and Gerardo L. Munck, 289–314. Lanham: Rowman & Littlefield.

Lysek, Jakub, Jiří Pánek, and Tomáš Lebeda. 2021. "Who Are the Voters and Where Are They? Using Spatial Statistics to Analyse Voting Patterns in the Parliamentary Elections of the Czech Republic." *Journal of Maps* 17(1): 33–38.

Madariaga, Aldo. 2020. *Neoliberal Resilience: Lessons in Democracy and Development from Latin America and Eastern Europe.* Princeton: Princeton University Press.

Madrid, Raul. 2011. "Ethnic Proximity and Ethnic Voting in Peru." *Journal of Latin American Studies* 43(2): 267–97.

2012. *The Rise of Ethnic Politics in Latin America.* New York: Cambridge University Press.

Madrid, Raúl L., Wendy Hunter, and Kurt Weyland. 2010. "The Policies and Performance of the Contestatory and Moderate Left." In *Leftist Governments in Latin America: Successes and Shortcomings*, edited by Kurt Weyland, Raúl L. Madrid, and Wendy Hunter, 140–80. New York: Cambridge University Press.

Mahoney, James. 2000. "Path Dependence in Historical Sociology." *Theory and Society* 29(4): 507–48.

2001a. *The Legacies of Liberalism: Path Dependence and Political Regimes in Central America.* Baltimore: The Johns Hopkins University Press.

2001b. "Path-Dependent Explanations of Regime Change: Central America in Comparative Perspective." *Studies in Comparative International Development* 36(1): 111–41.

Mahoney, James, and Richard Snyder. 1999. "Rethinking Agency and Structure in the Study of Regime Change." *Studies in Comparative International Development* 34(2): 3–32.

Mainwaring, Scott, and Timothy Scully, eds. 1995. *Building Democratic Institutions: Party Systems in Latin America.* Palo Alto: Stanford University Press.

Mainwaring, Scott, and Mariano Torcal. 2005. "Party System Institutionalization and Party System Theory after the Third Wave of Democratization." Working Paper No. 319. Notre Dame: Kellogg Institute for International Studies.

Mair, Peter. 2002. "Populist Democracy vs. Party Democracy." In *Democracies and the Populist Challenge*, edited by Yves Mény and Yves Surel, 81–98. New York: Palgrave Macmillan.

Majone, Giandomenico. 1998. "Europe's Democratic Deficit." *European Law Journal* 4(1): 5–28.

Malewska-Szałygin, Anna. 2017. *Social Imaginaries of the State and Central Authority in Polish Highland Villages, 1999–2005.* Newcastle upon Tyne: Cambridge Scholars Publishing.

2021. "Countermovements: Rural Social Imaginaries Confronting Neoliberal Economics and Politics in Southern Poland." *Europe-Asia Studies* 73(9): 1641–57.

Malová, Darina. 2017. *Strengthening Social Democracy in the Visegrád Countries: Limits and Challenges Faced by SMER-SD*. Prague and Bratislava: Friedrich Ebert Stiftung.

March, Luke. 2011. *Radical Left Parties in Europe*. New York: Routledge.

Markowski, Radosław. 1997. "Political Parties and Ideological Spaces in East Central Europe." *Communist and Post-Communist Studies* 30(3): 221–54.

2002. "The Polish SLD in the 1990s: From Opposition to Incumbents and Back." In *The Communist Successor Parties of Central and Eastern Europe*, edited by András Bozóki and John T. Ishiyama, 51–88. Armonk: M.E. Sharpe.

2006. "The Polish Elections of 2005: Pure Chaos or a Restructuring of the Party System?" *West European Politics* 29(4): 814–32.

2008. "The 2007 Polish Parliamentary Election: Some Structuring, Still a Lot of Chaos." *West European Politics* 31(5): 1055–68.

2016. "The Polish Parliamentary Election of 2015: A Free and Fair Election That Results in Unfair Political Consequences." *West European Politics* 39(6): 1311–22.

2020. "Plurality Support for Democratic Decay: The 2019 Polish Parliamentary Election." *West European Politics* 43(7): 1513–25.

Marks, Gary, Liesbet Hooghe, Maira Nelson, and Erica Edwards. 2006. "Party Competition and European Integration in the East and West: Different Structure, Same Causality." *Comparative Political Studies* 32(2): 155–75.

Marušiak, Juraj. 2005. "SMER – From Pragmatism to Social Democracy? Seeking Identity." In *Trajectories of the Left: Social Democratic and (Ex-)Communist Parties in Contemporary Europe: Between Past and Future*, edited by Lubomír Kopeček, 165–77. Brno: Institute for Comparative Political Research, Masaryk University.

2021. "'Slovak, Not Brussels Social Democracy'. Europeanization/De-Europeanization and the Ideological Development of Smer-SD before 2020 Parliamentary Elections in Slovakia." *Czech Journal of Political Science* 1(February): 37–58.

Maškarinec, Pavel. 2017. "A Spatial Analysis of Czech Parliamentary Elections, 2006–2013." *Europe-Asia Studies* 69(3): 426–57.

Matějů, Petr, and Blanka Řeháková. 1997. "Turning Left or Class Realignment? Analysis of the Changing Relationship between Class and Party in the Czech Republic, 1992–96." *East European Politics and Societies* 11(3): 501–42.

Matiuta, Cristina. 2018. "Political Cleavages in Post-Communist Europe. Romania as a Case Study." *Yearbook of the Institute of East-Central Europe* 16(3): 147–64.

Mattioli, Fabio. 2018. "Financialization without Liquidity: In-Kind Payments, Forced Credit, and Authoritarianism at the Periphery of Europe." *Journal of the Royal Anthropological Institute* 24(3): 568–88.

2020. *Dark Finance: Illiquidity and Authoritarianism at the Margins of Europe*. Stanford: Stanford University Press.

McClintock, Cynthia. 2013. "Populism in Peru: From APRA to Ollanta Humala." In *Latin American Populism in the Twenty-First Century*, edited by Carlos de la Torre and Cynthia J. Arnson, 203–37. Washington and Baltimore: Woodrow Wilson Center Press and The Johns Hopkins University Press.

McFaul, Michael. 2002. "The Fourth Wave of Democracy and Dictatorship: Noncooperative Transitions in the Postcommunist World." *World Politics* 54(2): 212–44.

McLean, Iain, and Alistair McMillan. 2003. *The Concise Oxford Dictionary of Politics.* 2nd ed. New York: Oxford University Press.

Mesežnikov, Grigorij, Oľga Gyárfášová, Martin Bútora, and Miroslav Kollár. 2008. "Slovakia." In *Populist Politics and Liberal Democracy in Central and Eastern Europe*, edited by Grigorij Mesežnikov, Oľga Gyárfášová, and Daniel Smilov, 101–30. Bratislava: Institute for Public Affairs.

Mijeski, Kenneth J., and Scott H. Beck. 2011. *Pachakutik and the Rise and Decline of the Ecuadorian Indigenous Movement.* Athens: Ohio University Press.

Mikloš, Ivan. 2014. "Slovakia: The Latecomer that Caught Up." In *The Great Rebirth: Lessons from the Victory of Capitalism over Communism*, edited by Anders Åslund and Simeon Djankov, 113–34. Washington: Peterson Institute for International Economics.

Milanovic, Branko. 2019. *Capitalism, Alone: The Future of the System that Rules the World.* Cambridge: Harvard University Press.

Millard, Frances. 1999. *Politics and Society in Poland.* New York: Routledge.

2002. "The Presidential Election in Poland, October 2000." *Electoral Studies* 21(2): 357–63.

2003. "The Parliamentary Elections in Poland, September 2001." *Electoral Studies* 22(2): 367–74.

2006. "Poland's Politics and the Travails of Transition after 2001: The 2005 Elections." *Europe-Asia Studies* 58(7): 1007–31.

2008. "Party Politics in Poland after the 2005 Election." In *Reinventing Poland: Economic and Political Transformation and Evolving National Identity*, edited by Martin Myant and Terry Cox, 65–82. London: Routledge.

2010. *Democratic Elections in Poland, 1991–2007.* New York: Routledge.

Minkenberg, Michael, ed. 2015. *Transforming the Transformation? The East European Radical Right in the Political Process.* New York: Routledge.

2017. *The Radical Right in Eastern Europe: Democracy under Siege?.* New York: Palgrave Macmillan.

Mishler, William, and Richard Rose. 2001. "What Are the Origins of Political Trust? Testing Institutional and Cultural Theories in Post-Communist Societies." *Comparative Political Studies* 34(1): 30–62.

Montúfar, César. 2013. "Rafael Correa and His Plebiscitary Citizens' Revolution." In *Latin American Populism in the Twenty-First Century*, edited by Carlos de la Torre and Cynthia J. Arnson, 295–323. Washington and Baltimore: Woodrow Wilson Center Press and The Johns Hopkins University Press.

Moravcsik, Andrew. 2002. "In Defense of the 'Democratic Deficit': Reassessing Legitimacy in the European Union." *Journal of Common Market Studies* 40(4): 603–24.

Morgan, W. B. 1992. "Economic Reform, the Free Market and Agriculture in Poland." *The Geographical Journal* 158(2): 145–56.

Morgenstern, Scott. 2017. *Are Politics Local? The Two Dimensions of Party Nationalization around the World.* New York: Cambridge University Press.

Mosley, Layna. 2013. "'Just Talk to People'? Interviews in Contemporary Political Science." In *Interview Research in Political Science*, edited by Layna Mosley, 1–28. Ithaca: Cornell University Press.

Mouffe, Chantal. 2018. *For a Left Populism.* London: Verso.

2022. *Towards a Green Democratic Revolution: Left Populism and the Power of Affects.* London: Verso.

Moyn, Samuel. 2023. *Liberalism against Itself: Cold War Intellectuals and the Making of Our Times*. New Haven: Yale University Press.

Mudde, Cas. 2004. "The Populist Zeitgeist." *Government and Opposition* 39(4): 542–63.

2007. *Populist Radical Right Parties in Europe*. New York: Cambridge University Press.

2016. "Europe's Populist Surge: A Long Time in the Making." *Foreign Affairs* 95(6): 25–30.

2021. "Populism in Europe: An Illiberal Democratic Response to Undemocratic Liberalism." *Government and Opposition* 56(4): 577–97.

Mudde, Cas, and Cristóbal Rovira Kaltwasser, eds. 2012. *Populism in Europe and the Americas: Threat or Corrective for Democracy?* New York: Cambridge University Press.

Mudde, Cas, and Cristóbal Rovira Kaltwasser, eds. 2013. "Exclusionary vs. Inclusionary Populism: Comparing Contemporary Europe and Latin America." *Government and Opposition* 48(2): 147–74.

Müller, Jan-Werner. 2021. *Democracy Rules*. New York: Farrar, Straus and Giroux.

Mungiu-Pippidi, Alina. 2001. "The Return of Populism – The 2000 Romanian Elections." *Government and Opposition* 36(2): 230–52.

2002. "The Romanian Postcommunist Parties: A Story of Success." In *The Communist Successor Parties of Central and Eastern Europe*, edited by András Bozóki and John T. Ishiyama, 188–205. Armonk: M.E. Sharpe.

Muñoz, Paula, and Eduardo Dargent. 2016. "Perú: El Fin del Optimismo." *Revista de Ciencia Política* 36(1): 313–38.

Mustillo, Thomas. 2012. "Ecuador Electoral Dataset – Legislative and Presidential Election Results, 1979–2006." Latin American Electronic Data Archive (LAEDA), The University of Texas at Austin. Accessed February 12, 2023. https:// repositories.lib.utexas.edu/handle/2152/16319.

Myant, Martin. 2003. *The Rise and Fall of Czech Capitalism: Economic Development in the Czech Republic since 1989*. Cheltenham: Edward Elgar Publishing.

Myant, Martin, and Jan Drahokoupil. 2011. *Transition Economies: Political Economy in Russia, Eastern Europe, and Central Asia*. Hoboken: John Wiley & Sons.

Nalepa, Monika. 2016. "Party Institutionalization and Legislative Organization: The Evolution of Agenda Power in the Polish Parliament." *Comparative Politics* 48(3): 353–72.

National Election Commission (PKW) of Poland. 2023. Elections and Referenda. Accessed February 2, 2024. https://pkw.gov.pl/wybory-i-referenda.

Nicholson, Tom. 2002. "Gašparovič: 'No Way' to Coalition with HZDS." *The Slovak Spectator*, September 2. Accessed June 14, 2023. https://spectator.sme .sk/c/20016931/gasparovic-no-way-to-coalition-with-hzds.html.

Ober, Josiah. 2017. *Demopolis: Democracy before Liberalism in Theory and Practice*. New York: Cambridge University Press.

O'Donnell, Guillermo. 1979. *Modernization and Bureaucratic-Authoritarianism: Studies in South American Politics*. 2nd ed. Berkeley: University of California Press.

O'Dwyer, Connor. 2006. *Runaway State-Building: Patronage Politics and Democratic Development*. Baltimore: Johns Hopkins University Press.

Offe, Claus. 1985. "New Social Movements: Challenging the Boundaries of Institutional Politics." *Social Research* 52(4): 817–68.

Oficina Nacional de Procesos Electorales (ONPE) del Perú. 2023. Plataforma Nacional de Datos Abiertos. Accessed October 21, 2023. www.gob.pe/onpe.

Olson, David M. 1993. "Dissolution of the State: Political Parties and the 1992 Election in Czechoslovakia." *Communist and Post-Communist Studies* 26(3): 301–14.

Orenstein, Mitchell A. 2001. *Out of the Red: Building Capitalism and Democracy in Postcommunist Europe*. Ann Arbor: The University of Michigan Press.

Orenstein, Mitchell A., and Bojan Bugarič. 2022. "Work, Family, Fatherland: The Political Economy of Populism in Central and Eastern Europe." *Journal of European Public Policy* 29(2): 176–95.

Organization for Economic Co-operation and Development (OECD). 2023. Data. Accessed May 5, 2023. www.oecd.org/en/data.html.

Osa, Maryjane. 1998. "Contention and Democracy: Labor Protest in Poland, 1989–1993." *Communist and Post-Communist Studies* 31(1): 29–42.

Ost, David. 2005. *The Defeat of Solidarity: Anger and Politics in Postcommunist Europe*. Ithaca: Cornell University Press.

2009. "The Invisibility and Centrality of Class after Communism." *International Journal of Politics, Culture, and Society* 22(4): 497–515.

2011. "'Illusory Corporatism' Ten Years Later." *Warsaw Forum of Economic Sociology* 2(3): 19–49.

2015a. "Class after Communism: Introduction to the Special Issue." *East European Politics and Societies* 29(3): 543–64.

2015b. "Stuck in the Past and the Future: Class Analysis in Postcommunist Poland." *East European Politics and Societies* 29(3): 610–24.

2018. "Workers and the Radical Right in Poland." *International Labor and Working-Class History* 93(Workers and Right-Wing Politics): 113–24.

2022. "Why (Which) Workers Often Oppose (Which) Democracy?" In *The Cambridge Handbook of Labor and Democracy*, edited by Angela B. Cornell and Mark Barenberg, 263–78. New York: Cambridge University Press.

Pankowski, Rafał. 2010. *The Populist Radical Right in Poland: The Patriots*. New York: Routledge.

Pappas, Takis S. 2014. "Populist Democracies: Post-Authoritarian Greece and Post-Communist Hungary." *Government and Opposition* 49(1): 1–23.

2016a. "Modern Populism: Research Advances, Conceptual and Methodological Pitfalls, and the Minimal Definition." In *Oxford Research Encyclopedia of Politics*, edited by William Thompson. Oxford: Oxford University Press.

2016b. "The Specter Haunting Europe: Distinguishing Liberal Democracy's Challengers." *Journal of Democracy* 27(4): 22–36.

2019. "Populists in Power." *Journal of Democracy* 30(2): 70–84.

Pehe, Jiri. 2018. "Explaining Eastern Europe: Czech Democracy under Pressure." *Journal of Democracy* 29(3): 65–77.

Pellen, Cédric. 2009. "The 1998–1999 Polish Peasant Demonstrations: Politization, Media Coverage and Personalization of a Protest Movement." *Politix* 86(2): 167–88.

Peters, Paul A., and Emily H. Skop. 2007. "Socio-Spatial Segregation in Metropolitan Lima, Peru." *Journal of Latin American Geography* 6(1): 149–71.

Pickel, Susanne. 2007. "Modernization, Cleavages and Voting Behavior in East Europe. An Analysis of Romanian Voting Behavior in Comparative Perspective." *Sociologie Românească* 2: 85–113.

Pickering, Paula M. 2009. "Explaining Support for Non-Nationalist Parties in Post-Conflict Societies in the Balkans." *Europe-Asia Studies* 61(4): 565–91.

Pienkos, Donald. 2001. "Interesting Times: Polish Politics and Elections, 1989–2001." *The Polish Review* 46(4): 431–39.

Pierson, Paul. 2000. "Increasing Returns, Path Dependence, and the Study of Politics." *The American Political Science Review* 94(2): 251–67.

Piketty, Thomas. 2020. *Capital and Ideology*. Cambridge: The Belknap Press of Harvard University Press.

Pink, Michael, and Adam Folvarčný. 2020. "The Czech Pirate Party: A New Alternative, Not Only for the Young." *Intersections: East European Journal of Society and Politics* 6(4): 176–96.

Pirro, Andrea L. P., and Ben Stanley. 2022. "Forging, Bending, and Breaking: Enacting the 'Illiberal Playbook' in Hungary and Poland." *Perspectives on Politics* 20(1): 86–101.

Plecitá-Vlachová, Klára, and Mary Stegmaier. 2003. "The Chamber of Deputies Election, Czech Republic 2002." *Electoral Studies* 22(4): 772–78.

2008. "The Parliamentary Election in the Czech Republic, June 2006." *Electoral Studies* 27(1): 179–84.

Plešivčák, Martin. 2013. "The Regional Dimension of the Socio-Political Urban-Rural Conflict in Slovakia." *AUC Geographica* 48(1): 47–58.

Poertner, Matthias. 2018. "Creating Partisans: The Organizational Roots of New Parties in Latin America." PhD dissertation. Berkeley: University of California.

Polanyi, Karl. (1944) 2001. *The Great Transformation: The Political and Economic Origins of Our Time*. 2nd ed. Boston: Beacon Press.

Polga-Hecimovich, John. 2014. "¿Hacia Una Superación del 'Cleavage' Regional? La Nacionalización de los Partidos Políticos Ecuatorianos desde el Retorno a la Democracia." *América Latina Hoy* 67: 91–118.

Polity5. 2020. Polity5 Annual Time Series, 1946–2018. Accessed September 9, 2023. www.systemicpeace.org/inscrdata.html.

Polk, Jonathan, Jan Rovny, Ryan Bakker, Erica Edwards, Liesbet Hooghe, Seth Jolly, Jelle Koedam, et al. 2017. "Explaining the Salience of Anti-Elitism and Reducing Political Corruption for Political Parties in Europe with the 2014 Chapel Hill Expert Survey Data." *Research and Politics* 4(1): 1–9.

Pop-Eleches, Cristian, and Grigore Pop-Eleches. 2012. "Targeted Government Spending and Political Preferences." *Quarterly Journal of Political Science* 7(3): 285–320.

Pop-Eleches, Grigore. 2001. "Romania's Politics of Dejection." *Journal of Democracy* 12(3): 156–69.

2007. "Historical Legacies and Post-Communist Regime Change." *Journal of Politics* 69(4): 908–26.

2008. "A Party for All Seasons: Electoral Adaptation of Romanian Communist Successor Parties." *Communist and Post-Communist Studies* 41(4): 465–79.

2009. *From Economic Crisis to Reform: IMF Programs in Latin America and Eastern Europe*. Princeton: Princeton University Press.

2010. "Throwing Out the Bums: Protest Voting and Anti-Establishment Parties after Communism." *World Politics* 62(2): 221–60.

2015. "Pre-Communist and Communist Developmental Legacies." *East European Politics and Societies* 29(2): 391–408.

Pop-Eleches, Grigore, and Joshua Tucker. 2017. *Communism's Shadow: Historical Legacies and Contemporary Political Attitudes*. Princeton: Princeton University Press.

Popescu, Marina. 1997. "A Change of Power in Romania: The Results and Significance of the November 1996 Election." *Government and Opposition* 32(2): 172–86.

2003. "The Parliamentary and Presidential Elections in Romania, November 2000." *Electoral Studies* 22(June): 325–35.

Powell, Eleanor Neff, and Joshua A. Tucker. 2014. "Revisiting Electoral Volatility in Post-Communist Countries: New Data, New Results and New Approaches." *British Journal of Political Science* 44(1): 123–47.

Pridham, Geoffrey. 2002. "EU Enlargement and Consolidating Democracy in Post-Communist States — Formality and Reality." *JCMS: Journal of Common Market Studies* 40(5): 953–73.

Przeworski, Adam. 1991. *Democracy and the Market: Political and Economic Reforms in Eastern Europe and Latin America*. New York: Cambridge University Press.

1996. "Public Support for Economic Reform in Poland." *Comparative Political Studies* 29(5): 520–43.

Puddington, Arch, ed. 2008. *Freedom in the World 2008: The Annual Survey of Political Rights and Civil Liberties*. Lanham: Rowman & Littlefield.

Pugh, Jonathan. 2009. "What Is Radical Politics Today?" In *What Is Radical Politics Today?* edited by Jonathan Pugh, 1–13. New York: Palgrave Macmillan.

Pula, Besnik. 2018. *Globalization under and after Socialism: The Evolution of Transnational Capital in Central and Eastern Europe*. Stanford: Stanford University Press.

2020. "Disembedded Politics: Neoliberal Reform and Labour Market Institutions in Central and Eastern Europe." *Government and Opposition* 55(4): 557–77.

Pytlas, Bartek. 2021. "Party Organisation of PiS in Poland: Between Electoral Rhetoric and Absolutist Practice." *Politics and Governance* 9(4): 340–53.

Quality of Government (QoG). 2023. QoG Data. Accessed February 12, 2024. www .gu.se/en/quality-government/qog-data.

Rae, Gavin. 2008. *Poland's Return to Capitalism: From the Socialist Bloc to the European Union*. New York: Taurus Academic Studies.

2016. "Public Capital and the Post-Communist Welfare State: The Case of Poland." *Polish Sociological Review* 194(2): 155–69.

Raimondi, Paolo. 1991. "Slovak Leader Shift Reinforces IMF Foes." *Executive Intelligence Review* 18(18): 7–8.

Ramonaitė, Ainė. 2020. "Mapping the Political Space in Lithuania: The Discrepancy between Party Elites and Party Supporters." *Journal of Baltic Studies* 51(4): 477–96.

Ratazjac, Waldemar. 2012. "Eastern Poland: A Belt of Poor Regions." *Aestimum*: 17–33.

Raymond, Christopher, and Moisés Arce. 2013. "The Politicization of Indigenous Identities in Peru." *Party Politics* 19(4): 555–76.

Riker, William H. 1982. "The Two-Party System and Duverger's Law: An Essay on the History of Political Science." *The American Political Science Review* 76(4): 753–66.

Ringdal, Kristen, and Teuta Starova. 2010. "Social Dimensions of Party Choice in Albania." *Südosteuropa* 58(1): 109–27.

Riofrancos, Thea. 2020. *Resource Radicals: From Petro-Nationalism to Post-Extractivism in Ecuador*. Durham: Duke University Press.

Roberts, Kenneth M. 1995. "Neoliberalism and the Transformation of Populism in Latin America: The Peruvian Case." *World Politics* 48(1): 82–116.

1996. "Economic Crisis and the Demise of the Legal Left in Peru." *Comparative Politics* 29(1): 69–92.

1998. *Deepening Democracy? The Modern Left and Social Movements in Chile and Peru.* Stanford: Stanford University Press.

2000. "Populism and Democracy in Latin America." Paper prepared for the conference "Challenges to Democracy in the Americas," Atlanta, October 16–18.

2006a. "Populism, Political Conflict, and Grass-Roots Organization in Latin America." *Comparative Politics* 38(2): 127–48.

2006b. "Do Parties Matter? Lessons from the Fujimori Experience." In *The Fujimori Legacy: The Rise of Electoral Authoritarianism in Peru*, edited by Julio F. Carrión, 81–101. University Park: The Pennsylvania State University Press.

2007. "Latin America's Populist Revival." *SAIS Review of International Affairs* 27(1): 3–15.

2013. "Market Reform, Programmatic (De)Alignment, and Party System Stability in Latin America." *Comparative Political Studies* 46(11): 1422–52.

2014. *Changing Course in Latin America: Party Systems in the Neoliberal Era.* New York: Cambridge University Press.

Rodrik, Dani. 2018. "Populism and the Economics of Globalization." *Journal of International Business Policy* 1(1–2): 12–33.

2021. "Why Does Globalization Fuel Populism? Economics, Culture, and the Rise of Right-Wing Populism." *Annual Review of Economics* 13(1): 133–70.

Rohrschneider, Robert, and Stephen Whitefield. 2009. "Understanding Cleavages in Party Systems: Issue Position and Issue Salience in 13 Post-Communist Democracies." *Comparative Political Studies* 42(2): 280–313.

Rogers, Samuel. 2019. "China, Hungary, and the Belgrade-Budapest Railway Upgrade: New Politically-Induced Dimensions of FDI and the Trajectory of Hungarian Economic Development." *Journal of East-West Business* 25(1): 84–106.

2020a. "Fidesz, the State-Subsumption of Domestic Business and the Emergence of Prebendalism: Capitalist Development in an 'Illiberal' Setting." *Post-Communist Economies* 32(5): 591–606.

2020b. "Hungarian Authoritarian Populism: A Neo-Gramscian Perspective." *East European Politics* 36(1): 107–23.

2024. *The Political Economy of Hungarian Authoritarian Populism: Capitalists without the Right Kind of Capital.* New York: Routledge.

Roper, Steven D. 2003. "Is There an Economic Basis for Post-Communist Voting? Evidence from Romanian Elections, 1992–2000." *East European Quarterly* 37(1): 85–100.

Rorty, Richard. 1998. *Achieving Our Country: Leftist Thought in Twentieth-Century America.* Cambridge: Harvard University Press.

Rosner, Andrzej, and Monika Stanny. 2017. "Socio-Economic Development in Rural Areas in Poland." Warsaw: The European Fund for the Development of Polish Villages Foundation and Institute of Rural and Agricultural Development, Polish Academy of Sciences.

Rosset, Jan. 2011. "The 2010 Presidential Election in Poland." *Electoral Studies* 30(1): 241–44.

Rovira Kaltwasser, Cristóbal, and Paul Taggart. 2016. "Dealing with Populists in Government: A Framework for Analysis." *Democratization* 23(2): 201–20.

Rovira Kaltwasser, Cristóbal, Paul A. Taggart, Paulina Ochoa Espejo, and Pierre Ostiguy, eds. 2017. *The Oxford Handbook of Populism*. New York: Oxford University Press.

Rovny, Jan. 2015. "Party Competition Structure in Eastern Europe: Aggregate Uniformity versus Idiosyncratic Diversity?" *East European Politics and Societies* 29(1): 40–60.

Rovny, Jan, and Jonathan Polk. 2017. "Stepping in the Same River Twice: Stability amidst Change in Eastern European Party Competition." *European Journal of Political Research* 56(1): 188–98.

Ruckert, Arne, Laura Macdonald, and Kristina R. Proulx. 2017. "Post-Neoliberalism in Latin America: A Conceptual Review." *Third World Quarterly* 38(7): 1583–1602.

Rupnik, Jacques. 2018. "Explaining Eastern Europe: The Crisis of Liberalism." *Journal of Democracy* 29(3): 24–38.

Rybář, Marek. 2014. "The Czech Presidential Elections, January 2013: Towards a More Powerful Head of State?" *Electoral Studies* 35(September): 378–81.

Rybář, Marek, and Kevin Deegan-Krause. 2008. "Slovakia's Communist Successor Parties in Comparative Perspective." *Communist and Post-Communist Studies* 41(4): 497–519.

2009. "Party Democracy and Party Competitiveness in Slovakia: Is There a Trade-Off?" Paper prepared for the joint sessions of the European Consortium for Political Research, Lisbon, April 14–19.

Rydgren, Jens. 2005. "Is Extreme Right-Wing Populism Contagious? Explaining the Emergence of a New Party Family." *European Journal of Political Research* 44(3): 413–37.

Sachs, Jeffrey. 1990. "Social Conflict and Populist Policies in Latin America." In *Labour Relations and Economic Performance*, edited by Renato Brunetta and Carlo Dell'Aringa, 137–69. London: The McMillan Press.

Santora, Marc. 2019. "Poland's Solidarity Movement Turns 30 in a Time of Increasing Divisions." *The New York Times*, June 4, sec. A.

Scheiring, Gábor. 2020a. "Left behind in the Hungarian Rustbelt: The Cultural Political Economy of Working-Class Neo-Nationalism." *Sociology* 54(6): 1159–77.

2020b. *The Retreat of Liberal Democracy: Authoritarian Capitalism and the Accumulative State in Hungary*. New York: Palgrave Macmillan.

2021a. "Dependent Development and Authoritarian State Capitalism: Democratic Backsliding and the Rise of the Accumulative State in Hungary." *Geoforum* 124(4): 267–78.

2021b. "Varieties of Dependency, Varieties of Populism: Neoliberalism and the Populist Countermovements in the Visegrád Four." *Europe-Asia Studies* 73(9): 1569–95.

2022. "The National-Populist Mutation of Neoliberalism in Dependent Economies: The Case of Viktor Orbán's Hungary." *Socio-Economic Review* 20(4): 1597–1623.

Scheiring, Gábor, and Kristóf Szombati. 2020. "From Neoliberal Disembedding to Authoritarian Re-Embedding: The Making of Illiberal Hegemony in Hungary." *International Sociology* 35(6): 721–38.

Schimmelfennig, Frank, and Ulrich Sedelmeier. 2004. "Governance by Conditionality: EU Rule Transfer to the Candidate Countries of Central and Eastern Europe." *Journal of European Public Policy* 11(4): 669–87.

Schmidt, Gregory. 2006. "All the President's Women: Fujimori and Gender Equity in Peruvian Politics." In *The Fujimori Legacy: The Rise of Electoral Authoritarianism in Peru*, edited by Julio Carrión, 150–77. University Park: The Pennsylvania State University Press.

Schwörer, Jakob. 2021. "Less Populist in Power? Online Communication of Populist Parties in Coalition Governments." *Government and Opposition* 57(3): 467–89.

Seawright, Jason. 2012. *Party-System Collapse: The Roots of Crisis in Peru and Venezuela*. Stanford: Stanford University Press.

Shafir, Michael. 2001. "The Greater Romania Party and the 2000 Elections in Romania: How Obvious Is the Obvious?" *The Romanian Journal of Society and Politics* 1(2): 91–126.

Sheahan, John. 2006. "Redirection of Peruvian Economic Strategy in the 1990s: Gains, Losses, and Clues for the Future." In *The Fujimori Legacy: The Rise of Electoral Authoritarianism in Peru*, edited by Julio F. Carrión, 178–200. University Park: The Pennsylvania State University Press.

Shields, Stuart. 2007a. "From Socialist Solidarity to Neo-Populist Neoliberalisation? The Paradoxes of Poland's Post-Communist Transition." *Capital and Class* 31(3): 159–78.

2007b. "Too Much Shock, Not Enough Therapy: Transnational Capital and the Social Implications of Poland's Ongoing Transition to a Market." *Competition and Change* 11(2): 155–78.

2012. *The International Political Economy of Transition: Neoliberal Hegemony and Eastern Central Europe's Transformation*. London: Routledge.

2015. "Neoliberalism Redux: Poland's Recombinant Populism and Its Alternatives." *Critical Sociology* 41(4–5): 659–78.

2021. "Domesticating Neoliberalism: 'Domification' and the Contradictions of the Populist Countermovement in Poland." *Europe-Asia Studies* 73(9): 1622–40.

Silva, Eduardo. 2009. *Challenging Neoliberalism in Latin America*. New York: Cambridge University Press.

Sirovátka, Tomáš, Lucie Novotná, and Steven Saxonberg. 2023. "Populism and Growing Welfare State Agenda: Elections of 2013 and 2017 in Czechia." *Czech Sociological Review* 59(3): 1–25.

Slater, Dan, and Erica Simmons. 2010. "Informative Regress: Critical Antecedents in Comparative Politics." *Comparative Political Studies* 43(7): 886–917.

Slobodian, Quinn. 2023. *Crack-Up Capitalism: Market Radicals and the Dream of a World without Democracy*. New York: Metropolitan Books.

2025. *Hayek's Bastards: Race, Gold, IQ, and the Capitalism of the Far Right*. Brooklyn: Zone Books.

Smyth, Regina. 2005. "The Communist Legacy in Post-Soviet Elections: Looking beyond Redemption." *Government and Opposition* 40(3): 464–69.

Snegovaya, Maria. 2022. "How Ex-Communist Left Parties Reformed and Lost." *West European Politics* 45(4): 716–43.

2024. *When Left Moves Right: The Decline of the Left and the Rise of the Populist Right in Postcommunist Europe*. New York: Oxford University Press.

Soifer, Hillel David. 2012. "The Causal Logic of Critical Junctures." *Comparative Political Studies* 45(12): 1572–97.

Sondergaard, Lars, and Mamta Murthi. 2012. *Skills, Not Just Diplomas: Managing Education for Results in Eastern Europe and Central Asia*. Washington: The World Bank.

Spáč, Peter, and Vlastimil Havlík. 2015. "Overcoming the Danger of Incumbency: The Case of Smer Party in Slovakia." Paper prepared for the general conference of the European Consortium for Political Research, Montreal, August 26–29.

St John, Ronald Bruce. 2010. *Toledo's Peru: Vision and Reality*. Gainesville: The University Press of Florida.

Stanley, Ben. 2015a. "Poland: The Long Arm of Transition." In *Europe Today: A Twenty-First Century Introduction*, edited by Ronald Tiersky and Erik Jones, 257–91. New York: Rowman and Littlefield.

2015b. "The Polish Self-Defense Party: From Agrarian Protest to the Politics of Populism." In *Rural Protest Groups and Populist Political Parties*, edited by Dirk Strijker, Gerrit Voerman, and Ida Terluin, 191–215. Wageningen: Wageningen Academic Publishers.

2016. "Confrontation by Default and Confrontation by Design: Strategic and Institutional Responses to Poland's Populist Coalition Government." *Democratization* 23(2): 263–82.

2023. "Poland: The Deconsolidation of Democracy." In *Europe Today: A Twenty-First Century Introduction*, edited by Erik Jones and Masha Hedberg, 192–220. New York: Rowman and Littlefield.

Stark, David, and Laszlo Bruszt. 1998. *Postsocialist Pathways: Transforming Politics and Property in East Central Europe*. New York: Cambridge University Press.

Statistical Office of the Slovak Republic (SOSR). 2023. Elections and Referenda. Accessed September 19, 2023. https://volby.statistics.sk/.

Stegmaier, Mary, and Lukáš Linek. 2014. "The Parliamentary Election in the Czech Republic, October 2013." *Electoral Studies* 35(September): 385–88.

Stegmaier, Mary, and Klára Vlachová. 2011. "The Parliamentary Election in the Czech Republic, June 2006." *Electoral Studies* 30(1): 238–41.

Stevenson Murer, Jeffrey. 2002. "Mainstreaming Extremism: The Romanian PDSR and the Bulgarian Socialists in Comparative Perspective." In *The Communist Successor Parties of Central and Eastern Europe*, edited by András Bozóki and John T. Ishiyama, 367–96. Armonk: M.E. Sharpe.

Stone, Randall W. 2002. *Lending Credibility: The International Monetary Fund and the Post-Communist Transition*. Princeton: Princeton University Press.

Streeck, Wolfgang. 2016. *How Will Capitalism End? Essays on a Failing System*. Brooklyn: Verso.

2024. *Taking Back Control? States and State Systems after Globalism*. Brooklyn: Verso.

Sum, Paul E. 2010. "The Radical Right in Romania: Political Party Evolution and the Distancing of Romania from Europe." *Communist and Post-Communist Studies* 43(1): 19–29.

Szacki, Jerzy. 1995. *Liberalism after Communism*. Budapest: Central European University Press.

Szczerbiak, Aleks. 1998. "Electoral Politics in Poland: The Parliamentary Elections of 1997." *The Journal of Communist Studies and Transition Politics* 14(3): 58–83.

2002. "Poland's Unexpected Political Earthquake: The September 2001 Parliamentary Election." *Journal of Communist Studies and Transition Politics* 18(3): 41–76.

2007. "'Social Poland' Defeats 'Liberal Poland'? The September–October 2005 Polish Parliamentary and Presidential Elections." *Journal of Communist Studies and Transition Politics* 23(2): 203–32.

2013. "Poland (Mainly) Chooses Stability and Continuity: The October 2011 Polish Parliamentary Election." *Perspectives on European Politics and Society* 14(4): 480–504.

2017. "An Anti-establishment Backlash That Shook up the Party System? The October 2015 Polish Parliamentary Election." *European Politics and Society* 18(4): 404–27.

Szikra, Dorottya. 2018. *Welfare for the Wealthy: The Social Policy of the Orbán-Regime, 2010–2017*. Budapest: Friedrich Ebert Stiftung.

Szombati, Kristóf. 2018. *The Revolt of the Provinces: Anti-Gypsyism and Right-Wing Politics in Hungary*. New York: Berghahn Books.

2021. "The Consolidation of Authoritarian Rule in Rural Hungary: Workfare and the Shift from Punitive Populist to Illiberal Paternalist Poverty Governance." *Europe-Asia Studies* 73(9): 1703–25.

Tansey, Oisín. 2007. "Process Tracing and Elite Interviewing: A Case for Non-Probability Sampling." *PS: Political Science and Politics* 40(4): 765–72.

Taras, Raymond. 1995. *Consolidating Democracy in Poland*. Boulder: Westview Press.

1998. "Voters, Parties, and Leaders." In *Transition to Democracy in Poland*, edited by Richard F. Staar, 47–73. New York: St. Martin's Press.

Tarrow, Sidney. 2010. "The Strategy of Paired Comparison: Toward a Theory of Practice." *Comparative Political Studies* 43(2): 230–59.

Tavits, Margit. 2005. "The Development of Stable Party Support: Electoral Dynamics in Post-Communist Europe." *American Journal of Political Science* 49(2): 283–98.

2013. *Post-Communist Democracies and Party Organization*. New York: Cambridge University Press.

Tavits, Margit, and Natalia Letki. 2009. "When Left Is Right: Party Ideology and Policy in Post-Communist Europe." *American Political Science Review* 103(4): 555–69.

Tavory, Iddo. 2020. "Interviews and Inference: Making Sense of Interview Data in Qualitative Research." *Qualitative Sociology* 43(4): 449–65.

Tepe, Sultan. 2019. "The Inclusion-Moderation Thesis: An Overview." In *Oxford Research Encyclopedia of Politics*, edited by William R. Thompson. Oxford: Oxford University Press.

Thelen, Kathleen. 2014. *Varieties of Liberalization and the New Politics of Social Solidarity*. New York: Cambridge University Press.

Thomeczek, Jan Philipp. 2023. "Moderate in Power, Populist in Opposition? Die Linke's Populist Communication in the German States." *Journal of Political Ideologies*, 1–20.

Thorp, Rosemary, and Maritza Paredes. 2010. *Ethnicity and the Persistence of Inequality: The Case of Peru*. New York: Palgrave Macmillan.

Tismaneanu, Vladimir. 1999. "Introduction." In *The Revolutions of 1989*, edited by Vladimir Tismaneanu, 1–16. New York: Routledge.

2007. "Leninist Legacies, Pluralist Dilemmas." *Journal of Democracy* 18(4): 34–39.

Tismaneanu, Vladimir, and Gail Kligman. 2001. "Romania's First Postcommunist Decade: From Iliescu to Iliescu." *East European Constitutional Review* 10(1): 78–85.

Toplišek, Alen. 2020. "The Political Economy of Populist Rule in Post-Crisis Europe: Hungary and Poland." *New Political Economy* 25(3): 388–403.

Transparency International. 2023. Corruption Perceptions Index. Accessed April 14, 2024. www.transparency.org/en/cpi/2024.

Traub, James. 2019. *What Was Liberalism?: The Past, Present, and Promise of a Noble Idea*. New York: Basic Books.

Tucker, Joshua A. 2006. *Regional Economic Voting: Russia, Poland, Hungary, Slovakia, and the Czech Republic, 1990–1999*. New York: Cambridge University Press.

Tuesta Soldevilla, Fernando. 2024. "Data Política." Blog de Fernando Tuesta Soldevilla. Accessed February 17, 2024. http://blog.pucp.edu.pe/blog/fernandotuesta/catpolitica/elecciones/.

Tworzecki, Hubert. 1996. *Parties and Politics in Post-1989 Poland*. Boulder: Westview Press.

  2012. "The Polish Parliamentary Elections of October 2011." *Electoral Studies* 31(3): 617–21.

  2019. "Poland: A Case of Top-Down Polarization." *The ANNALS of the American Academy of Political and Social Science* 681(1): 97–119.

Učeň, Peter. 2001. "Slovakia." *European Journal of Political Research* 40(3–4): 402–12.

United Nations (UN). 2023a. UN Data. https://data.un.org/. Accessed March 3, 2023.

  2023b. UN Direction of Trade Statistics. Accessed August 18, 2023. www.unccd.int/resources/knowledge-sharing-system/direction-trade-statistics-dots.

United Nations High Commissioner for Refugees (UNHCR). 2023. Refugee Data Finder. Accessed March 13, 2023. www.unhcr.org/refugee-statistics/download.

United Nations Development Program (UNDP). 2024. Human Development Index (HDI). Accessed February 15, 2024. https://hdr.undp.org/data-center/human-development-index#/indicies/HDI.

Vachudova, Milada Anna. 2005. *Europe Undivided: Democracy, Leverage, and Integration after Communism*. Oxford: Oxford University Press.

  2008a. "Center-Right Parties and Political Outcomes in East-Central Europe." *Party Politics* 14(4): 387–405.

  2008b. "Tempered by the EU? Political Parties and Party Systems before and after Accession." *Journal of European Public Policy* 15(6): 861–79.

  2020. "Ethnopopulism and Democratic Backsliding in Central Europe." *East European Politics* 36(3): 318–40.

Valdez, Sarah. 2011. "Subsidizing the Cost of Collective Action: International Organizations and Protest among Polish Farmers during Democratic Transition." *Social Forces* 90(2): 475–95.

Van Cott, Donna Lee. 2005. *From Movements to Parties in Latin America: The Evolution of Ethnic Politics*. New York: Cambridge University Press.

Varoufakis, Yanis. 2012. "The Modest Proposal and the Democratic Deficit." Thoughts for the Post-2008 World (blog), April 18. Accessed May 17, 2023. www.yanisvaroufakis.eu/2012/04/18/the-modest-proposal-and-the-democratic-deficit/.

  2023. *Technofeudalism: What Killed Capitalism*. Brooklyn: Melville House.

Vera Rojas, Sofía, and Santiago Llanos-Escobar. 2016. "Ecuador: Democracia después de Nueve Años de la Revolución Ciudadana de Rafael Correa." *Revista de Ciencia Política* 36(1): 347–65.

Vergara, Alberto, and Daniel Encinas. 2016. "Continuity by Surprise: Explaining Institutional Stability in Contemporary Peru." *Latin American Research Review* 51(1): 159–80.

Vergara, Alberto, and Aaron Watanabe. 2019. "Presidents without Roots: Understanding the Peruvian Paradox." *Latin American Perspectives* 46(5): 25–43.

Viteri, Maria Amelia. 2020. "Anti-gender Policies in Latin America: The Case of Ecuador." *LASA Forum* 51(2): 42–46.

Volintiru, Clara, and George Stefan. 2016. "Social Roots: How Romania's Social Democrats Won the 2016 Election." EUROPP: European Politics and Policy (blog), December 21. Accessed March 27, 2023. https://blogs.lse.ac.uk/europpblog/2016/12/21/social-roots-romania-2016-election/.

Vos, Rob. 2002. "Ecuador: Economic Liberalization, Adjustment and Poverty, 1988–99." In *Economic Liberalization, Distribution, and Poverty: Latin America in the 1990s*, edited by Rob Vos, Lance Taylor, and Ricardo Paes de Barros, 259–313. Northampton: Edward Elgar Publishing.

Ward, James Mace. 2013. *Priest, Politician, Collaborator: Jozef Tiso and the Making of Fascist Slovakia*. Ithaca: Cornell University Press.

Weisbrot, Mark, Jake Johnson, and Lara Merling. 2017. *Decade of Reform: Ecuador's Macroeconomic Policies, Institutional Changes, and Results*. Washington: Center for Economic Policy Research.

Wesełowski, Włodzimierz, and Edmund Wnuk-Lipiński. 1992. "Transformation of Social Order and Legitimization of Inequalities." In *Escape from Socialism: The Polish Route*, edited by Walter D. Connor and Piotr Płoszajski, 83–95. Armonk: M.E. Sharpe.

Weyland, Kurt. 1999. "Neoliberal Populism in Latin America and Eastern Europe." *Comparative Politics* 31(4): 379–401.

2009. "The Rise of Latin America's Two Lefts: Insights from Rentier State Theory." *Comparative Politics* 41(2): 145–64.

2010. "The Performance of Leftist Governments in Latin America: Conceptual and Theoretical Issues." In *Leftist Governments in Latin America: Successes and Shortcomings*, edited by Kurt Weyland, Raúl L. Madrid, and Wendy Hunter, 1–27. New York: Cambridge University Press.

White, Jonathan, and Lea Ypi. 2016. *The Meaning of Partisanship*. New York: Oxford University Press.

Whitefield, Stephen, and Robert Rohrschneider. 2015. "The Salience of European Integration to Party Competition: Western and Eastern Europe Compared." *East European Politics and Societies* 29(1): 12–39.

Wiesehomeier, Nina, and Kenneth Benoit. 2009. "Presidents, Parties, and Policy Competition." *The Journal of Politics* 71(4): 1435–47.

Wightman, Gordon. 2001. "Slovakia Ten Years after the Collapse of Communist Rule." In *Party Development and Democratic Change in Post-Communist Europe: The First Decade*, edited by Paul G. Lewis, 126–40. London: Frank Cass Publishers.

Wineroither, David, and Gilg Seeber. 2018. "Three Worlds of Representation: A Linkage-Based Typology of Parties in Western and Eastern Europe." *East European Politics and Societies* 32(3): 493–517.

Wittenberg, Jason. 2006. *Crucibles of Political Loyalty: Church Institutions and Electoral Continuity in Hungary*. Cambridge: Cambridge University Press.

2015. "Conceptualizing Historical Legacies." *East European Politics and Societies* 29(2): 366–78.

World Bank Group. 2023a. World Development Indicators. Accessed August 8, 2023. https://databank.worldbank.org/source/world-development-indicators.

2023b. Worldwide Governance Indicators. Accessed August 15, 2023. www.worldbank.org/en/publication/worldwide-governance-indicators.

World Inequality Database (WID). 2023. Data. Accessed August 20, 2023. https://wid.world/data/.

World Values Survey (WVS). 2023. Data and Documentation. Accessed April 4, 2023. www.worldvaluessurvey.org/WVSContents.jsp.

Wyss, Johana. 2021. "Exploring Populism through the Politics of Commemoration." *Europe-Asia Studies* 73(9): 1683–1702.

Yashar, Deborah J. 2005. *Contesting Citizenship in Latin America: The Rise of Indigenous Movements and the Postliberal Challenge*. New York: Cambridge University Press.

Zakaria, Fareed. 1997. "The Rise of Illiberal Democracy." *Foreign Affairs* 76(6): 22–43.

Zamosc, Leon. 2007. "The Indian Movement and Political Democracy in Ecuador." *Latin American Politics and Society* 49(3): 1–34.

Zarycki, Tomasz. 2015. "The Electoral Geography of Poland: Between Stable Spatial Structures and Their Changing Interpretations." *Erdkunde* 69(2): 107–24.

Ziblatt, Daniel, and Nick Biziouras. 2002. "Doomed to Be Radicals? Organization, Ideology, and the Communist Successor Parties in East Central Europe." In *The Communist Successor Parties of Central and Eastern Europe*, edited by András Bozóki and John T. Ishiyama, 287–302. Armonk: M.E. Sharpe.

Żmija, Dariusz. 2015. "Economic Poverty in Rural Areas of Poland." *Acta Scientiarum Polonorum. Oeconomia* 14(3): 167–75.

Żmija, Katarzyna, and Dariusz Żmija. 2014. "The Development of Rural Areas in Poland under Transformation Conditions." *Problems of Small Agricultural Holdings* 3(2): 53–63.

Zubek, Radosław. 2008. "Poland: From Pacesetter to Semi-Permanent Outsider." In *The Euro at Ten: Europeanization, Power, and Convergence*, edited by Kenneth Dyson, 292–306. Oxford: Oxford University Press.

Index

For EU product safety concerns, contact us at Calle de José Abascal, 56–1°, 28003 Madrid, Spain or eugpsr@cambridge.org.